TOWARDS SUSTAINABLE SOCIETY ON UBIQUITOUS NETWORKS

IFIP – The International Federation for Information Processing

IFIP was founded in 1960 under the auspices of UNESCO, following the First World Computer Congress held in Paris the previous year. An umbrella organization for societies working in information processing, IFIP's aim is two-fold: to support information processing within its member countries and to encourage technology transfer to developing nations. As its mission statement clearly states,

> *IFIP's mission is to be the leading, truly international, apolitical organization which encourages and assists in the development, exploitation and application of information technology for the benefit of all people.*

IFIP is a non-profitmaking organization, run almost solely by 2500 volunteers. It operates through a number of technical committees, which organize events and publications. IFIP's events range from an international congress to local seminars, but the most important are:

- The IFIP World Computer Congress, held every second year;
- Open conferences;
- Working conferences.

The flagship event is the IFIP World Computer Congress, at which both invited and contributed papers are presented. Contributed papers are rigorously refereed and the rejection rate is high.

As with the Congress, participation in the open conferences is open to all and papers may be invited or submitted. Again, submitted papers are stringently refereed.

The working conferences are structured differently. They are usually run by a working group and attendance is small and by invitation only. Their purpose is to create an atmosphere conducive to innovation and development. Refereeing is less rigorous and papers are subjected to extensive group discussion.

Publications arising from IFIP events vary. The papers presented at the IFIP World Computer Congress and at open conferences are published as conference proceedings, while the results of the working conferences are often published as collections of selected and edited papers.

Any national society whose primary activity is in information may apply to become a full member of IFIP, although full membership is restricted to one society per country. Full members are entitled to vote at the annual General Assembly, National societies preferring a less committed involvement may apply for associate or corresponding membership. Associate members enjoy the same benefits as full members, but without voting rights. Corresponding members are not represented in IFIP bodies. Affiliated membership is open to non-national societies, and individual and honorary membership schemes are also offered.

TOWARDS SUSTAINABLE SOCIETY ON UBIQUITOUS NETWORKS

The 8th IFIP Conference on e-Business, e-Services, and e-Society (I3E 2008), September 24-16, 2008, Tokyo, Japan

Edited by

Makoto Oya
Shonan Institute of Technology
Japan

Ryuya Uda
Tokyo University of Technology
Japan

Chizuko Yasunobu
Hitachi Consulting Co., Ltd.
Japan

Springer

Editors

Makoto Oya
Shonan Institute of Technology
Japan

Ryuya Uda
Tokyo University of Technology
Japan

Chizuko Yasunobu
Hitachi Consulting Co., Ltd.
Japan

p. cm. (IFIP International Federation for InformationProcessing, a Springer Series in Computer Science)

ISSN: 1571-5736 / 1861-2288 (Internet)

ISBN: 978-1-4419-4672-0 eISBN: 978-0-387-85691-9

Printed on acid-free paper

springer.com

Contents

Keynotes

Organized Session

eService on Healthcare and Social Innovation

Research Track

User Behavior Modeling

Information Overload and Recommendation Systems

Trust and Security

Service Oriented Computing and Web Services

P2P Co-Operation and Content Management

Ubiquitous, Mobile and Pervasive Services

e-Health and e-Education

e-Government (G2G, G2B and G2C)

Legal, Societal and Cultural Issues

Industrial and Administration Track

Local Government ICT Platform in Japan

Infrastructure and Implementation

General Chair's Message

Welcome to I3E 2008; the 8th IFIP Conference on e-Business, e-Services, and e-Society sponsored by the three IFIP Technical Committees, TC6, TC8, and TC11. I3E 2008 represents the continuation of a tradition that evolved from the first conference convened in Zurich (Switzerland) in 2001, and that has since journeyed across the world. From Lisbon (Portugal) in 2002, to Sao Paulo (Brazil) in 2003, Toulouse (France) in 2004, Poznan (Poland) in 2005, Turku (Finland) in 2006, and Wuhan (China) in 2007. This year, I3E 2008 will be held from the 24th to 26th September 2008 in the center of Tokyo; a capital city characterized by a mixture of modern technology and traditional culture.

The members of the I3E 2008 Organizing Committee proposed that our e-society, which is based on ubiquitous networks, should be sustainable and that discussions directed at the achievement of a sustainable e-society should be initiated. We therefore decided on the slogan of "Towards Sustainable Society on Ubiquitous Networks" for I3E 2008.

The conference provides users, engineers and scientists in academia, industry and government with a forum within which they can present their latest findings concerned with the applications of e-business, e-services, and e-society and the underlying technology to support those applications. The conference will host three keynotes, one organized session and two panel discussions, as well as regular paper sessions comprising a research track and an industrial and administration track. The title of the organized session is "e-Services on Healthcare and Social Innovation" and the organizer is Prof. Osamu Sudoh from the University of Tokyo. The titles of the panel discussions are "How P2P technology drives e-Society" and "Smart cards and tags can create Ubiquitous Network Society?", and the organizers of the panel discussions are Dr. Tadao Saito, Professor Emeritus at the University of Tokyo, and Prof. Shiro Sakata from Chiba University, respectively.

We would like to thank the members of the Steering Committee, Prof. Wojciech Cellary from the Poznan University of Economics in Poland, Prof. Winfried Lamersdorf from the University of Hamburg in Germany, and Prof. Reima Suomi from the Turku School of Economics in Finland for their continued and generous support.

We are also grateful to the members of the Program Committee for voluntarily reviewing contributed manuscripts and appreciate the assistance of other Organizing Committee members for their efforts in preparing this conference, especially Dr. Motohisa Funabashi, Chair of the Local Steering Committee.

We would also like to thank the Ministry of Internal Affairs and Communications for providing the impetus for the conference and for promoting the e-Society, the Association for the Promotion of Public Local Information for managing the financial aspects of the conference, and the National Institute of Information and Communications Technology for supporting finance for the conference.

Finally, to the attendees, thank you for your participation in I3E 2008, and welcome to Tokyo. I hope you enjoy the conference and your stay in Japan.

Ryoichi Sasaki
I3E 2008 General Chair
Tokyo Denki University

Program Committee Chair's Message

The basic technologies required to carry out various services over the Internet have matured greatly. e-Business, e-Services, and e-Government are now applied to a large number of real systems around the world. In effect, we are creating a global e-Society.

The popularization of e-technologies has brought with it new challenges and issues in various fields. These include user behavior models, filtering and recommendation systems to overcome information overload, security and trust issues, P2P cooperation and contents delivery or management, SOA and SaaS, Web autonomy and self-organization, legal and ethical issues, and societal and cultural issues, such as the digital divide. These issues and challenges need to be considered in order to actualize the next generation of people-centric Internet services. We are certain the papers and presentations at this conference will timely address these important issues.

The evaluation and acceptance of papers for this conference was a lengthy and involved process. After initial submissions, papers were screened by two or more reviewers. The results were then openly discussed by members of the Program Committee using a collaborative Web system. As a result, twenty-five papers were selected for the research track and four papers were chosen for the industrial and administration track. All of the chosen research papers relate to the issues and challenges just mentioned above, while the industry and administration papers give a number of suggestions for future research directions. All should lead to discussion that will contribute to the realization of a sustainable society on ubiquitous networks.

At this time we would like to thank the members of the Program Committee and reviewers for their hard work. We would also like to take this opportunity to acknowledge the Steering Committee members for their cooperation, and the editors whose efforts have produced a superb conference publication. Finally, we would particularly like to thank Thomas Baignères and Matthieu Finiasz for providing iChair, the Web-based collaborative review system – an excellent example of how we e-Academics can work together for the benefit of everyone.

Makoto Oya
I3E 2008 Program Committee Chair
Shonan Institute of Technology

Ryuya Uda
I3E 2008 Program Committee Vice Chair
Tokyo University of Technology

Organizing Committees

Honorary General Chair
Tadao Saito, Professor Emeritus of The University of Tokyo, Toyota InfoTechnology Center Co., Japan

General Chair
Ryoichi Sasaki, Tokyo Denki University, Japan

Program Committee Chair
Makoto Oya, Shonan Institute of Technology, Japan

Program Committee Vice Chair
Ryuya Uda, Tokyo University of Technology, Japan

Local Steering Committee Co-Chairs
Motohisa Funabashi, Hitachi, Ltd., Japan
Terutoshi Sano, The Association for Promotion of Public Local Information, Japan

Local Steering Committee Vice Chair
Ken Kobayashi, Hitachi, Ltd., Japan

Local Steering Committee Secretary
Kunihiko Miyazaki, Hitachi, Ltd., Japan

Finance Co-Chairs
Hiroshi Yajima, Tokyo Denki University, Japan
Shigehisa Honma, The Association for Promotion of Public Local Information, Japan

Local Arrangements Chair
Isao Echizen, National Institute of Informatics, Japan

Local Arrangements Vice Chair
Soichi Furuya, Hitachi, Ltd., Japan

Publication Chair
Chizuko Yasunobu, Hitachi Consulting Co., Ltd., Japan

Publication Vice Chairs
Katsunari Yoshioka, Yokohama National University, Japan
Junji Nakazato, National Institute of Information and Communications Technology, Japan

Publicity Chair
Hiroshi Yoshiura, University of Electro-Communications, Japan

Panel Chair
Shiro Sakata, Chiba University, Japan

Organized Session Chair
Osamu Sudoh, The University of Tokyo, Japan

Members
Toyoyuki Kobayashi, NTT Communications Corporation, Japan
Hirokazu Konishi, NEC Corporation, Japan
Yuichi Matsushima, National Institute of Information and Communications Technology, Japan
Masahiko Narita, Advanced Institute of Industrial Technology, Japan

Liaison Chairs

IFIP:	Wojciech Cellary,	Poznan University of Economics, Poland
Europe:	Volker Tschammer,	FhG FOKUS, Germany
North America:	Narcyz Roztocki,	State University of New York At New Paltz, USA
South America:	Claudia Bauzer Medeiros,	University of Campinas, Brazil
Asia-Pacific:	Wee Keong Ng,	Nanyang Technological University, Singapore

Steering Committee
Wojciech Cellary, Poznan University of Economics, Poland
Winfried Lamersdorf, University of Hamburg, Germany
Reima Suomi, Turku School of Economics, Finland

Program Committee

Esma Aïmeur,	Université de Montréal, Canada
Masanori Akiyoshi,	Osaka University, Japan
Americo Nobre Amorim,	Ufpe/FIR, Brazil
Markus Bick,	ESCP-EAP European School of Management, Berlin, Germany
Melanie Bicking,	Universität Koblenz-Landau, Germany
Regis Cabral,	FEPRO Piteå, Sweden
Kok-Wai Chew,	Multimedia University, Malaysia
Sharon Dawes,	University at Albany, SUNY, USA
Dirk Deschoolmeester,	Universität Ghent, Belgium
Naoki Endo,	Toshiba Solutions Co., Japan
Simone Fischer-Hübner,	Karlstad University, Sweden
Motohisa Funabashi,	Hitachi, Ltd., Japan
Rüdiger Grimm,	Universität Koblenz-Landau, Germany
J. Felix Hampe,	University of Koblenz-Landau, Germany
Ayako Hiramatsu,	Osaka Sangyo University, Japan
Birgit Hofreiter,	University of Vienna, Austria
Jie Huang,	Zhongnan University of Economics and Law, PRC
Rei Itsuki,	Hiroshima International University, Japan
Tomasz Janowski,	United Nations University, Macao
Marijn Janssen,	Delft University of Technology, Netherlands
Atsushi Kanai,	Hosei University, Japan
Naoyuki Karasawa,	Niigata University, Japan
Dipak Khakhar,	Lund University, Institute for Informatics, Sweden
Ranjan Kini,	Indiana University Northwest, USA
Dimitri Konstantas,	University of Geneva, Switzerland
Irene Krebs,	Brandenburg University of Technology Cottbus, Germany
Hiromitsu Kurisu,	Hitachi, Ltd., Japan
Winfried Lamersdorf,	Universität Hamburg, Fachbereich Informatik, Germany
Hongxiu Li,	Turku School of Economics, Finland

External Reviewers

Rilwan Basanya,	United Nations University, Macao
Steve Capell,	Red Wahoo, Australia
Remi Chandran,	United Nations University, Macao
Nick Cook,	Newcastle University, UK
Jairo Dornelas,	UFPE, Brazil
Elsa Estevez,	United Nations University, Macao
Matthias Fluegge,	Fraunhofer Fokus, Germany
Carlos Molina-Jimenez,	Newcastle University, UK
Alexander Pokahr,	Universität Hamburg, Informatics Department, Germany
Teppo Räisänen,	University of Oulu, Finland
Hisao Sakazaki,	Hitachi, Ltd., Japan
Sonja Zaplata,	Universität Hamburg, Informatics Department, Germany

Future Outlook on Mobile and Ubiquitous Services

Dr. Takeshi Mizuike

Vice President, Chief Executive Director, Technology Development Center,

KDDI R&D Laboratories Inc.

Mobile communication service, which started from a simple cellular-phone now provides wide variety of applications. One of the most useful features is capability to access internet applications from mobile environment with a reasonable price and without any knowledge of computer literacy. In addition to e-mail and Web access, currently available applications on mobile handsets include digital camera, music player, GPS navigation, digital broadcast receiver, IC card payment and so on. Future trend of mobile services is introduced with focus on further expansion of such application areas along with new technologies to support new service development. One of the important aspects is a function as a personal portal device. A mobile user can generate his/her own personal information in a so-called ubiquitous environment. For example, a "Life-log" trial system has been developed as a mobile application. Short-range communication links such as RF-ID tag and Bluetooth may also be utilized to enhance capability of mobile applications. Another important aspect is integration with other services such as fixed broadband communication services and digital broadcasting. Next generation wireless and network technologies will provide infrastructure to support such new services in mobile environment. Service platform will then be a key factor for successful implementation of new application concepts. A special attention is also paid to additional requirements such as information security, advanced human machine interface and batteries.

Takeshi Mizuike was born in 1953 in Tokyo, Japan. He graduated from the University of Tokyo in 1977. He also received M.S. degree from Stanford University and Ph. D degree from the University of Tokyo, in 1981 and 1999, respectively. He joined KDD Co. Ltd. (Currently KDDI Corporation) in 1977 and conducted a research on radio communication systems and network planning at its R&D Laboratories. After management work for strategic technology planning at KDDI Headquarters, he is now chief executive director of Technology Development Center at KDDI R&D Laboratories. He is a Fellow of Institute of Electronic, Information and Communication Engineers of Japan and a Senior member of IEEE. He contributed to ITU-R standardization activities as a former Vice-chairman of Study Group 8 for mobile service. He is a recipient of the research achievement award from the minister of education and science of Japan in 2003.

How salesforce.com Changes Information Technology

Adam Gross

Vice President of Platform and Developer Marketing, salesforce.com

Imagine a new approach where you no longer need hardware or software to run your business applications. Imagine not having to worry about high availability and disaster recovery. Imagine being able to focus 100 percent of your energy figuring out what features your users want and actually being able to deliver them. These are the promises and reality of Platform as a Service , a new way to harness the power of cloud computing for enterprise application development and delivery. Sound too good to be true? In this session, Adam Gross, vice president of platform and developer marketing, salesforce.com, will cover the key components of the Cloud Computing architecture and profile several companies who have put them to work to build better applications, faster, at a fraction of the cost.

Adam Gross is vice president of Platform and Developer Marketing at salesforce.com. At the company, Gross focuses on bringing platform, integration and development technologies to developers, ISVs and companies around the world to build on-demand applications on the Force.com platform and deliver them through the AppExchange marketplace. This work includes launching the company's first Web services API, which has grown to become one of the most popular business Web services available, accounting for over 50 percent of all of salesforce.com's traffic.

Prior to salesforce.com, Adam was an early innovator in the Web services market, serving as Vice President of Product Marketing at GrandCentral Communications (recently acquired by Google). Prior to GrandCentral, Gross co-founded Personify, a San Francisco-based software company that provided personalization and analytics systems for some of the largest sites on the Web, and served as a technology analyst in Stanford Research Institute's Media Futures Program. Gross holds a B.S. in New Media Systems and Policy from Carnegie Mellon University.

Gross is an accomplished speaker, having recently presented at some of the industry's most popular business and technology conferences including:

- O'Reilly Emerging Technology Conference
- MIT Technology Review Emerging Technology Conference
- InfoWorld SOA Executive Forum
- NYPHP Conference
- eBay's Developer Conference
- IBD Network – Web 2.0 and the Enterprise
- Web 2.0 Expo

SOUNDS FROM UTOPIA
Critical Issues of the Web 2.0 Perspective in the Network Society

Prof. Dr. Jan A.G.M. van Dijk

Department of Media, Communication and Organization, University of Twente

Every decade sounds from utopia return to the discussion about the social consequences of the Internet. This medium would be substantially more (inter)active, creative, participatory, direct and equal as compared to traditional media. Moreover, on the Internet things would be created in a network of cooperation, and not primarily by individuals and market or government organizations. Finally, the Internet is supposed to compensate for lost community and sociability. With the Web 2.0 these utopian sounds reappear in a new shape. However, this time the Internet has substantially changed. There are not only many more participants but they also seem to be more active on the web than ever before. With an open mind to the new opportunities Professor van Dijk has discussed the remaining critical issues of the Web 2.0 perspective. Such are:

- Who actually controls the Internet? The business world, governments or the users and their organizations? His answer: after a predominance of public and user organizations from the 1990s onwards control of the Internet has shifted to the business world and governments. They define the framework of user generated content in Web 2.0.
- The inequality of participation: the digital divide. Large parts of the population, even in high-tech countries are not able to participate and contribute for a lack of access and digital skills.
- Do really new forms of sociability appear? In the context of so-called 'network individualization' new forms of sociability appear such as social networking sites and online communities. However, they offer no revolution but increasingly integrate with traditional offline social forms.
- The assault on quality media. The rise of free user generated content in a.o. newssites, video, music and information exchange sites, encyclopedias threatens current business models of quality media as users appear to make no difference evaluating their content. New business models and calls for quality editorship are to be expected.

- The quality of web content that seems to dissolve all differences between experts and lay persons. This is a threat to the current information elite and contemporary business models on the Internet. Increasingly they will have to (im)prove themselves and respond to the continuing need of intermediary information agents.
- Does the Internet offer wise crowds or stupid mobs? Both will appear. Wise crowds will be limited and organized; stupid mobs will be widespread and unorganized.

The speaker has consistently applied these general issues to their significance for developing E-services by businesses and governments.

Jan A.G.M. van Dijk is professor of communication science at the University of Twente, the Netherlands and head of the Department of Media, Communication and Organization. His teaching chair is called The Sociology of the Information Society.

Van Dijk is investigating the social aspects of information and communication technology since 1984. His research specializes in social, cultural and political/policy issues. At the end of the 1980s he coined the term network society and made an inventory of the anticipated social consequences of ICTs and the Internet. His key publication in this respect is the continually updated book The Network Society (1999, 2006, Dutch editions: 1991, 1994, 1997, 2001), translated in several languages. Other, more recent books in English are Digital Democracy (2000), Information and Communication Technology in Organizations (2005) and The Deepening Divide, Inequality in the Information Society (2005), all Sage Publications.

Van Dijk is considered to be an expert on the field of the social consequences of the new media, in particular information inequality (the so-called 'digital divide'), privacy and security, (digital) democracy and social cohesion.

Van Dijk leads a research program about E-government and is strongly engaged in policy discussions. He is an advisory of the European Commission and several Dutch ministries, government organizations and municipalities.

Personal website: http://www.gw.utwente.nl/vandijk

eService Innovation and Sensor Based Healthcare

Osamu Sudoh[1] **Sozo Inoue**[2] **Naoki Nakashima**[3]

[1]Graduate School of Interdisciplinary Informatics, Univ. Tokyo,
7-3-1 Hongo, Bunkyo-ku, Tokyo, Japan, 113-0033
sudoh@iii.u-tokyo.ac.jp

[2]Library, Kyushu Univ.,
6-10-1 Hakozaki, Higashi-ku, Fukuoka, Japan, 812-8580
sozo@lib.kyushu-u.ac.jp

[3]Kyushu Univ. Hospital,
3-1-1, Maidashi, Higashi-ku, Fukuoka, Japan, 812-8582
nnaoki@info.med.kyushu-u.ac.jp

Abstract. This paper discusses eServices using frontier applications, which targets medical domain applications using sensor network, along with New standardized health check system introduced to Japanese nations recently. We clarify the ubiquitous aspects of this application, and address challenges for ubiquitous innovation. We also describe the experience of introducing and operating the system with a real field trial.

1 Introduction

There is growing momentum today around the world to encourage innovations based on information networks. As defined by Joseph A. Shumpeter in The Theory of Economic Development in 1926, innovation is the creation of value through unprecedented combinations of the means of production, resources, the workforce and other components. It is open innovation that is now rapidly proliferating around the globe. Unlike innovation based solely on internal resources, open innovation involves collaboration among multiple players, making effective use of external resources on the basis of networks. In other words, new value is created not by a single unusual talent

---

Please use the following format when citing this chapter:

Sudoh, O., Inoue, S., Nakajima, N., 2008, in IFIP International Federation for Information Processing, Volume 286; Towards Sustainable Society on Ubiquitous Networks, eds. Oya, M., Uda, R., Yasunobu, C., (Boston: Springer), pp. 1–14.

but by stepping up interaction among multiple players that are able to work with latent creative abilities. The architecture of participation and interaction is therefore the key to open innovation.

From the perspective of open innovation discussed above, all organizations including administrative, medical, educational and research bodies will need to make fundamental considerations. So this paper discusses New Public eServices using frontier applications, especially Medical eService using sensor network.

2 Open Innovation and eServices

It is necessary for us to envision a new paradigm for open innovation which will be utilized to achieve sustainable social development. In the new paradigm, e-Government and Local e-government should be emphasized as a core function. The infrastructure must be developed into a platform so that it can be applied to the entire society.

Joint outsourcing helps multiple government agencies and local bodies utilize common information systems. However, each information system has a number of identical software modules. In the framework of common infrastructure for e-Government and Local e-government built based upon SOA (Service Oriented Architecture), common functions are built into modules so that efficiency and transparency in administrative systems can be developed. The following section explains social transformation via a wider-area collaboration of Local e-government.

SOA is a group of independent software modules, each of which is structured to support the requirements of a certain job process and/or common functionality across entire job functions. They are reusable and distributed over the network. The relationships against the modules are assigned by controllers to suit overall system architecture. Duplicate investment can be avoided with SOA, and a drastic decrease in cost can be achieved.

The concept of Local e-government can be strategically developed for the regional growth of the society. SOA is used to modularize software applications which will have varied usage not only for administrative processes but also for administrations in public facilities, hospitals, schools, and day care centers. The outsourcing of SOA-based systems with data centers will greatly contribute to the performance improvement of local SMEs.

The concept of e-Government initiatives can be a driving force for complete transformation of the regional community. To achieve this goal, it is important for us to utilize not only administrative information systems but also medical, welfare, educational institutions and facilities to actively utilize information facilities and infrastructure. Even local private corporations and households should participate.

In many advanced countries, aging society has become a serious social issue. In this context, it is important to prevent the increase of medical costs and to consider preventive health. Various research projects for preventive medicine utilizing IT are currently underway in the world.

We have also taken part of the development of a health management test bed using sensor networks, which is to serve as an empirical research platform. The primary goal of the research is to organize a preventive health system to curb deterioration due to various adult diseases, such as high blood pressure, diabetes, kidney disease, and cardiac illness, to prevent complications, and to support secondary prevention for the improvement of health condition. Wearable bio-sensors and earthed indoor sensors are in place to obtain patient's ecological data. The data is transmitted from Mote client to the data center via IP-VPN. Data is made anonymous before being sent over remote grids. Advanced data analysis is performed for a large volume of collected data pertaining to body movements, and is reported by the system to designated doctors. This is to support medical diagnosis and consultation by doctors for health management.

If the research produces certain outcomes, it will be upgraded into a larger empirical initiative using the research infrastructure of the sensor network and ASP, which is used to introduce preventive health services and security services.

Several leading municipalities are developing SOA-based information infrastructure in a joint effort. The Japanese medical insurance system has been reformed recently to prevent the increase of medical costs, through health prevention and management efforts in local communities. Therefore, the management of medical and health-related information at the community level has become an important issue. In this regard, it is possible to take a strategic approach to the evolution of local communities by incorporating the community model based on the sensor network infrastructure into the entire Local e-government scheme.

The SOA concept is being promoted by these leading local governments, in which software is modularized and used for a variety of purposes. Software modules are not only for government administration but also public facilities, hospitals, and daycare centers. If the aforementioned local health management architecture using sensor networks is linked to this joint SOA initiative, the local information infrastructure would increase optimal efficiency in management of medical and welfare facilities where new quality services could be created.

This paper will show the innovative capability of medical eService that should be based on SOA and ASP.

3 Healthcare

3.1 Background

The results of the national nutrition survey study in 2006, conducted by the Ministry of Health, Labour and Welfare, showed that 8.2 million people have diabetes, and if those in the diabetes-prone group are added, that figure would be 18.7 million people among the total Japanese population of 127 million people. Along with the increase in diabetes, there have also been alarming increases in other diseases caused by had life-style habits hypertension and dyslipidemia. Approximately 39.7 million have hypertension and 14.1 million have dyslipidemia. These three diseases are considered to be major causative factors in the two diseases that account for the second and third ranking causes of death in Japan, myocardial infarction and brain stroke, respectively. Additionally, uncontrolled diabetes causes chronic renal failure, and leads hemodialysis, which spends 5 million yen per year x person. Recent studies have shown that obesity with visceral fat accumulation, which is commonly known as "metabolic syndrome", is the main cause of diabetes, hypertension and dyslipidemia. The survey shows 19.4 million have metabolic syndrome if those in prone group are added. That means that this is an age in which we must call metabolic syndrome the national disease.

In the typical course, obesity begins in their 20's to 40's, developing to lifestyle diseases in their 40's to 60's. As the results, elderly people spend higher medical cost by causing atherosclerotic diseases, or by hemodialysis. Younger onset of these serious diseases leads to the decrease of working resources.

Accordingly, in order to avoid contracting these life threatening diseases, to inhibit increasing medical cost, and to keep productivity, the first issue of priority is the prevention of obesity and the control of metabolic syndrome.

New Standardized Health Check-up System (Particular Health Check-up System; PHCS)

In June 2006, the Japanese government amended the Medical Care Law to establish an annual health check-up/management system for all citizens aged 40 – 74 years. This system will greatly affect insurers because it will cover 57 million citizens and will involve all insurers from April 2008. Insurers will be penalized economically from 2013 when stated goals are not achieved. All Japanese have basic health care insurance.

The annual health check-up is described as follows:

1. Questionnaire (inquiry pertaining to weight change, smoking, exercise).

2. Physical examination (height, weight [body mass index], waist, blood pressure).

3. Blood chemistry tests (Triglyceride, HDL-cholesterol, LDL-cholesterol, GOT, GPT, γ-GTP, Cre, blood glucose (fasting or postprandial), HbA1c, uric acid).

Stratification involves two steps. On the basis of results, participants are assigned to one of three risk groups. The waist and body mass index determine the first assignment. Risk factors identified by blood chemistry tests and smoking history are tallied, and participants are assigned to the "information provided group", "motivation support group", or the "aggressive support group" (Fig.1).

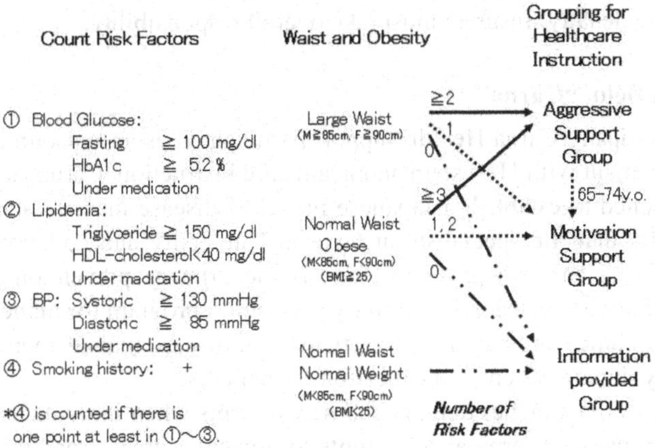

Fig.1 Stratification into risk groups according to the results of physical examination and blood chemistry tests (ref.[5]).

Insurers need to provide healthcare instruction once to individuals assigned to the motivation support group, and repeatedly to individuals assign to the aggressive support group. The information provided group is not given health instruction. A physician, a health nurse, or a registered dietitian should provide the first healthcare instruction each year. Non-face-to-face instruction via telephone or information and communication technology (ICT) system is allowed for additional instruction on the aggressive support group. Insurers do not need to provide healthcare instruction to the person who is under medication of lifestyle disease when he/she is classified into the motivation support group or the aggressive support group.

All data obtained from the PHCS will be digitized in a standard protocol as HL7 CDA and in standard cords as JLAC 10. Insurers will have to maintain records for each insured person as long as he or she remains insured. The records will contain health check-up and instruction data. If the individual changes insurer as he changes occupation, the former insurers will transfer the data to the new insurer so that there is no gap in the record. With these systems in place, it is anticipated that the Japanese government have access to huge amounts of anonymous data that can be used for statistical purposes. Insurers can keep the data without anonymising it because, for example, they have to analyze it together with the receipt data from the medical institutions. Insurers will be able to store data more effectively when the on-line reimbursement project is fully achieved in 2011.

The Japanese government suggests that the insurer pay an additional 10% contribution to medical cost of aged person (age 75 year or over) if it does not achieve the stated goals or be rewarded by a 10% discount if stated goals are achieved from 2013. The Japanese government is asking for a 25% decrease in the number of diabetes and pre-diabetes patients per insurer for example.

Insurers will be allowed to outsource the required tasks to healthcare provider companies. Thus, many tasks will be outsourced to Internet data centers.

The initial action of insurers will be the engagement of a health-care provider company for outsourcing. After registration of the covered citizens, the health-care provider will begin service. If the providers do not produce adequate outcomes, insurers must pay the penalty. Insurers must take overall responsibility.

Our Research field, "Carna"

A venture company Carna Health Support participated as an outsourcing company for data management with IT system and healthcare instruction. Carna Health Support originally launched to establish a Japanese model of disease management in diabetic field in 2006 by diabetic specialists in Kyushu University and collaborator companies. Thus, Carna has two programs, one is the primary prevention program for PHCS, and another is the secondary/tertiary prevention program for diabetes mellitus.

To motivate clinics and patients to participate in disease management, Carna supports the family doctor system and education for patients.

For clinics, Carna matches doctors and new patients when individuals are affected with a lifestyle disease. Carna also attempts to prevent patient dropout by telephone contact, support patient education and detection of early-stage complications by means of periodic questionnaires, and facilitate medical specialists' cooperation according to the timing described in the critical pathway system.

For patients, Carna promotes guideline medical care described in the critical pathway, report the results of blood tests quickly, and provide 'Carna points' as rewards for the patient's efforts (for instance, regular clinic visits) and for improvement in their diabetic condition (HbA1c). Carna exchanges the points for coupons with which they can obtain certified health-related products such as healthy foods and exercise goods.

(1) Critical pathways for quality control, for appropriate matching of services to individuals, and for adaptation to the political direction in Japan.

Carna developed a region-related, outcome-oriented critical pathway as the core competency in the call center. Carna also standardized workflow in the call center calling 'algorithm'. The critical pathways and the parts of the algorithm are digitized. Carna prepared an education system with structured questionnaires and comprehensive teaching materials, which are closely related to the personalized critical pathway.

Carna had two kinds of outcome-oriented critical pathways by the end of 2006. One is for the primary prevention program (lifestyle improvement program). The other is for the secondary/tertiary prevention program for diabetes mellitus.

Features of the critical pathway for lifestyle improvement program edge are described below;

- Using five kinds of critical pathway matching each stage of Prochaska stage model (pre-contemplation stage, contemplation stage, preparation stage, action stage, maintenance stage) .
- Matching the framework of the PHCS

Features of the critical pathway for diabetes mellitus (secondary/tertiary prevention) that Carna has developed are described below;

- Scheduling of medical services based on clinical guidelines produced by the Japanese Diabetic Society.

- Supporting general care of diabetic outpatients including timely reminders of the need to visit medical specialists such as an ophthalmologist, and a diabetologist.
- Using 'the overlay method' to create an optimal personalized critical pathway for each patient. A personalized critical pathway is created by overlay with a basic sheet for regular examination, and optional sheets matching patient's treatments, the severity of the diabetic complications, and the patient's level of knowledge. Carna can create 2,880 different of critical pathways.
- Modifying continuously as the patient's condition

(2) Personalized communication based-on patient characteristics

Patients' responses to interventions vary because the basic characters of patients vary. For successful intervention, Carna determines the patient's character type during the registration process, and Carna depends on this information to personalize our communication with the patient. This approach may also decrease stress of the call center staff.

(3) Other algorithms and ICT system for efficient and secure data management

Carna developed other algorithms ICT system as shown in Fig.2. Carna used application service provider system for ICT to input participant records.

Carna is using an Internet data center in Fukuoka city, Japan, for database servers. Carna sends data over the Internet via virtual private network from the call center.

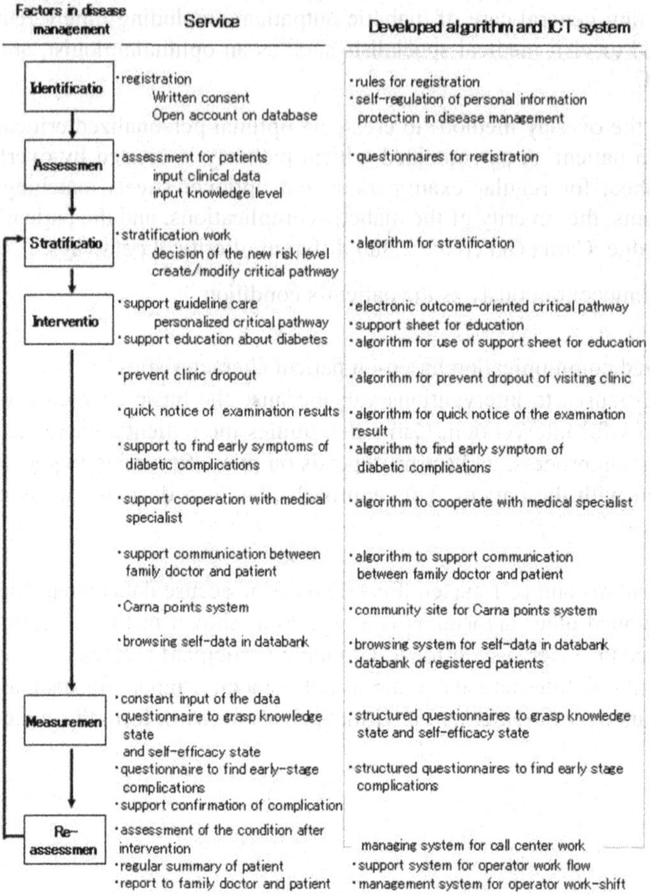

Fig. 2 Disease management services and rules, algorithms, and ICT system in the secondary/tertiary prevention program for diabetes mellitus (ref.[5])

(4) Ethical considerations

Carna quantified the risk of disclosure in terms of information value, threat arising from inadequate ICT security, and areas of vulnerability and showed that the highest risk was posed by databases containing individual patient profiles. Consequently, We believes that we need regulations pertaining to the provision of health information and that we need general classifications for various types of patient information that we deal with in disease management work.

3.2 SOA Based Healthcare using Sensor Network

We aim to develop a SOA based healthcare system of Canra which manages effective PHCS, integrated with sensor networks. Using sensor network with vital sensors, the activities and lifestyles of patients/citizens can collected in an easy and accurate manner, and therefore effective healthcare can be possible.

However, since the entire system will be highly complex system, the following issues have to be considered.

Scalability

Since the medical check system is to be applied to massive populations in long term, the system has to handle huge amount of data. Distributed architecture which can process massive data will be needed. Especially, maintenance cost in an wide area distribution should be seriously considered.

Heterogeneity

The system should handle various kinds of data, such as manually input data, sequential motion sensor data, and periodical vital sensor data. Along with this, sensors and networking devices will also be heterogeneous to meet with the varieties of required data and reliability.

Reliability

Because of the variety of data and of the requirement for long battery life of mobile sensor devices, there should appear trade-offs between accuracy of data and energy consumption. For example, we can analyze the movement of an patient more accurately and more in real time if we could obtain frequent motion data from an accelerometer, but it results in severe battery life. Optimal balance of these parameters should be discovered for reliability of data.

Human Friendliness

Since the system is to be used in the daily lives of patients, it should be highly user-friendly as much as stress free to patients. It has the following two aspects:

- Human interfaces such as web interfaces should be easy to use, and easy to be embedded to the patients' lifestyles, so as in the case of blog systems.
- Vital sensor devices should be non-intrusive, small as much as possible, and even free in the way of attaching to the body. For example, a heart rate sensor attached to the finger keeps the patient away from desk work.

Security and Privacy Management

The data handled in the system are sometimes highly privacy-sensitive ones. Therefore, complete security and adequate personal data access control are the necessary.

Flexibility

This is the most important feature. Although we addressed the above requirement for the system, we still do not know how much we should decide the qualitative or quantitative parameters or implementations from so many design options.

It means that we fundamentally need many experiences and trials, that we should adopt the style of rapid development based on the feedbacks from the trials. Here, the reason why SOA, which realizes highly modularized composition of service functions, is crucial in this healthcare domain.

4 Experience

In this section, the experience aimed for effective medical check systems are described. In the experience, sensor network was introduced for automatically monitoring the activity of patients, and for advising the patients adequately. Moreover, the obtained data from the sensors as well as manually recorded data can be used for medical knowledge discovery which is unknown so far.

4.1 Design

For simplicity, we classify the users of the system into two roles: patients, and data analyst. *Patients* are the users who resulted in the need for continuous care by specific medical check. *Data analysts* are the users who analyze the data from the sensors along with the manually recorded data, and correspond to physician, health adviser in the specific medical check system, and medical researcher in actual situation.

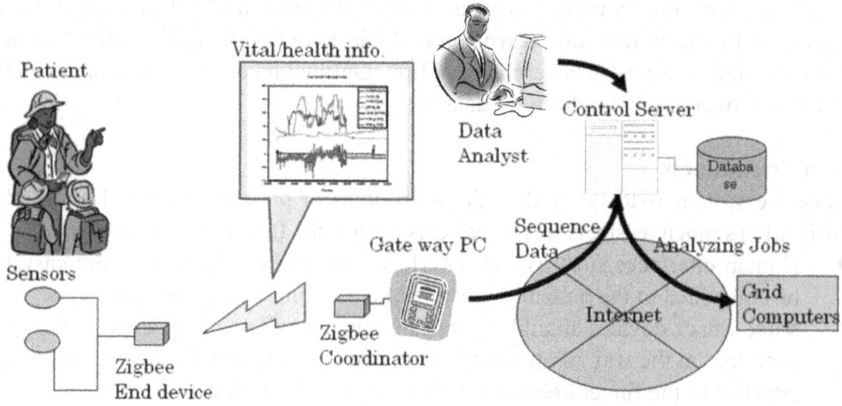

Fig.3 System and Network Architecture

Fig. 3 is the system and network architecture of the system. The system consists of sensors, zigbee[8] end devices, zigbee coordinator, gateway PC, control server, database, and grid computers. The use cases of the system are described in the following.

Patient

Patients have sensor end devices in their lives. End devices attached with sensors acquire vital data of the patients periodically, and send them to zigbee coordinator through routers.

Routers, coordinators, and gateways are placed in offices and homes, and receive data from the end devices, and send to the control server. Gateway PCs also accept manual inputs from the patients.

Data Analyst

Data analysts do data analysis, or data mining using the data gathered to the control server.

The control server stores the data from gateway PCs to the database systems, and throws analysis/mining jobs by data analysts to grid computers, with the data, and receives the answer.

4.2 Consequence

Based on the architecture introduced above, we tried a first-step experience, where basic design options, such as communication protocols, communication throughput, human friendliness of sensor devices, sensor measurement methods, are discovered with reasonably small amount of population in a single place.

The trial was done in a building which has a hospital and a fitness club at once. 3 patients participated at one time, and repeated 3 times for independent groups, which means 9 patients in total.

The trial was scheduled as the following:

1st day: medical check (Fig. 4(a))

In the first day, the patients took full-fledged medical check, including blood, urinalysis, ECG, X-ray, body consumption, BMI, blood pressure, and CPX(cardiopulmonary exercise).

Especially, CPX (Fig.4(a)) has an important factor. In CPX, an adequate heart rate can be calculated from variety of measurements such as the rate of O2 and CO2 in breath during an exercise. This value of heart rate can be used in the exercises in the following days.

2nd~7th day: exercise and dietary program (Fig.4 (b))

From the next day, the patients take fitness exercises, including body stretch, aerobic exercise, and muscle training, for about 2 hours.

Besides, the patients are managed dietary program. 2 of the meals in a day are designated by a dietitian, and diet soup and diet frozen food are sent to the home of the patients. And what they ate in the rest of the day are interviewed and recorded by the dietitian. To be accurate, this is done from the 1st day.

8th day: measurement of the effects (Fig.4(c))

After the days of exercises and dietary program, the effect of the exercises and diets are evaluated by measuring the change of blood factors, urinalysis, body composition, BMI, and blood pressure.

(a)1st day (b)2nd~7th day (c) 8th day

Fig. 4 Scene of trial

Sensor and zigbee devices

For this trial, we used the following sensor devices

- 2D / 3D accelerometers
- Temperature, humidity, and light sensors
- Heart rate sensors (non-zigbee)
- Heart rate sensors (non-wireless)

Fig. shows one type of the sensor zigbee devices, which has 2D accelerometers, temperature, humidity, and light sensors, and gateway PC.

Fig. 5 Sensor Zigbee devices and gateway PC

Obtained Data

Through the trial, obtained data are the following:

- Medical check of the 1st day, such as blood tests, body/athletic abilities, body compositions, urinalysis, and thoracic pictures,
- CPX data of the 1st day(
- Lifestyle related inqury to the patients
- Record of excercises from 2nd to 7th days, such as weight of before/after, blood pressure of before/after, and, time, number, expected calorie of each exercise item.
- Sensor data of exercise hours(
- Calorie intake during the dietary program, and,
- The change of blood test, BMI, body composition in the 8th day.

After all, detailed data for analysis or data mining could be successfully obtained through the trial.

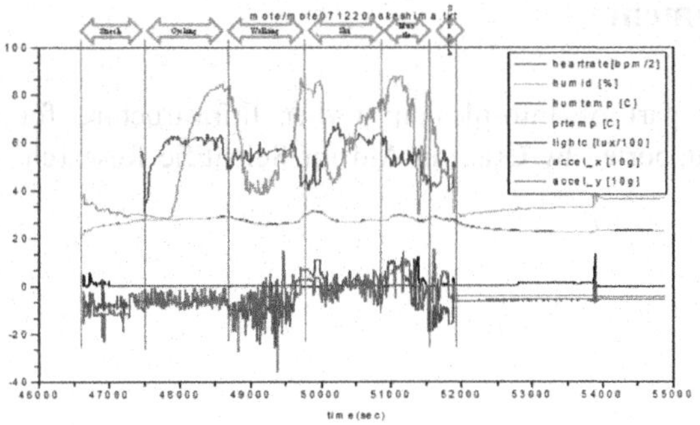

Fig. 6 Example of sensor data

5 Conclusion

Here, we discuss the aspects of SOA in the sensor based medical domain we experienced.

First of all, SOA is often discussed in the context of web systems, which means online and homogeneous system. However, we tried ubiquitous environment where network is not always online, and many kinds of small devices which sometimes has no programmability to developers. It addresses many future challenges to SOA environments.

For scalability, we acknowledged the ease of maintenance of zigbee protocol. Multi-hop communication can extend the communication area, and easy handshake protocol reduces the time and maintenance cost of reconnect.

For heterogeneity, the only device types we could adapt to was one which has open source OS , and on site functionality of updating software. This kind of flexibility must be required although it might affect the device cost and power consumption.

For reliability, we could reduce the sampling frequency of accelerometer to several Hz while keeping the accuracy of activity recognition, which leaded to the longer battery life.

For human friendliness, not only intrusive sensors which we did not use, but also types of sensors which had to be fixed on specific places of a body, such as a heart rate sensor on the chest or on the finger, and an accelerometer which was designated to be fixed on the back, was hated by patients. On the other hands, sensors which are designated to be placed in any place on the body such as a pocket, were easier to use, while they reported practically accurate data, such as an accelerometer, temperature, and humidity sensors.

Security and privacy management, and flexibility on the server side are the future challenges to be discussed to fit SOA.

Acknowledgement

This work is a part of Info-plosion: Cyber Infrastructure for the Information-explosion Era, supported by Grant-in-Aid for Scientific Research on Priority Areas, MEXT, Japan.

References

[1] Council on Competitiveness ed. (2005) Innovate America, Council on Competitiveness US.
[2] Gregory G. Curtin, Michael H. Sommer and Veronika Vis-Sommer eds. (2003) The World of E-Government, The Haworth Press
[3] Japanese Ministry of Health, Labour and Welfare: Particular health check-up/instruction, http://www.mhlw.go.jp/bunya/kenkou/seikatsu/pdf/02.pdf
[4] Kobayashi, K., Nakashima, N., Inoguchi, T., Nishida, D., Tanaka, N., Hoshino, A., Hamada, M., Kozuma, Y., Nakaguma, H., Matsushita, R., Soejima, H., Takayanagi, R., Nawata, H.(2006) Development of a new critical pathway for regional medical network for outpatients with diabetes mellitus. J. Japan Diab. Soc. 49: 817 – 824.
[5] Nakashima, N., Kobayashi, K., Inoguchi, T., Nishida, D., Tanaka, N., Nakazono, H., Hoshino, A., Soejima, H., Takayanagi, R., Nawata, H.(2007) "A Japanese Model of Disease Management," Stud Health Technol Inform, 129: 1174-8.
[6] Sudoh, O. (2007) Community Governance and Sensor Network in the Era of Info-Explosion, Tongji University ed., Proceedings of International Symposium on Urban Governance and Community Development, Shanghai, pp.161-183
[7] Sudoh, O. ed. (2005) Digital Economy and Social Design, Springer-Verlag
[8] Zigbee Alliance, http://www.zigbee.org/

Decision Making Model for Online Music Service Users

Ayako Hiramatsu, Takahiro Yamasaki, Kazuo Nose

Osaka Sangyo University,

3-1-1 Nakagaito, Daito, Osaka 574-8530, Japan

ayako@ise.osaka-sandai.ac.jp, takahiro@eic.osaka-sandai.ac.jp,

nose@ise.osaka-sandai.ac.jp

Abstract. This paper describes a consumer behavior model for online shopping, especially online music services, because they are the most popular online shopping service in Japan. Based on Howard's consumer decision model, questionnaires about decision making for online music services were given to 282 students. The questionnaire results show that almost 90% of respondents have downloaded from online music services, and high school students use such services slightly more than university students. This paper analyzes the questionnaire results by structure equation modeling and examines the relationships between the factors in Howard's model.

1 Introduction

Internet penetration in Japan is remarkable. In 2006 its penetration rate was 68.5%, and the number of Internet users was estimated at 87.54 million (White paper 2007). With the Internet's diffusion, the popularity of e-shopping continues to increase. 63.7% of all Internet users have been using e-shopping for more than two years (Internet Association Japan 2005, 2006), and these numbers are still growing. For marketing, understanding the behavior of e-shopping users is crucial.

To understand consumer behavior, user models are often constructed by analyzing the behavior data of users. Concerning Internet users, there have been some researches about online game models (Hsu and Lu 2004) and e-shopping users (Shih 2004) based on the Technology Acceptance Model (TAM) (Liu 2007). Farag et al. also researched a model that analyzed relationships between e-shops and real shops

Please use the following format when citing this chapter:

Hiramatsu, A., Yamasaki, T., Nose, K., 2008, in IFIP International Federation for Information Processing, Volume 286; Towards Sustainable Society on Ubiquitous Networks, eds. Oya, M., Uda, R., Yasunobu, C., (Boston: Springer), pp. 15–25.

(2007). Moreover, Watanabe and Iwasaki analyzed why consumers buy PCs through the Internet (2007). However, decision making processes based on various factors and the relationship between them have not been analyzed much, due to such difficulties as direct observation and analysis of the subjective conditions of users.

Our research aims to understand how consumers make e-shopping decisions. Consumer behaviors for real shops (Evans et al. 2006) were researched. Based on Howard's famous consumer decision model (1989), we examined decision making processes in online shopping. The target of this analysis was narrowed to online music services, which are the most popular online shopping service. Questionnaires about decision making for online music services were done with Japanese consumers. The questionnaire results were analyzed by structure equation modeling (Schumacker and Loman 2004) (Kline 2005) to examine the relationships between the factors in Howard's model.

2 Decision Making Process of Consumers

The Howard-Sheth buying behavior model presented in 1969 is one important model that explains consumer decision making. It explains the complexity of the consumer decision making process for incomplete information with an S-O-R paradigm that consists of three components: stimulus-organism-response. In this model, consumers are motivated by perceiving a stimulus, and then they shift to purchase after composing concepts to learn purchases. Furthermore, it is hypothesized that the problem is simplified as learning continues. As a result of experimental researches based on this model, Howard proposed the simple consumer decision model shown in Figure 1.

This simple consumer decision model is comprised of six interrelated components, as shown in Figure 1: information (F), brand recognition (B), attitude toward the brand (A), confidence in judging the brand (C), intention (I), and purchase (P). The three central components (B, A, and C) comprise the buyer's brand image and the ABCs of consumer behavior.

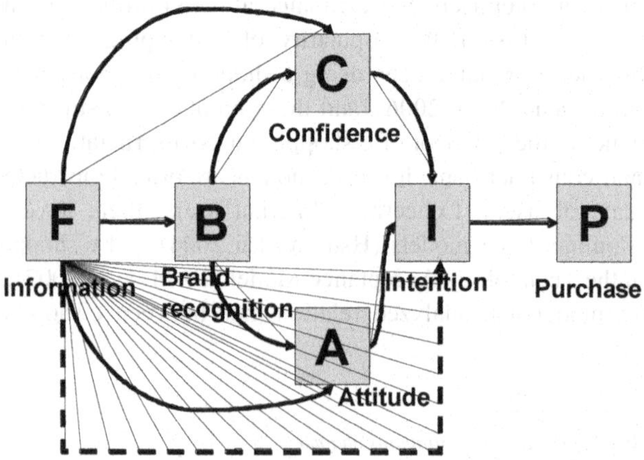

Figure1: Howard's consumer decision model modified for routine problem solving

"Information" (F) is what is received and stored. The perception is stored, not the stimulus. "Brand recognition" (B) reflects the extent to which the consumer knows enough about the brand to distinguish it from others. "Confidence" (C) is the consumer's degree of certainty that his/her evaluative judgment of a brand, whether favorable or unfavorable, is correct. "Attitude" (A), the second part of brand image, is the extent to which consumers expect the brand to satisfy their particular needs. "Intention" (I) is a mental state that reflects the consumer's plan to buy a specified number of units of a particular brand in a specified time period. "Purchase" (P) shows whether the consumer really does buy the brand. The influence from "information" (F) to "intention" (I) is connected by a dotted line. This arrow is added in routine problem solving cases when consumers repeatedly buy a low-price or a daily product.

3 Analysis Target

3.1 Online Music Service

With annual growth of about 2% since 2003, the size of the visual contents market was estimated in 2005 at approximately 11.3 trillion yen (about $ 0.1 trillion), broken down as follows: visual contents/5.3 trillion yen, audio contents/1.0 trillion, and text contents/5.0 trillion (White paper, 2007). Moreover, the music or game contents market has especially expanded. The usage rate of musical contents is 10.9%, which is the highest among such various contents as visual contents, audio contents, and text contents, of contents by Internet with PCs. Even using contents through mobile Internet, the usage rate of musical ring tones is the highest with 15.6% and the rate of downloading songs is 14.0%, which is second. Based on this present condition, we chose online music services as our research subject for online shopping through Internet.

3.2 Survey Items

To adapt Howard's model to online music services, we considered the following survey items. Channels for acquiring information about online music services are considered communication among friends and families, information from such media as television, radio, and magazines, and such Internet sources as e-mails and web pages. "Brand recognition" corresponds to musicians and online music service providers. For "Confidence", we considered confidence in artists and providers. "Attitude" items include sound quality, price, payment methods, data size, and outtakes or live versions. "Intention" included consumer's income, popularity, season, and advertising campaign. "Purchase" shows whether consumers really buy the music. This experiment examined the degree of experience with online music services.

4 Questionnaire Survey

4.1 Survey Condition

The questionnaires asked participants to indicate their degree of agreement with the above items based on a five-point scale: 5-strongly agree, 4-agree, 3-neutral, 2-disagree, and 1-strongly disagree. The question details are shown in the appendix. 282 consumers (164 university students, 106 high school students, and 12 others) answered the questionnaires.

Table1: Results of download medium

	All	High school students	University students
Mobile phone	44.0%	64.2%	29.3%
PC	22.0%	9.4%	29.9%
Both	23.8%	19.8%	27.4%
Others	10.3%	6.6%	13.4%

Table2: Number of download experiences

	All	High school students	University students
51～	37.9%	38.7%	37.8%
11～50	25.2%	28.3%	23.8%
2～10	23.8%	25.5%	23.2%
1	2.5%	0.9%	1.2%
0	10.6%	6.6%	14.0%

Table 1 shows the ratios of download media. Many respondents use mobile phones. From Table 1, more than 80% of high school students and over 50% of university students use mobile phones, including respondents who use both PCs and mobile phones. Table 2 shows the numbers of download experiences from online music services. Almost 90% of students have downloaded music.

4.2 Questionnaire Results

The questionnaire results are shown in Table 3-a, 3-b. The symbols on the left row correspond to the number of the questions shown in the appendix.

Table 3-a: Questionnaire results

	Strongly agree	Agree	Neutral	Disagree	Strongly disagree
F101	17.4%	34.0%	27.0%	9.9%	11.7%
F102	7.1%	28.0%	35.8%	12.4%	16.7%
F201	8.2%	24.1%	31.2%	17.4%	19.1%
F202	2.5%	15.6%	36.2%	19.1%	26.6%
F301	4.6%	5.3%	24.1%	18.1%	**47.9%**
F302	2.8%	13.5%	27.3%	20.9%	**35.5%**
F303	6.4%	14.2%	24.5%	17.0%	**37.9%**
F401	14.9%	35.1%	24.1%	13.5%	12.4%
F402	24.5%	25.2%	20.9%	14.2%	15.2%
F403	24.8%	29.8%	23.4%	8.2%	13.8%
F404	17.4%	32.6%	26.6%	12.4%	11.0%
F501	8.5%	27.7%	33.3%	13.1%	17.4%
F502	15.2%	20.9%	34.0%	14.2%	15.6%
F601	9.2%	14.5%	27.0%	17.4%	**31.9%**
F602	11.7%	17.4%	26.2%	14.2%	**30.5%**
F603	11.3%	13.1%	29.1%	14.2%	**32.3%**
F701	17.0%	29.4%	22.7%	13.5%	17.4%
F702	11.0%	27.3%	31.9%	16.0%	13.8%
F703	18.1%	22.7%	26.6%	13.1%	19.5%
B101	6.0%	16.0%	24.5%	**21.3%**	**32.3%**
B102	27.7%	29.4%	23.4%	9.2%	10.3%
C101	4.3%	13.1%	42.6%	21.3%	18.8%
C102	13.5%	22.3%	41.1%	13.8%	9.2%
A101	48.6%	23.0%	14.2%	5.7%	8.5%

The results of Information questions reveal that many students don't think information by e-mail is very important. Furthermore, information by radio is not important because students do not usually listen to radio. Such information from Internet as web logs and web pages is relatively important. Direct word-of-mouth is more important than word-of-mouth by Internet. The most important information comes from TV; clearly, students are greatly influenced by TV.

As the results of "Brand recognition" questions, students pay much more attention to the musicians than delivery providers. Since consumers cannot directly examine the products of online shopping, it is often asserted that the reliability of the online stores is very important. However, with online music services, consumers can listen to trial songs as products, providing them a change to examine products almost directly. Therefore, consumers care about songs as products, but they have little concern about the reliability of providers.

The "Confidence" results for indirect purchases suggest that consumers do not have confidence that they will be satisfied with products and providers. Therefore, many respondents answered "Neutral."

Table 3-b: Questionnaire results

	Strongly agree	Agree	Neutral	Disagree	Strongly disagree
A102	44.3%	17.7%	14.9%	8.9%	14.2%
A201	58.5%	22.0%	11.7%	4.3%	3.5%
A202	21.6%	19.1%	27.0%	17.4%	14.9%
A203	12.1%	13.1%	18.4%	**23.8%**	**32.6%**
A301	56.7%	19.5%	13.5%	4.3%	6.0%
A302	16.0%	12.4%	30.9%	16.0%	24.8%
A303	19.9%	21.3%	27.0%	11.3%	20.6%
A401	41.5%	19.1%	20.6%	8.5%	10.3%
I101	47.2%	25.5%	14.5%	7.1%	5.7%
I102	39.4%	23.0%	25.5%	5.3%	6.7%
I201	7.1%	6.4%	18.8%	23.4%	**44.3%**
I202	5.3%	5.3%	21.3%	19.5%	**48.6%**
I301	19.9%	18.8%	24.1%	14.2%	23.0%
I302	31.2%	25.5%	19.1%	9.9%	14.2%
I303	27.7%	22.7%	22.3%	10.3%	17.0%
I304	17.0%	18.1%	28.7%	14.9%	21.3%
I401	14.5%	14.9%	24.5%	18.4%	27.7%
I402	31.9%	19.9%	20.6%	9.6%	18.1%

Regarding questions about "Attitude," consumers are naturally interested in price. Trial services, sound quality, and data size are clearly important. Opinions are divided about accounting systems.

For questions about "Intention," consumers want to repeatedly download and buy songs. Many consumers also want to download new releases or hit songs. Because the price of one song is cheap or because they can be billed for their purchases, the opportunity of income does not equal the opportunity of downloading.

5 Analysis by Structural Equation Modeling

We verified Howard's consumer decision model as a hypothesis for the decision making process of online music service users by structural equation modeling with the questionnaire results.

In the questionnaire, each component of the model has several questions. Since "Information" and "Intention" have more questions, we analyzed the factors of these two components to extract the main factors before structural equation modeling. The factor analysis results suggest that "Information" consists of three factors: "TV," "Radio," and "Consumer Generated Media (CGM)." "Intention" consists of two factors: "Popularity" and "Campaign." These factors are latent variables for structural equation modeling.

"Brand recognition" and "Confidence" are treated as latent variables. The questions about each component are observed variables for the corresponding components. For "Purchase" as a latent variable, the experience of download is an observed variable.

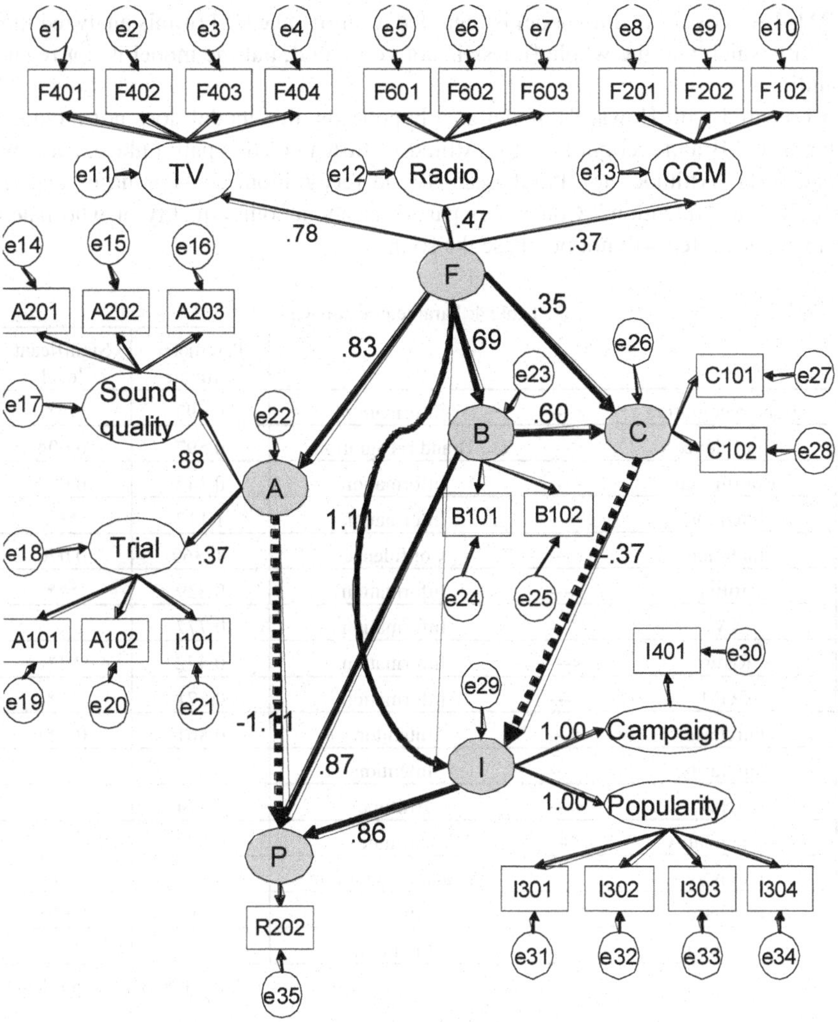

Figure 2: Consumer decision model as analysis result

"Attitude" in the questionnaires consists of nine questions. Since questions about services included in "Intention" are fit for "Attitude" due to the contents, two questions are assigned to "Attitude," but not to "Intention." Therefore "Attitude" consists of 11 questions. Among them, questions about data size and accounting system are not related to other factors and are difficult to explain with questionnaire results. For that reason, "Attitude" consists of two factors: "Sound quality" and "Trial."

Figure 2 shows the analysis results of structural equation modeling. Table 4 shows the estimated parameters between the latent variables. The following are the fit criteria of this model. The goodness of fit index (GFI) is 0.865, the comparative fit index (CFI) is 0.912, and the root mean square error of approximation (RMSEA) is 0.058. If the GFI and CFI values are 1.0, the model perfectly fits to the data. Empirically, a desirable value is over 0.95 or 0.9. The RMSEA value is desirable if it is less than 0.05: if RMSEA is over 0.1, the model is regarded as unfit. The GFI of this analyzed model is a little small and the whole fitness is not very good, but the model is not regarded as unfit.

Compared with Howard's model as a hypothesis, this model does not include the paths from "Brand recognition" to "Attitude." Instead of this path failure, paths were added from "Attitude" to "Purchase," "Brand recognition" to "Purchase" and from "Attitude" to "Intention." Consumers particular about sound quality or who listen to trial versions often will not purchase the song.

Table 4: Parameter estimates

			Parameter estimate	Significant level
Brand recognition	<---	Information	0.693	***
Confidence	<---	Brand recognition	0.597	0.002
Confidence	<---	Information	0.346	0.037
Intention	<---	Information	1.112	***
Intention	<---	Confidence	-0.369	0.076
Attitude	<---	Information	0.829	***
TV	<---	Information	0.777	
Radio	<---	Information	0.472	***
CGM	<---	Information	0.371	***
Purchase	<---	Intention	0.861	0.027
Popularity	<---	Intention	1	
Trial	<---	Attitude	0.374	
Sound quality	<---	Attitude	0.882	***
Purchase	<---	Brand recognition	0.874	0.02
Purchase	<---	Attitude	-1.11	0.095
Campaign	<---	Intention	1	***

*** : 0.001significant level

The following are the indirect effects from "Information" to "Purchase:"

- By Attitude: -0.92
- By Brand recognition: 0.60
- By Brand recognition and Confidence and Intention: -0.13
- By Confidence and Intention: -0.11
- By Intention: 0.95

There are negative effects by "Attitude" or "Confidence." The large effect from "Information" to "Intention" can be explained by the many experienced consumers who regard downloading music as a *normal* thing. Moreover, the positive effect from "Information" to "Purchase" by "Brand recognition" can be explained by simple purchases that are decided as soon as information is acquired. From the above analysis, in online music services, consumers decide to purchase immediately after information acquisition; on the other hand, the close examination of "Attitude" and "Confidence" discourages consumers from buying music.

6 Conclusion

This paper described a consumer behavior model for online music services, the most popular online service in Japan. Based on Howard's consumer decision model, we designed a hypothetical model of a consumer decision model for online music services. The proposed hypothetical model was examined with questionnaire data. As a result of analysis, the model slightly differed from the hypothetical model. However, since its fitness is not very good, it must be improved. Moreover, this questionnaire was only given to students, so we need to include different populations.

References

Martin Evans, Ahmad Jamal, and Gordon Foxall (2006) *Consumer Behavior*, John Wiley & Sons.

Sendy Farag, Tim Schwanen, Martin Dijst, and Jan Faber (2007) "Shopping online and/or in-store? A structural equation model of the relationships between e-shopping and in-store shopping," *Transportation Research Part A*, 41, pp.125-141.

John A. Howard (1989) *Buyer Behavior in Marketing Strategy*, Prentice Hall.

Chin-Lung Hsu and His-Peng Lu (2004) "Why do people play on-line games? An extended TAM with social influences and flow experience," *Information & Management*, 41, pp.853-868.

Internet Association Japan (2006) *Internet white paper 2006*, Impress.

Internet Association Japan (2005) *Internet white paper 2005*, Impress.

Rex B. Kline (2005) *Principles and Practice of Structural Equation Modeling*, The Guilford Press.

Chuanlan Liu (2007) *Modeling Consumer Adoption of The Internet as a Shopping Medium*, Cambria Press.

Randall E. Schumacker and Richard G. Lomax (2004) *A Beginner's Guide to Structural Equation Modeling*, Lawrence Erlbaum Associates.

Hung-Pin Shih (2004) "An empirical study on predicting user acceptance of e-shopping on the Web," I*nformation & Management* , 41, pp.351-368.

Kazuo Watanabe and Kunihiko Iwasaki (2007) "Factors Affecting Consumer Decisions about Purchases at Online Shops and Stores," *Proceedings of IEEE CEC/EEE 2007*, pp80-87.

White paper (2007) *Information and Communications in Japan* http://www.johotsusintokei.soumu.go.jp/whitepaper/ja/h19/index.html

Appendix

[Questions]

"Information"

- Direct word-of-mouth

F101: Do you think word-of-mouth information from your friends is important?
F102: Do you think word-of-mouth information from your family is important?

- Word-of mouth by Internet

F201: Do you think the information from web logs or BBS without registration systems is important?
F202: Do you think the information from BBS with registration systems is important?

- E-mail

F301: Do you think direct mail is important?
F302: Do you think the information from e-mails for members only is important?
F303: Do you think the information from fan clubs is important?

- TV

F401: Do you think the information from TV commercials is important?
F402: Do you want to get TV programs theme songs?
F403: Do you think the information in musical TV programs is important?
F404: Do you want to get movie theme songs?

- Magazines

F501: Do you think the advertisements in magazines are important?
F502: Do you think articles about musicians in magazines are important?

- Radio

F601: Do you think the information from radio commercials is important?
F602: Do you think the information from radio music programs is important?
F603: Do you think information about musicians from special radio programs is important?

- Web pages

F701: Do you think the information of hit charts on web pages is important?
F702: Do you think the information from video delivery web sites is important?
F703: Do you think the information in musician web sites is important?

"Brand recognition"

B101: Do you try to learn a lot about music delivery providers?
B102: Do you try to learn a lot about the musicians whose songs you are downloading?

"Confidence"

C101: Do you have confidence in the reliability of delivery providers before purchasing?

C102: Do you have confidence that you will be satisfied with a particular musician's songs before downloading?

"Attitude"

- Trial

A101: Do you think a trial service in delivery sites is important?

A102: Even if you know the song, do you listen to a trial of it?

- Sound quality

A201: Do you pay attention to sound quality?

A202: Do you think such alternative versions as live recordings and outtakes are important?

A203: Are you satisfied with the sound quality by which you can judge the song?

- Accounting system

A301: Do you think price is important?

A302: Do you think a monthly fee is a better accounting system?

A303: Do you prefer payment per song as an accounting system?

- Data size

A401: Do you consider the data size of songs?

"Intention"

- Service

I101: Do you think the possibility of re-download is important?

I102: Do you think the payment method is important?

- Money

I201: When you have extra money, do you want to download a song soon?

I202: On payday, do you want to download a song soon?

- Motivation

I301: Do you want to download seasonable songs?

I302: Do you want to download new releases?

I303: Do you want to download hit songs?

I304: Do you want to download award-winning songs?

- Campaign

I401: If you can get one free song by purchasing of ten as part of a special campaign, do you want to download?

I402: If you can get unlimited songs much for 300 yen (about $2.7) for a limited time, do you want to download?

Intraday-scale Long Interval Method of Classifying Intramonth-Scale Revisiting Mobile Users

Toshihiko Yamakami

ACCESS, 2-8-16 Sarugaku-cho, Chiyoda-ku, Tokyo, 101-0064 Japan,
e-mail: Toshihiko.Yamakami@access-company.com

Abstract Penetration of the mobile Internet has increased its visibility worldwide. This enables analysis of detailed time-dimensional user behavior data. It also increases the industry need to identify and retain mobile users with strong loyalty to a particular mobile Web site. The author proposes an intramonth-scale revisit classification method for identifying intramonth-scale, revisiting mobile users. The author performs a case study and the result shows that the proposed method shows 87 % classifier accuracy. The author discusses a trade-off between classifier accuracy and a true positive ratio.

1 Introduction

The mobile Internet has increased its visibility in Web-based services. A major Japanese social network service provider published a press release in 2007 revealing that access from handsets had exceeded that from PCs. The mobile technology provider's long-held dream, that the mobile Internet will play a crucial key role in the Internet, is coming true. The mobile Internet is characterized by its 24-hour characteristic. It is available for 24 hours a day. This means that it is crucial to identify user behaviors in a time dimension. Mobile Internet users are "easy-come, easy-go", therefore, content providers require a new methodology to identify mobile users with strong loyalty to their mobile Web sites. In this paper, the author proposes an intraday-scale long interval method of identifying intramonth-scale, revisiting users.

Please use the following format when citing this chapter:

Yamakami, T., 2008 in IFIP International Federation for Information Processing, Volume 286; Towards Sustainable Society on Ubiquitous Networks, eds. Oya, M., Uda, R., Yasunobu, C., (Boston: Springer), pp. 27–36.

2 Purpose and Related Works

2.1 Purpose

The purpose of this research is to coin a new methodology for identifying intramonth-scale revisiting mobile users.

2.2 Related Works

Mining data streams is a field of increasing interest due to the growing importance of its applications and the dissemination of data stream generators. Research dealing with continuously generated, massive amounts of data quickly caught the attention of researchers in recent years [2] [4].

Web mining has become a hot research topic as services on the Web have emerged in the last decade [10] [5]. However, many techniques used for the PC Internet cannot be applied to the mobile Internet because the lifetime of each item is short due to screen size limitations.

Mobile clickstream analysis is a relatively unexplored field of research because SMS or WML1.3-based mobile Internet sites are still used in many countries. The WML deck consists of multiple cards, where many user clicks are absorbed by the client and are not available to the server.

The dynamics and volatility of mobile Internet services prevented long-term observational studies. Considering the fast growth of the mobile Internet, it is an important research topic to be covered. Halvey has performed the first large-scale mobile Internet analysis. He has reported a positive relationship to the day of the week in the mobile clickstream [3]. Church has performed sessions and queries analysis of mobile Internet searching with large real-world data [1]. The author conducted a regularity study on the mobile clickstream and reported 80 % accuracy in users that revisited the following month using statistical data on regularity [6] It showed an 80 % true positive ratio for regularity in long-term mobile web access [8]. However, this research covered only day-scale behavior.

The author proposed an early version of the time slot method, to identify regular users with a long interval of intraday Web visits [9]. The method was coined on the conjecture that the users who come to a web service twice in one day tend to return to the service in the following month [7]. From the empirical results, it appeared to be a promising method. The method identifies a regular user with an explicit partition among the active time slots. The limitation of the previous study is that the case studies were applied only to pay-per-month services. Services requiring subscription without a fee are not covered in past literature. These services have a large degree of volatile users and have an increased need to identify the users with strong loyalty. The originality of this research is to verify the method using services that do not charge content fees.

2.3 A Regularity-oriented Service Model

The author proposes a regularity-oriented service model as illustrated in Fig. 1 [7]. The service consists of two parts: pattern identification and service customization. This paper deals with the former one. The possible customization services are illustrated in Table 1. These services can be used to enclose regular users or to improve content based on the navigation patterns of regular users.

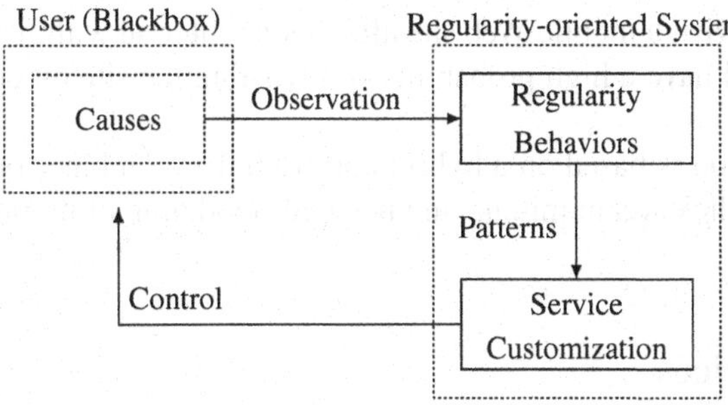

Fig. 1 Regularity-oriented service model.

Table 1 Customization services.

service	description
Menu customization	reflecting user patterns
Content rating & ranking	rating based on the navigations of regular users
Classified user service	additional service to enclose regular users

Regularity is important not only in subscription-based services, but also in mobile advertising. IDC predicts that mobile advertising will prosper in the next 5-10 years. Unique mobile-specific features in advertising include the mind-share of the Web site driving users to advertisements. Measurement of user mind-share can become an additional new feature for Internet advertising.

3 Long Interval Method

3.1 Assumptions

Past literature indicated the assumption that users who revisit a mobile Web site after a long interval within one day will have a high probability of revisiting the site in the following month.

In this paper, the author attempts to propose a method based on the assumption that users who revisit a mobile Web site after a long interval within the first visit day of the month will have a high probability of revisiting the site on other days within that month.

This assumption is based on a hybrid approach that combines quantitative measures in mobile clickstream mining and behavior modeling of mobile users.

3.2 Paid Services

The author proposes a long interval method for paid services as follows: [7]

Key Idea When a user returns to a particular web site after a long interval within a day, it is likely that he/she will return to the web site in the following month.
Long Interval Method: A method of classifying users using a long interval within one day from their click logs.
Regular Monthly Users: Group of users who will revisit the particular Web site in the following month.
Regularity classification: Two classifications, "regular"(positive) or "non-regular" (negative).
Regularity true/false evaluation: Whether a user marked as "regular" will revisit a specific mobile site in the following month.

The processing flow of classification is depicted as follows:

1. For month(m), take a sequence of clicks from clickstream for each user.
2. For each sequence, calculate the interval sequence.
3. For each interval sequence, filter out long intervals using a threshold value to identify intervals during one day.
4. Use the range-threshold for a long interval to classify it as positive (interval exists in the predefined range-threshold) or negative (no interval falls within the range-threshold).

The method provides an 88–92 % true positive ratio, however, it shows poor classifier accuracy.

3.3 Non-paid Services

Measuring user regularity is difficult for non-paid services. The author proposes a simple long interval method to measure the probability of revisiting within the same month.

First Visit Long Interval Method: A user is marked as "regular" (positive) when the user returns to a particular mobile Web side on his/her first visit day.
Regularity classification: Two classifications, "regular"(positive) or "non-regular" (negative).
Regularity true/false evaluation: Whether a user marked as "regular" will revisit a specific mobile site by the end of the month.

The processing flow is as follows:

1. For month(m), take a sequence of clicks from clickstream for each user.
2. For each sequence, calculate the interval sequence.
3. Take the first visit day interval, which is the interval before the predefined threshold value (e.g. 24 hours) in the sequence.
4. Use the range-threshold for the long interval to classify it as positive (interval exists in the predefined range-threshold) or negative (no interval falls within the range-threshold).

3.4 Classification Procedure

The classifier determines for each user whether more than the threshold value is found in the first visit day. If a long intraday interval is found, the user is marked as "will revisit", otherwise, that user is marked as "will not revisit".

The accuracy of the classifier shows the number of users in true positive and true negative classifications divided by the total number of users. The true positive ratio shows the number of users who revisited after a day-scale interval (in this case study, one day), divided by the total number of users that are marked as "will revisit". The false positive ratio shows the number of users who did not revisit after a day-scale interval divided by the total number of users that are marked as "will revisit". The true negative ratio shows the number of users who did not revisit after a day-scale interval divided by the total number of users that are marked as "will not revisit". The false negative ratio shows the number of users who revisited after a day-scale interval, divided by the total number of users that are marked as "will not revisit".

4 Case Study

4.1 Data Set

The subject of observation is a commercial car information service on the mobile Internet. This service also provides a car-auction service. The service was launched in June 2000. In June 2000, after filtering out non-mobile user identifiers, 514,180 clicks were associated with mobile user identifiers. 43,562 unique user identifiers were logged.

Basically, the service was converted from a PC Internet car information service to Compact HTML, a dialect of HTML for the mobile Internet. Although it is a commercial service, it does not charge a fee. Since it is a specialized service for a specific domain, it has a specific user segment. In relation to the nature of the accompanying auction service, the web traffic varied from month to month. The peak month and bottom month volume fluctuated at a ratio of one to nine, and had one to three volume fluctuations during the period of June 2000 to May 2001.

The service provided a used car value search, car purchase requests, a used car market value search, and a car auction service.

The service is up and operating now, however the service menus have changed over the span of time. The recent clickstream logs were not available for this research.

4.2 Results

The classification accuracy of the commercial mobile service in June 2000 is depicted in Table 2. The classifier accuracy (including both true positive and true negative), true positive, false positive, true negative, and false positive ratios are shown in the table. The internal threshold was set in the range of 2–720 minutes. Revisits are evaluated based on whether a user will return back to this specific mobile site after a certain threshold value. In this case study, the threshold value is 24 hours.

As interval threshold values increase, the classifier accuracy also increases. When interval threshold values are too small, it is difficult to get good classifier accuracy because unexpected intervals will impact the accuracy.

As interval threshold values increase, the true positive ratios improve. It should be noted that the true positive ratio does not reach 50 % even with the largest threshold value, 720 minutes (12 hours). The true positive ratio is poor in this proposed method.

As interval threshold values increase, the true negative ratios slowly decrease. The difference is not big, 91.77 % with a 2-minute threshold, and 88.88 % with a 720-minute threshold.

The classifier accuracy is driven by the true negative value, therefore, the classifier accuracy cannot exceed 88.88 % with a 720-minute threshold.

This shows a poor true positive ratio. The author attributes that the reason for the poor true positive ratio to a limitation of the first visit day analysis. First visit day analysis can give a good indication of "departing" users. However, there may be other users whose long-interval revisit patterns are shown on subsequent visit days, which are not used for classification. The first visit day analysis offers an advantage in terms of processing performance because the classifier needs to deal with the first visit day only. There is a trade-off between this performance advantage and a poor true positive ratio.

Considering the trade-off between classification accuracy and a true positive ratio, it is considered appropriate to use 12 hours as a threshold value. However, there is not a great difference between 1 hour and 12 hours because the true positive ratio is still under 50 %.

In order to improve the true positive ratio, a hybrid approach is needed to compensate the true positive ratio.

Table 2 Classification Accuracy in June 2000.

interval threshold (minutes)	classifier accuracy	true positive	false positive	true negative	false positive
2	73.76 %	22.83 %	77.17 %	91.77 %	8.23 %
3	79.67 %	26.58 %	73.42 %	91.08 %	8.92 %
5	83.06 %	30.24 %	69.76 %	90.54 %	9.46 %
10	85.07 %	33.96 %	66.04 %	90.13 %	9.87 %
20	85.75 %	35.85 %	64.15 %	89.98 %	10.02 %
40	86.05 %	36.81 %	63.19 %	89.89 %	10.11 %
60	86.24 %	37.41 %	62.59 %	89.82 %	10.18 %
120	86.51 %	37.98 %	62.02 %	89.62 %	10.38 %
240	86.82 %	38.90 %	61.10 %	89.41 %	10.59 %
480	87.18 %	40.22 %	59.78 %	89.13 %	10.87 %
720	87.42 %	41.25 %	58.75 %	88.88 %	11.12 %

5 Discussion

5.1 Usefulness of a Behavior-Based Hybrid Approach

The case study demonstrates the positive result on the assumption of a relationship between multiple visits with a long interval on the first visit day and the probability of revisiting on another day within the month.

It indicates that first day behavior can be used for user classification. It is a valuable finding for exploring mobile user behavior, which is characteristically "easy come, easy-go". This has a certain effect on performance that avoids large-scale computation because first day analysis is easier than other methods of analysis that utilize click logs with a long span of time.

This also suggests the implication that behavior modeling can improve data-intensive mobile data mining by using a high-level behavior assumption that is derived from long-term observations. The increasing size of mobile click logs provides a challenge for mobile data mining. The promising result from this hybrid approach for behavior modeling and data analysis is a step forward for further mobile data mining, especially in terms of user regularity.

5.2 Limitations

These results were obtained within the scope of a specific service. The characteristics that were encountered could be service-specific or user group profile-specific.

The data were obtained from mobile clickstreams in 2000. Comparisons with the latest mobile clickstreams are needed in order to trace the recent results.

It should be also noted that the periodical update of content during a day is a basic, unchanging mobile service pattern. The data obtained in 2000 are applicable as long as this basic service pattern persists. The services observed in 2000 are up and in commercial operation today, however, the most recent data were unavailable for this research.

5.3 Applicability

The identification of users with a high revisit ratio can be utilized for many mobile applications including user interface customization and content evaluation. It is important to identify which applications can use this measure to realize value-added services on the mobile Internet.

The revisit ratio can be used as a litmus test to measure the effectiveness of new services or new user interfaces. It is difficult to capture user feedback on a mobile Web site because the user interface is limited and users often do not want to provide additional input for service feedbacks. Content providers can also use the navigation patterns of loyal users to identify the key services and content on their site. Content providers can introduce new user interfaces or new services and evaluate them based on behavior changes among loyal users.

Also, it is feasible for content providers to differentiate between users with high retention and others in their services. This could improve a mobile Web site's capability to capture users.

The mobile Internet has an "easy-come and easy-gone" characteristic, therefore, applications such as these, which gain indirect feedback from users, are very valuable.

A major Japanese wireless carrier announced in a press release recently that they made their unique user identifier system available to both official and non-official carrier sites, starting in March 2008. This will leverage the applicability of the proposed method because the user identifier is available to all content providers.

5.4 Cross-service Comparison

There are distinguishable differences between the news service studied in past literature and the car information service observed in this paper. It is interesting to note that the news service in the literature reported a high true positive ratio and poor classifier accuracy. In contrast, the case study in this paper shows high classifier accuracy and a poor true positive ratio. The differences are depicted in Table 3.

Table 3 Cross-service comparison.

	news service	car information service
intra-month log volume	rather stable	fluctuating
fee	monthly fee (partially free)	free
target	paid experience	all
true positive ratio	high	low
classifier accuracy	low	high

Stable and general services are considered to have a high true positive rate using the intraday interval method, and fluctuated and specific-preference services have a high true negative ratio and a poor true positive ratio.

Although the contrast is interesting, the fundamental cause of this differentiation cannot be identified from this study alone. Further analysis of this difference remains for further studies.

6 Conclusion

The mobile Internet is characterized by "easy-come and easy-gone" users. The mobile Internet has a unique perspective on this from the dimension of time. The author proposed an intraday long interval method for identifying users with a high probability of revisiting on an intramonth scale. The case study showed classifier accuracy of 90 % with commercial data from 2000.

This method can be applied to a wide range of mobile data services, assuming only a user identifier and time stamps in clickstreams. This method can be applied in the first month of deployment because it uses intraday behavior and intramonth prediction.

This method can be utilized to distinguish users with different loyalties to a specific mobile Web site. Therefore, it enables the tracking of user clickstreams with a higher probability of revisiting in order to identify preferred content and services, which, in turn, facilitates the timely improvement of mobile Web content.

References

1. Church, K., Smyth, B., Cotter, P., Bradley, K.: Mobile information access: A study of emerging search behavior on the mobile internet. ACM Transactions on the Web (TWEB) **1**(1), Article 4 (2007)
2. Gaber, M.M., Zaslavsky, A., Krishnaswamy, S.: Mining data streams: a review. ACM SIGMOD Record **34**(2), 18–26 (2005)
3. Halvey, M., Keane, M., Smyth, B.: Predicting navigation patterns on the mobile-internet using time of the week. In: WWW2005, pp. 958–959. ACM Press (2005)
4. Jiang, N., Gruenwald, L.: Research issues in data stream association rule mining. ACM SIGMOD Record **35**(1), 14–19 (2006)
5. Liu, J., Zhang, S., Yang, J.: Characterizing web usage regularities with information foraging agents. IEEE Transactions on Knowledge and Data Engineering **16**(5) (2004)
6. Yamakami, T.: Regularity analysis using time slot counting in the mobile clickstream. In: Proceedings of DEXA2006 workshops, pp. 55–59. IEEE Computer Society (2006)
7. Yamakami, T.: A long interval method to identify regular monthly mobile internet users. In: AINA2008 Workshops/Symposium (WAMIS 2008), pp. 1625–1630. IEEE Computer Society Press (2008)
8. Yamakami, T.: A stream-mining-oriented user identification algorithm based on a day-scale click regularity assumption. Journal of Information Processing **49**(7), xxx–xxx (2008)
9. Yamakami, T.: A time slot count in window method suitable for long-term regularity-based user classification for mobile internet. In: MUE 2008, pp. 25–29. IEEE Computer Society Press (2008)
10. Zaiane, O.R., Man Xin, J.H.: Discovering web access patterns and trends by applying olap and data mining technology on web logs. In: ADL '98. IEEE Computer Society (1998)

The Study of Customer Segmentation Examined by Catastrophe Model

Yu-Kai Huang

Institute of Publishing and Culture Enterprise Management

osilo.huang@gmail.com

Abstract. Convenience stores in Taiwan have made remarkable successes with retail delivery services by integrating E-commerce and logistics systems to form a new retail delivery model: "On-line shopping with pick-ups at convenience stores." Although choice behavior has been discussed in marketing, few studies describe the non-linear characteristic of choice behavior. The catastrophe model was used to analyze the linkages between customer satisfaction and switching cost on pick-up point service loyalty. The results indicated that the switching cost plays the splitting factor in the catastrophe model, and a high switching cost makes the discontinuous choice behavior. In the cusp catastrophe mode, "Reselection electronic map" is the main index of the splitting factor. Nevertheless, "The quality of relative service concerning the electronic map" is the main index of the normal factor. It has been expected that a catastrophe approach to discontinuous behavior has made clearly abundant implications. Based on the findings of loyalty in the application of cusp catastrophe theory, the cusp catastrophe model is an appropriate model to know the process of loyalty. It suggests that other researchers could consider the cusp catastrophe theory and other nonlinear techniques, especially for standard approaches not adequately to capture the underlying dynamic.

1 Introduction

The Internet has provided people with a new medium for social activities and has also opened up entirely new features of social reality. In Taiwan, convenience stores,

---

Please use the following format when citing this chapter:

Huang, Y. –K., 2008, in IFIP International Federation for Information Processing, Volume 286; Towards Sustainable Society on Ubiquitous Networks, eds. Oya, M., Uda, R., Yasunobu, C., (Boston: Springer), pp. 37–48.

which are widely distributed, provide a 24-hour purchasing environment for customers. Up to date, the convenience stores have integrated E-commerce with logistics system to form a new retail delivery model: "On-line shopping in an electronic store and pick-up goods in a convenience store." Because convenience stores remain open 24 hours a day even on holidays, on-line shoppers can pick up goods according to their schedules. In Taiwan, portal sites such as Yahoo.com and Pchome.com are providing retail delivery services for on-line customers and have made many remarkable successes.

Taiwan's history of retailing delivery of e-commerce is not long. CVS.com (CVS.com is a joint venture by four families of convenience stores including Family.com, Hi-Life.com, Okcvs.com and Nikomart.com) is an RD provider that began service in the beginning of 2000 in Taiwan, while 7-11.com joined the market at the end of 2000. Because of safe method of payment way and the quick delivery, RD services by convenience stores have become a substantial provider of the electronic commerce logistics in Taiwan. Currently, over 1,200,000 per month orders are completed by the electronic commerce with retail delivery model. Figure 1 shows the retailing structure.

For a RD (Retailing Delivery) system provider, the business volume of the RD service is mostly based on store locations. Therefore, it is difficult for the provider to provide different services for customers. Generally speaking, 7-11 has the greatest share in the E-commerce retail delivery market. It has captured 70% of the market while the other convenience stores only account for 30% of the market. Due to the difficulty for retail delivery providers to make a difference on the operation process, the customer loyalty has become an important issue for marketing practitioners.

The RD system provides an easy on-line shopping process, safe pick-up points and quick delivery service for e-retailing. The retailing delivery includes four functions: (1) e-map, (2) packing process, (3) delivery system and (4) pick-up point. Figure 1 displays the concept of retailing delivery system.

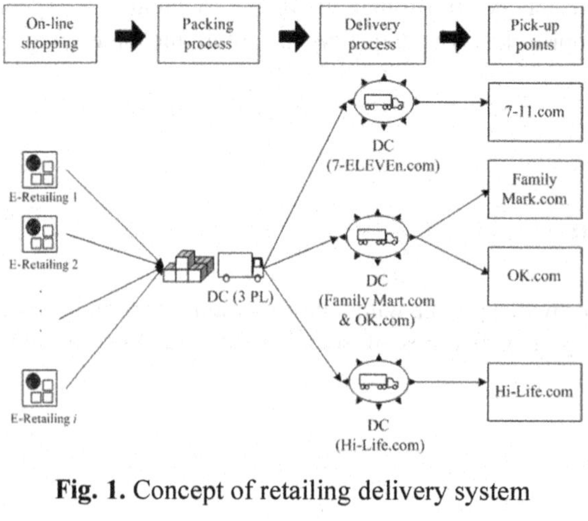

Fig. 1. Concept of retailing delivery system

In the electronic commercial environment, customer preferences are very diverse, and their loyalty level is very low. Companies should acknowledge the changes in customer demand patterns quickly and respond to consumer's behavior appropriately. Thus, an important issue is why consumers vary in, how they divide into their purchases across outlets, and how outlets can gain a greater share of consumer expenditures. It is necessary to use management experience and research results to create an overall picture of the relationships between loyalty and satisfaction. The research issues are included in the following:

1. Applying the catastrophe theory and modeling a Catastrophe Cusp Model to the consumer behavior on the pick-up point choice.
2. Using the Cusp Catastrophe Model for developing loyalty strategies.

2 Theoretical Foundation and Research Method

2.1 Cusp Catastrophe Model

Catastrophe theory is a mathematical theory that describes the relation between two sets of variables, control variables and behavioural variables (state variables), is so-called gradient system. In the gradient system, with fixed value of the control variables, the system always seeks an equilibrium state which means that the value of the behavioural variable changes until the minimum or maximum of a certain quantity is obtained.

Catastrophe theory was developed and popularized in the early 1970's. Initially, it attracted attention very quickly in 1978; an entire issue of behavioral science was devoted to the approach. After a period of criticism, the catastrophe theory is well established and widely applied. Today the theory is very much alive. Numerous nonlinear phenomena that exhibit discontinuous jumps in behavior have been modeled by using the theory, for instance in the field of chemistry [1], physics [2-5], psychology [6] and in the social sciences [7-10]. The models' strengths include that complex behavior can be captured by using significantly fewer nonlinear equations than the number of linear equations needed to describe the same phenomena.

Catastrophes are bifurcations between different equilibria and fixed-point attractors. It is a topological branch of mathematics developed to study and classifies phenomena characterized by sudden shifts in behavior arising from small change in circumstance. The theory specifies that small changes in control parameters across critical thresholds will cause stable equilibria either to disappear, or to bifurcate into multiple equilibria, some of which are stable.

The catastrophe structure most commonly has been applied the cusp model [10]. Figure 2 shows the basic form of the deterministic cusp model generated. Each catastrophe model can be formalized by potential or gradient structures, a potential function $F(x, c)$ is a function of both the system state x and the control parameter(s) c. The Cusp Catastrophe Model consists of one behavior variable and only two control variables. The potential is represented by Eq. (1), the equilibria of Eq. (1) is three-dimensional [7].

$$F(u,v,x) = -\frac{1}{4}x^4 + \frac{1}{2}ux^2 + vx \qquad (1)$$

Where the state variable x is controllability, and u and v are environmental control parameters. As a stable equilibrium state x for this potential gives relative value x of a function F (u, v, x), a set of point (u, v, x) is defined as Eq. (2),

$$\frac{\partial F}{\partial x} = -x^3 + ux + v = 0\ ;\ M_F : \left\{(u,v,x) \,\middle|\, -x^3 + ux + v = 0\right\} \qquad (2)$$

Where M_F is said to be cusp catastrophe manifolded. The values of x in correspondence to which attains a local maximum or minimum satisfies the condition as Eq. (3),

$$3x^2 + u = 0 \qquad (3)$$

Eliminating x from Eq. (2) and Eq. (3), the bifurcation set is express by Eq. (4).

$$4u^3 = 27v^2 \qquad (4)$$

A switch in topology takes place at the values of u and v satisfying Eq. (4), which constitute the catastrophe set. In the equation Eq. (3) x is the state variable, and u, v are control parameters. The parameter u determines whether the system has one or can have two stable equilibria. When $u > 0$ only one stable equilibrium can exit whatever the value of v. When $u < 0$ it depends upon the value of v whether the system has a single low level of stable equilibrium, or a low level and a high level equilibria, or a single high level of equilibrium.

According to the different variable sets, three different cases can be defined. Case 1: There is one stable equilibrium point; Case 2: There are two stable and one unstable equilibrium point; or Case 3: There is one stable equilibrium point, and one at which an instantaneous jump in the state variable occurrence.

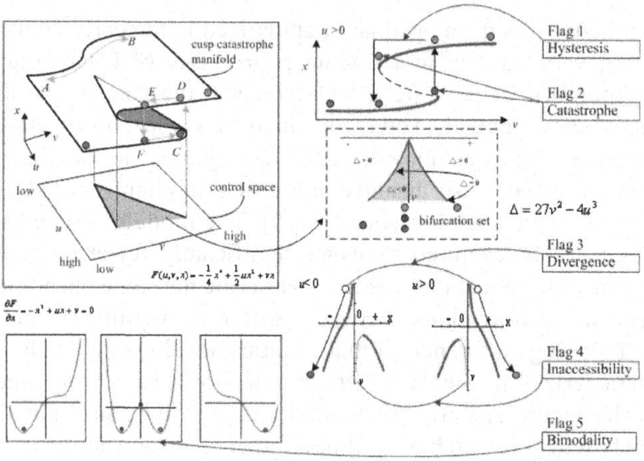

Fig. 2. A Cusp Catastrophe Model and its Five Different Flags

Changes in the control or independent variables (v-right/left movement, and u-back/front movement) cause the changes in the behavior or dependent variable (x-vertical movement). If u is low, smooth changes in v occur in proportion to change in x as shown by examining the travel of point A and B in Figure 2. When u is high (past the singularity) changes in v producing relatively small changes in x until a threshold is reached when there is a sudden discontinuous shift in x. This is depicted by the path from point C to D in Figure 2. Note, that a reversal in v back to the point of the shift in x, will not cause x to return back to its original position, since v will have to move well past to cause x to shift back. This is shown as the movement from point C to E.

2.2 Approaches for Estimating Catastrophe Models

GEMCAT approaches have been successfully applied in a number of different organizational research contexts [7, 11]. Next, the GEMCAT approach is described in some details. Oliva *et al.*'s [12] GEMCAT approach allows all variables in a catastrophe to be latent composites. To accomplish this, the variable X, Y, and Z in the canonical cusp is presented by Equation (5),

$$f(x,y,z) = \frac{1}{4}z^4 - \frac{1}{2}yz^2 - xz \tag{5}$$

Let:

$i = 1\ldots I$ dependent variables;

$j = 1\ldots J$ "splitting" independent variables;

$k = 1\ldots K$ "normal" independent vatiables;

$t = 1\ldots T$ observations;

Z_{it} = the value of the i-th dependent variable on observation t;

Y_{it} = the value of the j-th splitting independent variable on observation t;

X_{kt} = the value of the k-th normal independent variable on observation t;

Now, define three "latent" unobservable variables:

$$Z_t^* = \sum_{i=1}^{I} \alpha_i Z_{it} \tag{6}$$

$$Y_t^* = \sum_{j=1}^{J} \beta_j Y_{jt} \tag{7}$$

$$X_t^* = \sum_{k=1}^{K} \gamma_k X_{kt} \tag{8}$$

Thus, the equation (5) can be redefined as these three "latent" unobservable constructs which can thus accommodate univariate or multivariate measurements for each type of variable. This allows the cusp catastrophe model to be rewritten as shown in Eq. (9):

$$f(X_t^*, Y_t^*, Z_t^*) = \frac{1}{4}Z_t^{*4} - X_t^* Z_t^* - \frac{1}{2}Y_t^* Z_t^{*2} \tag{9}$$

In these terms, the estimation problem, given $X = X_{kt}, \mathrm{Y} = \mathrm{Y}_{jt}$ and $\mathrm{Z} = Z_{it}$, and its derivative set equal to zero can be stated as:

$$\frac{\partial f(X_t^*, Y_t^*, Z_t^*)}{\partial Z_t^*} = Z_t^{*3} - X_t^* - Y_t^* Z_t^* = 0 \tag{10}$$

From equation Eq. (10) the estimating goal is to minimize Eq. (11):

$$\mathrm{Min}_{\alpha i, \beta j, \gamma k} \Phi = \left\| e_t^2 \right\| = \sum_{t=1}^{T} \left[Z_t^{*3} - X_t^* - Y_t^* Z_t^* \right]^2 \tag{11}$$

where the e_t = error. That is, for a given empirical data on various specified dependent, splitting, and normal variables, one wishes to estimate the impact coefficients that define their respective latent variables, which make Φ as close to zero as possible. Minimizing Φ is equivalent to find the best fitting cusp catastrophe surface to the empirical data.

More recently, Lange *et al.* (2000) developed an improved version of the algorithm called GEMCAT II (the GEMCAT II software is developed in Delphi V3.0), which provides greater speed, efficiency, utility and flexibility in terms of analysis and testing [13]. GEMCAT II uses a combination of the Downhill Simplex method and Powell's Conjugate Gradient approach. GEMCAT estimates the various indicator weights by minimizing the total squared residual (Φ) across observations; the default procedure is to run the Downhill Simplex.

3 Data Analysis and Results

3.1 Operationalized of Variable and Data Set

According to the research by Feng and Huang [14], the two most relevant variables influencing the loyalty of a pick-point are switching cost and service quality. With these two variables, the loyalty dynamics may be conceptualized in terms of the cusp catastrophe model. In our hypothesized model, loyalty is the dependent variable z, service quality is a normal variable v, whereas the switching cost is a bifurcation variable u. Cusp catastrophe theory uses a continuous parameter to describe discrete morphology behavior. In a cusp catastrophe model framework, after the intensities of the normal factor and splitting factor are determined, model fitting and dynamical analyses are then performed.

GEMCAT allows x, u, v in the cusp catastrophe model to represent "latent" variables consisting of arbitrary linear combinations of more elementary "indicator" variable. Our operationalizations of the dependent and independent indicator are measure is as follows:

1. Loyalty (X^*):
   $\triangle x_1$: relative loyalty by repurchase
   $\triangle x_2$: relative loyalty by personal partiality
   $\triangle x_3$: relative loyalty by verbal communications
   $\triangle x_4$: relative loyalty by the partialities of other services
2. Service Quality (V^*)
   $\triangle v_1$: relative service quality concerning the electronic map
   $\triangle v_2$: relative service quality concerning the e-tracking
   $\triangle v_3$: relative service quality concerning the service attitude
   $\triangle v_4$: relative service quality concerning the marketing program
3. Switching Cost (U^*)
   u_1: switching cost concerning the personal custom
   u_2: switching cost concerning the electronic map
   u_3: switching cost concerning the distance

The data for the study were collected from an on-line survey that a pop-window invitation contained an embedded URL linkage to the website hosting. Participants who completed the questionnaires were given coupons of 100NT through cellular phone announcements. Survey responds were rated on a five-point Likert scale. The survey lasted for six weeks and was collected 11,462 responds in total. A random sample of 1,500 responses generated from those who had experiences of picking up on-line ordered merchandises at convenience stores was selected because of the restriction of GEMCAT Ⅱ. For instance, the latent variables in a cusp catastrophe model take the following general form:

$$X_t^* = \alpha_1 \Delta x_{1t} + \alpha_2 \Delta x_{2t} + \alpha_3 \Delta x_{3t} + \alpha_4 \Delta x_{4t} \text{，} t = 1, 2, \ldots, 1500 \tag{12}$$

$$V_t^* = \gamma_1 \Delta v_{1t} + \gamma_2 \Delta v_{2t} + \gamma_3 \Delta v_{3t} + \gamma_4 \Delta v_{4t} \text{，} t = 1, 2, \ldots, 1500 \tag{13}$$

$$U_t^* = \beta_1 u_{1t} + \beta_2 u_{2t} + \beta_3 u_{3t} \text{，} t = 1, 2, \ldots, 1500 \tag{14}$$

3.2 Model Fit and Analysis Results

Data were fitted using GEMCAT II version 1.3, yielding the average squared difference Φ/N = 0.000929 between the actual and the predicted X^*, where N represents the number of cases. Substitution of these weights into Eq. (15)-Eq. (18) yields,

$$X^* = \Delta x_1 + 0.2813 \cdot \Delta x_2 + 0.2175 \cdot \Delta x_3 + 0.1981 \cdot \Delta x_4 \tag{15}$$

$$U^* = 0.074 \cdot u_1 + 0.2952 \cdot u_2 + 0.761 \cdot u_3 \tag{16}$$

$$V^* = 0.0615 \cdot \Delta v_1 + 0.0089 \cdot \Delta v_2 + 0.032 \cdot \Delta v_3 + 0.0021 \cdot \Delta v_4 \tag{17}$$

$$Min\Phi = \left\| e_t^2 \right\| = \sum_{t=1}^{1500} \left[Z_t^{*3} - X_t^* - Y_t^* Z_t^* \right]^2 = 2.871 \tag{18}$$

Figure 3 shows the relationships between control variables and dependent variable. Figure 4 explains the distribution situation in the control space of our study samples; the x-axis shows the relative service quality of CVS.com and 7-11.com, while the y-axis expresses the switching cost.

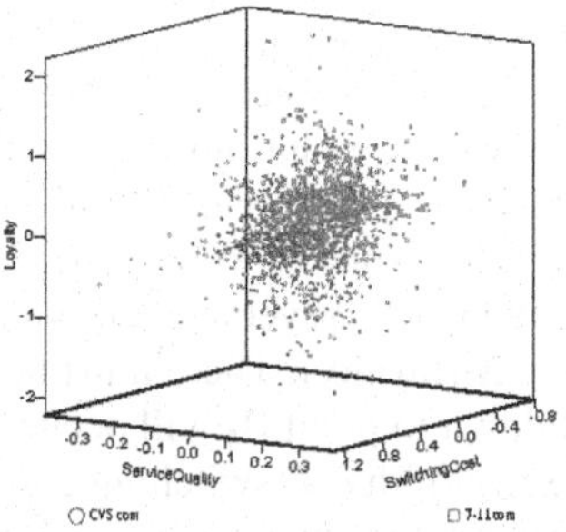

Fig. 3. Relationships between Control Variables and Dependent Variable

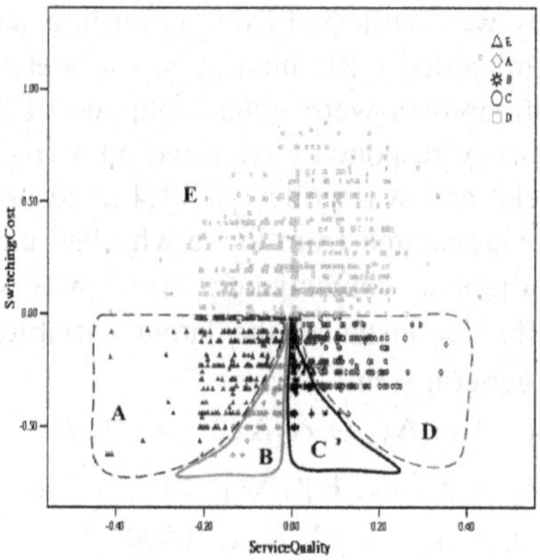

Fig. 4. Control Space Separate from Different Control Set

4 Discussion and Implications

In the previous section, we have demonstrated the efficacy of GEMCAT Ⅱ for testing catastrophe models; next, we will discuss the nonlinear behavior of our behavior model developed by the cusp catastrophe model using software developed of this thesis. Figure 5 presents our mapping of the control variables onto the catastrophe surface structure. The projection of the fold curve into parameter space C yields the catastrophe set K. The b_4 and b_3 are trajectories in C that determine corresponding trajectories B_4 and B_3 of equilibrium behavior.

System dynamics occur on the surface of the model in Figure 5. Changes in position result form changes in U (switching cost) and V (service quality), causing changes in X (loyalty). If U's magnitude is small, then smooth change occurs in X (loyalty), directly proportional to change in X (loyalty), as depicted by Path D as shown in Figure 5. Small difference in the initial starting positions (e.g., Points A_1 and A_2) can result in vastly different values for X (loyalty) as the magnitude of the U (switching cost) variable increases beyond the point where the pleat starts. This can be seen in Figure 5, where A_1 is driven downward, and A_2 is driven upward. At high values of U (switching cost), large changes in V (service quality) will produce relatively small changes in X. At some point, however, a sudden discontinuous shift in X (loyalty) will occur that reverses system behavior from its previous state. This is shown by examining the travel from Point B_4 to B_3 as depicted by Path C in Figure 5. Note that once the shift has happened, reversing the values of V will not cause a substantial downward change in X (loyalty). There must be a significant reversal in U (switching cost) before a shift down to point B_4 will occur. These lags in response are aggravated or mitigated by the size of the U (switching cost) variable. Within the cusp area, the dependent variable can take on two possible values for a given (V, U) pair. This characteristic allows the modeling of lag effects (hystereses).

Moving from the more tactical issues discussed in the illustration to more strategic issues pertaining to service strategy in general, our research indicates that, depending on switching cost, the relation between service quality and loyalty can be nonlinear, at least for some facets of service. This finding has important implications for loyalty strategies and decisions on how to deploy a limited budget across different opportunities to enhance service, given that competitors are making similar decisions. The cusp catastrophe model have five important features, we develop our four different types of loyalty strategies via the catastrophe characteristic and the hysteresis characteristic in this section as shown in Figure 6.

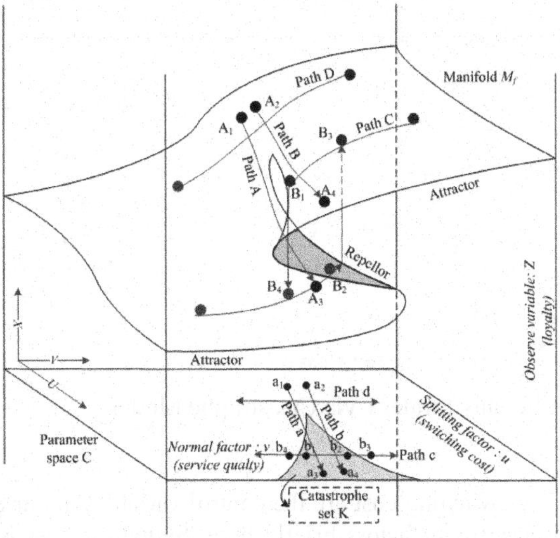

Fig. 5. Behavior Manifold of the Cusp Catastrophe Model

We take CVS.com as an example and develop loyalty strategies via the cusp catastrophe model. Clustering analysis to identify convertible consumers is the first step of developing loyalty strategy. As shown in Figure 6, it is difficult for any strategies to change a consumer if he or she is very satisfied with 7-11.com or switching cost is very high. Idea-convertible consumers must have medium switching cost and there should be difference in service quality between 7-11.com and CVS.com (see Figure 6).

According to our analysis above, switching cost and service quality are the two main factors influencing loyalty. That is, when perceived switching costs are low, dissatisfied consumers should be more likely to defect than satisfied customers because perceived switching benefits outweigh perceived switching costs. Simply speaking, when perceived switching costs are high, customers may remain in spite of their dissatisfaction owing to the perceived switching benefits. Thus, the relationship between customer satisfaction and loyalty is stronger for customers with high switching costs than for those with low switching costs.

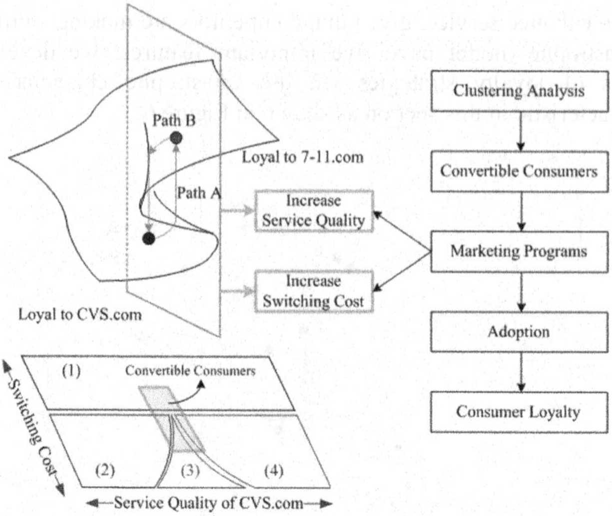

Fig. 6. Developing Loyalty Strategy via Catastrophe Model

Service quality and switching cost are the control variables in our cusp catastrophe model; we will discuss these factors briefly here. Switching cost is the customer's perception of loss in terms of time, money, and psychological costs when switching. Many studies argued that it is defined as perceived risks when switching service providers, the potential losses are of financial, performance-related, social, psychological, and safety-related nature. When a customer changes a service provider, there exists some uncertain perceived risks that a new supplier might not perform the core service at a level equal to, or better than, the current supplier. Clearly, switching costs seem to be an important element when deciding whether to switch a service provider or not. Because the indicator u_3 (switching cost concerning the distance) has the greatest impact on loyalty among the different indicators of switching cost, one of these loyalty strategies will be related to indicator u_3.

From the short-term point of view, indicator v_4 (marketing program) is the most important factor among the four indicators of service quality of the control variables $u_{i.}$. Sales promotions can encourage consumers to either buy larger quantities of the promoted product or buy that product at an earlier time. By definition, the objective of sales promotions is to offer a direct incentive that affects consumers to accelerate their purchase.

5 Conclusions

Catastrophe Theory (CT) is a theory of great generality that can provide useful insights as to how behavior may radically change as a result of varying smoothly control variables. The theory describes how small, continuous changes in control parameters can have sudden, discontinuous effects on dependent variables. The cusp catastrophe model needs one behavior variable and two controllable variables. This study conducts an online survey of those in Taiwan who have experience in online shopping and goods pick-up at convenience stores, in order to investigate how customer satisfaction and switching cost influence customer loyalty, we study the pick-up point loyalty intentions of existing customers for two convenience stores.

The purpose of this study was to explore the relationships between service quality, switching cost and loyalty using a nonlinear dynamic modeling approach. In accordance with the catastrophe theory, results were analyzed using the program GEMCAT II. The contributions of our work are as follows.

1. In the cusp catastrophe model, "Reselection electronic map" is the main index of the splitting factor. "Relative service quality concerning the electronic map" is the main index of the normal factor.
2. These characteristics including bimodality, hysteresis and catastrophe are all present in our research data.
3. With high switching cost, whether a person is satisfied or dissatisfied, it is very difficult to change to the opposite state. On the other hand, if a change is effected, our model would predict that it will persist with the same degree of "inertia" which maintains the original state.
4. According to the previous findings of loyalty within the application of the cusp catastrophe theory, the cusp catastrophe model is an appropriate model for understanding the process of loyalty.

We hope that we made clear that the catastrophe approach to discontinuous behavior has fruitful implications. Catastrophe theory concerns qualitative behavior of continuous variables. It suggests a complex relation between continuous and categorical variables, which falls outside the scope of standard categorical models and data-analytical methods. It is suggested that other researchers could consider the cusp catastrophe theory and other nonlinear techniques, especially when standard approaches do not adequately capture the underlying dynamics.

References

1. D.J. Wales, A microscopic basis for the global appearance of energy landscapes, *Science*, Vol. 293 (2001), pp. 2067-2070.
2. S. Qin, J.J. Jiao, S. Wang and H. Long, A nonlinear catastrophe model of instability of planar-slip slop and chaotic dynamical mechanisms of its evolutionary process, *International Journal of Solids and Structures*, Vol 38 (2001), pp. 8093-8109.
3. D. Aerts, M. Czachor, L. Gabora, M. Kuna, A. Posiewnil, J. Pykacz and M. Syty, Quantum morphogenesis: A variation on Thom's catastrophe theory, *Physical Review E*, Vol. 67 (2003), pp. 1-13.
4. X.A. Lignous, G.A.R. Parke, J.E. Harding and A.N. Kounadis, A comprehensive catastrophe theory for non-linear buckling of simple system exhibiting fold and cusp catastrophe, *International Journal for Numerical Methods in Engineering*, Vol. 54 (2002), pp. 175-193.
5. T.Y. Kenneth and S.O. Cheung, A catastrophe model of construction conflict behavior, *Building and Environment*, Vol.41 (2006), pp. 438-447.
6. I.N. Stewart and P.L. Peregoy, Catastrophe theory modeling in psychology, *Psychological Bulletin,* Vol. 94 (1982), pp. 336-362.
7. T.A. Oliva, R. L. Oliver and I.C. MacMillian, A Catastrophe Model for Developing Service Satisfaction Strategies, *Journal of Marketing*, Vol. 56 (1992), pp. 83-95.
8. M. Smith, R.A. Lancioni and T.A. Oliva, The effects of management inertia on the supply chain performance of produce-to-stock firms, *Industrial Marketing Management*, Vol. 24 (2005), pp.614-628.

9. W. Dou and S. Ghose, A dynamic nonlinear model of online retail competition using cusp catastrophe theory, *Journal of Business Research*, Vol. 59 (2006), pp.838-848.
10. G.G. Haveman and T.A. Oliva, Organization design, inertia, and the dynamics of competitive response, *Organization Science*, Vol. 4 (1993), pp. 181-208.
11. G.K. Kalph and T.A. Oliva, Multivariate Catastrophe Model Estimation: Method and Application, *Academy of Management Journal*, Vol. 37 (1994), pp. 206-221.
12. T.A. Olvia, W.S. Desarbo, D.L. Day and K. Jedidi, GEMCAT: A GEneral Multivariate methodology for estimating CATastrophe models, *Behavior Science*, Vol.32 (1987), pp. 121-137.
13. L. Lange, S. McDade and T.A. Oliva, Technological Choice and Network Externalities: A Catastrophe Model Analysis of Firm Software Adoption for Competing Operating Systems, *Structural Change and Economic Dynamics*, Vol. 12 (2001), pp. 9-57.
14. C.M. Feng and Y.K. Huang, The Choice Behavior Analysis of the Pick-up Point for the E-commerce Retailing Delivery, *Journal of the Eastern Asia Society for Transportation Studies*, Vol. 6 (2005), pp. 2778 – 2793.

A Procedure of How to Conduct Research in Transparent Mobile Recommendations

Mike Radmacher
Chair of Mobile Business & Multilateral Security,
Gräfstr.78, 60054 Frankfurt am Main, Germany,
mike.radmacher@m-chair.net

Abstract. The information overflow of today's information society can be overcome by the usage of recommender systems. Due to the fact that most recommender systems act as black boxes, trust in a system decrease, especially when a recommendation failed. Recommender systems usually don't offer any insight into the systems logic and cannot be questioned as it is normal for a recommendation process between humans. Transparency, which is about explaining to the user why a recommendation is made, supports the user in a way of understanding the reasoning behind a recommendation. Within a mobile environment, it is possible to address the user more individualized but transparency needs a completely different way of visualization and interaction. The paper in hand aims at setting up a process model on how to address transparency in mobile recommendations and therefore introduce into a complex new area of research, recommender systems didn't address in the past.

1. Introduction

Today's information society which includes the emergence of the information flow, confronts the user with the conflict between getting the information he is looking for and spending the time he is able to, while searching for what he is interested in [1, 2]. "To give customers exactly what they want, you first have to learn what that is. It sounds simple, but it's not" [3]. At this time, recommender systems

---

Please use the following format when citing this chapter:

Radmacher, M., 2008, in IFIP International Federation for Information Processing, Volume 286, Towards Sustainable Society on Ubiquitous Networks, eds. Oya, M., Uda, R., Yasunobu, C., (Boston: Springer), pp. 49–60.

gain significant importance by supporting the user to find what he is actually looking for. Sometimes this also means to support the service provider for "suggesting ... those products which best suit his needs and preferences in a particular situation and context" [4].

Recommender systems are well known in the academia as well as in practice over the last 20 years. GroupLense [5], MovieLense [6], Video Recommender [7], Ringo [8] and Fab [9] are only a few systems that are developed by researchers. Some websites like Amazon.com, CDNow.com, Barnes & Nobel, MovieFinder.com, Pandora.com, TiVo.com, Netlix.com or Launch.com have also made successful use of recommender systems [11].

But when we talk about transparency as the explanation why a particularly recommendation is made, most of the recommender systems act as black boxes [12]. They cannot be questioned [11] and the systems logic behind the recommendation isn't visible. Trust in a recommender system decreases if the recommendation failed without any reasons. Transparency which can explain how the system works [13,14,15], enables the user to make a more accurate judgment of the true quality of a recommended item [16]. In a mobile environment, transparency is even more important due to the processing of personal information e.g. location data, time of usage, interests, and other situational dependent information that can be used to offer a more individualized recommendation [17,18]. Processing this information, especially location data, needs mostly users' approval [19, 20].

The paper in hand sets up a procedure on how to address transparency in mobile recommendations and therefore introduce a complex new area of research, recommender systems didn't address in the past.

The paper is structured as follows: The section "Theoretical Framework" gives an overview about transparency in the area of recommender systems and demonstrates its importance as well as its novelty. The section "Research Methodology" discusses the underlying research approach, related to design research, research questions, artifacts as well as the created procedure on how to investigate transparency in mobile recommendations. The four following sections are describing each phase of the procedure, while the last section sums up the contribution of what is learned and how further questions can be addressed in more detail.

2. Theoretical Framework

Research in the area of recommender systems is performed over the last 20 years in a few different areas. The algorithm refinement, the analysis of user behavior and the consideration of user feedback are typically distinguished.

Algorithm refinement is conducted on the one hand by optimizing recommender techniques like rule-based filtering, content-based filtering, collaborative filtering and hybrid approaches [9,21,22,23,24] and on the other hand by addressing new application areas with specific domain related input vector e.g. music [25] or video [5.6]. The analysis of user behavior is accomplished by classical research separated into the active way which asks the user explicitly about his behavior [26] and the passive way [27,28] where the behavior is derived by indirectly information collection and interpretation. The third path of research in recommender systems addresses the consideration of user feedback, often given by the buzzword "recommendation by critique" [4,29].

All these topics are of importance but for a while it has recognized that a new aspect called transparency also plays an important role of the acceptance and usage of recommender systems.

Using recommender systems means, users typically disclose some personal opinions e.g. in the form of ratings. Based on these ratings, a recommendation e.g. for movies, books other products is made. The user has the possibility to accept or reject the recommendation. Over the years literature indicated that recommender systems are not always be trusted by users [11,12,21]. Most of the recommender systems act as black boxes, not offering any insight into the systems logic or justifications for recommendations and cannot be questioned [11,12,22]. Recommendations are often correct, but also occasionally very wrong [11]. There are no indicators given when trusting a recommendation and when to doubt one from a user's point of view [11]. In addition a user is very sensible when it comes to recommendations in an area he is not familiar with [12]. But when a user doesn't trust a recommender system, he will not disclose personal information.

By offering transparency which is about explaining to the user why a recommendation is made, the user will trust a service provider more than before [10,12,30]. In case something went wrong, the level of trust normally decreases, but when transparency is offered to understand what happened, trust does not have to decrease. Transparency explains how a system works [30], enables more accurate judgment of the quality of a recommended item [13]. It offers a higher acceptance of recommendations and can increase sales [12]. The user can question the recommendation which also helps the system to refine the recommendation process [11]. Transparency is even more important in a mobile environment because personal information e.g. location data, time of usage, interests, and other situational dependent information can be used to offer a more individualized recommendation [17,18]. Its processing needs mostly users' approval [19, 20]. Transparency provides a method to check if personal privacy policies are respected. Furthermore, in a mobile environment, transparency also needs a completely different way of visualization and interaction [31].

The aim of this contribution is to offer a guideline on conducting research in the area of transparent mobile recommendations - a reference procedure that allows designing transparent mobile recommendations as well as its integration into classical recommender processes, which includes the refinement of recommender processes by user feedback, collected through the questioning of transparent recommendations.

3. Research Methodology

The current section addresses the research methodology of this paper in form of a research procedure. Furthermore, research questions, artifacts and hypotheses are defined.

3.1 Research Approach

The underlying methodology of this research paper is based on design research [32][33][34]. A design research based process model [35] is chosen (figure 1) to address the research questions. The procedure is separated into six stages. Every single stage is related (in brackets) to the design research approach by Hevner et al. [32] and Takeda et al. [33].

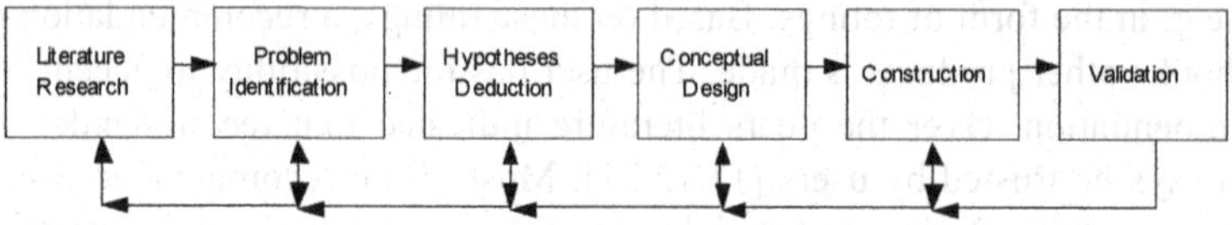

Fig. 1. Research progress related to design research [35]

It starts with the literature research, followed by the problem identification (awareness of a problem). The hypotheses deduction and a first conceptual design (suggestions) are part of the third and fourth stages. Stage five is about the construction (development) of a specific artifact and the procedure concludes with the evaluation (evaluation) in stage six. The focus in this paper lies on stages four and five.

The literature research (stage 1) and the problem identification (stage 2) are already given by the introduction as well as by the theoretical framework and will not be extended by this article. The research questions are below. Hypotheses (stage 3) are not part of this contribution. The main contribution of this paper is a process model that supports the conceptual design (stage 4) as well as the construction (stage 5), which includes addressing the artifacts mentioned below. The validation (stage 6) of specific artifacts is also not part of this article.

3.2 Research Questions & Artifacts

In order to design a transparent communication process between user and service provider for mobile recommendations a couple of research questions are defined. Based on the literature it is indicated that transparency is a new and relevant topic in recommender system's research, especially in the area of mobile recommendations [10,11,12]. The following research questions (RS) are defined:

- (RS1) How can transparency be defined (e.g. characteristics) and realized (e.g. design elements) in a mobile environment by considering its advantages and limitations?
- (RS2) How do we design a communication process between user and service provider that makes mobile recommendations more transparent to users?
- (RS3) How can transparency be integrated in order to refine mobile recommendation processes?
- (RS4) How to operate the model of transparency in real-life applications?

According to the design research approach the following artifacts have to be designed:

- (A1) By addressing RS1 the concept of transparency for a mobile environment is defined that includes the consideration of questions from a data processing point of view as well as general legal conditions.
- (A2) Answering RS2 and RS3 comprises the systematic and engineering course of action to develop and integrate a software component that enables transparency within mobile recommendations.
- (A3) The prototype based development of a transparent mobile event recommender system documents the applicableness of the artifact instantiation in (2).

3.3 Process Model

The designed process model covers the research questions as well as the artifacts and supports the conceptual design (stage 4, section 3.1) as well as the construction (stage 5, section 3.2) of transparent mobile recommendations. This section contains a briefly overview while chapter 4-7 is given more detailed information.

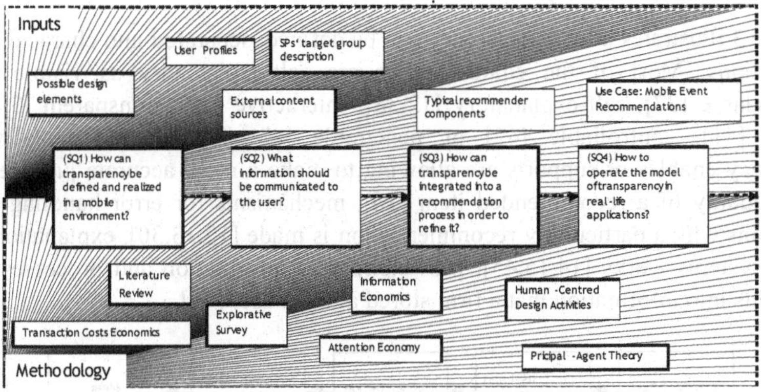

Fig. 2. Process model for how to conduct research of transparent mobile recommendations

The process model is separated into three different sections. First, the input vectors, second, the methodology and third, the four different questions that have to be addressed when you are trying to establish transparency in recommender systems.

Input vectors are information that are used to answer one of the four questions. The different methodologies approaches are used to provide a scientific basis by already well known approaches. The questions that have to be addressed are distinguished into four aspects. The first one discuses how information should be presented, the second what kind of information is relevant to the user, the third addressed the integration of transparency in already existing recommender systems and finally the fourth, the construction of a real life application which states its realization.

The following section addresses each question by demonstrating how the question can be answered by using input values as well as different methodology approaches.

4. Representation of Transparency (1)

When you start thinking about how a mobile recommendation can be made transparent from a user's point of view, at first it is important to know what transparency is about (input values).

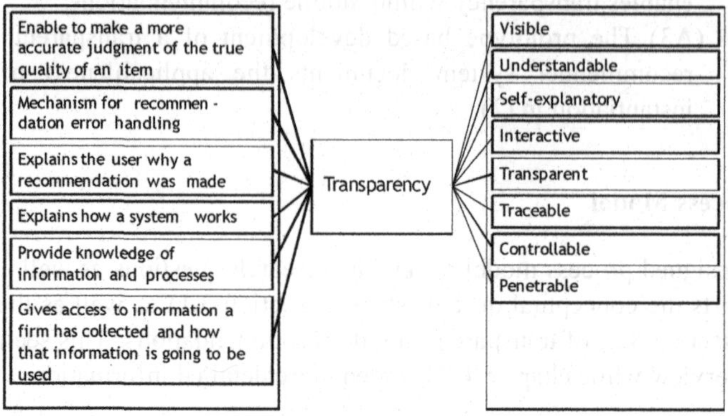

Fig. 3. How is transparency defined?

Figure 3 illustrates how transparency can be defined, separated into characteristics and functions. Most of the characteristics are self-explanatory as visible [36], understandable [37], self-explanatory [12,38], interactive [13], transparent [39,40], traceable [41], controllable [42] or penetrable [43,44]. The functions which transparency enables or supports are allowing to make a more accurate judgment of the true quality of a recommended item [16], mechanisms for error handling [11], explanations why a particularly recommendation is made [12,13,30], explanations on how the systems works [14,15,45], provisioning of information and processes [30] and insights into information that a firm stored about a user [46].

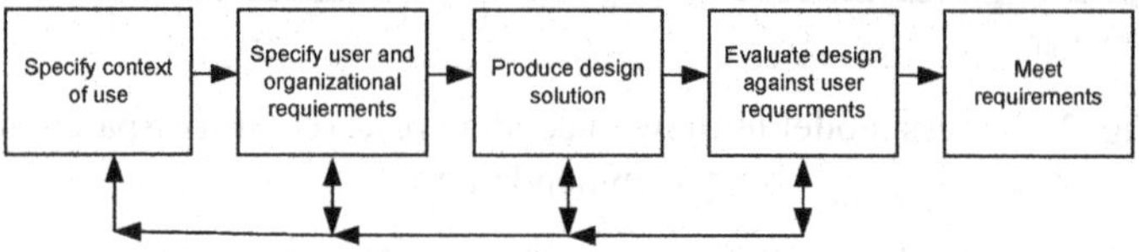

Fig. 4. Human-Centred Design Activities [47]

After knowing what transparency is about, the development of a user interface that offers transparent mobile recommendation is part of the ongoing research. The Human-Centred Design Activities (methodology) procedure given by figure 4, illustrates a guideline on how to design a mobile user interface. After specifying the context of use, requirements as e.g. the functions and the characteristics of a transparent mobile recommendation are specified. Based on these requirements a few different design solutions distinguished by e.g. using different style element as text, video, audio, images or changing the amount of displayed information e.g. only 3 explanations for each recommendation or 4 or 5, are developed and evaluated by using e.g. user trials in order to check if the initial requirements are meet. The result should be a user interface that allows the representation of transparent mobile recommendations.

5. Information Relevance (2)

After the investigation of how transparency is defined and how to represent transparent mobile recommendations in chapter 4, it is also important to know what kind of information is relevant from the user's point of view. First, the information that can be used (input values) to be visualized is separated into available information and relevant information.

The available information is e.g. the service provider target group description which can include for instance age, gender, professionalism, occupation group, income, basic setting, interests, work attitude, personality, country, region, location, frequency of use or brand loyalty [48]. In addition there is user generated information as part of the available information as e.g. information that is stored in user profiles [35]. Such information can be a pseudonym, age, interest or other. Direct user feedback by for instance explicit answering of questions as "was the recommendation helpful?", indirect user feedback by deriving the user's behavior through surf behavior, mouse movements, scroll behavior, retention period or iris movements [27] and information of a user as e.g. location information provided by a third party, completes the picture of the available information.

Relevant information is typically the kind of information the user concerns about most. By looking into the already established research approaches (methodology) three different theories can help to answer this question. First the attention economy [1,2] which is based on the limited attention of a user. The high amount of available information cannot be searched by humans because their capacity is limited. Therefore it is important the offer the user a set of information that is probably interesting for him by filtering out irrelevant information. The transaction costs theory [49] also supports the question about the information relevance from a user's perspective. Looking for information takes time which produces costs. Finding relevant information is a less time consuming step and will reduce search costs. The third theory is about risk and uncertain [50]. An Information that is provided for instance by a recommender engine has to be trustful. The user should have the possibility to check if the recommendation is right.

Trying to find a match between the service provider target group description and the user profile attributes involves a matching process which can be typically described by figure 5.

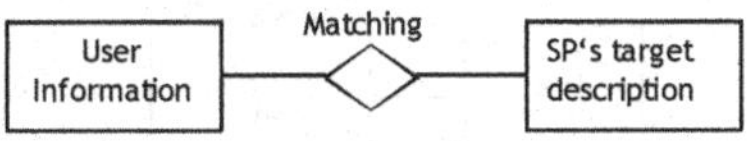

Fig. 5. Matching Process

The classical matching can be done rule-based as given below:

IF

user_profile_attribute$_{i1}$(UPA$_{i1}$) = service_provider_attribute$_{j1}$ (SPA$_{j1}$)

AND/OR IF

user_profile_attribute$_{i2}$(UPA$_{i2}$) = service_provider_attribute$_{j2}$ (SPA$_{j2}$)

AND/OR IF

user_profile_attribute$_{in}$(UPA$_{in}$) = service_provider_attribute$_{jm}$ (SPA$_{jm}$)

THEN match

ELSE no match

Due to the fact that each user attribute has its specific relevance, each attribute needs to have a weight which expresses the relevance. A user profile (UP_i) consists of several user attribute (UPA). $UP_i = \{UPA_{i1}, \ldots UPA_{in}\}$. Each attribute has a name ($UPAN_i$) and a weight ($UPAW_i$) which indicates its importance to the user. $UPA_i = \{(UPAN_{i1}, UPAW_{i1}), \ldots, (UPAN_{in}, UPAW_{in})\}$.

The main question that has to be answered by individual research is what factors have an impact on user's relevance in a specific application area. $UPAW_i = \{ A_i + B_i + C_i + D_i + E_i + \ldots \}$

6. Integration of Transparency (3)

The question of the integration of transparency has to investigate the structure of traditional recommender systems. The following structure of a recommender system is derived by literature research.

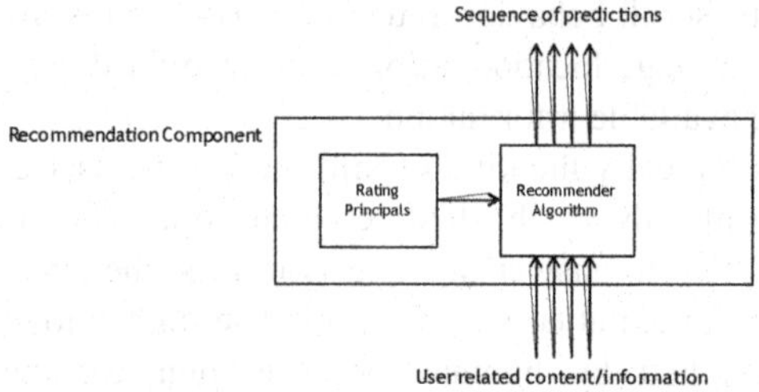

Fig. 6. Classical Recommender System

A classical recommender system always consists of user related information as input, a recommendation algorithm, rating principals the algorithm is operating on and a sequence of predictions as output [51]. In order to offer transparency within recommendations, the following enhancements are proposed.

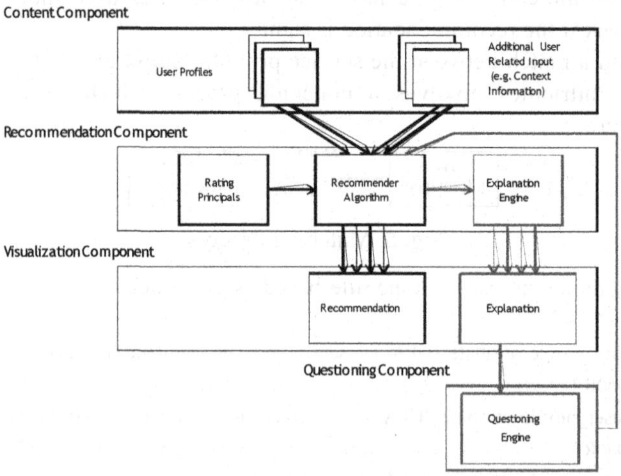

Fig. 7. Transparency in classical recommender systems

The proposed architecture comprises three additional components: the explanation engine, the explanation and the questioning engine. The explanation engine is located within the recommendation component. After the recommender algorithm generated the recommendation, information about the system conclusion is transferred to the explanation engine which main task is the processing for the explanation. The component called explanation which is located in the visualization component is responsible for the visualization of the underlying conclusion. The visualization can be performed by e.g. different style elements as mentioned at the end of section 4. The questioning engine allows to critique the system assumption for a particularly recommendation. Remember that transparency should help the user to understand why a particularly recommendation was made, especially in the case of a wrong recommendation.

By offering transparency new direct user feedback is generated that can be used to refine existing recommendations.

7. Real-Life Application Scenario (4)

The last part of the process model, described in section 3, is the development of a real life application that is operating on the previously findings. The application that is chosen is a transparent mobile event recommender system, called MoReCa.

Events are typically every kind of activity users can participate in, e.g. movies, concerts, lectures, meetings, dinners and others. An event is minimally described by its name, a location where it takes place and a time when it starts and ends. Why an event is recommended to a user can have several reasons. An event can be recommended based on user's interests, on the distance between the event's location and the user's current position, due to the fact that a couple of friends already accepted the recommendation or the user's calendar is just empty. The event, in this case the movie "Spiderman 4", is described by its name, the location, the date and the time. By asking the system why this recommendation is made, MoReCa will display explanations for the recommendation, given by figure 8.

Fig. 8. Transparency in mobile event recommendations

An explanation, in this example, consists of a icon and textual description and enables the possible to give explicit feedback in the form of yes the explanation is right, no it is wrong, it is inappropriate for this recommendation or by changing the order to express the relevance of an explanation.

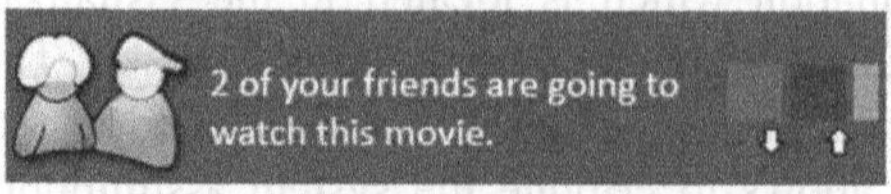

Fig. 8. Transparent explanation of a mobile event recommendation

This representation of transparent recommendations can allow being more tolerant against wrong recommendations and providing active user feedback to refine recommendations.

8. Conclusion and Outlook

The paper in hand discussed the important and relevance of transparency in mobile recommendations in order to establish a more human like recommendation process. When it comes to a mobile environment transparency is completely new, especially its visualization and integration into mobile recommender systems. Furthermore the article offered a procedure that demonstrates how research of transparency for mobile recommendations can be conducted.

Based on this procedure the development of a real life application, a transparency mobile event recommender system, is an ongoing development, which will be evaluated at the end of 2008.

According the research approach in section 3.1, the work this paper presented has covered the fourth and fifth stages.

References

1. J.K. Bleicher and K. Hickethier, Aufmerksamkeit, Medien und Ökonomie. Lit, 2002.
2. G. Franck, Ökonomie der Aufmerksamkeit. Carl Hanser, 1998.
3. P. Zipkin, The limits of mass customization, Sloan Management Review 42,3, 2001, pp. 81-87.
4. Q.N. Nguyen and F. Ricci, User Preferences Initialization and Integration in Critique-Based Mobile Recommender Systems, AIMS, Nottingham, UK, 2004.
5. J.A. Konstan, B.N. Miller, D. Maltz, J.L. Herlocker, R. Gordon, E. Prairie and J. Riedl, GroupLens: applying collaborative filtering to Usenet news, Communications of the ACM, Vol.40, No.3, 1997, pp. 77 – 87.
6. B.J. Dahlen, J.A. Konstan, J.L. Herlocker, N. Good, A. Borchers and J. Riedl. Jump- starting movielens: User benefits of starting a collaborative filtering system with "dead data", University of Minnesota TR 98-017, 1998.
7. W.C. Hill, L. Stead, M. Rosenstein and G.W. Furnas: Recommending and Evaluating Choices in a Virtual Community of Use, CHI 1995, pp. 194-201.

8. U. Shardanand and P. Maes, Social Information Filtering: Algorithms for Automating "Word of Mouth", Conference on Human Factors in Computing Systems, 1995.
9. M. Balabanović and Y. Shoham, Fab: content-based, collaborative recommendation. Communications of the ACM, Vol.40, No.3, 1997, pp. 66-73.
10. M. Hingston, User Firendly Recommender Systems, University of Sydney, School of Information Technologies, 2006.
11. J.L. Herlocker, J.A. Konstan and J. Riedl, Explaining collaborative filtering recommendations, ACM conference on CSCW, 2001, pp. 241 – 250.
12. R. Sinha, and K. Swearingen, The role of transparency in recommender systems, Conference on Human Factors in Computing Systems, Minneapolis, Minnesota, USA, 2002, pp. 830-831.
13. N. Tintarev and J. Masthoff, A Survey of Explanations in Recommender Systems, Workshop on Recommender Systems and Intelligent User Interfaces associated with ICDE'07, Instanbul, Turkey, 2007.
14. N. Tintarev, Explanations of Recommendations, ACM Recommender Systems, Minneapolis, Minnesota, USA, 2007, pp. 203-206.
15. J. Muramatsu and W. Pratt, Transparent Queries: investigation users' mental models of search engines, ACM SIGIR conference on research and development in information retrieval, New Orleans, Louisiana, United States, 2001, pp. 217 – 224.
16. M. Bilgic R.J. Mooney, Explaining Recommendations: Satisfaction vs. Promotion, Beyond Personalization 2005: A Workshop at the International Conference on Intelligent User Interfaces, San Diego, CA, 2005.
17. S. Figge, Innovatives Mobile Marketing - Kontextabhängige Kundenansprache mit Hilfe mobiler Portale, in Rannenberg, Kai (Hrsg.): Schriften zum Mobile Commerce und zur Mobilkommunikation; Hamburg 2006.
18. A. Albers, An Electronic Market Framework for context-sensitive Mobile Consumer Profiles in the Marketing Domain, AMCIS, Keystone, USA August 2007.
19. M. Radmacher, J. Zibuschka, T. Scherner, L. Fritsch and K. Rannenberg, Privatsphärenfreundliche topozentrische Dienste unter Berücksichtigung rechtlicher, technischer und wirtschaftlicher Restriktionen, WI, Karlsruhe, 2007.
20. J. Zibuschka, L. Fritsch, M. Radmacher, T. Scherner and K. Rannenberg, Privacy-Friendly LBS: A Prototype-supported Case Study, AMCIS, Keystone, USA August 2007.
21. P. Resnick and H.R. Varian, Recommender Systems, Communications of the ACM, Vol.40, No.3, 1997, pp.56-58.
22. R. van Meteren and M. van Someren, Using Content-Based Filtering for Recommendation, University of Amsterdam, Netherlands, 2000.
23. H. Eui-Hong and G. Karypis: Feature-based recommendation system. CIKM 2005, pp. 446-452.
24. B. Sarwar, G. Karypis, J. Konstan and J. Riedl, Item-based collaborative filtering recommendation algorithms, 10th international conference on WWW, 2001, pp. 285-295.
25. J. Donaldson, A Hybrid Social-Acoustic Recommendation System for Popular Music, ACM Recommender Systems, Minneapolis, Minnesota, USA, 2007, pp. 187-190.
26. L.M. Quiroga and M. Mostafa, An experiment in building profiles in information filtering: the role of context of user relevance feedback, Information Processing and Management Vol.38, No.5, 2002.
27. X. Fu, Evaluating Sources of Implicit Feedback in Web Search. ACM Recommender Systems, Minneapolis, Minnesota, USA, 2007, pp. 191-194.
28. S. Jung, J.L. Herlocker and J.Webster, Click data as implicit relevance feedback in web search, Inf. Process. Manage. Vol.43, No.3, 2007, pp. 791-807.
29. P. Pu, User-Involved Preference Elicitation, IJCAI Workshop on Configuration, Gentilly Cedex, France, 2003.

30. K. Swearingen and R. Sinha, Beyond Algorithms: An HCI Perspective on Recommender Systems. SIGIR workshop on Recommender Systems, New Orleans, LA, USA, 2001.
31. M. Radmacher, Elicitation of profile attributes by transparent communication, ACM Recommender Systems, Minneapolis, Minnesota, USA, 2007, pp. 199-202.
32. A.R. Hevner, et.al., Design Science Information Systems Research, MIS Quarterly, Vol.28, No.1, 2004, pp. 75-105.
33. H. Takeda, et. al., Modeling Design Processes, AI Magazine, 1990, pp. 37-48.
34. V. Vaishnavi and B. Kuechler, Design Research in Information Systems, AIS, 2006.
35. M. Radmacher, Adaptive Customer Profiles For Context Aware Services in a Mobile Environment, In IFIP International Federation for Information Processing, Volume 251, Integration and Innovation Orient to E-Society Volume 1, Wang, W. (Eds), (Boston: Springer), pp. 390-399; Wuhan, China.
36. J. Koenemann and N. Belkin, A case for interaction: A study of interactive information retrieval behavior and effectiveness, in Proceedings of the Human Factors in Computing Systems Conference, NY, 1991.
37. S. Maaß, Transparenz. Eine zentrale software-ergonomische Forderung, Report Nr. FBI-HH-B-170/94, Hamburg, 1994.
38. J. Wandmacher, Software-Ergonomie, de Gruyter, Berlin, 1993.
39. S. Bødker, Through the Interface- a Human Activity Approach to User, Interface Design, Dissertation, Aarhus University 1987.
40. D.A., Norman, The Invisible Computer: Why Good Products Can Fail, the Personal Computer is So Complex, and Information Appliances Are the Solution. Cambridge, MIT Press, 1998.
41. M. Fritter, Towards More "Natural" Interactive Systems, International Journal of Man-Machine Studies, 11, 1979, pp. 339-350.
42. M. Frese, A Theory of Control and Complexity: Implications for Software-Design and Integration of Computer Systems into the Work Place, in: M. Frese, E. Ulich, W. Dzida (Hrsg.), Psychological Issues of HCI in the Work Place. Elsevier Science, Amsterdam, 1987, pp. 313-337.
43. P. Spinas, N. Troy, E. Ulich, Leitfaden zur Einführung und Gestaltung von Arbeit mit Bildschirmsystemen, München, 1983.
44. H. Oberquelle. Situationsbedingte und benutzerorientierte Anpaßbarkeit von Groupware, in A. Hartmann, T. Herrmann, M. Rohde, V. Wulf (Hrsg.), Menschengerechte Groupware - Software-ergonomische Gestaltung und partizipative Umsetzung, Chapter of the ACM, 42, Teubner, Stuttgart, 1994, S. 31-49.
45. S. Maaß, Why Systems Transparency?, in T. R.G. Green, S. J. Payne, G. C. van der Veer (Hrsg.). The Psychology of Computer Use. Academic Press, London, 1983, pp.19-28.
46. N.F. Awad and M.S. Krishnan, The Personalization Privacy Paradox: An Empirical Evaluation Of Information Transparency and the Willingness to be Profiled Online for Personalization, MIS Quarterly, Vol.30, No. 1, 2006, pp.13-28.
47. S. Love, Understanding Mobile Human-Computer Interaction, Butterworth Heinemann, Great Britain, 2005.
48. P. Kotler, and F. Bliemel, Marketing-Management, Schaeffer-Poeschel, Auflage10., überarb. und aktualisierte Aufl, Stuttgart, ISBN: 9783791016894, 2001.
49. O. L. Williamson, Organization Theory: From Chester Barnard to the Present and Beyond, Oxford University Press US, ISBN 0195098307, 1985.
50. T. Ripperger, Ökonomik des Vertrauens - Analyse eines Organisationsprinzips, Mohr Siebeck Verlag Tübingen 1998.
51. P. Resnick and R. Sami, The Influence Limiter: Provably Manipulation-Resistant Recommender Systems, ACM Recommender Systems, Minneapolis, Minnesota, USA, 2007, pp. 17-24.

Development of Recommender Systems Using User Preference Tendencies: An Algorithm for Diversifying Recommendation

Yuki Ogawa[1], Hirohiko Suwa[1], Hitoshi Yamamoto[2], Isamu Okada[3], Toshizumi Ohta[1]

[1]University of Electro-Communications, Graduate School of Information Systems

Chofu-shi, 81,182-8585 Tokyo, Japan. ogawa@ohta.is.uec.ac.jp

[2]Rissho University, Faculty of Business Administration

[3]Soka University, Faculty of Business Administration

Abstract. Many e-commerce sites use a recommendation system to filter the specific information that a user wants out of an overload of information. Currently, the usefulness of the recommendation is defined by its accuracy. However, findings that users are not satisfied only with accuracy have been reported. We consider that a recommendation having only accuracy is unsatisfactory. For this reason, we define the usefulness of a recommendation as its ability to recommend an item that the user does not know, but may like. To improve user satisfaction levels with recommendation lists, we propose an alternative recommendation algorithm that increases the diversity of the recommended items. We examined items that appeal to several different taste tendencies to create a list and achieved diversity in that list. First, we created a similarity network of items by using item rating data. Second, we clustered the items in the network and identified the topics that appealed to the same preference tendency. Our proposed algorithm was able to include items covering several topics in the recommendation list. To evaluate the effect on user satisfaction levels, we used our algorithm to make a recommendation list for DVD items carried by Amazon.co.jp and conducted a questionnaire survey. The results showed higher levels of user satisfaction with our list than a list created using Collaborative Filtering (CF).

Please use the following format when citing this chapter:

Ogawa, Y., Suwa, H., Yamamoto, H., Okada, I., Ohta, T., 2008, in IFIP International Federation for Information Processing, Volume 286; Towards Sustainable Society on Ubiquitous Networks, eds. Oya, M., Uda, R., Yasunobu, C., (Boston: Springer), pp. 61–73.

1. Introduction

The massive growth of the Internet has made an enormous amount of information available to us. However, it is becoming very difficult for users to acquire an applicable one. Therefore, some techniques such as information filtering have been introduced to address this issue. Recommender systems filter information that is useful to a user from a large amount of information. Many e-commerce sites use recommender systems to filter specific information that users want out of an overload of information [2]. For example, Amazon.com is a good example of the success of recommender systems [1]. Over the past several years, a considerable amount of research has been conducted on recommendation systems. In general, the usefulness of the recommendation is measured based on its accuracy [3]. Although a high recommendation accuracy can indicate a user's favorite items, there is a fault in that only similar items will be recommended. Several studies have reported that users might not be satisfied with a recommendation even though it exhibits high recommendation accuracy [4].

For this reason, we consider that a recommendation having only accuracy is unsatisfactory. The serendipity of a recommendation is an important element when considering a user's long-term profits. A recommendation that brings serendipity to users would solve the problem of "user weariness" and would lead to exploitation of users' tastes. The viewpoint of the diversity of the recommendation as well as its accuracy should be required for future recommender systems.

The purpose of this research is to introduce diversity into recommendations, and to build useful recommender systems for users. For this purpose, we define the usefulness of a recommendation as its ability to recommend items that the user does not know, but may like. To improve user satisfaction levels with recommendation lists, we propose an alternative recommendation algorithm that increases the diversity of recommended items.

2. Related Works

2.1. Existing Recommender Systems

Recommender systems are based on two general techniques: Content-based Filtering and Collaborative Filtering [5, 6]. Content-based Filtering is a technique in which items are recommended if their feature information is similar to feature information based on user preferences [7, 8]. The quality of recommendation of content-based filtering does not depend on the number of users. Therefore, this technique is advantageous in that recommendations are stable even in the early stage of performance. However, it has some problems such as the difficulty of extracting feature information on items, or how an item's feature information is described. Moreover, there is a fault in that the items recommended will be alike. Collaborative Filtering is a technique of selecting recommendation items based on users' information whose tastes are similar [9, 10]. The degree of similarity is calculated by information obtained on item ratings. This technique is applicable also to the item of a different kind. However, the disadvantage is that much information is needed on item evaluations in order to understand users' tastes [8].

In addition, a technique using a hybrid system that unifies Content-based Filtering and Collaborative Filtering has also been proposed [11, 12]. Many of these recommendation system studies, however, are aiming at increasing the accuracy of recommendations. We emphasize that the problem is not about accuracy alone.

2.2. Research on Diversity of Recommendations

Shimizu et al. [13] proposed a Collaborative Filtering technique based on known/unknown information in users' items, in order to recommend favorite items that users do not know. An experiment focusing on novelty indicated that their technique was able to recommend many favorite items that users did not know compared to other collaborative filtering techniques. However, this technique is difficult to actually use because acquiring the information on unknown items is hard: Users do not answer, "I don't know" for an unknown item. Moreover, the validity of recommendations is also brought into question in their research because only the evaluation of the novelty was tested. An evaluation of recommendations should consider direct evaluations by users.

Ziegler et al. [4] proposed an index that calculates the degree of similarity of items in a recommendation list using category information on the items (classification of genres and authors). Moreover, they proposed a diversification technique that minimizes the degree of similarity of items in the recommendation list using their index. The results of a questionnaire experiment show that the degree of user satisfaction improved by introducing diversification into the recommendation. However, there is a fault in that the applicable scope must be limited since the technique demands category information on items. The items had similar relationships to each other that could not be expressed with manual category classification. The similarities between items varied, for example, market trends and similarities of movie themes. Therefore, diversification of genres in a recommendation list is not necessarily useful for users.

The target of our research is to provide recommendations with diversity that are useful to users, , which means recommendations of favorite items that users did not know, i.e., were "unknown" to them. Therefore, we tried to develop a method of diversified recommendation in consideration of user preferences.

3. Diversification of Recommendation by Diversification of Preference Tendency

Recommending items that have different taste tendencies would be an effective method for recommending an item unknown to the user. For this reason, we propose a recommendation algorithm that diversifies the preference tendency of items in recommendation lists. Presumption of preference tendency requires information on users' item rating data. The method is as follows. First, we create a similarity network of items by using users' item rating data. Second, we cluster the items in the network and identify topics that appeal to the same preference tendency. Finally, we create a recommendation list that is diversified so that it might contain several different topics. The proposed technique is designed to recommend unknown items to users by using a little information about the users.

3.1. Outline of Our Algorithm

Figure 1 illustrates the overall concept of our recommendation technique. The proposed technique is divided into three steps.

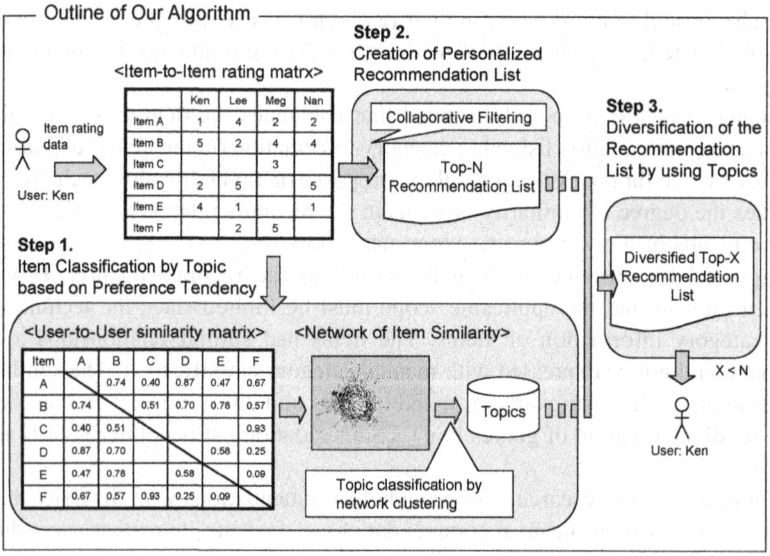

Fig. 1 Overall concept of recommendation technique

- Step 1: Grouping of items according to topic by using preference tendency
- Step 2: Creation of personalized recommendation list
- Step 3: Diversification of recommendation list by using topics

In Step 1, we classify topics according to users' item rating data in order to acquire classification information on the item that reflects users' tastes. In this classification, we express a network of similar relationships of users' tastes of items by using the rating data. Next, we cluster the network and classify the items as topics to ensure that the taste tendencies are similar.

In Step 2, we create a personalized recommendation list. To raise the degree of user satisfaction, both diversity and accuracy of a recommendation list are required [4]. We make a personalized recommendation list by using user-based Collaborative Filtering. Thereby, an accurate list is created.

In Step 3, we select items of different preference tendency from the recommendation list in Step 2. Preference tendency in this paper is defined as topic information acquired using Step 1. Based on the above steps, we make a recommendation list that is compatible in accuracy and diversity.

3.2. Item Classification by Topic Based on Preference Tendency (Step 1)

We propose a technique to classify topics that involves clustering an item network. Some related studies have been done on network categorization. Toda et al. [15] proposed a method of extracting topics from document sets by using graphic analysis. Matsuo et al. [16] analyzed researcher communities from a network of collaboration-related papers. Yuta et al. [17] analyzed a community consisting of linked relationships in social networking systems (SNS). These studies are useful for discovering potential communities and topics, and for categorizing information that changes topicality. Moreover, calculation of the degree of similarity between items by using user item rating data, which also adopts Item-based collaborative filtering, is effective in recommending similar items [18]. As mentioned above, we found that topics could be classified into preference tendency according to network clustering of item similarities. A networking method for topic classification is described in section 3.2.1. Then, we explain a method of network clustering in 3.2.2.

3.2.1. Network of Item Similarity

We use a weighted undirected network to classify topics. The network describes an item as a node and the similarity between rating data of items as an edge. The network is constructed as follows. First, we calculate an item-to-item similar value matrix using equation (1) from a user-to-item rating value matrix. Next, we construct a weighted network by connecting items with the edges. Thereby, we create a similar item network which reflects the user's preference tendency. In equation (1), $r_{i,a}$ is a rating value over user's U_i item I_a.

$$sim(I_a, I_b) = \frac{\sum_i r_{i,a} r_{i,b}}{\sqrt{\sum_i (r_{i,a})^2}\sqrt{\sum_i (r_{i,b})^2}} \quad (1)$$

3.2.2. Topic classification by Network Clustering

The topic classification is performed using a clustering algorithm of Newman [19] to apply the similar item network constructed in section 3.2.1. Newman proposed an index of modularity Q, which evaluates clustering performance, and proposed a clustering technique using the index [19, 20]. The value of Q is obtained by subtracting a theoretical value of the rate of a link in the module at the time of assuming that it is a random network, from the actual measurement of the probability that a link exists between the nodes in a module. The Q increases if links in the module are dense and those between modules are sparse. This is why the Q value is regarded as a useful index by which the performance of clustering can be evaluated objectively. Newman stated that an independent modular structure emerges when the Q value became larger than 0.3. The Q value formula is expressed in equation (2). In this equation, C is the total of a cluster, m is the number of edges that exist in the whole network, and l_{ij} is the number of edges of cluster i and cluster j.

$$Q = \sum_i^C \left(\frac{li}{m} - a_i^2 \right) \quad (2)$$

$$a_i = \sum_j e_{ij}$$

$$e_{ij} = \frac{l_{ij}}{2m}$$

This clustering technique is a greedy algorithm that continues the merger with the node from which the increased value (ΔQ) of Q serves as the maximum. In an initial state, one node is one cluster. Although this algorithm is used to calculate semi-optimal rather than optimal solutions, it has been used in many studies [17, 22] to perform effective clustering because of the computational complexity of $O(n\, m^2)$. Equation (3) is the formula of ΔQ_{ij}, which is an incremental value of Q when combining clusters i and j.

$$\Delta Q_{ij} = 2\left(e_{ij} - a_i a_j\right) \quad (3)$$

Although the above-mentioned equation is applied as the clustering technique in a non-weighted network, it can also be applied in weighted networks [21]. Moreover, if weight is set as an edge, it has been reported that the size of a cluster can be equalized and improved [22].

For the above reason, we think that the proposed technique is effective for classifying item groups that have similar ratings into topics.

3.3. Creation of Personalized Recommendation List (Step 2)

The second step involves creating the personalized recommendation list. This is because both diversity and accuracy (personalized) are required for a recommendation list in order to raise the degree of user satisfaction [4]. Therefore, we create the personalized recommendation list using user-based Collaborative Filtering.

User-based Collaborative Filtering is a technique applied to discover user groups, in which users have similar likings, and to recommend favorite items of the user group. This technique has two processes: calculating the degree of similarity, and calculating a prediction rating value. In the first process, the degree of similarity is calculated between users using user's item rating, in order to find users with preference similar to those who are recommended. The Pearson correlation coefficient [9] is often used for this calculation. In the second process, the prediction rating value P of a non-rated item is calculated based on the rating of a similar user. A prediction rating value is calculated for every user, and the top-N items of this value become the recommendation list. Equation (4) is the formula of the prediction rating value of User U_x's non-rated item I_a, and *ave* (r_x) is the average of all the rating values User U_x voted on. Moreover, $\Sigma_k \in K$ is User U_x and top K neighborhood users with a high degree of similarity.

$$P_{x,a} = ave(r_x) + \frac{\sum_{k \in K} sim(x,k)(r_{x,a} - ave(r_k))}{\sum_{k \in K} |sim(x,k)|} \quad (4)$$

3.4. Diversification of Recommendation List by Using Topics (Step 3)

In order to achieve diverse recommendations, we select the items of a different preference tendency using topic information and the personalized recommendation list. First, we classify the personalized list according to topic. Next, by calculating the average of the prediction rating value of the item for every topic, we determine the priority of a topic. Finally, we choose one item in order of a topic with a high priority, and add it to the recommendation list. We repeat this process for all of the items that are finally recommended. Using this process, we create diverse recommendation lists with several different topics.

4. Evaluation of Recommendation List

We evaluate a recommendation list using a questionnaire on user degree-of-satisfaction. Conventionally, precision and recall are often used as an index of the accuracy of a recommendation list [3]. However, these evaluation indices are indices of accuracy, and they depend on the first evaluation of an item. An evaluation of a recommendation must evaluate which has discovered the user's potential interest. Therefore, precision and recall alone are not sufficient for evaluating a user's potential interest.

In this research, our target recommendation is a recommendation with diversity that is useful for a user, that is, a recommendation that recommends favorite items that may be unknown to the user. Therefore, we use a questionnaire to evaluate whether the proposed technique can recommend "favorite items unknown to a user."

Specifically, we evaluate the distribution of items and the average rating value of items in a recommendation list that were unknown to the user.

5. Evaluation Experiment

To evaluate our technique, we compare recommendations obtained by using the proposed technique and an existing technique (collaborative filtering).

5.1. Experiment Outline

5.1.1. Experimenter

The experiment was conducted using 14 university students as experimenter.

5.1.2. Data Set

In this experiment, 1,000 DVD items listed in Amazon.co.jp were used as an item set. We selected the item of the sales high order in consideration of the rate of a genre. In addition to the item evaluations obtained from the experimenter, we used item evaluations by 1,609 Amazon.co.jp reviewers as evaluation information.. The number of reviews used was 5,692, and the average rating value was 4.2. These data were acquired using Amazon API [23]. We conducted the crawling between 2007/4/18 - 2007/4/20.

5.1.3. Experimental Procedure

The procedure of the experiment is described below.

(1) Collection of item evaluation data

To obtain data on a user's present tastes, we had each user evaluate items. First, we showed experimenter a list of 30 DVD items at random. Next, the experimenter was asked to evaluate whether an item was "known" or "unknown", and to rank items as "favorite" items (on a scale of 1-5).

(2) Classification of a topic

We classified the topics based on taste tendencies from item rating information. First, we created a similar-item network using item rating information obtained from experimenter and Amazon.co.jp reviewers. Next, we clustered this network and classified items as a topic.

(3) Creation of diversified recommendation list

We created the diversified recommendation list using the topic information from (2). First, the top 50 items were selected by user-based Collaborative Filtering in the data from (1) using the item (seen or known, although not looked at) that the user knew. Next, we used the topic information from (2) and the top 50 items, and created the diversified recommendation list of top X items (X∈ [10, 20, 30, 40, 50]).

(4) Evaluation of user degree of satisfaction

To evaluate the diversified recommendation list, we showed a user the recommendation list created in (3), and obtained data on the user degree of satisfaction. Each user answered known/unknown on the evaluation (seen or known although not looked at, or did not know), and indicated favorites (on a scale of 1-5) for each item on the recommendation list.

5.2. Experimental Result

5.2.1. Result of Topic Classification

We created an item network similar to that in Fig. 2 using the collected item rating data. Table 2 shows the results of clustering this network. As a result of the topic classification by clustering, 659 items out of 1000 were connected as one network. High clustering performance (Q= 0.43) was achieved as a result of the clustering in this network. Moreover, the topics were alike in genre, series, etc., and they reflected the preference tendency to some extent.

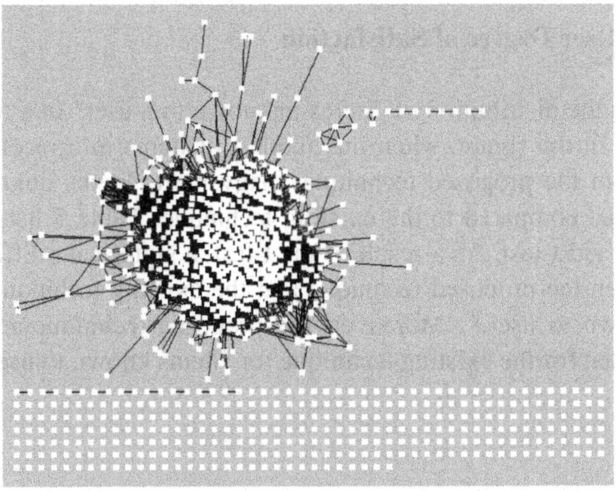

Fig. 2 Network of item similarity

Table 2 Result of clustering

Extracted number of topics	343
Number of items in 1 topic (ave.)	2.92
Number of items of the maximum network	659
Modularity of the maximum network	0.43

5.2.2. Results of Diversification of Recommendation List

Table 4 shows the number of topics in a recommendation list. As the table indicates, the recommendation list created by using the proposed technique was able to cover all the topics with only the top 20 items in a recommendation list.

Table 4 Kinds of topics in recommendation list (Top-X items)

Top-X	Kinds of topics in a recommendation list	
	Diversification of Topics (DT)	Collaborative Filtering (CF)
10	9.9	5.9
20	16.1	10.1
30	16.1	13.2
40	16.1	14.9
50	16.1	16.1

5.2.3. Results of User Degree of Satisfaction

Fig. 3 shows the distribution of "items unknown to a user" in a recommendation list. As indicated in the figure, when the number of items in a recommendation list was 10-40, as with the proposed technique, many more "items unknown to a user" were recommended compared to the existing technique. Table 5 lists the average of item rating value and t-test. As a result of the t-test, a significant difference (*p<.05) was found between the proposed technique and the existing technique in the top 20-30 "items unknown to user." Moreover, the proposed technique acquired a rating value as high as that for the existing technique for "items known to user."

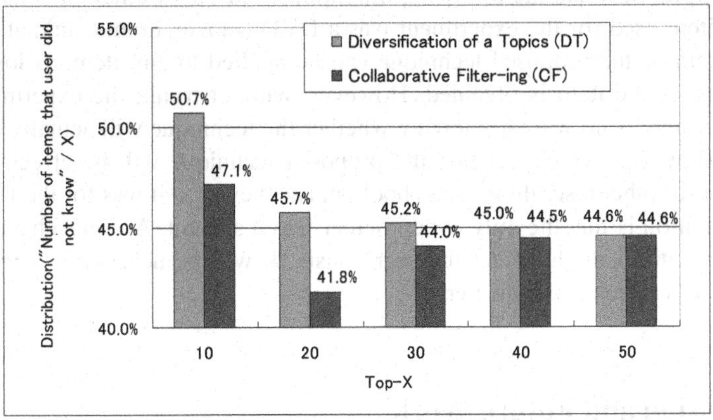

Fig. 3 Distribution of items unknown to user in a recommendation list

Table 5 Results of rating value (user average) and t-test

Top-X	Items known to user			Items unknown to user		
	DT	CF	*p* value	DT	CF	*p* value
10	3.35	3.67	.074	2.86	2.71	.085
20	3.67	3.63	.732	2.87	2.67	.040*
30	3.69	3.63	.429	2.86	2.70	.026*
40	3.67	3.67	.912	2.82	2.81	.809
50	3.67	3.67	—	2.80	2.80	—

* $p < .05$

6. Discussion

In this research, our target recommendation was a recommendation with diversity that is useful for a user. Specifically, our goal was to recommend favorite items that a user does not know. From the viewpoint of recommending "items unknown to a user," the proposed technique was able to recommend more "items unknown to a user" than the existing technique, based on the results in Fig. 3. Moreover, for "favorite items unknown to a user," the proposed technique recommended items with a higher evaluation than those recommended by the existing technique, based on the results of Table 5. For this reason, when we select an item from each topic, we think that giving priority to and choosing an item with the highest predicted rating value leads to the recommendation of items the user is interested in. As mentioned above, it can be said that the proposed technique, which diversifies the topic based on the preference tendency in a recommendation list, was an effective technique for recommending "favorite items unknown to a user."

This experiment had the following limitations. The first limitation is that the only type of item used for the experiment was a DVD (movie, drama, animation, etc.). The algorithm of the proposed technique can be applied to any item, as long as the user's rating of the item is obtained. However, without trying the experiment with other items, there is no way of knowing whether the technique will actually be useful for users. However, we expect that the proposed technique will be effective to the same extent for other tasty things (e.g. book, music, news) as it was for the DVD. The second limitation is that the only experimenter was a student. A user's characteristics (e.g. age, vocation) might affect the user's taste. It will be necessary to try the experiment with various experimenters.

7. Conclusion and Future Work

The purpose of this research was to introduce diversity in recommendations, and to build recommender systems useful for users. In order to improve the user degree of satisfaction of a recommendation list, we proposed a recommendation algorithm that raises the diversity in a recommendation list. Specifically, we achieve diversity of recommendation by keeping items that reflect a different preference tendency on a recommendation list. The process of the proposed technique was as follows. First, we created a similarity network of items by using item rating data. Second, we clustered the items in the network and identified the topics that appealed to the same preference tendency. Finally, we created a diversified recommendation list that might have several different topics. Our proposed algorithm can include items that cover several topics in the recommendation list. To evaluate the effect on user satisfaction levels, we used our algorithm to make a recommendation list for DVD items listed on Amazon.co.jp and conducted a questionnaire survey. From the viewpoint of diverse recommendations, the proposed technique was able to recommend more "favorite items unknown to user," than the existing technique.

We will expand our research in the future as follows. The first objective is to create a recommendation list that is personalized using methods other than user-based collaborative filtering. This is because collaborative filtering has a "rating value sparse problem" [12] and a "cold-start problem". In the "rating value sparse problem," a deviation occurs in the evaluated item. In the "cold-start problem," it is not possible to create a recommendation that a user is satisfied with in the early stage of employment when there is little user's item rating data. A solution may be reached by using a default rating for items the user is not evaluating. The second objective is to solution of the problem of trade-off in accuracy and diversity. The usefulness of a recommendation may be different according to a user's properties, a user's situation, and the kind of item. It will be necessary to consider these properties and to consider how the balance of accuracy and diversity should be adjusted.

References

1. Linden, G.., Smith, B. and York, J.: Amazon.com Recommendations: Item-to-Item Collaborative Filtering, IEEE Internet Computing, Vol.7, No.1 (2003)

2. Schafer, J., Konstan, J.A. and Riedl, J.: E - Commerce recommendation applications, Data Mining and Knowledge Discovery, Vol.5, pp.115- 153 (2001)
3. Sarwar, B., Karypis, G.., Konstan, J. and Riedl, J.: Application of dimensionality reduction in recommender system, Proc. of ACM WebKDD Workshop (2000)
4. Ziegler, C., NcNee, S.M., Konstan, J.A. and Lausen, G..: Improving Recommendation Lists through Topic Diversification, Proc. of WWW2005, pp.22-32 (2005)
5. Ramakrishnan, N.: PIPE :Web Personalization by Partial Evaluation, IEEE Internet Computing, Vol.4, No.6, pp.21-31 (2000)
6. Riecken, D.: Personalized Views of Personalization, Comm. ACM, Vol.43, No.8, pp.26-158 (2000)
7. Pazzani, M., Muramatsu, J. and Billsus, D.: Syskill and webert: Identifying interesting web sites, Proc. of Thirteenth National Conf. on Artificial Intelligence, pp.54-61, (1996)
8. Mooney, R.J. and Roy, L.: Content-Based Book Recommending Using Learning for Text Categorization, Proc. of ACM SIGIR' 99 Workshop Recommender Systems: Algorithms and Evaluation, (1999)
9. Resnick, P., Iacovou, N., Suchak, M., Bergstorm, P. and Riedl, J.: GroupLens: an open architecture for collaborative filtering of netnews, Proc. of ACM Conf. on Computer Supported Cooperative Work, pp.175-186 (1994)
10. Resnick, P. and Varian, H.: Recommender systems, Comm. ACM, Vol.40, No.3, pp.56-58 (1997)
11. Balabanovic M. and Shoham, Y.: Fab: Content-based, collaborative recommendation, Comm. ACM, Vol.40, No.3, pp.66- 72 (1997)
12. Claypool, M., Gokhale, A., Miranda, T., Murnikov, P., Netes, D. and Sartin, M.: Combining Content-Based and Collaborative Filters in an Online Newspaper, Proc. of ACM SIGIR' 99 Workshop Recommender Systems: Algorithms and Evaluation (1999)
13. Shimizu, T., Hijikata, Y. and Nishida, S.: A Basic Study on Discovery-oriented Algorithm for Collaborative Filtering, IPSJ SIG Notes, Vol.2006, No.59, pp.53-60 (2006)
14. Herlocker, J., Konstan, J., and Riedl, J.: Explaining Collaborative Filtering Recommendations, Proc. of CSCW' 00, pp.241-250 (2000)
15. Toda, H., Kitagawa, H., Fujimura., Ko., Kataoka, R. and Oku masahiro.: Topic Structure Mining for Document Sets Using Graph Structure, The IEICE transactions on information and systems, Vol.J90-D, No.2, pp.292-310 (2007)
16. Matsuo, Y., Tomobe, H., Hashida, K., Nakashima, H. and Ishizuka, M.: Social Network Extraction from the Web information, Transactions of the Japanese Society for Artificial Intelligence. AI, Vol.20, No.1E, pp.46-56 (2005)
17. Yuta, K., Ono, N. and Fujiwara, Y.: Structural Analysis of Human Network in Social Networking Services, Transactions of Information Processing Society of Japan, Vol.47, No.3, pp.865-874 (2006)
18. Sarwar, B., Karypis, G., Konstan, J. and Riedl, J.: Item-Based Collaborative Filtering Recommendation Algorithms, Proc. 10th International World Wide Web Conf, pp.285-295 (2001)
19. Newman, M.E.J.: Fast algorithm for detecting community structure in networks, Phys. Rev. E, Vol.69, 066133 (2004)
20. Newman, M.E.J.: Detecting community structure in networks, Eur. Phys. J. B38, pp.321-330 (2004)
21. Newman, M.E.J.: Analysis of weighted networks, Phys. Rev. E70, 056131 (2004)
22. Ando, J. and Yoshii, S.: Discussion about Community Extraction Methods for WWW Navigation, IEICE technical report. Artificial intelligence and knowledge-based processing, Vol.2006, No.2, pp.115-122 (2006)
23. Amazon Web Services: http://www.amazon.com/gp/aws/landing.html

Cryptographic Approch for Workflow Systems

Yasuo Hatano[1], Kunihiko Miyazaki[1], Toshinobu Kaneko[2]

[1] Systems Development Laboratory, Hitachi, Ltd., 292, Yoshida-cho, Totsuka-ku, Yokohama-shi, Kanagawa-ken, 244-0817,
[2] Tokyo University of Science, 2641, Yamazaki, Noda-shi, Chiba-ken, 278-8510,
e-mail: {yasuo.hatano.bn, kunihiko.miyazaki.zt}@hitachi.com, kaneko@ee.noda.tus.ac.jp

Abstract This paper proposes encryption schemes to enforce the order of the procedure in a workflow system. In workflow systems, it is important to perform a procedure according to an order that is given by some regulation. In addition, it is desired that each reviewer checks a necessary part of a document to admit the application because the document sometime contains privacy information, e.g., name, birthday, income and so on. There is a procedure in a workflow system which it is sufficient to pass if one of two reviewers admits the document. More generally, there is a procedure in a workflow system that can be passed if k of n reviewers admit the document, which we call a "threshold procedure". By applying a cryptographic technique, e.g., a multiple encryption and secret sharing, this paper gives a method to realize various procedures in workflow systems, i.e., controlling the order of reviewers, disclosing a part of document selectively, and a threshold procedure. Conventional workflow systems control their procedure by a server, which we consider a trusted one. This implies that an administrator might tamper a procedure. The proposed schemes help us to enforce a procedure even if he/she is not trustworthy.

Please use the following format when citing this chapter:

Hatano, Y., Miyazaki, K., Kaneko, T., 2008 in IFIP International Federation for Information Processing, Volume 286; Towards Sustainable Society on Ubiquitous Networks, eds. Oya, M., Uda, R., Yasunobu, C., (Boston: Springer), pp. 75–86.

1 Introduction

1.1 Background

Workflow systems provide an automated procedure for a business process and they are used to computerize and to automate various procedures in a company. Recent accounting scandals in various countries have resulted in the passage of several laws establishing or enhancing standards for corporate financial reporting and record keeping. Typical examples are the Sarbanes-Oxley (SOX) Act in the United State[1] and the Japanese version of that act, the Financial Commodities Exchange Act[2]. They require companies to establish internal control and workflow systems are one of the important components to establish effective internal controls, because workflow systems give us a proper method to perform a procedure of a business process. In a procedure in a business process, various reviewers need to check a submitted document from an employee (applicant) and it is important to control the reviewing order which is defined by the business process.

To control the reviewing order is required not only for a business process in a company but also for a procedure performed through several corporations. In a one-stop service of public institutions, a procedure is sometime performed through several offices. For instance, if we apply a procedure to buy a car in Japan by a one-stop service, the procedure needs to access systems of several offices because, in the physical procedure, we first have to submit a certificate of a parking area to a police office and then submit an application to issue a car number to Distinct Transport Bureau. Other examples of procedures performed through several corporations are the one to issue a credit card and to claim a payment of insurance. To issue a credit card, the credit card company needs to check an applicant by credit facilities and then issues a credit card after checking the application in the card company.

Workflow systems are usually constructed with a server, which we consider a trusted one, and the server manages reviewers, the document and the status of an application in a procedure and controls the order of the procedure. In this paper, we show a cryptographic technique to support a workflow system. We first propose a basic construction to enforce the order of a procedure by adopting a multiple encryption and then we propose enhanced constructions for threshold procedures and for partial disclosure of a document. Note that we call procedures that can be passed if k of m reviewers admit the application "threshold procedures".

To realize a threshold procedure has several advantages for workflow systems. One advantage is that, by combining basic constructions and threshold procedures, we can construct any kinds of procedures for workflow systems even if the order of a procedure is complicated. Another advantage is that a threshold procedure allows us to make a pass for a substitute reviewer. Even if a regular reviewer is absent, e.g., a manager travels on business, a substitute reviewer, e.g., an assistant manager, can admit a document by a threshold procedure.

Moreover, the partial disclosure of a document in a procedure is important because some documents in workflow systems contain sensitive information, e.g., name and birthday, and it is desired that such information is disclosed to only proper reviewers. For instance, a credit card application contains sensitive information like a name, birthday, annual income, bank account number, PIN number and so on. As we mentioned in the above, in a procedure to issue a credit card, the card company needs to check an application by credit facilities. The card company, however, should not submit the whole information for credit facilities. In this case, the card company should hide the PIN number for credit facilities and should hide the income and PIN number for a bank. In this paper, we give a method to realize threshold procedures by using a secret sharing[15] and also show partial disclosure of a document in a procedure by adopting hybrid encryption schemes[5, 8].

As we mentioned in the above, conventional workflow systems use a server, which we consider a trusted one, and the server controls the order of a procedure. Such systems, however, imply that an administrator of a server might tamper a procedure and associated log entries that are important evidence for a procedure. Hence if the administrator is not trustworthy, nobody knows whether the procedure have been done properly or not. This means that internal control does not achieve if we do not trust an administrator of a workflow system. In addition, if a workflow system is collaborated with several corporations, e.g., one-stop services and credit card applications, it is hard to manage a whole procedure because there are several administrators. Using the proposed method, we can construct a workflow system that strongly protects the order of a procedure by a cryptographic technique. This enables us to enforce a procedure even if an administrator is not trustworthy. In addition, the proposed schemes facilitate constructing a procedure collaborated with several corporations because the order of the procedure can be decided only by an applicant or a reception.

1.2 Related Work

As we mentioned in the above, we adopt a multiple encryption to control the reviewing order of a procedure. A multiple encryption is used for improving security[16]. Encrypting a plaintext by several encryption algorithms, information of the plaintext will not be leaked even if one of the encryption algorithms is broken.

Another application of multiple encryptions is "onion routing"[13], which is a technique to hide receiver's information in a network communication. When Alice sends a message to Bob by using onion routing, she first chooses several routers and encrypts traffic information to Bob such that the received router can know only information about the next router. Since each router can know only the information about the next router, Alice can hide the information about the receiver Bob that she wants to send the message to.

Proxy re-encryption schemes[9] are methods that allow proxies to transform a ciphertext which has been encrypted for one party, so that it may be decrypted by another. Dodis proposed two framework of proxy re-encryption schemes, called "unidirectional proxy re-encryption" and "bidirectional proxy re-encryption", and proposed using a multiple encryption as a simple construction for a unidirectional proxy encryption[9].

The goals of related works introduced in the above are not the control of the reviewing order. To construct a workflow system, we propose encryption schemes that enable us to control an order of reviewers and show enhanced schemes to perform a threshold procedure and to disclose a necessary part of a document in a procedure. Using the proposed methods, we can construct various procedures with the order control by a cryptographic protection.

2 Preliminary

In this paper, we use the following notation.

- u_i : i-th reviewer.
- M_i : Plaintext browsed by i-th reviewer.
- C_i : Ciphertext received by i-th reviewer.
- n : Number of reviewer.
- *hash* : Cryptographic hash function.
- *Concat* : Concatenation function.
- *Parse* : Parser.
- KeyGen : Key generation algorithm.
- Enc : Encryption algorithm.
- Dec : Decryption algorithm.
- $\mathtt{SE} = (\mathtt{KeyGen}, \mathtt{Enc}, \mathtt{Dec})$: Symmetric key cryptosystem.
- $\mathtt{PE} = (\mathtt{KeyGen}, \mathtt{Enc}, \mathtt{Dec})$: Asymmetric key cryptosystem.

Note that, KeyGen is a probabilistic algorithm, which takes a security parameter and which outputs a secret key for symmetric key cryptosystems or private/public key pair for asymmetric key cryptosystems. Enc is a probabilistic algorithm that takes a plaintext and encryption key, i.e., a secret key for symmetric key cryptosystems and a public key for asymmetric key cryptosystems, and that outputs a ciphertext. Dec is a deterministic algorithm that takes a ciphertext and a decryption key, i.e., a secret key for symmetric key cryptosystems and a private key for asymmetric key cryptosystems, and that outputs the resulting plaintext or the invalid ciphertext $\perp$.

In the following, we use the notation ES.Alg to denote the algorithm Alg of ES. For instance, SE.KeyGen denotes the key generation algorithm KeyGen of a symmetric cryptosystem SE.

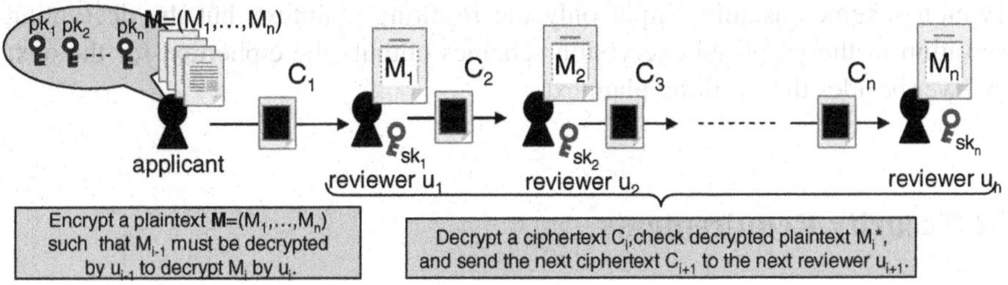

Fig. 1 Cryptographic Approach for Workflow System

3 Cryptographic Approach for Workflow Systems

3.1 Encryption Schemes with Reviewing Order Control

In this paper, we propose encryption schemes that enable us to enforce a reviewing order (see Fig. 1). In the proposed schemes, a sender(applicant) designates several reviewers and encrypts a plaintext $\mathbf{M} = (M_1, \ldots, M_n)$ by public keys of reviewers such that the reviewer $u_i (i = 2, \ldots, n)$ can only read the plaintext M_i after u_{i-1} read the plaintext M_{i-1}.

A reviewer u_i receives her/his ciphertext C_i and decrypts it with her/his private key sk_i. The decryption algorithm outputs the ciphertext C_{i+1} for the next reviewer u_{i+1} besides the decrypted plaintext M_i^* and the reviewer u_i reads M_i^* and sends C_{i+1} to the next reviewer u_{i+1}. Note that we call the proposed schemes as "Encryption Schemes with Reviewing Order Control (ESROC)" and that denote this as $\mathtt{ESROC} = (\mathtt{KeyGen}, \mathtt{Enc}, \mathtt{Dec})$. We describe the algorithm of ESROC in the following.

Key Generation Algorithm `KeyGen`:
Probabilistic algorithm that takes a security parameter and that outputs a set of public/private key pairs (PK, SK). Note that $PK = (pk_1, \ldots, pk_n)$ and $SK = (sk_1, \ldots, sk_n)$ respectively denote a set of public keys and private keys and (pk_i, sk_i) denotes a public/private key pair for reviewer u_i.

Encryption Algorithm `Enc`:
Probabilistic algorithm which accepts a plaintext $\mathbf{M} = (M_1, \ldots, M_n)$ and a set of encryption keys PK and which outputs a ciphertext C_1 for the first reviewer u_1.

Decryption Algorithm `Dec`:
Deterministic algorithm which accepts a ciphertext C_i for the i-th reviewer u_i and the reviewer's private key sk_i and which outputs the decrypted plaintext M_i^* and the ciphertext C_{i+1} for the next reviewer u_{i+1}. The decryption algorithm outputs invalid ciphertext $\perp$ if the decryption process fails.

The difference from conventional encryption schemes and the proposed schemes is in the decryption algorithm `Dec`. The decryption algorithm of conventional encryption schemes usually output only the resulting plaintext, but the decryption algorithm in the proposed encryption schemes outputs the ciphertext for the next reviewer besides the resulting plaintext.

3.2 Security Requirements

The proposed schemes are required that a ciphertext is decrypted according to the order that is defined by applicant who encrypts a plaintext. Moreover, the decrypted plaintext M_i^* can be read by only the reviewer u_i. Therefore the proposed schemes must have the following properties.

- Order Robustness
  It is infeasible to cheat the reviewing order for any probabilistic polynomial time (PPT) adversaries. More precisely, it is infeasible for any PPT adversaries to compute a ciphertext $C_i'(\neq C_i)$ which generates C_{i+1} by $\mathtt{ESROC.Dec}_{sk_i}(C_i)$.
- Confidentiality
  It is infeasible for any PPT adversaries to know any information about the plaintext M_i. More precisely, for a plaintext pair $\mathbf{M}^{(0)}$ and $\mathbf{M}^{(1)}$, where $\mathbf{M}^{(b)} = (M_1, \ldots, M_i^{(b)}, \ldots, M_n)$ $(b = \{0,1\})$, it is infeasible for any PPT adversaries to decide which plaintext, $\mathbf{M}^{(0)}$ or $\mathbf{M}^{(1)}$, is encrypted.

The notion of confidentiality is equivalent to indistinguishability (IND) notion for public key encryption schemes[6]. In addition, the notion of order robustness contains the notion of plaintext awareness (PA), which is another security notion for public key encryption schemes[6]. Therefore, from the result in [6], a secure encryption as the proposed schemes implies a secure public key encryption in the sense of IND-CCA2 (INDistinguishability against adaptive chosen ciphertext attacks). It should be noted that, for a secure encryption as the proposed schemes, it is not enough to be just an IND-CCA2 secure encryption because an IND-CCA2 secure public key encryption is not always a PA secure public key encryption although an public key encryption which is PA and IND-CPA secure is an IND-CCA2 secure public key encryption (see [6]).

4 Basis Construction

4.1 Construction

In this section, we propose a basic construction for ESROC. The proposed method in this section, we adopt the conventional asymmetric key cryptosystem and construct an ESROC by using a multiple encryption.

The encryption algorithm of the basic construction encrypts the i-th plaintext M_i with a ciphertext C_{i+1}, which is a ciphertext for the next reviewer u_{i+1}, and outputs a ciphertext C_{i-1} for the previous reviewer u_{i-1}. The decryption algorithm decrypts a ciphertext C_i by the private key sk_i of the i-th reviewer. The output of the decryption algorithm consists of two components: one is the decrypted plaintext M_i^* and the other is the ciphertext C_{i+1} for the next reviewer u_{i+1}. We show this construction in Fig. 2[1].

As shown in Fig. 2, in the basic construction, the number of reviewers increases size of a target ciphertext. Therefore, in practice, hybrid encryption schemes, e.g., [5, 8], is suitable to construct a basic construction.

$\mathtt{ESROC.KeyGen}(\lambda, n)$
  for $i = 1$ to n do
    $(pk_i, sk_i) \leftarrow \mathtt{PE.KeyGen}(\lambda)$;
  end for;
  output (PK, SK);

$\mathtt{ESROC.Enc}(\mathbf{M}; pk_1, \ldots, pk_n)$
  $C_{n+1} \xleftarrow{R} \{0,1\}^L$;
  for $i = n$ to 1 do
    $C_i \leftarrow \mathtt{PE.Enc}(C_{i+1} || M_i; pk_i)$;
  end for;
  output C_1;

$\mathtt{ESROC.Dec}(C_i; sk_i)$;
  $C \leftarrow \mathtt{PE.Dec}(C_i; sk_i)$;
  $(C_{i+1} || M_i^*) \leftarrow Parse(C)$
  output (C_{i+1}, M_i^*);

Fig. 2 Basic Construction

4.2 Security

A ciphertext C_i is generated from a plaintext M_i and a ciphertext C_{i+1} by the encryption algorithm of an asymmetric key cryptosystem PE.Enc. If the asymmetric key cryptosystem PE is secure enough, i.e., it is PA and IND-CPA secure(see [6]), we can say that the basic construction described in this section has the property of order robustness and confidentiality. Note that, even if an adversary know some private keys except the one for a target block i, the basic construction is secure.

[1] More generally, each reviewer can use different asymmetric key cryptosystems in a basic construction. Note that if the security of an asymmetric key cryptosystem depends on the message length, the security parameter must be carefully chosen.

5 Enhanced Constructions

5.1 Construction for Threshold Procedure

5.1.1 Improvement of the basic construction

There are some procedures in a workflow system such that several reviewers check a document and the order of them is not defined. For instance, there are two reviewers, $u^{(1)}$ and $u^{(2)}$ in a procedure and both reviewer have to admit the document but $u^{(1)}$ may admit before $u^{(2)}$ and $u^{(2)}$ may admit before $u^{(1)}$. In addition, there is a case where it is sufficient to pass a procedure if one of two reviewers admits the document. More generally, those procedures is described as the one that is passed if k of m reviewers admit the document and we call such procedures as (m,k) threshold procedures. By using threshold procedures, we can construct various procedures even if a procedure is complicated. In this subsection, we enhance the basic construction for (m,k) threshold procedures.

To improve the basic construction for a threshold procedure, we apply the Shamir's secret sharing[15] to the basic construction. We show the proposed construction for an (m,k) threshold procedure in Fig. 4. Note that, in Fig. 4, i-th reviewers in the (m,k) threshold procedure denotes $u_i^{(1)},\ldots,u_i^{(m)}$ and the private and pubic key of a reviewer $u_i^{(j)}(j=1,\ldots,m)$ denote $sk_i^{(j)}$ and $pk_i^{(j)}$, respectively. The set of reviewers, whose ciphertexts $C_i^{(x)}(x=1,\ldots,m)$ are received by reviewer u_{i+1}, denotes $\mathscr{U}_i \subseteq \{u_i^{(1)},\ldots,u_i^{(m)}\}$, where the number of elements in $\mathscr{U}_i$ is greater than or equal to k. Although we adopt a secret sharing for a threshold procedure, we may adopt all-or-nothing transform (AONT)[14] instead of secret sharing if a procedure requires that all of m reviewers admit the document.

5.1.2 Security

As we showed in Fig. 4, we divide an $(i+1)$-th ciphertext $C_{(i+1)}$ into m ciphertexts $C_{i+1}^{(1)},\ldots,C_{i+1}^{(m)}$ by using a secret sharing. Because of the property of secret sharing schemes, the $(i+1)$-th reviewer can recover the ciphertext $C_{(i+1)}$ if and only if he/she receives at least k ciphertexts in m ciphertexts, $C_{i+1}^{(1)},\ldots,C_{i+1}^{(m)}$. Since a ciphertext $C_{i+1}^{(j)}$ is given by the reviewer $u_{i+1}^{(j)}$, we can realize an (m,k) threshold procedure.

As we showed in Fig. 4, all of ciphertexts $C_i^{(j)}$, $C_{i+1}^{(j)}$ and C_{i+2} around a threshold procedure are obtained by decrypting the previous ciphertext $C_{i-1}^{(j)}$, $C_i^{(j)}$ and C_{i+1}, respectively. Therefore, from the same reason of the basic construction, if the asymmetric key cryptosystem PE is secure enough, the proposed construction in Fig. 4 is also secure.

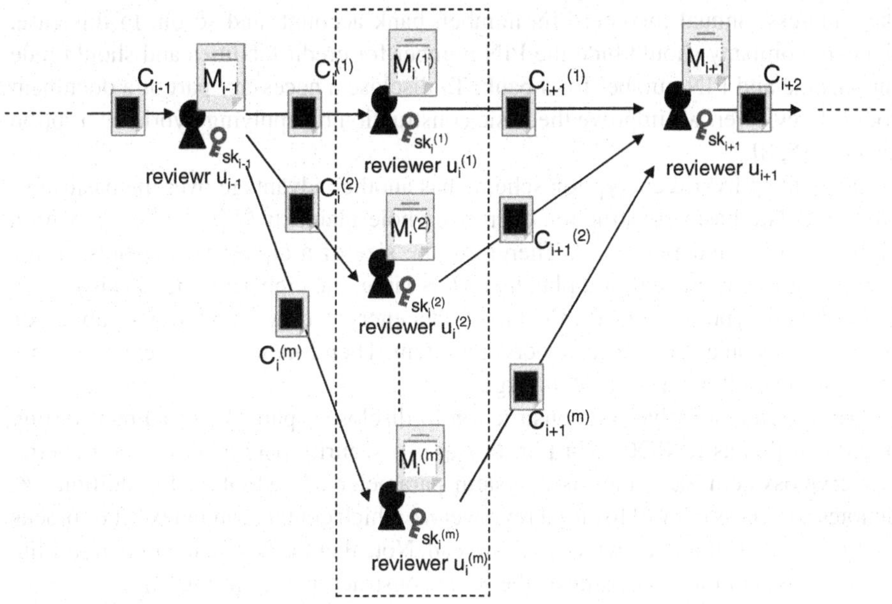

Fig. 3 Threshold Procedure

[Modification of Encryption Algorithm]

(1) $j = i+1$

  $a_0 \leftarrow C_j;$

  for $l = 1$ to k do $a_l \stackrel{R}{\leftarrow} \{0,1\}^*$; end for;

  for $x = 1$ to m do

    $C_j^{(x)} \leftarrow f(x) = a_0 + a_1 x + a_2 x^2 + \ldots + a_k x^k;$

    $C_{j-1}^{(x)} \leftarrow \mathtt{PE.Enc}(C_j^{(x)} || M_{j-1}^{(x)}, pk_j^{(x)});$

  end for;

(2) $j = i$

  $C_j \leftarrow (C_{j-1}^{(1)} || C_{j-1}^{(2)} || \ldots || C_{j-1}^{(m)});$

  $C_{j-1} \leftarrow \mathtt{PE.Enc}(C_j || M_{j-1}, pk_{j-1});$

[Modification of Decryption Algorithm]

(1) $j = i-1$

  $C \leftarrow \mathtt{PE.Dec}(C_j, sk_j);$

  $(C_{j+1}^{(1)} || C_{j+1}^{(2)} || \ldots || C_{j+1}^{(m)} || M_j) \leftarrow Parse(C)$

  output $C_{j+1}^{(1)}, C_{j+1}^{(2)}, \ldots, C_{j+1}^{(m)}, M_j;$

(2) $j = i$

  $C \leftarrow \mathtt{PE.Dec}(C_j^{(x)}, sk_j);$

  $(C_{j+1}^{(x)} || M_j^{(x)}) \leftarrow Parse(C);$

  output $C_{j+1}^{(x)} || M_j^{(x)};$

(3) $j = i+1$

$$C_j \leftarrow \sum_{x \in \mathscr{U}_j} \left(C_j^{(x)} \prod_{z \in \mathscr{U}_j, z \neq x} \frac{-z}{x-z} \right);$$

  $C \leftarrow \mathscr{D}(C_j, sk_j);$

  $(C_{j+1} || M_j) \leftarrow Parse(C);$

  output $C_{j+1} || M_j;$

Fig. 4 Modification for Threshold Procedure

5.2 Practical Construction with Privacy Protection

5.2.1 Construction based on hybrid encryption schemes

A document in a procedure sometime contains sensitive information and therefore reviewers must not know some of them even if they check the application. For instance, a credit card application contains sensitive information such as name, birthday, address, annual income, PIN number, bank account, and so on. In this case, the card company should hide the PIN number for credit facilities and should hide the income and PIN number for a bank. To disclose a necessary part of a document for each reviewer, we improve the basic construction by applying hybrid encryption schemes[5, 8].

Applying a hybrid encryption scheme has another advantage over the basic construction. The basic construction encrypts whole plaintext $M_i (i = 1, \ldots, n)$ with a ciphertext C_{i-1} independently. Therefore, the size of a ciphertext depends on the number of reviewers and, if a plaintext M_i is large, the ciphertext size is also large. In hybrid encryption schemes, the target data encrypted by a reviewer's public key is secret keys on a symmetric key cryptosystem. Therefore the ciphertext size is not increased even if a plaintext M_i is large.

We describe an enhanced construction to disclose a part of a document in Fig. 6 and call this as ESROC$^+$. In Fig. 6, λ_{SE} is a security parameter of a symmetric key cryptosystem SE, which is a system parameter of ESROC$^+$. In addition, $\mathscr{B}_i$ denotes an access control list for a reviewer u_i, which contains an index set of blocks m_j $(j = 1, \ldots, s)$ that the reviewer u_i can read. Note that the key generation algorithm of this construction is the same as the basic construction (see in Fig. 2).

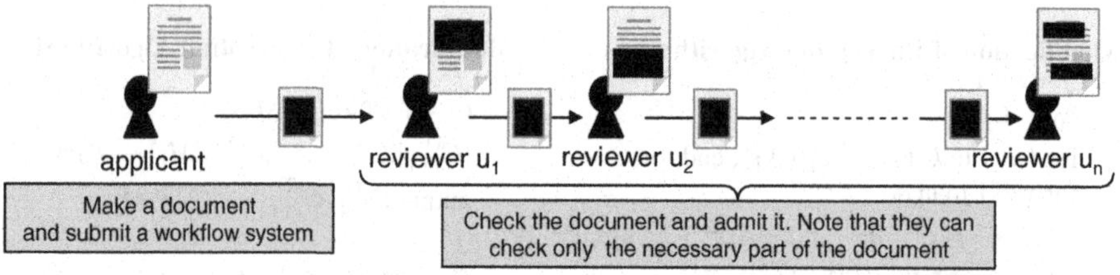
applicant
reviewer u1
reviewer u2
reviewer un
Make a document
and submit a workflow system
Check the document and admit it. Note that they can
check only the necessary part of the document

Fig. 5 Construction with Privacy Protection

$\mathtt{ESDOS}^+.\mathtt{Enc}(M; pk_1, \ldots, pk_n)$
  for $i = 1$ to s do
    $k_i \leftarrow \mathtt{SE.KeyGen}(\lambda_{\mathrm{SE}})$; $c_i \leftarrow \mathtt{SE.Enc}(m_i, k_i)$;
  end for;
  for $i = 1$ to n do
    $K_i \leftarrow Concat(hash(C), \mathscr{B}_i, \{k_j | j \in \mathscr{B}_i\})$;
      $(C = (c_1, \ldots, c_n))$
  end for;
  $C'_1 \leftarrow \mathtt{ESROC.Enc}(K, pk_1, \ldots, pk_n)$
    $(K = (K_1, \ldots, K_s))$;
  output $C_1 = (C'_1, C)$;

$\mathtt{ESDOS}^+.\mathtt{Dec}(C_i; sk_i)$
  $(C'_i, C) \leftarrow Parse(C_i)$;
  for $i = 1$ to s do $m^*_i \leftarrow$ NULL; end for;
  $(C'_{i+1}, K^*_i) \leftarrow \mathtt{ESROC.Dec}(C_i; sk_i)$;
  $(H^*, \mathscr{B}_i, \{k_j | j \in \mathscr{B}_i\}) \leftarrow Parse(K^*_i)$;
  if $H^* \neq hash(C)$ then output $\perp$;
  foreach $j \in \mathscr{B}_i$ do
    $m^*_j \leftarrow \mathtt{SE.Dec}(c_j, k_j)$;
  end foreach;
  output (C_{i+1}, M^*_i)
    $(C_{i+1} = (C'_{i+1}, C), M^*_i = (m^*_1, \ldots, m^*_s))$;

Fig. 6 Construction with Privacy Protection

5.2.2 Security

The scheme described in Fig. 6 is the same as the hybrid construction except the extra information, a ciphertext C_{i+1} and several secret keys of a symmetric key cryptosystem, are encrypted by a public key pk_i in the scheme in Fig. 6. From the result of a hybrid encryption schemes (see [5, 8, 11]), we can easily know that such extra information has no influence for the security. Therefore, from the same reason of the basic construction, if the asymmetric key cryptosystem PE and the symmetric key cryptosystem are secure enough, the proposed construction in Fig. 6 is also secure.

Note that, in the above discussion, we do not consider that an adversary regenerates the ciphertext. This is because, if an adversary who has some private key knows the whole information from ciphertexts except C_i, he/she can easily create a ciphertext C_i', which is different from C_i but generates the same resulting plaintext M_i^* as the target ciphertext C_i. In order to protect this "regeneration attack', it might be useful to attach a digital signature of the applicant with a document.

6 Conclusion

In this paper, we propose encryption schemes to enforce the order of reviewers in a workflow system. We give a basic construction and enhance it for a threshold procedure and for disclosing a necessary part of a document for each reviewer. The enhanced constructions help us to describe various procedures in a workflow system.

Conventional workflow systems are constructed with a server, which we consider a trusted one, to control the order, documents and reviewers in a procedure. Such workflow systems imply that an administrator might tamper a procedure. However, the proposed schemes strongly protect sensitive information in a document and the order of reviewers in a procedure even if the administrator is not trustworthy. Hence, the proposed schemes are especially useful for a procedure in which some reviewers belong to different corporations, e.g., a one-stop service of public institutions, or in which a corporation outsources some processes, e.g., credit facilities for a credit card application of credit card companies.

In practice, if we construct a procedure by the proposed schemes, we have to consider maintenance of the procedure, e.g., key management, changing the procedure and so on. To construct and evaluate a workflow system by using the proposed schemes is one of our future works.

References

1. "The Sarbanes-Oxley Act.", 2002.
2. Financial Services Agency, "Financial Instruments and Exchange Law", 2006. http://www.fsa.go.jp/common/diet/164/index.html (in Japanese)

3. "Private Information Protection Law", http://www.kantei.go.jp/jp/it/privacy/houseika/hourituan/ (in Japanese)
4. XML encryption, http://www.w3.org/TR/xmlenc-core/
5. M. Abe, R. Gennaro and K. Kurosawa, "Tag-KEM/DEM: A New Framework Hybrid Encryption", IACR Cryptology ePrint Archive: Report 2005/027, 2005. Available at http://eprint.iacr.org/2005/027
6. M. Bellare, A. Desai, D. Pointcheval and P. Rogaway, "Relations Among Notions of Security for Public-Key Encryption Schemes", Advances in Cryptology – CRYPTO'98, Lecture Note in Computer Science, Vol. 1462 (LNCS 1462), pp.26-46, Springer-Verlag, 1998.
7. M. Bellare, A. Boldyreva and J. Staddon, "Multi-Recipient Encryption Schemes: Security Notions and Randomness Re-Use", Public Key Cryptography – PKC 2003, Lecture Notes in Computer Science Vol.2567 (LNCS 2567), pp.85-99, Springer–Verlag, 2003
8. R. Cramer and V. Shoup, "Design and Analysis of Practical Public-Key Encryption Schemes Secure against Adaptive Chosen Ciphertext Attack", SIAM Journal on Computing archive, Vol. 33 , Issue 1, Society for Industrial and Applied Mathematics Philadelphia, PA, USA, pp. 167-226, Society for Industrial and Applied Mathematics, 2004.
9. Y. Dodis and A. Ivan, "Proxy cryptography revisited", In Proceedings of the 10th Annual Network and Distributed System Security Symposium (NDSS), February 2003.
10. Y. Hatano and K. Miyazaki, "An Encryption Method for Multiple Receivers with Different Roles", IEICE Technical Report, ISEC2005-167, 2006. (In Japanese)
11. Y. Hatano, K. Miyazaki and Toshinobu Kaneko, "A Study on Extended Multi-Recipient Encryption: Security Notion and Constructions", IEICE Technical Report, ISEC2007-88, 2007. (In Japanese)
12. R. Impagliazzo and M. Luby, "One-way functions are essential for complexity based cryptography", Proceedings of the 30th Symposium on Foundations of Computer Science, pp. 230-235, 1989.
13. M. G. Reed, P. F. Syverson and D. M. Goldshlag, "Anonymous Connections and Onion Routing", IEEE Journal on Special Areas in Communications, vol. 16, No. 4, pp. 482-494, 1998.
14. R. Rivest, "All-Or-Nothing encryption and the package transform", Fast Software Encryption '97, Lecture Notes on Computer Science, vol. 1267, pp. 210-218, Springer-Verlag, 1997.
15. A. Shamir, "How to share a secret", communications of the ACM, 22(11), pp.612-613, 1979.
16. R. Zhang, G. Hanaoka, J. Shikata and Hideki Imai, "On the Security of Multiple Encryption or CCA-security+CCA-security=CCA-security", Public Key Cryptography - PKC 2004, 7th International Workshop on Theory and Practice in Public Key Cryptography, Lecture Notes on Computer Science, vol. 2947 (LNCS 2947), pp.360-374, 2004.

A Fuzzy Model for Scalable Trust in E-Commerce

Zhaohao Sun[1], Xifeng Guo[2], Shuliang Zhao[1]

[1] School of Computer Science and Technology, College of Mathematics and Information Science, Hebei Normal University, Shijiazhuang, China, 050016

Email: zhsun@ieee.org, zhaoshuliang@sina.com

[2] Dept. of Computer Science, Hebei North University, Zhangjiakou, China, 075000

Email: gxf32366970@163.com

Abstract. With the rapid development of e-commerce and the expansion of e-commerce system scale, scalable trust in e-commerce becomes critical. This article examines scalable trust of multiagent e-commerce system (MECS) and proposes a fuzzy model for scalable trust in e-commerce. It also discusses the realization of scalable trust from the viewpoint of engineering. The proposed approach will facilitate research and development of trust, multiagent systems, e-commerce and e-services.

1. Introduction

Trust is significant for healthy development of e-commerce 1-9. Castelfranchi and Tan assert that e-commerce can be successful only if the general public trusts in the virtual environment, because lack of trust in security is one of the main reasons for e-consumers and companies not to engage in e-commerce 3. Therefore, trust has received an increasing attention in e-commerce and information technology (IT). For example, Finnie and Sun examine trust in e-supply chains 4. Koufaris and Hampton-Sosa examine how the website experience can influence customer trust in the company itself through customer beliefs about the website [8]. Pavlou integrates trust with the technology acceptance model to explore the customer acceptance of e-commerce [14]. Salm et al examine trust in e-commerce and notice that "many customers may still not trust vendors when shopping online" [15]. Slyke, Belanger and Comunale look at the impact of trust on the adoption of Web-based shopping [16].

Please use the following format when citing this chapter:

Sun, Z., Guo, X., Zhao, S., 2008, in IFIP International Federation for Information Processing, Volume 286; Towards Sustainable Society on Ubiquitous Networks, eds. Oya, M., Uda, R., Yasunobu, C., (Boston: Springer), pp. 87–97.

Sun et al introduce experience-based trust, knowledge-based trust, reasoning-based trust and hybrid trust in e-commerce and discuss their interrelationships in the context of multiagent e-commerce systems [17]. Verhagen et al examine the relationship between consumer perceptions of trust and the attitude towards purchasing at a consumer-to-consumer e-marketplace [24]. Uslaner discusses trust online and trust offline [23]. Xiu and Liu introduce a formal definition of trust and discuss the properties of trust relation [28]. Xiong and Liu propose a formal reputation-based trust model by combining amount of satisfaction, number of interaction and balance factor of trust in a peer-to-peer e-communities [29]. Yan et al consider that the consumers' trust in e-commerce system includes system-based trust and institution-based trust [30]. Then they discuss the relationship between trust and control, and suggest that trust without control is unstable and dangerous [31]. However, they have not examined how to propagate the trust of agents from individual through group to the whole system.

Trust has been extensively discussed in multiagent e-commerce system (MECS) [4, 23, 24]. Schmidt et al apply a fuzzy trust model to an e-commerce platform [34]. Wong and Sycara address two forms of trust i.e. trust that agents will not misbehave and trust that agents are really delegates of whom they claim to be [25]. Wu et al show that trust can be established if agents learn which other agents exhibit poor behavior and hence which agents do not to be trusted [26]. However, they have not examined scalable trust in MECS, which are of practical significance for multiagent e-commerce and e-services. Zhao and Sun discuss scalable trust in e-commerce from the viewpoint of sociology and engineering [32]. However, they have not provided formal investigation into scalable trust in MECS. This article will fill this gap by examining scalable trust in e-commerce, in particular in MECS, and propose a fuzzy model for scalable trust in MECS. It also discusses the realization of scalable trust from the viewpoint of engineering.

The rest part of this article is organized as follows: Section 2 provides the fundamentals of trust in e-commerce. Section 3 examines scalable trust in e-commerce. Section 4 looks at engineering-based scalable trust for MECS. Section 5 proposes an intelligent model of trust in e-commerce. Section 6 introduces a measure and evaluation of trust. Section 7 proposes a fuzzy logic based model for scalable trust in e-commerce. Section 8 concludes the article with some concluding remarks and future work.

2. Fundamentals of Trust in E-Commerce

This section first reviews the definitions of trust in e-commerce, and then proposes an ontology for trust in e-commerce.

There are many definitions of trust that have been proposed in the literature. Slyke et al define trust in e-sellers (web merchants) as the "truster's expectation about the motives and behaviors of a trustee", where truster is e-customer, and trustee is e-seller [13]. More generally, trust indicates a positive belief or expectation about the perceived reliability of, dependability of and confidence in a person, an intelligent agent, organization, company, object, or process [13]. Therefore, trust is the expectation that arises within a community based on commonly sharing norms from one member to another of that community.

Ramchurn et al [12] define trust as "a belief an agent has that the other party will do what it says it will (being honest and reliable) or reciprocate (being reciprocative for the common good of both), given an opportunity to defect to get higher payoffs". They conceptualize trust as (a) individual-level trust (agent believes in honesty or reciprocation of interaction partners) and (b) system-level trust (the agents are forced to be trustworthy by the system). They further characterize individual-level trust models as learning (evolution) based, reputation-based or socio-cognitive based. Learning models are based on interactions with other agents. Reputation-based models work by asking other agents of their opinion of potential partners.

Generally, trust can also be classified into strategic trust and moralistic trust [23]. Strategic trust is the trust that reflects our experience or willingness with particular people doing particular things (e.g. specific exchanges) [13]. This kind of trust can be called business trust or transaction trust [35], and then it is fragile and temporary [13]. Strategic trust can help us decide whether a specific website is safe and our information secure is there, etc. [23]. Strategic trust can be improved by references from past and current customers [13]. One reason for amazon.com's success with online books selling is that it provides the peer (customers') reviews for almost every book available at amazon.com. The customer can read the peer reviews (as references) before buying the book.

Moralistic trust is the durable optimistic view that strangers are well-intentioned [13], which is a more general value we learn early in life. This kind of trust will give us sufficient faith to take risks on the Web in the first place [23].

Tan and Thoen [35] propose a generic model of trust for e-commerce consisting of two basic components: Party trust and control trust based on the idea that the trust in a transaction with another party depends on the trust in the other party (party trust) and trust in the control mechanism (control trust) that ensure the successful performance of the e-transaction.

Party trust and control trust constitute transaction trust [35], because transaction trust is a kind of strategic trust. Therefore, party trust and control trust can also be considered as strategic trust, as shown in Figure 1. Further, party trust and control trust are supplementary to each other, because if there is not enough party trust between each other, then a control trust mechanism is prescribed.

It should be noted that trust ontology, proposed in Figure 1, is the first attempt for understanding of trust in e-commerce. The proposed trust ontology will be gradually elaborated in the future.

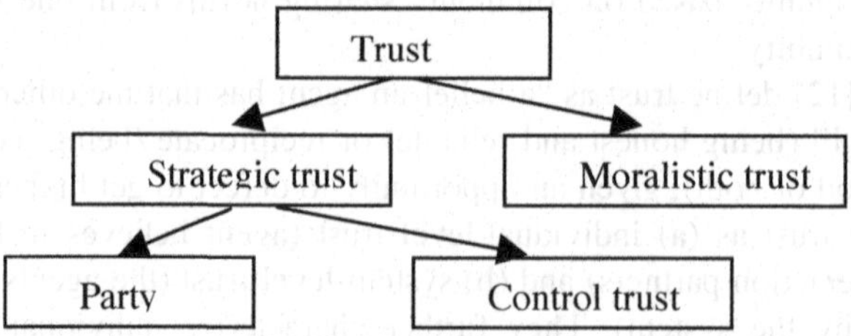

Figure 1. An ontology of trust in e-commerce

3. Scalable Trust in E-Commerce

There are definitions about scalability in many fields [7]. For brevity, we consider the scalable system as the system can deal with the increase of users and resources under the condition of neither remarkably decreasing system performance nor notably increasing management complexity [32].

Based on the definition of scalable system, the scalability of multiagent system (MAS) is when the system parameters change, such as agent number, heterogeneous agent, task scale and task heterogeneity, the system performance does not remarkably decrease, for instance, the declining of task accomplishment ratio, the shortage of resources. Then the scalable trust of MAS can be defined as the trust that can fit for the system parameter changes, that is, these changes cannot lead to the input's remarkable increase and the output's remarkable decrease [32].

Scalable trust can also be considered as trust propagation. That is, the trust between one agent and another is extended to that between one agent and an agent team. The scalable trust between agents within a MAS is the trust that can fit for the remarkable expanding of the MAS system scale and the big increase of agent numbers, provided that the system still keeps appropriate efficiency and modest extra cost.

4. Engineering-Based Scalable Trust for MECS

Scalable trust in the MECS can be treated through trust propagation from the sociology and engineering perspectives respectively [32]. In what follows, we look at the engineering-based scalable trust for MECS.

From the engineering perspective, with the drastic increasing of the agent number in the MECS, the non-scalability of the existed interaction-based trust models will lead to that the trust model has to maintain an enormous agent interaction database. The storage cost of the agent interaction experiences and the cost of selecting trusted agent also increase drastically, and finally these models cannot meet the requirement of the large scale application environment.

How to generalize the individual interaction-based trust to the network-based trust becomes significant for scalability of the system. The existing reputation-based trust models [6, 12, 33] provide the trust recommendation mechanism to make the individual interaction-based trust generalize to interaction network. It is important for these models to have the ability of efficiently processing the dishonest recommendation information in the system in order to guarantee the scalability of trust successful.

From the scalability viewpoint, the lowest level of trust is the individual interaction-based trust (or individual-level trust) [32]. This trust is just between individuals or agents themselves, one's trust in others cannot influence the trust building or computing of another individual's trust in others. Network-based trust is at a higher level, and group-based trust is at a higher level than the network-based trust. The critical issue of the propagation from individual-level trust to network-based trust is that an individual's trust in others can efficiently contribute to the trust construction of another individual's trust in others in the network. The transformation from network-based trust to group-based trust requires at least one group head that represents the group to interact with others. How to propagate the network-based trust to the group-based trust, and how to successfully build the group-based trust models are still open problems.

The still higher level trust is organization-based trust [32]. The differences of group and organization mainly are: (1) in organization, the relationship between members and the task representation are based on economic exchange, such as wage and salary, and they are regulated by contracts. The loyalty to the controller is strengthened through the punishment to the contract violation. (2) Trust of the non-organization member to the organization members is free from organization individuals. (3) Organization members must act according to organization rules. It is still lack of sound contributions on how to propagate group-based trust to organization-based trust.

The top level scalable trust is institution-based trust. By using trustworthy ways generalizing signals and symbols, such as personal skill, ability, etc., makes them not rely on group or organization that they belong to. For example, in our real life, the education diploma and driving license subjecting to one organization are these signals or symbols. The key of the realization of institution-based trust is to make the generalized signals and symbols trustful.

From the viewpoint of engineering, to make the trust scalable, it is necessary study: (1) the distributed storage and transmission of the interaction data and the recommendation information. (2) The distributed generation of one agent's trust value to others [10, 27].

5. An Intelligent Model of Trust in E-Commerce

In this section we will provide an intelligent model of trust in e-commerce from a viewpoint of knowledge based systems [17].

We assume that P is an agent and Q is another agent. P has a knowledge set K_P, which can be considered as the knowledge base in a knowledge-based agent [19], a set of reasoning methods R_P, which can be considered the problem-solving methods or strategies. Q has also a knowledge base K_Q and a reasoning set R_Q. Therefore, from a viewpoint of knowledge based systems [11], the behavior of P and Q *will be decided by* (K_P, R_P) *and* (K_Q, R_Q) *under the same environment*.

In the most general case, one of the necessary conditions for "agent *P* trusts agent *Q*" is that agent *Q* has more knowledge and reasoning methods or problem solving methods than agent *P*, because this is the important premise of agent *P* placing confidence in agent *Q* [2]. In other words, a necessary condition for "agent *P* trusts agent *Q*" is that at the time *t*, agent *P* and agent *Q* satisfy [17]:

$$K_P \subseteq K_Q \quad \text{and} \quad R_P \subseteq R_Q \quad \ldots\ldots\ldots\ldots\ldots\ldots\ldots (1)$$

Based on (1), we can see that trust as a binary relation satisfies [17]:

1. Reflectivity. Agent *P* trusts agent *P* itself.
2. Anti-symmetry. If agent *P* trusts agent *Q*, and agent *Q* trusts agent *P*, then *P*=*Q*. This is usually inconsistent in reality, because in e-commerce, agent *P* and agent *Q* can trust each other for an e-transaction. However, there are really many cases in e-commerce, in which agent *P* trusts agent *Q* whereas agent *Q* might not trust agent *P* [2]. This model (1) is more suitable for the latter case. This is the limitation of this model. However, if one agrees that trust is temporary, whereas distrust or mistrust is ubiquitous, then this model is still of practical significance.
3. Transitivity. If agent *P* trust agent *Q*, and agent *Q* trust agent *R*, then agent *P* trust agent *R*. For example, it is very common in e-commerce if customer *A* trusts his friend *B*, and *B* trusts eBay.com, then *A* trusts eBay.com. This is a kind of transitive trust or trust propagation in customer-to-business e-commerce. However, trust is not transitive in some cases. For instance, customer *A* trusts his friend *B*, and *B* trusts an e-commerce website, however, *A* does not trust this website.

Therefore, a trust relation is conditionally symmetric and transitive [28].

It should be noted that Xiu and Liu [28] also discuss the common properties of trust as a binary relation, and they argue that a trust relation is reflexive and only symmetric, and transitive conditionally, which is consistent with the above discussion. However, their formal definition of trust is based on the action of agent and its effect (action-effect), whereas our formal definition is based on the viewpoint of knowledge base systems.

In reality, the condition (1) can be weakened to three different possibilities that lead to "agent P trusts agent Q" [17].

1. $K_P \subseteq K_Q$
2. $R_P \subseteq R_Q$
3. $K_P \subseteq K_Q$ and $R_P \subseteq R_Q$

The first possibility is that "agent P trusts agent Q" because agent Q has more knowledge, data, information, and experience than agent P. For example, in a primary school, a student trusts his teacher, because the latter has more knowledge and experience than himself. Therefore, the trust resulting from this possibility is called *knowledge-based trust*, or agent P trusts agent Q *with respect to knowledge. In other words*, knowledge-based trust is based on one's knowledge and experience about competencies, motives, and goals of the agent [2, 17].

The second possibility is that "agent P trusts agent Q" because agent Q has more reasoning methods or problem solving methods than agent P. For example, in a system development team, a young team member trusts his team leader, because the latter has more problem solving methods than the former in systems analysis. Therefore, the trust resulting from the second possibility is called *reasoning-based trust*, or agent P trusts agent Q *with respect to reasoning. This implies that* this trust is based on one's reasoning and problem solving abilities [2, 28].

The third possibility is that "agent P trusts agent Q" because agent Q has more knowledge, experience and reasoning methods or problem solving methods than agent P. For example, a patient trusts an experienced doctor working in a clinic, because the doctor has more knowledge, experience and methods in diagnosis and treatment. Therefore, the trust resulting from the third possibility is called *hybrid trust*, or agent P trusts agent Q *hybridly. In other words,* hybrid trust is a combination of knowledge-based trust and reasoning-based trust [17].

6. Measure and Evaluation of Trust

Tweedale and Cutler examine trust in multiagent systems and notice the measure of trust [22]. However, they have not gone into it. In what follows, we will introduce a unified measure of trust based on the discussion of the previous section.

Generally, let the cardinality (size) of knowledge set K and reasoning methods set R be $|K|$ and $|R|$ respectively, which can be considered as a membership of $|K|$ and $|R|$ and ranged in [0, 1] respectively [33]. Then the trust degree of agent P in agent Q can be denoted as:

$$T(P,Q) = \alpha(1-\frac{|K_P|}{|K_Q|}) + (1-\alpha)(1-\frac{|R_P|}{|R_Q|}) \quad \cdots\cdots\cdots\cdots (2)$$

Where, when $\alpha = 1$, $T(P, Q)$ is the knowledge-based trust degree of agent P in agent Q. When $\alpha = 0$, $T(P, Q)$ is the reasoning-based trust degree of agent P in agent Q. When $0 < \alpha < 1$, $T(P, Q)$ is the hybrid trust degree of agent P in agent Q. For example, if knowledge-based trust degree of agent P in agent Q is 0.8, the reasoning-based trust degree of agent P in agent Q is 0.4, and $\alpha = 0.7$, then hybrid trust degree of agent P in agent Q is $T(P,Q) = 0.7 \times 0.8 + 0.3 \times 0.4 = 0.68$.

Further, $1=\frac{|K_P|}{|K_Q|}$ implies that agent P's trust degree is greater whenever the size of knowledge set of the agent Q is greater than that of agent P taking into account (1). Similarly, $1=\frac{|R_P|}{|R_Q|}$ implies that agent P's trust degree is greater whenever the size of reasoning methods of the agent Q is greater than that of agent P. The key idea behind it is that agent P easily trust agent Q if the latter has more knowledge and experience or problem solving ability than agent P taking into account (1). This case usually happens when a student trusts his teacher. With the age increasing the trust between any two persons will be decreasing based on (2), because they have similar knowledge and experience or problem solving ability. In other words, it is more difficult for one to trust others in the adult world. Therefore, $1=\frac{|K_P|}{|K_Q|}$ or $1=\frac{|R_P|}{|R_Q|}$ will be decreasing when the size of knowledge set of the agent P approaches to that of agent Q or the size of reasoning methods of the agent P approaches to that of agent Q. Therefore, the trust value proposed in (2) is of practical significance. For brevity, we use $T(P, Q)$ to denote either knowledge-based trust degree or reasoning-based trust degree or hybrid trust degree and do not differ one from another without specification.

It should be noted that Xiu and Liu assert that "trust evaluation result should be a Boolean value" [28], which has been extended and revised by the above discussion based on fuzzy logic [33].

7. Scalable Trust in E-Commerce: A Fuzzy Logic Perspective

Scalable trust has drawn some attention in e-commerce [2, 29, 32]. However, how to measure scalable trust in order to realize trust propagation from individual trust to system trust is still a big issue. This section will fill this gap based on the fuzzy operation (max-min) [33].

We consider the scalable trust in the following scenario: agent P trust in agent Q_1, Q_2,..., Q_n, which are all the agents within a MAS or MECS, that is, $Q = \{Q_1, Q_2,..., Q_n\}$. The question is what trust degree of agent P is in Q.

For any $i \subseteq \{1, 2,..., n\}$, the trust degree of agent P in agent Q_i is $T(P, Q_i)$, and then the maximal trust degree of agent P in the agent team Q can be denoted as

$$T(P,Q)_{max} = Max\{T(P,Q_i), i \subseteq \{1,2,...,n\}\} \text{ .... } (3)$$

and the minimal trust degree of agent P in agent team Q can be denoted as

$$T(P,Q)_{min} = Min\{T(P,Q_i), i \subseteq \{1,2,...,n\}\} \text{ .... } (4)$$

The maximal trust degree of agent P in agent team Q implies that the agent P trust the agent team Q with a trust degree $T(P, Q_K)$ and $\exists K \in \{1,2,...,n\}$ that satisfies

$$\text{For any } i \subseteq \{1, 2, ..., n\}, \ T(P,Q_K) = T(P,Q_i) \text{ .... } (5)$$

Therefore, this trust can be considered as "blind trust", because if the agent P trusts one agent of the agent team Q with the maximal trust degree, then he trusts the whole agent team in the MAS with the maximal trust degree. An e-commerce owner or vendor hopes that his customers trust his company employers with the maximal trust degree based on (3).

The minimal trust degree of agent P in the agent team Q implies that the agent P trusts the agent team Q with a trust value $T(P, Q_K)$ and $\exists K \in \{1,2,...,n\}$ that satisfies

$$\text{For any } i \subseteq \{1, 2, ..., n\}, \ T(P,Q_K) = T(P,Q_i) \text{ .... } (6)$$

This trust can be considered as "hostile trust", because he trusts the whole agent team Q in the MAS with the minimal trust degree that an agent within the MAS possesses. Currently, e-commerce owners or vendors try their best to avoid this trust degree that customers use to their companies based on customer relationship management and customer experience management [19].

The above two different trust propagations or scalable trusts represents two extreme cases. In reality, the trust degree of agent P in the agent team Q in the MAS or MECS will be in the interval of $[T(P,Q)_{min}, T(P,Q)_{max}]$. This fuzzy-based model can be used to propagate trust from individual-level through network-level and group-level as well as organization-level to institution or system level in a hierarchical way.

In the rest of this section we illustrate the maximal trust and minimal trust with the following example.

Let agent P be an e-customer who is visiting a MECS to buy an MP5 online. The MECS consists of a web client agent (a website) Q_1, a data provider agent (Q_2), and e-transaction agent (Q_3), the trust degree of agent P in these three agents are $T(P, Q_1) = 0.7$, $T(P, Q_2) = 0.9$, $T(P, Q_3) = 0.4$ respectively. Then

$$T(P,Q)_{\max} = Max\{0.7,0.9,0.4\} = 0.9 \quad \text{(7)}$$

and

$$T(P,Q)_{\min} = Min\{0.7,0.9,0.4\} = 0.4 \quad \text{(8)}$$

If this customer uses $T(P,Q)_{\max} = 0.9$ as his trust degree to the MECS, then he will buy the MP5 because he has tried for some time to buy an MP5. However, if he uses $T(P,Q)_{\min} = 0.4$ as his trust degree to the MECS, then he is heavily concerned about the security of the e-transaction, and believes that the information from the data provider agent is incomplete or distorted, then he will not buy this product.

8. Concluding Remarks

This paper examined scalable trust in e-commerce, discussed the realization of scalable trust from the viewpoint of engineering, and proposed a fuzzy logic-based model for scalable trust in e-commerce. The proposed approach will facilitate research and development of trust, multiagent systems, e-commerce and e-services. In future work, we will further examine scalable trust in e-commerce and e-services in more detail and develop a spiral model for scalable trust in e-commerce and e-services. We will also look into scalable trust management and scalable trust protocol for e-commerce.

Acknowledgements

This research is partially supported by a special professor research grant of Hebei Normal University and research grants of Science and Technology Department of Hebei Province, China, under Grant No. 06213537 and No. 05213571; the Nature Science Foundation of Beijing, China, under Grant No. 9072001.

References

1. Award NF, Fitzhgerald K (2005) The deceptive behaviors that offend us most about spyware. Comm of the ACM 48(8): 55-60

2. Branchaud M, Flinn S (2004) xTrust: A Scalable Trust Management Infrastructure. In: Proc 2nd Annual Conf on Privacy, Security and Trust, pp. 207-218. Fredericton, New Brunswick, Canada, 14-15 October
3. Castelfranchi C, Tan YH (eds) (2001) Trust and Deception in Virtual Societies. Kluwer Academic Publishers, Norwell MA, USA
4. Finnie G, Sun Z (2007) Negotiation, trust and experience management in e-supply chains. In Zhang Q (ed) E-Supply Chain Technologies and Management, pp. 172-193. Information Science Reference (IGI), Hershey PA, USA
5. Jones AJI, Firozabadi BS (2005) On the characterization of a trusting agent, aspects of a formal approach, www.sics.se/spot/document/TrustingAgent.ps. Accessed 08 April 2008
6. Kamvar SD, Schlosser MT (2005) EigenRep: Reputation management in P2P networks. In: Lawrence S (ed) Proc. 12th Int'l World Wide Web Conf. Budapest: ACM Press, pp.123~134.
7. Kenneth PB (2006) Scalable trust: engineering challenge or complexity barrier? STC'06, November 3, 2006, Alexandria, Virginia, USA
8. Koufaris M, Hampton-Sosa W (2002) Customer trust online: Examining the role of the experience with the Web site. CIS-2002-05, the CIS Working Paper Series, Zicklin School of Business, Baruch College
9. McKnight DH, Choudhury V, Kacmar C (2002) The impact of initial customer trust on intentions to transact with a web site: A trust building model. J Strategic Inform Syst 11: 297-323.
10. Hassan MW, McClatchey R, Willers I (2007) A scalable evidence based self-managing framework for trust management. Electronic Notes in Theoretical Computing Science 179: 59-73
11. Nilsson NJ (1998) Artificial Intelligence: A New Synthesis. Morgan Kaufmann Publishers, San Francisco
12. Ramchurn SD, Huynh D, Jennings NR (2004) Trust in multi-agent systems. The Knowledge Engineering Review 19(1): 1-25
13. Schneiderman B (2000) Designing trust into online experiences. Comm of the ACM 43(12): 57-59
14. Pavlou PA (2003) Customer acceptance of electronic commerce: Integrating trust and risk with the technology acceptance model. Intl J Electronic Commerce 7(3): 135-161
15. Salam AF, Iyer L, Palvia P, Singh R (2005) Trust in e-commerce, Comm of The ACM 48(2): 73-77
16. Slyke CV, Belanger F, Comunale CL (2004) Factors influencing the adoption of web-based shopping: The impact of trust. ACM SIGMIS Database 35(2): 32 - 49
17. Sun Z, Lu S, Han J, Finnie G (2007) Experience-based trust in e-commerce. In Wang W, et al (eds) Integration and Innovation Orient to E-Society. Proc 7th IFIP Intl Conf on E-commerce, E-services & E-society (I3E2007), Vol. 1, Oct 10-12, Wuhan, Springer, Boston, pp. 643-651
18. Sun Z, Finnie G (2004) Experience based reasoning for recognizing fraud and deception. In: Proc. Intl Conf on Hybrid Intell Syst (HIS'04), pp. 80-85. December 6-8, Kitakyushu, Japan, IEEE Press
19. Sun Z, Finnie G (2004) Intelligent Techniques in E-Commerce: A Case Based Reasoning Perspective. Springer-Verlag, Berlin Heidelberg
20. Sun Z, Finnie G (2007) A fuzzy logic approach to experience based reasoning, Intl J Intell Syst 22 (8): 867-889
21. Sun Z, Finnie G (2005) MEBRS: A multiagent architecture for an experience based reasoning system. LNAI 3681, pp. 972-978. Springer, Berlin
22. Tweedale J, Cutler P (2006) Trust in multiagent systems. LNCS 4252, pp. 479-485. Springer, Berlin Heidelberg
23. Uslaner EM (2004) Trust online, trust offline. Comm of The ACM 47(4): 28-29
24. Verhagen T, Meents S, Tan YH (2006) Perceived risk and trust associated with purchasing at electronic marketplaces. European J of Inform Syst 15: 542-555
25. Wong HC, Sycara K (1999) Adding security and trust to multi-agent systems. In: Proc Autonomous Agents '99 Workshop on Deception, Fraud, and Trust in Agent Societies, pp. 149-161
26. Wu DJ, Kimbrough S, Zhong F (2002) Artificial agents play the Mad Mex trust game: a computational approach. In: Sprague R H (ed) 35th Hawaii Intl Conf System Sciences (HICSS–35), pp. 389- 398. IEEE Press, Hawaii

27. Wu Y (2006) The problems and approaches of trust in B2C e-commerce system. J Commercial Research, 11:198-200 (in Chinese).
28. Xiu D, Liu Z (2005) A formal definition for trust in distributed systems. LNCS 3650, pp. 482-489. Springer Verlag, Berlin Heidelberg
29. Xiong L, Liu L (2002) Building trust in decentralized peer-to-peer electronic communities. In: Proc Intl Conf Electronic Commerce Research (ICECR-5), Montreal, Canada, October
30. Yan Z, Guan S, Mi J (2005) Problem and proposition of empirical study on B2C e-commerce trust. J Soft Science 19(2): 43-45 (in Chinese)
31. Yan Z, Guan S, Mi J (2006) Research on the relation between trust and control and its application in e-commerce. J Scie of Scie & Management of Scie & Techn 6: 5-31 (in Chinese)
32. Zhao Z, Sun Z (2008) Scalable trust in e-commerce. In: Proc. ISECS2008, IEEE Press. In press
33. Zimmermann HJ (1996) Fuzzy Set Theory and its Applications. Kluwer, Boston
34. Schmidt S, Steele R, Dillion T, Chang E (2005) Applying a fuzzy trust model to e-commerce systems. LNAI 3809, pp 318-329. Springer, Berlin.
35. Tan YH, Thoen W (2001) Toward a generic model of trust for electronic commerce. Intl J of Electronic Commerce 5(2): 61-74.

Extending RBAC for Large Enterprises and Its Quantitative Risk Evaluation

Seiichi Kondo[1], Mizuho Iwaihara[2], Masatoshi Yoshikawa[2], Masashi Torato[3]

[1]Mitsubishi Electric Corporation, Kamakura-city, Kanagawa, Japan
Kondo.Seiichi@dr.MitsubishiElectric.co.jp
[2]Kyoto University, Sakyo-ku, Kyoto, Japan
{iwaihara, yoshikawa}@i.kyoto-u.ac.jp
[3]Mitsubishi Electric Information System, Kamakura, Kanagawa, Japan
torato-masashi@mdis.co.jp

Abstract. Systems and security products based on the RBAC model have been widely introduced to enterprises. Especially, the demands on enforcement of enterprise-level security policies and total identity management are rapidly growing. The RBAC model needs to be extended to deal with various circumstances of large enterprises, such as geographical distribution and heterogeneous environments including physical access control. In this paper, we introduce a new RBAC model, suitable for single sign-on systems. This model optimizes evaluation of rule-based RBAC so that total operation costs and productivity can be improved.

Furthermore, to select most cost-effective RBAC extensions for enterprise-wide requirements, we propose a quantitative risk evaluation method based on fault trees. We construct fault trees having security violation and productivity loss as top events, and RBAC standard functions and security incidents as basic events. Probabilities of the top events are computed for given RBAC models and operation environments. We apply this method to a real enterprise system using the above RBAC extension and the proposed model realizes more safety and productivity over the base model.

Please use the following format when citing this chapter:

Kondo, S., Iwaihara, M., Yoshikawa, M., Torato, M., 2008, in IFIP International Federation for Information Processing, Volume 286; Towards Sustainable Society on Ubiquitous Networks, eds. Oya, M., Uda, R., Yasunobu, C., (Boston: Springer), pp. 99–112.

1 Introduction

Total and centralized management of identities and access control of large enterprises has been in focus, due to the increasing demands on corporate governance over information securities. Access control policies based on the role-based access control (RBAC) model [1][2][3] are becoming widely accepted and deployed to corporate information systems. However, as the RBAC is applied to many situations, we encounter a number of new challenges. We need to deal with geographically distributed, heterogeneous security objects, while consistencies of access control information have to be maintained in such a distributed environment. We need to find solutions which take into account the tradeoffs between total cost of system development, operations, and threat-levels of security events.

In a distributed enterprise-wide system, the task of provisioning changes on access control information such as roles and privileges becomes a big challenge, where changes are caused by various reasons, such as hiring, retirement and reallocation of personnel, installation of new facilities, and amendment of security policies. However, since there are various practical constraints in computing and distributing such changes, delays in reflecting the changes are inevitable. Delays in authorizing privileges will lead to productivity loss, while delays in revocation of privileges will lead to the risk of unauthorized access by non-admitted users. We propose a new extended RBAC model which can prevent or reduce such risks. It can be used for providing access control information efficiently by utilizing organizational and position information expressed in rules, so that changes on privileges are computed at authorization time instead of the time changes occur, having the effect of reducing provisioning cost.

The original RBAC model has been extended in various directions to deal with new requirements and target systems, such as Enterprise RBAC [4][5], rule-based approach [6][7][8], including this paper. However, it is hard to say a particular model fits given requirements with admissible costs, because there is not an established way of comparing RBAC extensions in terms of safety and cost effectiveness. Extended RBAC models have been compared with existing ones by qualitative analysis or by evaluation on a particular implementation [9]. In this paper, we propose a systematic and qualitative risk evaluation method for RBAC models, consisting of the following elements: (1) Common fault trees [14][15] are constructed based on the core functions of RBAC, augmented with functions for enterprise-level RBAC, and risk events obtained from past accidents and incidents[11][12]13]. (2) Subtrees necessary for evaluation are selected from the common fault trees systematically constructed at (1), and logic programs are generated from the AND-OR constructs of the fault trees. (3) Risk values are computed from the program of (2) by entering basic parameters to the program, where some parameters are obtained by measuring performance of a particular target system, while some parameters are obtained from empirical knowledge and surveys through questionnaires [11][13]. Using this evaluation method, we can quantitatively estimate in which circumstance our proposed model can prevent or reduce risks quantitatively.

The rest of this paper is organized as follows: In Section 2, we survey technologies related to management of access control information. In Section 3, we present quantitative risk evaluation method for RBAC and its extensions. In Section 4, we present a RBAC extension for large enterprises and apply the quantitative evaluation

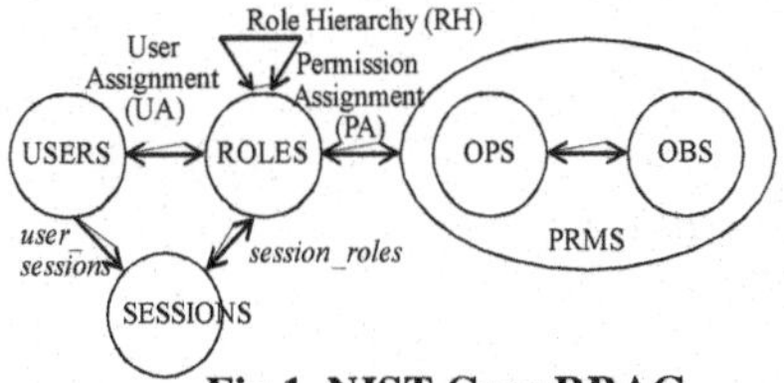

Fig.1. NIST Core RBAC

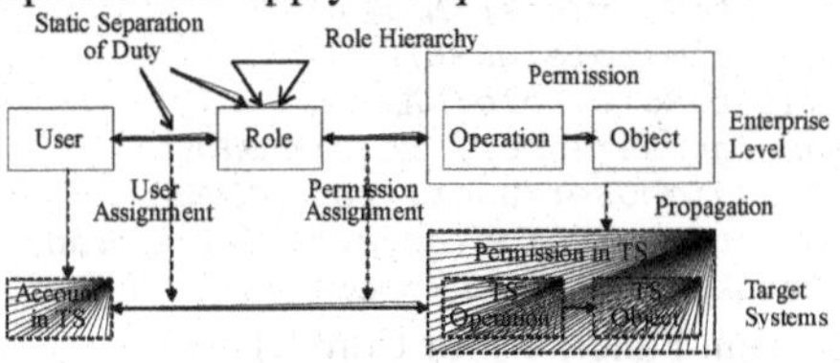

Fig.2. Enterprise RBAC Model

method of Section 3. Section 5 is a conclusion.

2 Related Technologies

In this section, we show basic definitions of RBAC models and related concepts to be used for our risk analysis.

2.1 Role-Based Access Control Model and its Variations

RBAC model [1][2][3] maintains the mapping between users and security objects via roles, instead of maintaining a direct mapping between them. This enables updates of user attributes such as organizations and positions, and security objects such as files and business applications, independently from each other. Fig.1 shows the standard model of the Hierarchical RBAC of NIST(National Institute of Standards and Technology)[2]. The following is the definition of the Core RBAC.
Definition1: Core RBAC

- $USERS, ROLES, OPS, and\ OBS$, users, roles, operations and objects, respectively.
- $UA \subseteq USERS \times ROLES$, a many-to-many mapping user-to-role assignment relation.
- $assigned\_users(r) = \{u \in USERS \mid (u,r) \in UA\}$, the mapping of role r onto a set of users.
- $PRMS = 2^{(OPS \times OBS)}$, the set of permissions.
- $PA \subseteq PRMS \times ROLES$, a many-to-many mapping permission-to-role assignment relation.
- $assigned\_permissions(r) = \{p \in PRMS \mid (p,r) \in PA\}$, the mapping of role r onto a set of permissions.
- $SESSIONS$, the set of sessions.
- $user\_sessions(u: USERS) \rightarrow 2^{SESSIONS}$, the mapping of user u onto a set of sessions.
- $session\_roles(s_i) \subseteq \{r \in ROLES \mid (session\_users(s_i), r) \in UA\}$, the mapping of session s onto a set of roles.
- $avail\_session\_perms(s: SESSIONS) \rightarrow 2^{PRMS}$, the permissions available to a user in a sessions.

The Core RBAC has the following Administrative Commands and System Functions, for managing and operating on the above constructs.
(1) Administrative Commands for Core RBAC

```
-AddUser(user:NAME)
-DeleteUser(user:Name)
-AddRole(role:NAME)
-DeleteRole(role:NAME)
-AssignUser(user, role:NAME)
-DeassignUser(user, role:NAME)
-GrantPermission(object, operation, role:NAME)
-RevokePermission(operation, object, role:NAME)
```

(2) System Functions for Core RBAC

```
-CreateSession(user:NAME; ars:2^NAMES; session:NAME)
-DeleteSession(user, session:NAME)
-AddActiveRole(user, session, role:NAME)
-DropActiveRole(user, session, role:NAME)
-CheckAccess(session, operation, object:NAME; out result:BOOLEAN)
```

Enterprise Role-Based Access Control (ERBAC) Model [4][5] has been proposed for user and access privilege management over all the systems of enterprise IT environment. The model can deal with multiple target systems, and its roles consist of combinations of diverse and system-specific privileges. Fig.2 depicts the ERBAC Model. We extend ERBAC for modeling provision of access control information. The extended ERBAC becomes the common underlying model for FTA (Fault Tree Analysis).

In the enterprise level, user assignments are usually defined using rules. In [6], the rule-based RBAC is shown, where rules defined over user attributes are evaluated at runtime to grant accesses. In this model, changes to attributes of users do not invoke changes to the user assignment, thus reducing operation costs of such changes, which are frequent in personnel changes. In [7], the Rule-Based Provisioning of RBAC is proposed, where dynamic rule-based assignment is used at the enterprise level, while static assignment is used at the target systems. In [8], a rule-based framework is proposed for role-based delegation and revocation. In [9], systematic control and management architecture of data integrity based on metadata management is shown.

2.2 Quantifying Costs and Risks of Security Policies

One of the reasons why there has been significant delay in adopting current information security measures to cooperate information systems is that the risks of IT security incidents are unclear, and thus it is hard to determine proper amount of investment. Therefore, quantitative assessment of security risks is in great demand. Risk quantification methods have been studied in several industrial sectors. In the banking sector, Basel Accord of 2004 (Basel II) [10] requires maintenance of regulatory capital reflecting three major components of risk that a bank faces: credit risk, operational risk and market risk. Basel II operational risk, which is newly added, includes the following event types related to information systems: internal/external frauds, software/hardware failures, and data entry errors.

The study of the economic impact of RBAC [11] gives quantitative definition of Operating Benefits OB_{it} per employee as follows:
i indexes industry, and t indexes year.
$OB_{it} = AC_{it} + PB_{it} + SB_{it}$
OB_{it} = operating benefits per employee

AC_{it} = administrative cost reductions per employee
PB_{it} = productivity benefits per employee
SB_{it} = security benefits per employee
The following three observations are reported as end-user benefits of RBAC:
(1) RBAC reduces administrative processing time.
(2) RBAC increases productivity.
(3) RBAC reduces the frequency and severity of security violations.

In (3), [12][13] are referred for the results of crime and security survey. In deriving (1), the following activities are quantitatively compared between RBAC and non-RBAC:

- Assigning existing privileges to new users,
- Changing existing users' privileges,
- Establishing new privileges for existing users, and
- Terminating privileges.

In order to operate these activities, delay time occurs from getting privileges to enabling them on real systems. The effect of downtime reduction is hard to be directly compared with (1), because if an employee is added, downtime for (2) is from the point s/he is added and to the point privileges are given to her/him. On the other hand, downtime for (1) is from the point when the administrator received change information and to the point the administrator reflects the change to the system. In this paper, we aim at measuring the effect to the system, so that we regard both (1) and (2) are productivity loss for employees. For (3), it is pointed out that the effort for reflecting security policies to the system is reduced as a benefit of introducing RBAC. This implies that the processing time reduction of (1) contributes to the reduction of time interval where access control states deviate from the security policies. For example, by reducing the time for terminating privileges, the probability of unauthorized access through the deviated access control states can be reduced.

2.3 Fault Trees for Security System Design and Analysis

FTA (Fault Tree Analysis)[14] has been utilized for safety-critical systems such as nuclear power plants, aircrafts, and artificial satellites. Recently, applications of FTA to analysis on failures and security of information systems are reported. In [15], design analysis of security-critical systems utilizing FTA is discussed.

Once a fault tree is constructed, the probability of the top event can be calculated as described in Fault Tree Handbook [14]. Thus construction of fault trees is important. In [15], it is pointed out that distinction of a system and components, and refinement of diversified security concerns are important issues.

The 12th Annual Computer Crime and Security survey [13] presents a list of twenty types of threats, including "Insider abuse of Net access," "Virus," "Laptop/mobile device theft". In this paper, we show construction of fault trees having core functions of RBAC as basic components, and also security violation and productivity loss as top events, and propose a framework for quantitatively analyzing cost effectiveness of RBAC variations, utilizing these fault trees.

3 Quantitative Analysis of Effectiveness of Applied RBAC Models

3.1 Overall Structure of Analysis

To incorporate access control policies based on an extended RBAC model, every functionality of the system has to meet the following requirements:

(1) Users unauthorized by the access control policies should not be able to execute requesting privileges.

(2) Users authorized by the access control policies should be able to execute requesting privileges.

The system may momentarily fall into invalid states due to significant events such as staff reallocation and accidents, and certain costs are expected to bring the system back into valid states. We try to measure these costs and the risks raised by the invalid states.

Faults regarding securities can be classified into direct and indirect faults. Direct faults are those which actually cause damage, while indirect faults are those which may not cause damage but cause violation of security rules which are intended to prevent such damage and imposed by the organization. If the system faces internal or external attacks while the settings of the system are violating company policies, damages are likely. Namely, the probabilities of incidents or accidents are strongly influenced by the probabilities of breach of company policies, which are in turn determined by the duration of exposure to dangerous states per unit time. The reduction of administrative processing time can contribute to improvement of securities. Therefore we use the probabilities of policy violation per unit time as basic components. For example, erroneous settings of access privileges and delayed effect of new settings due to slow processing time can be considered as basic components.

3.2 Basic Steps of Analysis

We propose a method for quantitatively evaluating given RBAC variations applied to given target systems. It proceeds by the following four steps:

(1) Constructing fault trees common to RBAC models: Defining fault trees having "security violation" and "productivity loss" as top events, and functions of the RBAC model and its variations as intermediate and basic events.

(2) Constructing model-specific fault trees: Selecting events relevant to the model under evaluation from the common fault trees of (1).

(3) Determining system and performance parameters: Event probabilities of basic and intermediate components are obtained from characteristics of the target system. In our model, probabilities are proportional to the ratio of elapsed time of basic and intermediate events to a unit time, such as a day.

(4) Implementing risk evaluation functions: The results of (1)(2)(3) are compiled into logic formulae or programs, and then evaluation results can be computed.

3.3 Target Access Control Systems

We consider functions of RBAC necessary for enterprise-level integrated access control systems, consisting of the following components:
(1) Enterprise-level Access Control System: administrates identity and access control information, observing enterprise-level security policies.
(2) Target Systems: execute application-specific access control by using information provisioned by the Enterprise-level Access Control System.
(3) Authorization Information Provider: provisions identity and access control information to target systems in the methods the target systems require. We need to be able to model two types of provisioning: batched prior provisioning and real-time change-triggered provisioning.

In the following, we discuss time cost in provisioning change information from the enterprise-level integratedly-managed databases to the target system. We assume that the following information is managed in the system at whole:
(1) User identifiers.
(2) User attributes (passwords, smart card information, certificates, etc)
(3) User groups (a group is a construct structuring users, corresponding to organizations, projects, qualifications, and positions, et al.)
(4) Enterprise-level roles
(5) Enterprise-level UA
(6) Enterprise-level permissions
(7) Enterprise-level PA

Upon execution of an administrative command, its resulting changes shall be provisioned and synchronized with the target systems. We need to classify the tasks of computing each element to be provisioned and the tasks of provisioning according to the above (1)-(7), and execute evaluation on these tasks and the synchronization method adopted by the evaluating model. Performance and cost evaluations are influenced by the ways of how changes on (1)-(7) are provisioned to the target systems. Changes may be provisioned in a separate or combined manner, and schedule-driven or change-driven manner. Fig.3 shows the case where the entire set of (1)-(7) is sent to the target system ts1. In Fig.3, when changes occur at the enterprise level, updated information of (1)-(7) is provisioned to ts1. UA(5) and PA(7) may be specified implicitly by rules implementing a policy. In this case, there are two choices: (a) rules

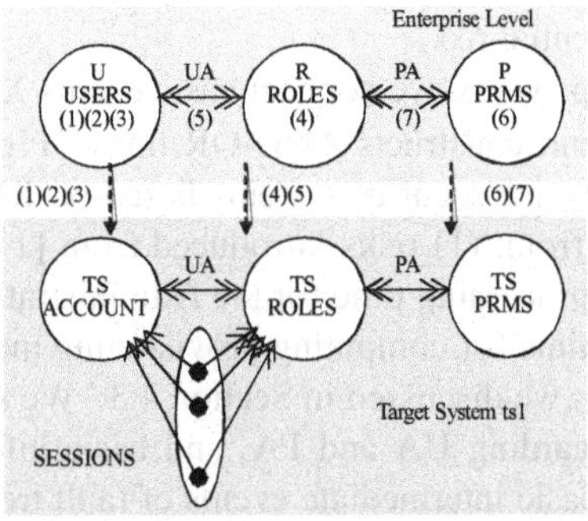

Fig.3. Enterprise-Level Role Provisioning

are evaluated to obtain concrete relationships between objects and the resultant relationships are provisioned, and (b) only rules are provisioned.

Upon comprehensive classification of the patterns of provisioning, we select patterns relevant to the operations of the evaluating model, and obtain the costs of the selected patterns. As an example, we consider User Addition as a frequent routine operation. It is executed by the following steps:

(1) Following the access policies, compute PRMS.
(2) Provision the user information.
(3) Provision permitted access control information.

We evaluate the performance cost of each step.

```
:- evaluate_user_provisioning(U_ID, U_Attr, APP_ID, add_user, Max_time,
Total_time).
evaluate_user_provisioning(U_ID, U_Attr, APP_ID, FuncName, Max_time,
Total_time) :-
   calculate_UA(U_ID, U_Attr, UA_List, UA_calculation_time),
   calculate_PA(UA_List, APP_ID, PA_List, PA_calculation_time),
   provision_U(APPID,FuncName,U_time),                 % (1)(2)(3)
   provision_R(APPID,FuncName,R_time),                 % (4)
   provision_P(APPID,FuncName,P_time),                 % (6)
   provision_UA(APPID,FuncName,UA_List,UA_time),       % (5)
   provision_PA(APPID,FuncName,PA_List,PA_time),       % (7)
   max([U_time,R_time,P_time,UA_time,PA_time], Max_time),
   sum([U_time,R_time,P_time,UA_time,PA_time], Total_time).
% provision_U(in,in,out).
provision_U(ts1,add_user,(measured_users_provisioning_time)).
provision_R(ts1,add_user,0).
provision_P(ts1,add_user, 0).
provision_UA(ts1,add_user,UA_List,(measured_ua_provisioning_time)).
provision_PA(ts1,add_user,_,0).
```

3.4 Risk Analysis Utilizing Common RBAC Fault Trees

Now we describe security threat analysis by constructing fault trees common to the RBAC model and its variations. As we pointed out in Section 3, we list up the following two top events.

TE1 (Security violation): An unauthorized user executes an operation (unauthorized access) - surfaced risk.

TE2 (Productivity loss): An authorized user is unable to execute a permitted operation (loss of opportunity) – potential risk.

Following the above top events, we connect basic events Xi (i=1, ···, n) described below to the top events, and constructs AND-OR trees. Fig.4 shows fault trees we constructed for large-enterprise security systems based on RBAC and ERBAC. We selected basic risk events from: (1) risks introduced from [11][12][13], and (2) risks arising from provisioning processing time for the Administrative Commands and System Functions of [2], and time for computing provisioning information specific to the evaluating RBAC model as we discussed in Section 4.3. We selected as the processes of evaluating the rules regarding UA and PA, and basic information such as users, roles, and permissions as basic intermediate events of fault trees. We can break down access control risks and productivity losses into these operations by considering processing time for executing low-level operations which are different in each model.

Top level risks are systematically placed in the fault trees according to causalities. In TE1, we introduce the risks shown in CSI Computer Crime and Security Survey [13], and focus on the risks A111 and A112 which have direct influence on RBAC. Under the assumption that the probabilities of these events happening per unit time are uniform, securities can be reinforced by reducing the time interval where unnecessary privileges exist during execution of RBAC functions.

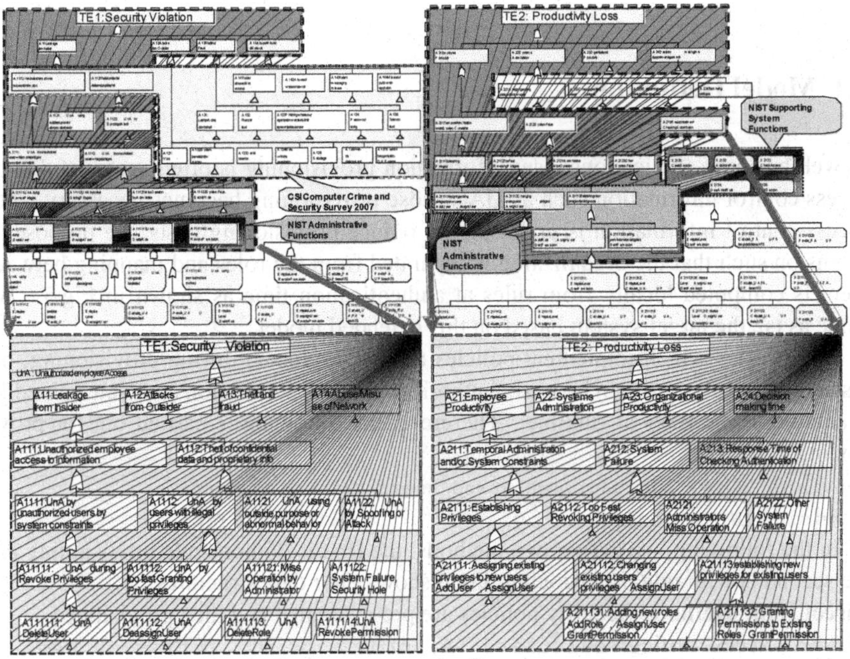

Fig.4. Common RBAC Fault Trees

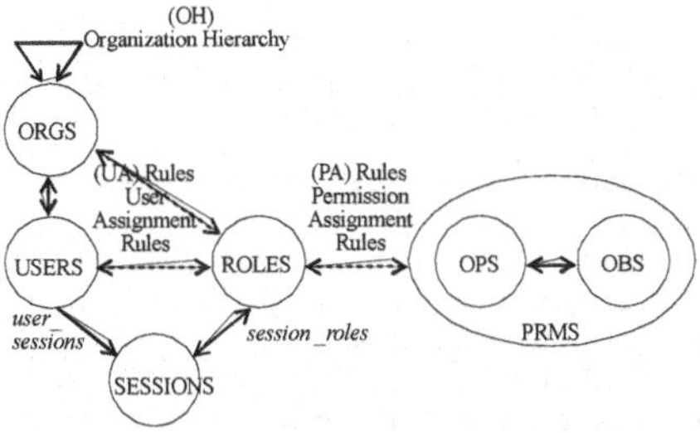

Fig.5. Rule-Based Hierarchical Organization RBAC

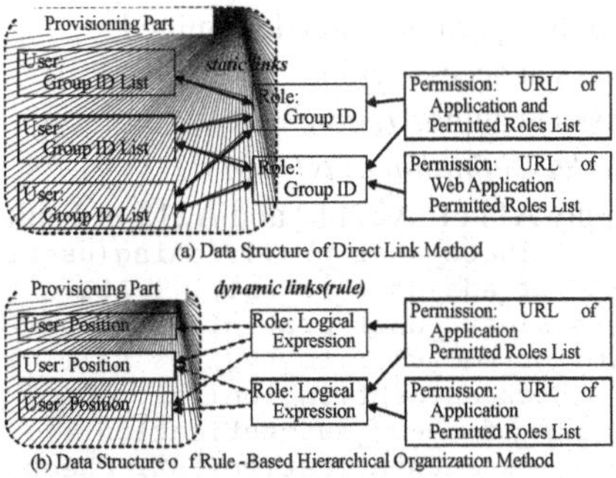

Fig.6. Provisioning Part for Add_User

4 Application to Rule-Based Hierarchical Organization RBAC and its Quantitative Evaluation

We consider the extension to the standard RBAC model, Rule-Based Hierarchical Organization RBAC for reducing batched prior provisioning costs. It is suitable for SSO (Single Sign On) of web applications. This model is implemented into real systems operating in enterprises of more than 50,000 employees, including manufacturing companies and financial companies. We apply the quantitative evaluation method of Section 3 to this system as case studies.

4.1 Model Definition

In web business applications, user information provisioning is often accompanied by access control information such as UA, whose provisioning becomes necessary when access control information is updated. To reduce provisioning costs, we propose an extension such that the organization is separated from the roles and mapping between them is computed locally from rules at authentication time as shown in Fig.5. We name as ts2 the target system based on this extended model.

In ts2, rules which implement policies are not evaluated during provisioning, but instead these rules are provisioned. Authorizations and permissions are determined by evaluating these rules at runtime. Therefore, the following is carried out for provisioning.

```
provision_U(ts2,add_user,(measured_users_provisioning_time)).
provision_UA(ts2,add_user,_,0).          % different from ts1
```

In the following, we define two methods, the first is without rule provisioning and the second is with rule provisioning. Fig.6 shows their data structures.

Direct Link Method: Security policies are pre-evaluated and then provisioned.
Tasks at access setting: `calculate_UA, provision_U, provision_UA`
Tasks at authorization: *`CheckAccess`*

Rule-Based Hierarchical Organization Method: Security policies are defined by rules, and only user information is provisioned. UA is computed at authentication and then permission is determined.
Tasks at access setting: `provision_U`
Tasks at authorization: `calculate_UA,` *`CheckAccess`*

Model Definition of ts1 and ts2

Apply A1111, A2111, and A213 of Fault Tree

```
:- evaluate_user_provisioning(user1, Attributes_list, ts1, add_user,
Time_of_Add_user_to_ts1). % A1111 and A2111 for ts1
:- evaluate_user_provisioning(user2, Attributes_list, ts2, add_user,
Time_of_Add_user_to_ts2). % A1111 and A2111 for ts2
:- check_authentication(ts1, check_on_demand_authorization,
  Time_of_check_authentication_1).    % A213 for ts1
:- check_authentication(ts2, check_on_demand_authorization,
 Time_of_check_authentication_2).    % A213 for ts2
:- check_authentication(ts1, check_authorization_on_authentication,
  Time_of_check_authentication_1).    % A213 for ts1
:- check_authentication(ts2, check_authorization_on_authentication,
```

Table 1. Data structure for measurement.

(a) Organization Structure

	Number of Organization	Number of Users	Position
Level1	4	4	Exective
Level2	6	48	Senior Manager
Level3	150	450	Manager
Level4	450	4,500	Employee
計	610	5,002	

(b) Objects, Permissions, and Rules

No. of objects	10
No. of role per object	2
total	16
No. of UA Rule	2
No. of belonging groups	10

Table 2. Measurement results.

	On-demand authorization		Authorization on authentication	
	Response Time (msec)	Throughput (transactions /sec)	Response Time (msec)	Throughput (transactions /sec)
Direct Link				
single	1.509	662.856	11.363	90.277
10	9.691	1,031.914	74.872	133.561
Rule Based				
single	1.575	645.856	12.210	81.486
10	9.942	1,005.874	79.561	125.690

```
Time_of_check_authentication_2).     % A213 for ts2
```

4.2 Evaluation

The differences of the two models are illuminated by the above definitions. We therefore compare performances according to the differences. Parameters of the fault trees regarding processing time are sampled from the running systems.

Table 1 shows statistics of the benchmarked systems, where users are 5,000, and the role hierarchy has five levels. Roles are automatically generated for each organization and each position, and each object is assigned with 16 roles as permissible. Rules for User Assignment consist of two terms, because most of real system implementations we encounter have rules of one or two terms combined by AND or OR. The target system implements two different authorization methods described below, and we compared response time and throughput for each model.

(1) On-demand authorization method

Authorization decision is carried out at the timing when a request for activating a web application is received with the URL of the application and the requesting user. This type of authorization is often used for opening connections upon clicks on links of pages.

- *Direct Link Method:* Belonging group lists, which are obtained by policy evaluation, are provisioned to the ID management database. These belonging group lists are held during user authorization. Upon a request for activating a web application, (1-1) roles that are approved for activation of the application are retrieved, and (1-2) authorization is made by directly comparing the roles with the belonging group lists.
- *Rule Based Hierarchical Organization Method:* No link indicating UA is held in the ID management database, but instead UA is stored as logical expressions. During user authorization, belonging organizations and positions are held. Upon an activation request of a web application, (2-1) roles approved for activation of the application are retrieved, and then (2-2) UA expressions containing these roles as terms are obtained, and finally (2-3) authorization is made by comparing the organizations and positions of the requesting user with the UA expressions.

(2) Authorization-on-authentication method

A list of permitted bossiness applications is constructed at the time a user is authenticated. Upon the timing one of these applications is activated, the list is referenced and authorization decision is made. We need to measure the time for constructing the list of permitted business applications. This authorization method is suitable for log-on to a portal site listing personalized applications, like EIP (Enterprise Information Portal).

• *Direct Link Method:* In this method, links between belonging group lists, which are obtained as a result of policy evaluation, and roles are provisioned to the ID management database. The following is executed during user authentication: (3-1) All the groups the user belongs to are retrieved, (3-2) roles approved for any of the business applications are retrieved, and (3-3) a list containing applications approved to the user is obtained from the direct links between those groups and roles.

• *Rule Based Hierarchical Organization Method:* There is no direct link indicating UA in the ID management database. Instead logical expressions are stored to the database. The following is executed during user authentication: (4-1) The organizations and positions of the authenticated user are retrieved, (4-2) roles approved for any of the business applications are retrieved, (4-3) UA expressions containing one of the roles as terms are retrieved, and finally (4-4) a list of applications approved to the user is constructed by comparing the organizations and positions of the user with the UA expressions.

Table 2 shows measurement results where an LDAP directory is used as the ID management database. The results show that the processing time of the rule based RBAC is 10 percent larger than that of the direct-link RBAC, while throughput has the opposite tendency.

We substitute these values for the following:

```
check_authentication(ts1, check_on_demand_authorization, 9.691).
check_authentication(ts2, check_on_demand_authorization, 9.942).
check_authentication(ts1, check_authorization_on_authentication,
74.872).
check_authentication(ts2, check_authorization_on_authentication,
79.561).
```

According to [11], authorization of existing privileges to new users occurs at the rate of 1.30 per year, per employee. Let us assume that 1 second is necessary for provisioning for a new user by a typical identity management product [16][17]. By assuming that the time for `provision_U` and `provision_UA` are equal, we obtain the following values.

```
provision_U(ts1,add_user, 500).
provision_UA(ts1,add_user,_,500).
provision_U(ts2,add_user,500.
provision_UA(ts2,add_user,_,0).
```

Assumption: 5 objects out of 10 objects are accessed per day, 200 days per year, and 10 users access concurrently.

On-demand authorization

```
  Productivity Loss of ts1 =
      1,000 (msec) * 5,000 * 1.3 +          % A2111 of Fault Tree
      9.691 (msec)   * 5 * 5,000 * 200      % A213
      = 54,955 sec
  Productivity Loss of ts2 =
      500 (msec) * 5,000 * 1.3 +            % A2111 of Fault Tree
      9.942 (msec)  * 5 * 5,000 * 200       % A213 of Fault Tree
      = 52,960 sec
```

Authorization on authentication

```
Productivity Loss of ts1 =
      1,000 (msec) * 5,000 * 1.3 +           % A2111 of Fault Tree
      74.872 (msec)   * 5,000 * 200          % A213 of Fault Tree
      = 81,372 sec
Productivity Loss of ts2 =
      500 (msec) * 5,000 * 1.3 +             % A2111 of Fault Tree
      79.561 (msec) * 5 * 5,000 * 200        % A213 of Fault Tree
      = 82,811 sec
```

The results are interpreted differently depending on the standpoint to tolerable risk. For example, the direct link method ts1 is justifiable if one-day delay can be accepted, or if creating accounts one day early and delaying release of them can be accepted. For the rule-based method ts2, it can be argued that 10 percent delay in processing time can be accepted and may not be regarded as productivity loss. This comes from the observation that while the total loss of productivity is obtained by the product of the amounts of employees and business days times 10 percent, the loss per user is a few seconds per day, which can be tolerated.

5 Conclusion

In this paper, we discussed extensions to RBAC to deal with circumstances of large enterprises, such as complexity of organizations, geographical diversities and heterogeneity of devices such as physical access control. To deploy RBAC for improving operability, convenience of employees, and security, we discussed designs of rule-based RBAC utilizing personnel affair information. Furthermore, to select most cost-effective RBAC extensions for enterprise-wide requirements, we proposed a quantitative risk evaluation method based on fault trees. We demonstrated usefulness of this RBAC risk evaluation method through application to the rule-based RBAC model, and presented cases where this model becomes advantageous. We think that this method is also applicable to enterprise-wide governance systems.

References

1. Feraiolo,D. and Kuhn,R., Role-Based Access Control, Communications of the 15th NIST-NSA National Computer Security Conference, 1992.
2. Ferraiolo,D., Sandhu,R., Gavrila,S., and Kuhn,R., Proposed NIST standard for Role-Based Access Control, ACM Transaction on Information and System Security, Vol.4 No.3, 2001.
3. Feraiolo,D., Kuhn,R., and Chandramouli,R., Role-Based Access Control Second Edition, Computer Security Series, ARTECH HOUSE, 2007.
4. Kern,A., Kuhlmann,M., Schaad,A., and Moffett,J., Observations on the role life-cycle in the context of enterprise security management, SACMAT'02, 2002.
5. Kern,A., Kuhlmann,M., Kuropka,R., and Ruthert,A., A meta model for authorisations in application security systems and their integation into RBAC administration, SACMAT'04, 2004.
6. Al-Kahtani, M. A. and Sandhu, R., A Model for Attribute-Based User-Role Assignment, 18th Annual Computer Security Applications Conference (ACSAC), 2002.
7. Kern,A. and Walhorn,C., Rule support for role-based access control, SACMAT'05, 2005.
8. Zhang,L., Ahn,G., and Chu,B. A rule-based framework for role-based delegation and revocation ACM Transactions on Information and system security (TISSEC), 2003.

9. Byun,J., Soh,Y., and Bertino,E. Systematic Control and Management of Data Integrity, SACMAT'06, 2006.
10. Bank for International Settlements (BIS), Basel II: Revised international capital framework, 2004.
11. Gallaher,M., O'Connor,A, and Kropp,B. The Economic Impact of Role-Based Access Control (NIST Planning Report 02-1), March 2002.
12. Briney,A., Security Focused, Information security, September 2000.
13. Computer Security Institute, CSI Survey 2007, The 12th Annual Computer Crime and Security Survey, 2007.
14. U.S. Nuclear regulatory Commission, Fault Tree Handbook, January 1981.
15. Brooke, P., and Paige, R., Fault trees for security system design and analysis, Computer & Security, Vol.23, No 3, 2003.
16. Sun Java System Identity Manager.
http://www.sun.com/software/roducts/identity_mgr/
17. IBM Tivoli Identity Manager.
http://www.ibm.com/software/tivoli/products/identity-mgr/

Presence-Based Runtime Composition of IMS Services Deployed in a SIP Servlet Platform

Juan Miguel Espinosa Carlín

Communication and Distributed Systems, RWTH Aachen University,
52074 Aachen, Germany,
e-mail: espinosa@i4.informatik.rwth-aachen.de

Abstract The IP Multimedia Subsystem (IMS) is aimed to enable the delivery of rich multimedia services in converged networks. Due to the current needs of the mobile telecommunications market to deliver tailored experiences to its users, IMS operators must be able to manage the interoperability and cooperation between the deployed services, in order to provide a high level of customization to their subscribers. With this goal in mind, this paper presents an extension to the Default Application Router introduced in the Java SIP Servlet API v1.1. The proposed Presence AR allows runtime changes in the precedence relationships and application subscriptions that build the composition chains, based on the Presence information of the users involved in the session.

1 Introduction

The convergence-driven need to seamlessly deliver services, has forced operators to adopt new approaches, like the Intelligent Networks, Web Services API's, and, most recently, the IP Multimedia Subsystem (IMS) [7]. In the context of the IMS architecture, Java SIP Servlets are a suitable option to implement a SIP Application Server (AS). In March 2003, the Java Community Process (JCP) released the Java SIP Servlet API (SSAPI), under the Java Specification Request (JSR) 116 [13], for building and deploying SIP applications. In such environment, a SIP Servlet container acts as an AS, and hosts one or more applications that are invoked according

Please use the following format when citing this chapter:

Espinosa Carlín, J. M., 2008, in IFIP International Federation for Information Processing, Volume 286; Towards Sustainable Society on Ubiquitous Networks, eds. Oya, M., Uda, R., Yasunobu, C., (Boston: Springer), pp. 113–124.

to specific mapping rules. Although the JSR 116 states that application composition is desirable, no standard compositions mechanisms are defined, and its definition is left entirely to the container implementation.

With the goal of promoting software modularity and reuse, the Java Community Process specified the SIP Servlet API v1.1 under the JSR 289 [15]. In the application composition framework of this specification, the core entity is the Application Router (AR), to which the container communicates to know the sequence in which the applications have to be invoked. Although the AR is essential for the proper operation of the container, the specification only provides the definition of a Default AR (DAR), which has no processing logic besides the declaration of the order in which applications will be invoked; the implementation of more powerful AR's that make use of complex rules and diverse data repositories, is left to the container implementations. With the goal of providing a richer component, this paper presents an extension that allows the AR to perform runtime composition, based on the Presence information associated to the users involved in a session.

The rest of this paper is structured as follows. Section 2 gives an overview of the available approaches for enabling IMS service composition. Then, Sect. 3 describes the proposed AR in detail. Section 4 presents the Proof-of-Concept prototype developed for implementing the Presence AR. Finally, the conclusions and an outline of future work are given in Sect. 5.

2 Available Approaches for IMS Service Composition

Although there are many techniques for enabling service composition in the IMS, most of them are based on at leat one of the approaches shown in Fig. 1.

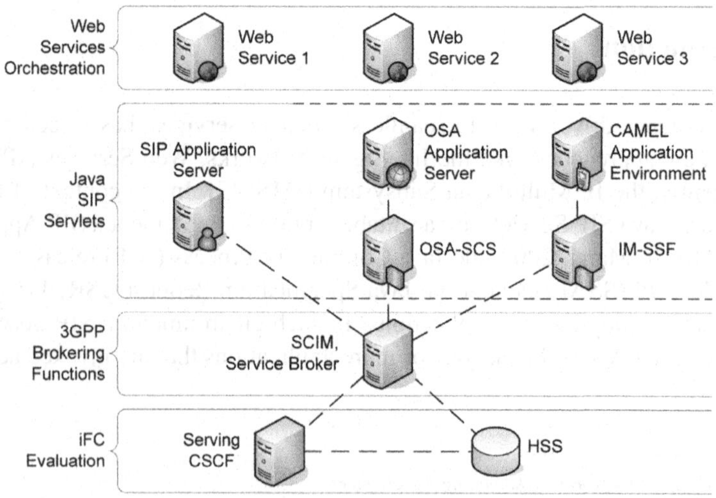

Fig. 1 Existing Approaches for IMS Service Composition

2.1 iFC Evaluation at the S-CSCF

For delivering services to the end users, the IMS makes use of the information stored in the user profiles residing in the HSS's. According to TS 23.218 [3], a service profile is composed by a Private User Identity to which the profile is applicable, and one or more service profiles associated to it. For each one of these service profiles, a Public User Identity (PUI) and zero or more initial Filter Criteria (iFC) are defined. iFC contain all the necessary information that helps the Serving Call-Session Control Function (S-CSCF) to decide when a specific AS must be involved in order to provide a service to the subscriber. iFC are evaluated by the S-CSCF for all those SIP requests that either create a dialog, or are stand-alone requests (e.g. `SUBSCRIBE`, `INVITE`, `OPTIONS`).

For the case in which there is more that one AS involved in the signaling path, the S-CSCF will forward the matched request to each one of them, according to the priority field of the iFC. Although this chaining mechanism is both efficient and reasonably simple, it only allows to sequence the interactions at the AS level. In order to coordinate the orchestration of individual services, a composing approach achieving refined granularity is needed [4].

2.2 3GPP Brokering Functions

The 3GPP has defined two entities aimed to deal with the feature interaction management in an IMS network. The first concept is the Service Capability Interaction Manager (SCIM), a function aimed to manage service capability coordination. The second one is the OSA/Parlay Service Broker (SB), aimed to broker OSA/Parlay applications, application hosted on SIP AS's, and services offered by legacy networks (e.g. CAMEL). Both components were supposed to be standalone entities placed between the S-CSCF and the AS, communicating with them via a SIP interface. However, the SCIM was never further defined, and for the case of the SB, the progress is being slowly documented in 3GPP TR 23.810 as part 3GPP Release 8.

Although these entities are theoretically able to manage the interaction of applications deployed in different domains (e.g. OSA/Parlay and CAMEL), a scenario in which such approach would be needed is not very realistic [4], notably limiting the practical use of both approaches.

2.3 Web Services Orchestration

Web Services orchestration is a topic on which a lot of research has been done in the past years. Based on the Universal Description, Discovery, and Integration (UDDI) for listing, on the Web Service Description Language (WSDL) for description, and on the Web Services Business Process Execution Language (BPEL) for orchestration, Web Services are a successful technology that allowed the IT community to realize key features behind the Service Oriented Architecture (SOA) concept.

Even though many efforts have been done for enabling the use of Web Services in the telecommunications environment [5], the process-driven nature of their orchestration techniques is not suitable for composing real-time communications services, being the later better described from an event-driven perspective [2].

2.4 Java SIP Servlets

The AR concept introduced in the JSR 289 allows for a clear separation between concerns and responsibilities, with developers implementing the application logic of the services, and deployers controlling the application selection and invocation order.

Because the container must support the invocation of originating applications for the caller and terminating applications for the callee, the specification introduces the concepts of `ORIGINATING` and `TERMINATING` routing regions. When the container queries the AR for the next application to invoke, it also sends the routing region in which the invocation has to be performed; a third `NEUTRAL` routing region is defined for applications that do not serve a particular subscriber.

As stated in the JSR 289, the Default AR (DAR) should be available in every compliant implementation, and should invoke applications driven by a properties file, in which the name of the property is the invoked SIP method, and the value of the property is the `SipRouterInfo` object converted into a string. The information contained by this string consists of the following [15]:

- The name of the application to be invoked, as identified by the application deployment descriptors.
- The subscriber's identity returned by the DAR, that can be any header present in the SIP request.
- The routing region in which the application has to be invoked (i.e. `ORIGINATING`, `TERMINATING`, or `NEUTRAL`).
- A SIP URI that indicates the route as returned by the AR.
- A route modifier, to indicate the direction to be followed in the invocation chain (i.e. `ROUTE`, `ROUTE_BACK`, or `NO_ROUTE`).
- A sting representing the AR's internal state. Because this information will be exclusively used by the AR, its contents are up to the individual DAR implementations.

An example of such configuration file is the following:

```
INVITE: ("OriginatingCallWaiting", "DAR:From",
        "ORIGINATING", "", "NO_ROUTE", "0"),
        ("CallForwarding", "DAR:To",
        "TERMINATING", "", "NO_ROUTE", "1")
```

For this example, the DAR is configured to invoke two applications on receiving an `INVITE` request, one for the originating region, and the other for the terminating region. The applications are identified by their names, and the returned subscriber identities are bonded with the contents of the `From` and `To` headers of the request.

The specification of the DAR is heavily based on the Distributed Feature Composition (DFC) algorithm [6], with the only available implementation, called the DFC-AR, being statically configured with no dependencies on external databases or other data stores [1]. DFC is realized from a pipe-and-filter perspective, in which multiple *feature boxes (FB's)* are linked by internal featureless calls, thus forming a sequences of FB's. In the context of the DFC-AR, these sequences are called *application chains*. A typical arrangement of feature boxes is shown in Fig. 2.

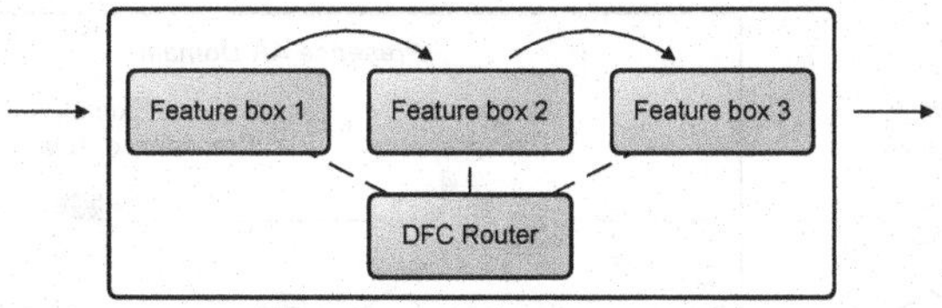

Fig. 2 Architecture of the Distributed Feature Composition

Table 1 shows a comparison between the described composition techniques in terms of the granularity offered by the approach, its provider interoperability, and the paradigm used for doing composition.

Table 1 Comparative Analysis of IMS Composition Approaches

Technique	Granularity	Interoperability	Paradigm
iFC Evaluation	Coarse	High (3GPP Standard)	Event-driven
3GPP Brokering Functions	Refined	Low (Propietary)	Event-driven
Web Services Orchestration	Refined	High (OASIS Standard)	Data-driven
JSR 289 Application Router	Refined	High (Java-based)	Event-driven

Because the SIP Servlet API builds on the well known API for deploying HTTP servlets, the programming model is already known to a considerably large community of developers; at the time of writing, there are at least five commercial and one open source implementations of the standard.

3 A Presence-Driven IMS Application Router

3.1 Functional Architecture

The proposed architecture for the Presence AR is shown in Fig. 3. A brief description of each of the entities is given next. For the aim of clarity, let's take the example of Alice establishing a call with Bob. Both of them have a contract to use the following services: *Speed Dial*, *Call Waiting*, *Call Forwarding*, *Voice Mail*, and *SMS*. Additionally, their IMS provider enables the *Enhanced Call* service, which composes the mentioned services depending on Alice's and Bob's Presence status.

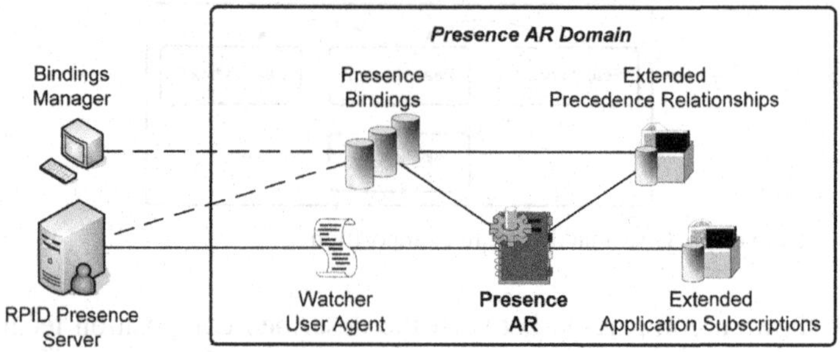

Fig. 3 The Presence Application Router

3.1.1 Extended Precedence Relationships

The application chains built by the DFC-AR are based on Precedence Relationships statically stored in an XML file. These relationships are enclosed within `<ordering>` elements, and establish a partial order among applications in each one of the routing regions. The higher an application name appears in the list, the higher priority that the application has in the region in which is listed. Due to the fact that not all the deployed applications keep a precedence relation with the others, it is absolutely valid that some applications are not listed on the relationships. Because the priority assigned to the applications is based on their proximity to the subscribers, applications with higher precedence will appear closer to the endpoints when invoked.

For the Presence AR, the idea is to reuse these relationships to give the AR alternative *Paths* inside an extended application chain: the taken Path will depend on the Presence information of the user being called. Because the published information represents only a weak form of contract, it does not ensure that it will always be possible to successfully contact the presentity, so a *Default Path* inside the extended chain has to be always defined. For the case of our example, a possible extended application chain built by the Extended Precedence Relationships is shown in Fig. 4.

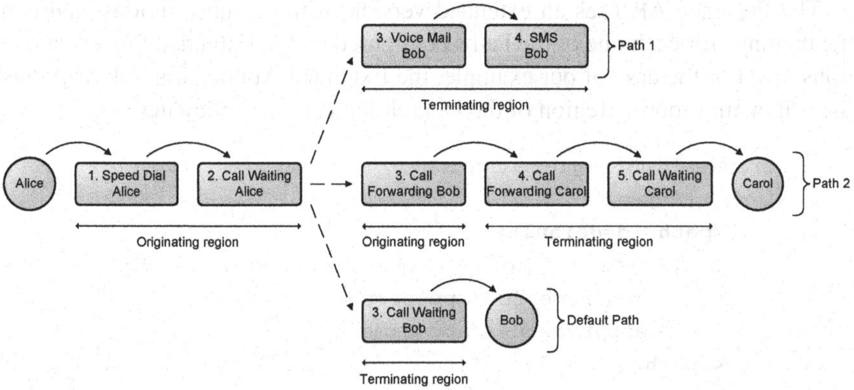

Fig. 4 Extended Application Chain for the Enhanced Call Service

The Extended Precedence Relationships configured on the Presence AR for Path 2 in both routing regions are structured as follows:

```
<originating-region>
  <ordering>
    <app-name>SD</app-name>
    <app-name>CW</app-name>
    <path id=2>
      <app-name>CF</app-name>
    </path>
  </ordering>
</originating-region>

<terminating-region>
  <ordering>
    <path id=2>
      <app-name>FW</app-name>
      <app-name>CW</app-name>
    </path>
  </ordering>
</terminating-region>
```

3.1.2 Extended Application Subscriptions

In the DFC-AR, the bindings between the received SIP requests and the invoked applications are statically configured by the Application Subscriptions. These Java regular expressions are called Address Patterns, and are enclosed by <mapping> XML elements that are evaluated against the From header, including its display-name portion for the case of the originating address, and against the Request-URI, for the case of the terminating address of the processed request.

The Presence AR uses an extended version of these subscriptions, and defines the bindings for each one of the Paths configured by the Extended Precedence Relationships. For the case of our example, the Extended Application Subscriptions for the originating routing region of the Default Path are the following:

```
<originating-region-mapping>
  <mapping>
    <path id=default>
      <address-pattern>.*sip:*</address-pattern>
        <app-name>SD</app-name>
        <app-name>CW</app-name>
    </path>
  </mapping>
</originating-region-mapping>
```

The additional subscriptions are configured as follows. For the originating region of Path 1, the Address Patterns contain the same two applications shown above (i.e. Speed Dial and Call Waiting), while for the originating region of Path 2, they contain one extra application (i.e. Call Forwarding). For the terminating routing region, the Address Patterns contain two applications for the first Path (i.e. Voice Mail and SMS), two for the second Path (i.e. Call Forwarding and Call Waiting), and one for the Default Path (i.e. Call Waiting).

3.1.3 Presence Bindings, Binding Manager, and Watcher User Agent

The Presence Bindings are managed through the Bindings Manager, and are defined to indicate the Presence AR which of the defined Paths has to be taken in the extended application chain, depending on whether or not specific parts of the conveyed Presence information meet certain criteria. These bindings are linked to both, the IMS Public User Identities (PUI's) stored in the HSS, and the Paths defined in the Extended Precedence Relationships. In order to get the Presence status of the users, the Presence AR implements a Watcher User Agent that fetches the data from the Presence Server. Assuming that the Rich Presence Information Data Format (RPID) [10] is used for publication, Bob could define the following Presence Bindings for the Enhanced Call service:

```
if ((RPID.person.place-type == residence) &&
  (RPID.person.activities == tv)) then path 1

if ((RPID.person.place-type == office) &&
  (RPID.person.activities == meeting)) then path 2
```

In case that the Presence data is provided by a large number of sources, the Presence AR can make use of already available mechanisms for integrating this information in a consistent and unified way [11].

3.1.4 Presence Application Router

The Presence AR is the key element of the proposed extension. At runtime, it fetches information from the Extended Precedence Relationships, from the Extended Application Subscriptions, from the Presence Bindings, and from the Watcher User Agent. It first verifies if one of the defined Paths is compatible with the received Presence information; if this is the case, the application chain enabled by the matched Path is used, and the first application in the chain is sent to the container. For example, if Bob's Presence indicates that he is at home watching TV, he doesn't want to be disturbed, so Alice will be rerouted to Bob's Voice Mail and Bob will receive and SMS indicating that Alice just tried to contact him (i.e. Path 1 in Fig. 4). In a second scenario, if Bob is at his office on a meeting, all his incoming calls are forwarded to his secretary, Carol (i.e. Path 2 in Fig. 4). Finally, if none of the defined paths is compatible with the current Presence status, or if the Presence service is currently unavailable, the service sets up a call with Bob, as indicated by the Default Path.

3.2 Deployment in an IMS Network

Figure 5 shows the placement of the Presence AR in a basic IMS deployment. On reception of an initial SIP request filtered through the iFC, the S-CSCF invokes the involved AS (i.e. the Servlet container). Next, the container queries the Presence AR to find out the order in which the services have to be invoked. Based on the chosen application chain, the Presence AR answers the container with the list of applications to be executed, together with the corresponding Routing Region (i.e. `ORIGINATING`, `TERMINATING`, or `NEUTRAL`) and the proper Routing Directive (i.e. `ROUTE`, `ROUTE_BACK`, or `NO_ROUTE`).

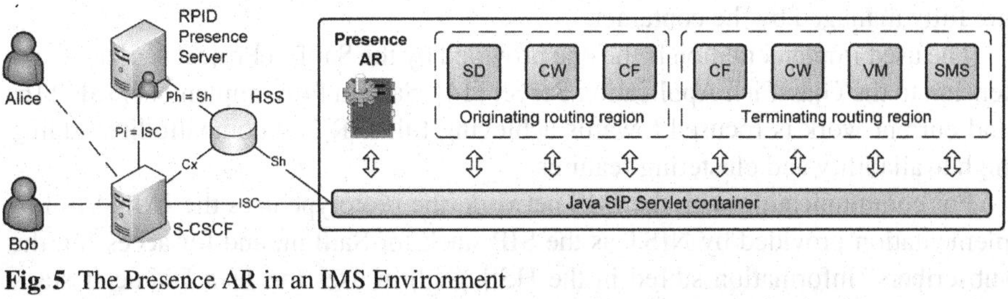

Fig. 5 The Presence AR in an IMS Environment

4 Proof-of-Concept Prototype

An overview of the prototype's architecture is shown in Fig. 6.

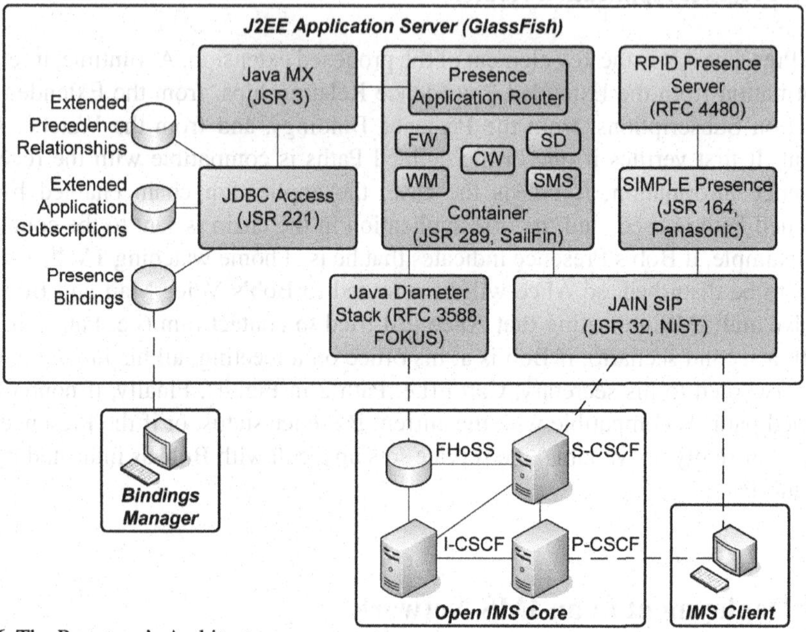

Fig. 6 The Prototype's Architecture

4.1 SIP Servlet Container

The abstraction level provided by the SSAPI is located between the transactions users and the SIP transaction layer. As such, it enables applications developers to access and control protocol details like the contents and the headers of the SIP messages, while issues as the formatting, retransmission, and correlation of the requests are fully managed by the container.

The used implementation is the one provided by the SailFin Project [16] as an extension to the GlassFish Application Server [14]. SailFin fully implements JSR 116, and current work is focused towards achieving full JSR 289 compatibility, adding high availability and clustering features.

For communicating with the IMS network, the prototype uses the JAIN SIP implementation provided by NIST as the SIP stack for SailFin, and for accessing the subscribers' information stored in the HSS, SailFin uses the Java Diameter stack developed by the FOKUS Fraunhofer Institute.

4.2 Application Router and Presence Server

Regarding the AR, four approaches were evaluated. The first one was SailFin's Alphabetical AR, which routes every initial SIP request to the deployed applications in alphabetical order. The second one was SailFin's DAR implementation, as defined in the Appendix C of the JSR 289. As already discussed, the DAR routes every initial request to the deployed applications based on the contents of the properties file. The third one was the DFC-AR, which is a DAR implementation based on the approach presented in [12]. These three AR's don't allow changing their behavior without modifying the source code and without doing a redeployment of the application, so they are not suited for the solution proposed in this paper.

A fourth option, taken as base for the Presence AR, is an AR that makes use of the Java Management Extensions (JMX) technology (JMX-AR), and is also included in the SailFin distribution. The JMX-AR offers a runtime configuration interface that allows to dynamically modify the application chains.

4.3 Data Repositories, Core IMS Network, and IMS Client

The Extended Application Subscriptions, the Extended Precedence Relationships, and the Presence Bindings, were deployed as Derby databases embeded through the GlassFish JDBC driver. Finally, the Bindings Manager was developed in Java Swing as a stand alone application, with the needed functionality to manipulate the Presence Bindings database.

For testing the Presence AR, a fully 3GPP compliant IMS environment based on the FOKUS Open IMS Core implementation [8] was deployed. For the IMS client, a prototype was developed in Java Swing, based on the UCT IMS Client Project [17]. The client was extended with the needed funtionality to manipulate the Presence information via XCAP [9], and an XCAP server developed at our research group was used.

5 Conclusions and Future Work

This paper presented an AR proposal based on the DAR specified by the JSR 289, and on the DFC-AR implementation presented in [12].

The Presence AR queries at runtime the Extended Precedence Relationships and the Extended Application Subscriptions associated with a composed service, and does the application routing based on bindings that relate specific portions of the published Presence information with Paths that have to be followed in an extended application chain. For the time being, only sequential application chains were considered. Additionally, a roadmap towards a Presence AR prototype implementation and its deployment in an IMS environment was also presented.

Further improvements on the Presence AR include the analysis and implementation of mechanisms that allow the composition of externally deployed applications, the structuring of hierarchical applications chains, and the cooperation between applications deployed in different environments.

References

1. Cheung, E., Purdy, K.H.: An Application Router for SIP Servlet Application Composition. IEEE International Conference on Communications, 2008. ICC '08 (2008)
2. Dinsing, T., Eriksson, G.A., Fikouras, I., Gronowski, K., Levenshteyn, R., Pettersson, P., Wiss, P.: Service composition in IMS using Java EE SIP servlet containers. Ericsson Review **3**, 92–96 (2007)
3. 3rd Generation Partnership Project: IP Multimedia (IM) session handling; IM call model; Stage 2. 3GPP TS 23.218 (2007)
4. Gourraud, C.: The IMS Latern. http://theimslantern.blogspot.com/ (2008). Last retrieved on 25.03.2008
5. Griffin, D., Pesch, D.: A Survey on Web Services in Telecommunications. IEEE Communications Magazine **45**(7), 28–35 (July 2007). DOI 10.1109/MCOM.2007.382657
6. Jackson, M., Zave, P.: Distributed Feature Composition: A Virtual Architecture for Telecommunications Services. IEEE Transactions on Software Engineering **24**(10), 831–847 (Oct 1998). DOI 10.1109/32.729683
7. Magedanz, T., Blum, N., Dutkowski, S.: Evolution of SOA Concepts in Telecommunications. Computer **40**(11), 46–50 (Nov. 2007). DOI 10.1109/MC.2007.384
8. Magedanz, T., Witaszek, D., Knuettel, K.: The IMS playground @ FOKUS-an open testbed for generation network multimedia services. First International Conference on Testbeds and Research Infrastructures for the Development of Networks and Communities, 2005. Tridentcom 2005 pp. 2–11 (23-25 Feb. 2005). DOI 10.1109/TRIDNT.2005.35
9. Rosenberg, J.: The Extensible Markup Language (XML) Configuration Access Protocol (XCAP). RFC 4825 (Proposed Standard) (2007). URL http://www.ietf.org/rfc/rfc4825.txt
10. Schulzrinne, H., Gurbani, V., Kyzivat, P., Rosenberg, J.: RPID: Rich Presence Extensions to the Presence Information Data Format (PIDF). RFC 4480 (Proposed Standard) (2006). URL http://www.ietf.org/rfc/rfc4480.txt
11. Shacham, R., Kellerer, W., Schulzrinne, H., Thakolsri, S.: Composition for Enhanced SIP Presence. 12th IEEE Symposium on Computers and Communications, 2007. ISCC 2007 pp. 203–210 (1-4 July 2007). DOI 10.1109/ISCC.2007.4381531
12. Smith, T.M., Bond, G.W.: ECharts for SIP servlets: a state-machine programming environment for VoIP applications. In: IPTComm '07: Proceedings of the 1st international conference on Principles, systems and applications of IP telecommunications, pp. 89–98. ACM, New York, NY, USA (2007). DOI http://doi.acm.org/10.1145/1326304.1326318
13. Sun Microsystems: Java Specification Request 116: SIP Servlet API. http://jcp.org/en/jsr/detail?id=116 (2003). Last retrieved on 20.04.2008
14. Sun Microsystems: GlassFish. http://glassfish.dev.java.net (2008). Last retrieved on the 20.04.2008
15. Sun Microsystems: Java Specification Request 289: SIP Servlet v1.1. http://jcp.org/en/jsr/detail?id=289 (2008). Last retrieved on 20.04.2008
16. Sun Microsystems: SailFin. http://sailfin.dev.java.net (2008). Last retrieved on the 20.04.2008
17. University of Cape Town: UCT IMS Client. http://uctimsclient.berlios.de (2007). Last retrieved on the 15.11.2007

A Service Oriented and Agent-Based Architecture for the e-Collaboration of SMEs

Ioannis Ignatiadis[1], Dimitrios Tektonidis[2], Adomas Svirskas[1,3], Jonathan Briggs[1], Stamatia-Ann Katriou[2], Adamantios Koumpis[2]

[1]Kingston University, Faculty of Computing, Information Systems and Mathematics, Penrhyn Road, SURREY KT1 2EE, UK

[2]ALTEC S.A. Research Programs Division, M. Kalou 6, Thessaloniki 546 29, GREECE

[3]Institut Eurécom, 2229 Route des Crêtes, Sophia-Antipolis 06560, FRANCE

Abstract The concept of a Service-Oriented Architecture (SOA) to flexibly address business needs with the use of Information Technology (IT) is increasingly being recognized as important for a company's agility and responsiveness to change. A SOA approach can also help to design more agile web portals, in order to enable companies to increase their responsiveness and adaptability with regards to addressing a business opportunity as a collaborative Virtual Organization (VO). Value can be added to the operations of such a VO with the use of Intelligent Agents to automate the processes of finding collaboration partners and negotiating the creation of VOs based on user-defined business rules. This paper discusses these concepts and their benefits for Virtual Organizations based on the work of a European Union (EU) co-funded Information Society Technologies (IST) project examining these issues for Small and Medium Enterprises (SMEs) in the European Enterprise Resource Planning (ERP) industry.

1 Introduction

Small and Medium-size Enterprises (SMEs) participating in today's global market are often ill-prepared in competing with their larger counterparts, who have established international activities with customers, suppliers and partners. The problems that

---

Please use the following format when citing this chapter:

Ignatiadis, I., Tektonidis, D., Svirskas, A., Briggs, J., Katriou, S. -A., Koumpis, A., 2008, in IFIP International Federation for Information Processing, Volume 286; Towards Sustainable Society on Ubiquitous Networks, eds. Oya, M., Uda, R., Yasunobu, C., (Boston: Springer), pp. 125–137.

SMEs in particular face have to do with limited partner networks in other countries, their narrow focus on specific geographic areas, and the limited amount of skills and resources to enable them to expand their activities and compete globally.

One way to overcome these limitations is to form a collaborative Virtual Organization (VO) with other companies facing the same problems but having complementary skills and resources. Such VOs are formed in response to more intensive competition, more specialized markets, faster technological change and shorter product (or service) life cycles (Aldrich 1999, Davidow and Malone 1992, Hagel and Armstrong 1997). The advantages for SMEs in forming and participating in such VOs include reduced operational and partner search costs, increased operational efficiency, increase of competitiveness against large corporations, and better meeting end customer needs by the sharing of knowledge and competencies among VO participants (Rautenstrauch 2002).

To support the formation and sustainability of online collaborations, a business model supported by an online collaboration platform must be implemented. In this paper we argue for the importance of using Service-Oriented Architecture (SOA) principles for the building of such platforms, as well as using intelligent software agents to automate some of the operations of the collaborative VOs. Our background is the European Union (EU) co-funded project Panda (PANDA-Project 2006) , where we examine the applicability of SOA and Intelligent Agents in the context of the creation and maintenance of e-collaborations in the European Enterprise Resource Planning (ERP) industry of SMEs.

In the sections that follow we first present background literature on the concepts of SOA and Intelligent Agents, followed by the description of the Panda project where these concepts are examined. We then present the SOA and Intelligent Agent-based architecture in the Panda project, followed by the discussion of its benefits. The paper is concluded with the current state of developments and future research in the Panda project.

2 Service-Oriented Architectures and Intelligent Agents

2.1 Service-Oriented Architectures

Service-Oriented Architecture (SOA) is an architectural style in which software applications are organized as a set of loosely coupled services (Harding 2007). The SOA paradigm enables to link business and computational resources (mainly organizations, applications and data) on demand. It is seen to be essential for delivering business agility and IT flexibility. It also facilitates the alignment of existing IT infrastructures to achieve (internal or external) enterprise connectivity, by removing redundancies, generating unified collaboration tools, and streamlining IT processes. The benefits from this approach are an increase in business agility to respond to future changes by adapting and reorganizing the existing services, as well as creating new services to fit in the existing IT architecture, in order to address changed business requirements. This applies to both internal operations, as well as external ones (e.g. providing new services to customers or changing the way the interactions with suppliers are carried out). A well-executed SOA implementation can bridge the gap between enterprise architecture and business strategy, with companies achieving a closer alignment of IT and the business, while in parallel implementing the robust reuse of existing technology and application code with agility and cost effectiveness (Laurent 2007).

Traditional systems were built as monoliths, making change complex, time-consuming and costly. The tight interconnection of such systems meant that even small changes could ripple across the applications and cause major rewriting (Tews 2007). The approach that SOA takes is that instead of tightly integrated application code, applications are built using loosely-coupled modules called "services", with each service describing an interface that can be accessed regardless of programming language, and without the need to access or understand the underlying code. Such services can be provided within enterprise applications, as interfaces to legacy systems, as new development, or from external providers in industry and government. From a business point of view, the goals are quicker time to market with innovative offerings, greater productivity, and reduced integration costs.

A SOA architecture is based on six assumptions (Brandl 2007): applications are loosely coupled; interface transactions are stateless; interface follows the RPC (remote procedure call) model; interface is message-based; messages use XML (eXtensible Markup Language) data; and interfaces may support both synchronous and asynchronous transactions. Viewed as an approach to building IT systems to match flexible business requirements, SOA connects applications across a network via a common communications protocol, allowing organizations to reuse old and future software, often with the help of Web Services (Brodkin 2007). SOA incorporates standards like SOAP (Simple Object Access Protocol) and XML, to deliver standard messaging formats and increased reuse of information assets at lower integration costs (Larrivee 2007).

2.2 Intelligent Agents

Service-Oriented Architectures do not provide any support for rational (semi-) automated selections when it comes to the creation of Virtual Organizations. Such rational selection is crucial for establishing and operating viable business formations. This issue can be addressed by enriching SOA with Intelligent Agents. Interests of individual VO members are represented by Intelligent Agents, acting according to customizable business rules. Although previous research on the role of Intelligent Agents in Virtual Organization has been carried out (e.g. Andrade et al. 2005, Guidi-Polanco et al. 2005, Oliveira and Rocha 2000, Petersen 2003, 2007, Svirskas et al. 2006), in this paper we are mostly concerned with the framing of Intelligent Agents within an overall SOA architecture, and the expected benefits of such an approach.

Practically this means exposing results of agent operations via standard Web Services interfaces, enabling easy integration of these results into ad-hoc mash-ups and portals. Maximilien and Singh (2005) distinguish between two primary classifications of consumer-to-provider interaction styles in services: *simple interactions and agent-mediated interactions*. Simple interactions occur directly between a service consumer and a service provider. Agent-mediated interactions use an intermediary agent that facilitates some aspects of the interaction. In our work we are mostly concerned with *agent-mediated interaction styles as they allow providing richer solutions*.

One also needs to make sure that these two types of entities (agents and services) coexist peacefully within a single architecture and interoperate properly. Maximilien & Singh propose a framework that augments a typical Service-Oriented Architecture with agents. Their principal idea is to install software agents between service consumers and each service that they consume. These consumer service agents expose the same interface as the service. However, they augment the service interface with agent-specific methods. The consumer communicates its needs via the augmented agent interface. Service method invocations are done via the service agent who, in turn, monitors and forwards all calls to the selected service.

The concept of multiple agents can also be useful in general-purpose Web Service composition. Maamar et al. (2005) present an agent-based and context-oriented approach that supports the composition of Web Services. To reduce the complexity featuring the composition of Web Services two concepts are put forward in their work, namely, software agent and context. During the composition process, software agents engage in conversations with their peers to agree on the Web Services that participate in this process. Conversations between agents take into account the execution context of the Web Services. The security of the computing resources on which the Web Services are executed constitutes another core component of the agent-based and context-oriented approach presented by Maamar et al.

The benefits of combining SOA and Intelligent Agents are foreseen to be increased adaptability and flexibility to organizational needs regarding VO processes. However, there is still much research to be done on the (business and technical) aspects of the combination of SOA and Intelligent Agents in the context of VOs. In addition, the standards associated with SOA (e.g. Web Services standards) are still to become mature and established. SOA may also not be particularly applicable in mission or safety-critical applications (Bloomberg and Schmelzer 2006). However, the use of these concepts in the Panda project, the associated architecture and the expected benefits are presented in the following sections.

3 The Panda Project

Panda (PANDA-Project 2006). examines e-collaboration in the European ERP industry of SMEs, facilitated with the formation and management of Virtual Organizations. Currently, the European ERP market (which is a major part of ICT business applications market in Europe – worth approximately €15 billion) is dominated by large multinational actors, most of them outside the EU, focusing on high-end market segments (ERP solutions for large multinational companies). However, as the high-end market has reached maturity, there is a shift of interest towards small and medium market segments (ERP solutions for small companies and SMEs).

Recognizing this potential for ERP value chains of SMEs, Panda aims to provide a powerful framework of e-business services, dedicated to addressing current inefficiencies in the operations of such value chains, as well as facilitating international e-collaborations based on local actors and alliances. Panda proposes the development of a new partnership based e-business model for SMEs such as ERP vendors, their national representatives, dealers and consultants. Panda also includes the development of a set of integrated supporting technologies in the form of a platform (portal) that will engage and involve local players in flexible multinational e-collaborations. These collaborations concern the provision of services towards an end customer (e.g. ERP implementations, upgrades, customizations, training, support, etc) which require the expertise of more than one partner.

The pilot installation of the prototype platform takes advantage of Panda's two large international 'informal' ERP value chains, comprising 2 ERP vendors (SMEs), 200 ERP national representatives and dealers and 50 IT consultants, who are active in 7 European countries (Greece, Romania, Bulgaria, Germany, Hungary, Finland and Sweden). The two value chains examined practically represent two different edges that appear in the ERP industry: (a) rigid - hierarchical value chain supporting a fully protected and licensed ERP product, (b) loose virtual community / value network of collaborating actors supporting an open source ERP solution.

The main functional requirements that arose from the users' perspective in Panda were the need to identify online suitable collaboration partners for participation in ERP projects, the efficient communication of the project's requirements and status, experience sharing from previous similar ERP projects, and standardization of contracts for international collaborations. Apart from the functional requirements however, other non-functional requirements which emerged as important were the flexibility of platform operations to match different value chain characteristics, while also allowing interoperability between platform architecture and partners' own systems. In addition, a degree of automation of operations carried out in the Panda platform as part of VO establishment was also deemed important. As such, the concepts of SOA and Intelligent Agents needed to be considered in the design of the architecture of the Panda platform. This architecture and its benefits are presented next.

4 E-Collaboration Architecture and Operations

4.1 System Architecture

Figure 1 illustrates Panda's SOA architecture (implemented with .NET Web Services) – the central point of user interaction is a portal (based on Microsoft Web Part's technology), accessed by human users and software agents. Interests of individual members of the Panda ecosystem are represented by Intelligent Agents (using FIPA standards and written in Java), acting according to customizable business rules (implemented using JBoss).

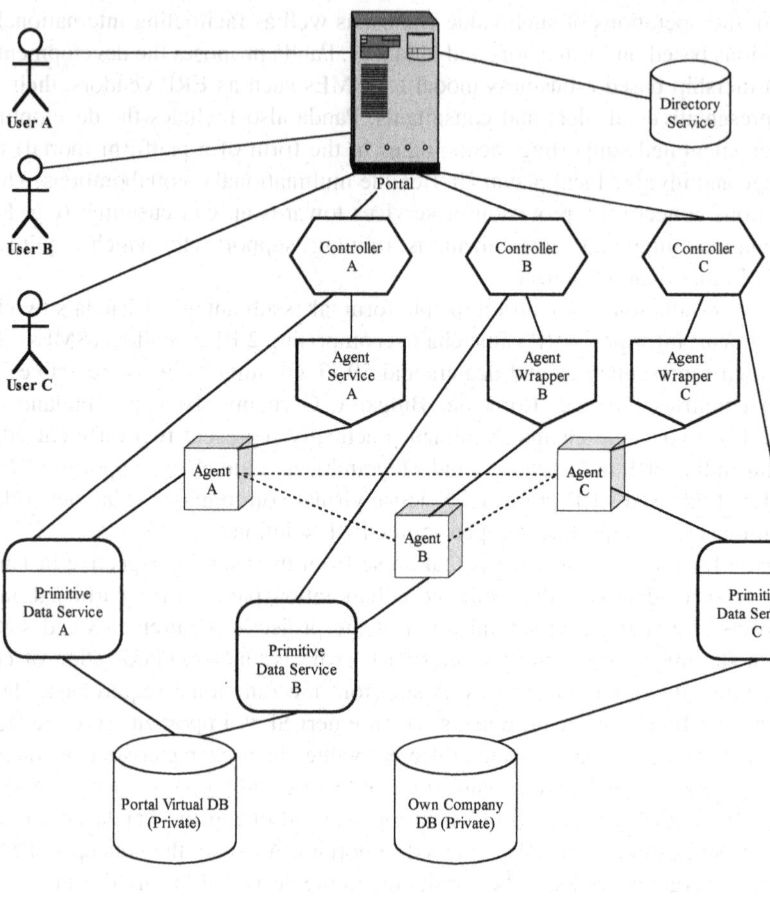

Fig. 1. Panda's SOA and agent-based architecture

The components that comprise the Panda platform are the following:

- Directory Service: A common repository containing login information, standard values like ERP modules, languages, industry sectors etc. The directory service can be accessed by a Web Service.
- Controller: User functionality in the portal that enables the creation and submission of requests to the Intelligent Agent.
- Agent Service: A Web Service that enables the submission of a Collaboration Request to the Agent and the acquisition of the list of the proposed VOs. This can also be implemented by a Web Service wrapper around agent functionality.
- Agent: The company's Intelligent Agent that undertakes the negotiations and the formation of the VOs. Agents communicate with each other to exchange information and engage in negotiations.

- Primitive Data Services: Set of simple Web Services that enable Agents and Controller to access the company's private repository (company database).
- Private repository (Company database): The repository that contains private information of the company like Company Profile, Collaboration Requests, Contracts etc. This can be a dedicated (virtual) storage within the portal, or can be at the company's legacy systems.

4.2 Agent Operations

The Panda agent system is composed of independent distributed instances of Partner Agent interacting with each other and with a set of centralized platform services. The main purpose of agents is to identify and negotiate with potential partners for collaboration in a VO, and suggest a number of such potential VOs based on various criteria such as price, deadlines of tasks, previous experiences and reputation of participants, etc. As such, the scope of agent contribution in Panda can be formulated as *agent-based negotiation towards VO formation using dynamic (semi-)private knowledge*. The agents consequently represent individual (distributed) actors participating in VO formation processes taking into account (i) individual private constrains and preferences (e.g. with regards to types of projects sought, availabilities of staff, pricing rules, etc) that are hidden to other actors, and (ii) minimization of disclosure of such private information.

Agents get active in the system once a Collaboration Request (CR) for the identification of suitable partners for collaborating in an ERP project is submitted in the system by a human user. Once a Collaboration Request (CR) has been created by a company in Panda and sent to potential partners via the corresponding agent, the companies that receive the request may begin negotiations by editing the request and sending a proposal back to the company via their agents. Further negotiations after the first response from the human users can be subsequently carried out automatically by agents (e.g. in terms of prices or deadlines). At the end of the negotiations the agent of the Collaboration Request issuer can create VO proposals that can be seen by the human user and one of these proposals potentially selected. The user who made the response proposal is then informed for his/her selection in a VO and the human requester of the collaboration can start composing a contract with his/her partner(s). Once the contract has been defined and agreed upon by all involved parties the project is then started. Project management activities can be carried out with an appropriate tool connected via Web Services to the Panda portal. At the end of the operations of the VO its results can be archived, and VO partners can rate each other with regards to their collaboration efficiency.

As has been mentioned, agents are involved in negotiations about CR details that lead to VO formation. Each agent is dedicated to a single company – the member of the value chain. The interaction amongst agents in Panda for the handling of Collaboration Requests (with human advisement) and VO proposals is shown in Figure 2 below.

In their negotiations, agents can be guided by user-defined business rules. Agents need to decide which of these rules are applicable in each type of negotiation, and need to flexibly adapt and prioritize those rules as the negotiations progress, potentially also guided by human input to correct decisions taken. Such rules can be set by each user to guide his/her agent, and can be implemented using a rules engine. Indicative user-defined business rules for the negotiation amongst agents can include for example:

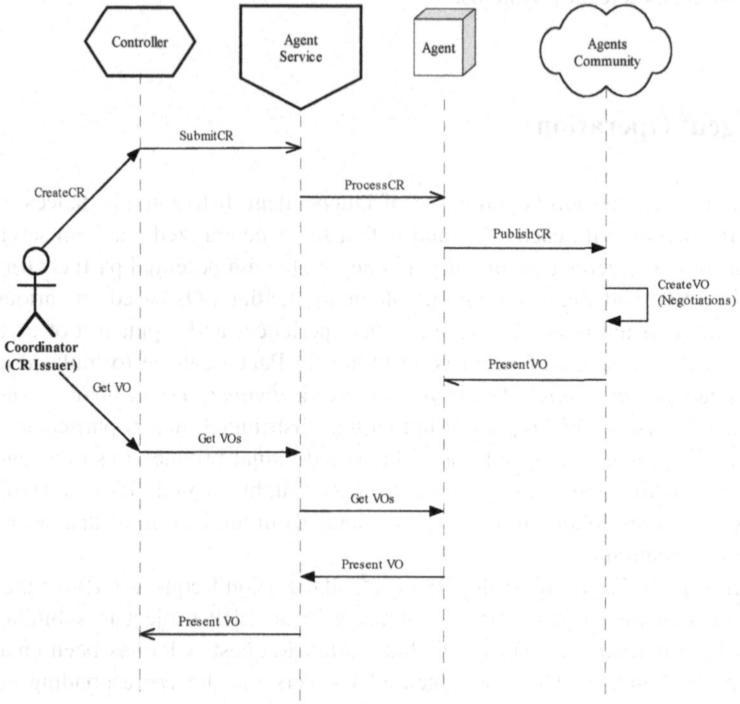

Fig. 2. Agent-based Collaboration Request (CR) processing and Virtual Organization (VO) handling

- My tolerance on price is -x% to +y%.
- I am prepared to wait x days to get a better price.
- I will pay more to finish the project sooner.
- Only consider partners in the same region/country as me.
- I do not want to deal with partners in my blacklist.
- I do not want to participate in projects less than x Euros.

These rules are represented in a JBoss rules engine, and agents need to decide the priority of each of these rules and resolve potential conflicts amongst the rules. As the negotiation amongst the agents is mainly based on price (and to a lesser degree deadlines of tasks), the majority of the business rules define strategies for negotiating the pricing arrangements amongst the partners.

4.3 SOA and Agent Benefits in Panda

The importance of adopting a Service-Oriented Architecture to increase an organization's agility and flexibility is becoming clearer for many organizations interested in gaining a competitive advantage by differentiating their services and becoming better prepared to respond to changes in their market (Bloomberg and Schmelzer 2006). Extending the SOA principles to a VO setting in the Panda project, it is argued that the SOA advantages can also be obtained for a conglomeration of companies coming together to synergistically exploit complementary skills and competencies. Although there is not a shortage of platforms for firms to collaborate online in particular industries or across industries, the advantages of adopting a SOA approach for such platforms offered by the adaptability and easy reconfigurability to match heterogeneous VOs' business requirements, need to be taken into consideration. The benefits of using a SOA approach in Panda in particular is the re-usability, interoperability and adaptation of the various Panda components to different value chains (e.g. with regards to how reputation or project management are handled), as well as companies' operational characteristics (e.g. with regards to how company profiles and company private data are handled). Different enterprises connecting to the Panda platform can exploit Web Service connectivity to pass their data (e.g. profiles, pricelists, etc) to and from the portal, as well as using data from the portal, implementing a "data as a service" layer. Services provided by the Panda platform can also be substituted by alternative ones, or new ones can be written, to ensure compatibility with different ERP value chain requirements, in addition for allowing for the possibility for the Panda platform to be exploited outside the ERP industry, implementing a "software as a service" layer. The SOA conceptual approach in Panda is depicted in Figure 3 below.

In contrast to costly and timely hardwiring of point-to-point connections between companies in order to promote interoperability and collaboration, a distributed SOA approach adopted in Panda enables companies to more flexibly participate in a platform that can consider the technical (infrastructure) and business (operational) capabilities of enterprises to enable them to efficiently engage in collaborative activities with other partners.

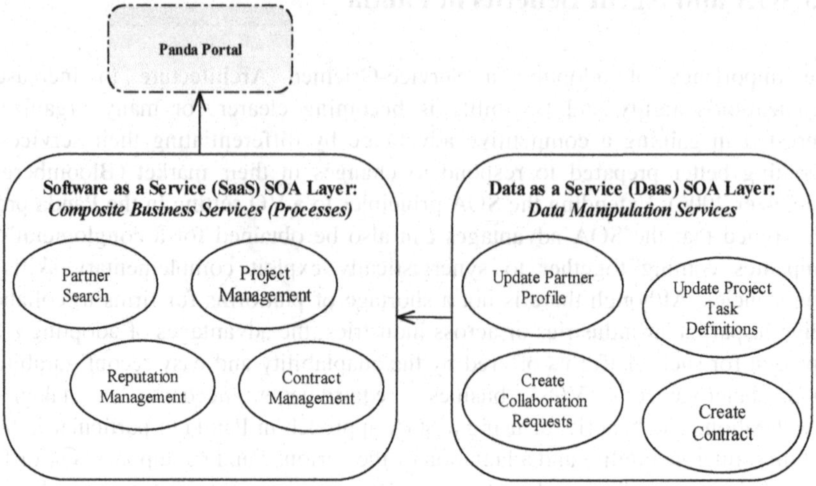

Fig. 3. SOA conceptual approach in Panda

In addition, in contrast to large ERP vendors (such as SAP, Oracle) having their own business ecosystems centered around the provision, installation, maintenance and support of their products, for SMEs in the ERP industry the participation in a flexible, adaptable, and partially automated (with Intelligent Agents) e-collaboration platform can increase their synergies, expand their activities and lower their costs of operation, making them better suited to compete with their larger counterparts.

With regards to Intelligent Agents, as has been mentioned these play the role of the partners' representatives for (semi-)automated negotiation that support the e-business acceleration in the ERP value chain domain. One of the goals is to provide negotiation-based matchmaking methods that take into account (i) limited information provision, (ii) multi criteria evaluation of proposals, (iii) private preferences and metrics (in terms of different weights for criteria used to find potential collaborators) for each participant. Using (static) public data, previous experience, or reputation mechanism, the collaboration requester's agent can carry out negotiations with a selected set of potential partners that provide the highest probability to match the requester's preferences. The peer-to-peer negotiation is used for gathering semi-private knowledge to be able to evaluate the participants (proposals are based on participants' private preferences and availability and can't be evaluated without negotiation) and construct VOs. The finalization of the matchmaking is done by the VO proposals evaluation and there is a possible backtracking when the evaluation gives non-satisfactory results. This automation of partner finding and VO creation processes (supported by human advisement) is expected to give significant time and cost savings for the relevant SMEs in the ERP industry.

5 Conclusions

The main concerns of Panda include: (1) taking prevailing best practices from SOA and associated issues (e.g. what can be provided as a service and in which level of abstraction, as well as interoperability at the data and software levels), and finding best ways to apply them to SMEs and their business needs regarding collaboration with other partners, (2) examining the degree to which processes within a VO can be automated with the use of Intelligent Agents.

It is expected that the combination of Intelligent Agents aiding in the automation of processes (such as negotiation-based matchmaking for the formation of VOs), together with the adoption of a SOA approach promoting flexibility, interoperability and adaptability to user needs, can contribute towards the building and maintenance of a community of member organizations with similar or complementary skills and competencies. At the time of writing of this paper a prototype system using SOA and Intelligent Agent principles was completed, and given to a number of SMEs in the European ERP industry for testing and practical evaluation of the expected benefits of such an approach. In addition, the issues of building security and trust in online environments (Dimitrakos et al. 2004, Ignatiadis et al. 2006, Msanjila and Afsarmanesh 2007) in order to increase collaboration, as well as adopting efficient and effective SOA governance (Bloomberg and Schmelzer 2006, Larrivee 2007, Laurent 2007), will also be examined in future stages of the project, together with the development of its business plan.

Although the Panda project is exemplified in the ERP industry, the concepts, business and developed technological aspects could also be applied in other settings where collaborative projects are implemented. This includes practically any business sector where business-oriented software solutions (i.e. software products coupled with value added services to form 'extended' solutions) are used. The applicability of Panda in these areas is also a matter of future research, together with examining Web 2.0 principles to increase collaboration amongst partners.

Acknowledgements

The authors of this paper wish to acknowledge the kind contribution of the European Commission towards funding of the Panda project.

References

Aldrich, D. F. (1999). *Mastering The Digital Marketplace*. Chichester: John Wiley.

Andrade, F., Neves, J., Novais, P., Machado, J., Abelha, A. (2005). *Legal Security and Credibility in Agent Based Virtual Enterprises*. Paper presented at the PRO-VE'05 - 6th IFIP Working Conference on Virtual Enterprises, Valencia, Spain, 26 - 28 September.

Bloomberg, J., Schmelzer, R. (2006). *Service Orient or Be Doomed!: How Service Orientation Will Change Your Business*. Hoboken, New Jersey: Wiley.

Brandl, D. (2007). SOA explained. *Control Engineering*, 54(8), 22-22.

Brodkin, J. (2007). Are SOAs saving anyone money? *Network World*, 24(28), 24-25.

Davidow, W. H., Malone, S. M. (1992). *The Virtual Corporation - Structuring And Revitalizing The Corporation For The 21st Century*. New York: Harper Collins.

Dimitrakos, T., Wilson, M., Ristol, S. (2004). *TrustCoM - A Trust and Contract Management Framework enabling Secure Collaborations in Dynamic Virtual Organisations*. Sophia Antipolis, France.

Guidi-Polanco, F., Cubillos, C., Menga, G. (2005). *The Global Automation Platform: An Agent-based Framework for Virtual Organizations*. Paper presented at the PRO-VE'05 - 6th IFIP Working Conference on Virtual Enterprises, Valencia, Spain, 26 - 28 September.

Hagel, J., Armstrong, A. (1997). *Net.Gain: Expanding Markets Through Virtual Communities*. Harvard: Harvard Business School Press.

Harding, C. (2007). An Open Marketplace for Services. *DM Review*, 17(9), 20-39.

Ignatiadis, I., Svirskas, A., Roberts, B., Tarabanis, K. (2006). Promoting Trust in B2B Virtual Organizations through Business and Technological Infrastructures. *International Journal of Networking and Virtual Organizations, Special Issue on: Trust Development and Management in Virtual Organizations*, 3(4), 395-411.

Larrivee, B. (2007). SOA: No Governance Needed. Or Is It? *AIIM E-DOC*, 21(5), 24-25.

Laurent, W. (2007). The Importance of SOA Governance. *DM Review*, 17(8), 38-38.

Maamar, Z., Mostefaoui, S. K., Yahyaoui, H. (2005). Toward an Agent-Based and Context-Oriented Approach for Web Services Composition. *IEEE Transactions on Knowledge and Data Engineering*, 17(5), 686 - 697.

Maximilien, E. M., Singh, M. P. (2005). *Toward web services interaction styles*. Paper presented at the 2005 IEEE International Conference on Services Computing (SCC'05), Orlando, Florida, USA, 11-15 July.

Msanjila, S. S., Afsarmanesh, H. (2007). *Towards Establishing Trust Relationships Among Organizations in VBEs*. Paper presented at the PRO-VE'07: 8th IFIP Working Conference on Virtual Enterprises, Guimaraes, Portugal, 10-12 September.

Oliveira, E., Rocha, A. P. (2000). Agents advanced features for negotiation in Electronic Commerce and Virtual Organisations formation process. In C. Sierra, F. Dignum (Eds.), *European Perspectives on Agent Mediated Electronic Commerce*: Springer-Verlag.

PANDA-Project. (2006). *EU IST-027169*. http://www.panda-project.com. Accessed April 2007.
Petersen, S. A. (2003). *An Agent-based Evaluation Framework for Supporting Virtual Enterprise Formation*. Paper presented at the Twelfth International Workshop on Enabling Technologies: Infrastructure for Collaborative Enterprises, Linz, Austria, 9-11 June.

Petersen, S. A. (2007). Virtual enterprise formation and partner selection: an analysis using case studies. *International Journal of Networking and Virtual Organizations*, 4(2), 201-215.

Rautenstrauch, T. (2002). *The Virtual Corporation: A Strategic Option For Small And Medium-Sized Enterprises (SMEs)*. Paper presented at the Association for Small Business and Entrepreneurship, St. Louis.

Svirskas, A., Ignatiadis, I., Roberts, B., Wilson, M. (2006). *Virtual Organization Management using Web Service Choreography and Software Agents*. Paper presented at the PRO-VE'06: 7th IFIP Working Conference on Virtual Enterprises, Helsinki, Finland.

Tews, R. (2007). Beyond IT: The business value of SOA. *AIIM E-DOC*, 21(5), 14-17.

Autonomous Web Services Based on Dynamic Model Harmonization

Makoto Oya

Information Science, Shonan Institute of Technology,

1-1-25, Tsujido Nishi-Kaigan, Fujisawa, 251-8511, Japan

Abstract. Web Services has become the infrastructure to connect business applications over the Internet. Under the current Web Services, however, stakeholder systems must follow the predefined rules for a particular business service including those about business protocols to send/receive messages and about system operation. Only the systems built strictly to follow the predefined rules can participate in the concerning service. This is insufficient when considering future eBusiness systems. More flexible mechanism is desired where freely built and autonomously running systems can exchange business messages without pre-agreed strict rules. We call it Autonomous Web Services (AWS) and proposed the framework called Dynamic Model Harmonization (DMH) with its algorithm, which dynamically adjusts different business process models between systems [1]. In this paper, we propose middleware technology that realizes AWS based on the DMH. The proposal includes the mechanism and specification to drive an application by a dynamically harmonized business process model, as well as the DMH algorithm extended in line with the proposed mechanism. In addition, the way to control very long transactions often appear in AWS environment is proposed, and messaging infrastructure for AWS is discussed based on the prototype implementation.

1 Introduction

As Web Services became enough matured and widely used, adjustment of business process among eBusiness/eCommerce systems has become a next important issue.

Please use the following format when citing this chapter:

Oya, M., 2008, in IFIP International Federation for Information Processing, Volume 286; Towards Sustainable Society on Ubiquitous Networks, eds. Oya, M., Uda, R., Yasunobu, C., (Boston: Springer), pp. 139–150.

Web Services is the technology to exchange data between applications in different systems over the Internet using HTTP/XML. There are two types of message exchange protocol, the RPC protocol that directly uses HTTP request-response protocol and the messaging protocol that asynchronously exchanges messages using additional protocol layer over HTTP. RPC is enough for simple information delivery. For full-scale commercial transactions, the messaging protocol is suitable in general because actual work often occurs after receiving HTTP-request and immediate HTTP-response with the result data is difficult to make. These protocols have been standardized and well established, such as SOAP/Framework [3] for the basic protocol, SOAP/RPC [4] for RPC, ebXML Messaging [5] and WS-Reliability [6] for the messaging protocol. WS-Reliability supports the reliable message delivery features, the duplicate elimination and the guaranteed message ordering, which are indispensable for the commercial message exchange.

Under the current Web Services technology, it is assumed that systems share an agreed model of business process to execute consistent exchange of business messages. The stakeholder systems must strictly follow the predefined rules for a particular service. The rules precisely define the business process including message formats and possible sequences of message delivery and may direct a specific operation rule of each system. Defining such common rules and forcing systems to follow them is possible in a particular enterprise or enterprise group, a particular domain group, or a community sharing a well-defined purpose. As a matter of fact, many business transaction systems are working under the current Web Services using business process description language such as BPMN and BPEL [7].

When considering eBusiness/eCommerce systems scattered over the world in the Internet, however, predefining or standardizing precise business process rules for various business transactions and forcing systems to be developed strictly according to them is not realistic and does not agree with the vision of the Internet. Improved flexible Web Services technology is needed where freely built and autonomously running systems can exchange business messages without predefined rules in order to pursue free and flexible network society for the future. We call this technology as *Autonomous Web Services* (*AWS*). Unknown systems, when they encounter in the Internet, adjust their business process models using their best effort and execute business transaction. They are not necessary to be developed in the way to follow specific rules or to subordinate to specific management servers. Loose common *environment* that is independent of particular services may exist, however, systems that are freely developed and autonomously running under such environment can execute business transaction on demand. This is the ultimate goal of AWS.

Two big challenges are addressed to realize AWS. The major challenge is how to dynamically adjust business process models and drive the application program as the adjusted model instructs. The other is, derived from systems' autonomy, how to control and maintain very long transactions that often occur between systems not sharing a unified operation rule. In order to solve the former challenge, we provided the method that dynamically generates business protocols [2], and then proposed the generalized framework called *Dynamic Model Harmonization* (*DMH*) and showed the detailed algorithm [1]. In DMH, systems expose their business process model descriptions including operation signatures and behavior. Two systems exchange their models when they encounter in the Internet. Each system harmonizes (i.e., dynamically modifies) its model adjusting to the partner's model, and then starts exchanging a series of business messages.

This paper proposes technology to enable middleware that realizes AWS based on DMH. We call this middleware as *AWS middleware*. The DMH algorithm proposed in [1] is extended to apply to middleware implementation. Mechanism to control applications according to the harmonized model is proposed. An application is broken into segments corresponding to each send/receive operation and the segments are driven by a harmonized model generated by DMH algorithm. A solution to the second challenge is also proposed, introducing two concepts, VL session and VL process.

The structure of this paper is: Section 2 explains the principle of DMH and proposes the extended DMH algorithm applicable to middleware technology. Section 3 mentions the overview and major problems of AWS middleware. Section 4 explains the proposed way of controlling application under DMH and provides details of model harmonization, control mechanism and programming model using an example. Section 5 mentions about VL transaction and messaging infrastructure, and discusses on the prototype implementation. Section 6 gives a short conclusion.

2 Dynamic Model Harmonization

The core of Autonomous Web Services (AWS) is Dynamic Model Harmonization (DMH). This section defines the basic principle of DMH, and proposes the extended DMH algorithm applicable to middleware control.

2.1 Principle of DMH

In the framework of DMH, each system exposes its external specification as a *model* M, which is represented by $M = (O, B)$, where:

- O is a set of *operations* op, where $op = (pattern, format)$.
- *pattern* indicates whether the operation is output (send) or input (receive).
- *format* specifies a type of output or input message.
- *behavior* B is, in general, represented as a finite state machine, namely
  $B = (S, F, \Phi)$, where
  $S\ (\subset O)$ is a set of starting operations,
  $F\ (\subset O)$ is a set of final operations, and
  Φ is a transition function.

DMH consists of the following four steps (**Fig.1** outlines these steps):

1. Two systems Z_1 and Z_2 expose each model $M_1 = (O_1, B_1)$ and $M_2 = (O_2, B_2)$.
2. Z_1 and Z_2 exchange the models when they encounter.
3. In each system, matching between the operations is examined and the model is modified (harmonized) to co-operate with the model of the opposite system. This process is called *DMH algorithm*.

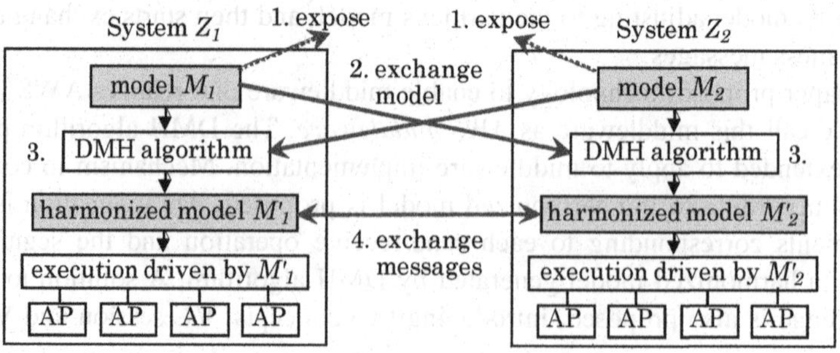

Fig. 1. Outline of Dynamic Model Harmonization

4. If resulting harmonized models M'_1 and M'_2 are not empty and operation mapping is determined, business transaction, i.e. a series of message exchanges, starts according to the harmonized model. Otherwise, business transaction is abandoned.

It is assumed that a type matching function t_match() is provided from the environment (see Section 1). When f is an output format and g is an input format, t_match(f, g) examines whether instances of f matches to g. As shown in [1], t_match() is appropriate to be defined as the following three value function:

t_match(f, g) = true (if all instances of f match to g), or
false (if some instance of f does not match to g), or
undefined (if cannot determine either true or false).

Various kinds of t_match() exist. Simplest one is when type names in the same name space are specified as *format* and they are stored in a specific portion of message texts. Value of t_match() is easily determined by examining type names equality. However, in more complex cases such as type is given by a complex XML schema, determination of t_match() may be limited in a certain range. DMH algorithm determines possible operation mapping by examining t_match() $\neq$ false taking this into consideration. Application of Web ontology is another potential approach for t_match() implementation. See more discussion in [1] and [2].

Note that the first element O in M corresponds to "interface" in WSDL2.0 [8]. The *pattern* corresponds to the MEP (message exchange pattern) though this paper restricts its value either 'input' or 'output' to simplify the discussion.

2.2 DMH Algorithm

In [1], a behavior was represented by a regular expression and a precise DMH algorithm was shown and verified. Here, a behavior is represented as a nondeterministic automaton, and an extended DMH algorithm in line with middleware control is proposed bellow. When a behavior B is restricted as a nondeterministic automaton, a transition function Φ is given by $\Phi(o)$ = (a subset of O) where $o \in O$. The proposed DMH algorithm is outlined as follows.

- First, for $M_1 = (O_1, B_1)$, B1 = (S_1, F_1, Φ_1), $M_2 = (O_2, B_2)$ and $B_2 = (S_2, F_2, \Phi_2)$, a product model M is built, such that $M = (O, B)$ where $O = O_1 \times O_2$, $B = (S, F, \Phi)$, $S = S_1 \times S_2$, $F = F_1 \times F_2$, $\Phi(o_1, o_2) = \Phi_1(o_1) \times \Phi_2(o_2)$.
- An operation matching function o_match(p, q) is defined as follows (where p, $q \in$O, fp and fq are formats of p and q respectively):

  - o_match(p, q) = false if both p and q are input or output,
  - o_match(p, q) = t_match(fp, fq) if p is output and q is input, and
  - o_match(p, q) = t_match(fq, fp) if p is input and q is output.

- Next, M is modified in the following three steps:

1. remove from O all pairs (o_1, o_2) satisfying o_match(o_1, o_2) = false.
2. reduce S, F and values of Φ to be subsets of O.
3. remove unnecessary nodes and paths from B (= (S, F, Φ)). Namely, remove from O all pairs (o_1, o_2) that are not reachable from S and all pairs (o_1, o_2) that do not reach to F. They are also removed from the domain and values of Φ.

- The resulted M (denoted M') is called a *harmonized co-operation model* (or simply a *harmonized model* when the context is clear). Z_1 part of M' (denoted M'_1) and Z_2 part of M' (denoted M'_2) are called harmonized models of Z_1 and Z_2.

At some status of the harmonized co-operation model and for some output operation of the system, if a destination input operation of the opposite system is not uniquely determined, we say "operation mapping is not determined". Precisely, it is the case when, for some $(o_1, o_2) \in$O, $\Phi(o_1, o_2)$ includes both (a, b_1) and (a, b_2) or both (b_1, a) and (b_2, a), where a is an output operation, and b_1 and b_2 are distinct input operations. Otherwise, we say "operation mapping is determined". If the harmonized co-operation model is not empty and operation mapping is determined, then it decides Z_1 and Z_2 are co-operative and business transaction is started. After starting, a series of message delivery is controlled according to the harmonized co-operation model.

3 AWS Middleware

This section proposes a middleware, called *AWS middleware*, realizing AWS based on the DMH framework and algorithm mentioned in the previous section.

3.1 Overview

AWS middleware constitutes a store-and-forward type asynchronous messaging system. Fig.2 shows the overview when systems Z_1 and Z_2 exchange messages over AWS middleware. Note that the internal structure of Z_2 is same as Z_1 but simplified in the figure. End points of messaging are called UA (user agent). UA has a unique name and plays as a primary entity of sending and receiving messages. A message sent by UA through AP (application program) is stored in the output queue (outQ), then, asynchronously delivered to the input queue (inQ) in the opposite system. The message in inQ is asynchronously taken out and passed to UA through AP. Reliable messaging, exactly once semantics and message ordering guarantee, is supported since AWS middleware handles business transaction.

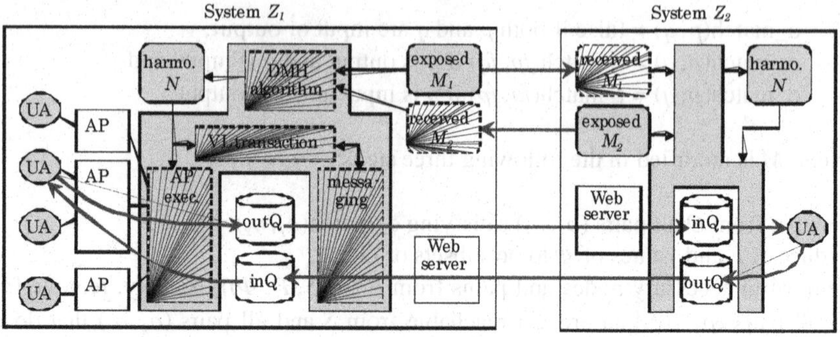

Fig. 2. AWS middleware overview

Messaging protocol of AWS middleware is built over HTTP and SOAP/Framework. Like ebXML Messaging [5], one one-way message delivery is processed by one HTTP request-response. A message taken out from outQ is sent to the Web server of the recipient system by HTTP POST request. If successfully stored in inQ, HTTP response is returned to the original system and the message is removed from outQ. If not successful, retry occurs. Asynchronous reliable messaging is implemented in this way. The protocol is natural extension of the current Web Services protocols and any additional existing Web Services technology is applicable. Security mechanism such as PKI, for instance, is applicable exploiting UA has a unique name.

3.2 Problems

Major problems to be solved are following three:

1. DMH driven application execution
   In system Z_1, AWS middleware generates a harmonized co-operation model N from its own model (M_1 in Fig.2) and a received model (M_2) from Z_2. Then it needs to control AP execution flow according to the contents of N. It is difficult if send/receive operations are embedded in AP. In addition, as a premise of such DMH driven execution control, it needs to separate operation mapping from AP, establishing independence of a model and program codes.
2. Control of very long transaction
   Comparing to short transaction processing such as online banking system, business transaction in the Internet does not require strict ACID but each transaction often continues during long period such as from price inquiry to delivery of goods. In AWS, each system has its own policy of system operation and administration. Life of transaction tends to be longer because of long waiting time to receive an expecting message. Even a message sending operation may be blocked because of a long

period of retry, several hours, several days, or more. Thus, a business transaction in AWS is much longer than that in the current well-managed Web Services business transaction system. AWS middleware needs to control such a very long transaction (VL transaction).

3. Messaging infrastructure
Messaging infrastructure itself does not have big issues since messaging is enough mature technology, except that retry algorithm and message queue implementation need special consideration in AWS middleware. Sending operation may accompany very long retry cycle as mentioned in 2 but AWS does not assume systems to share a single messaging policy. AWS middleware needs to decide times and interval of retry based on runtime negotiation and dynamic control. In addition, reliable and dependable implementation of inQ and outQ is required because message queues keep large number of messages during long period, even beyond system shutdown time.

We focus on the problem 1 in this paper and propose our solution in the next section. The problems 2 and 3 are discussed in Section 5.

4 DMH Driven Application Execution

Differently from usual client-server communication, under the framework of DMH, output operations are exposed as well as input operations. An application sends a message to an output operation of its own system instead of an input operation of the opposite system. Operation mapping is automatically determined by AWS middleware using DMH algorithm as mentioned in2.2. Application does not need to know operations of opposite systems and independence and autonomy of a system are improved. Moreover, to separate program codes and a model, AWS middleware supports a *program configuration file* to specify methods and message format handling classes corresponding to each operation in the model.

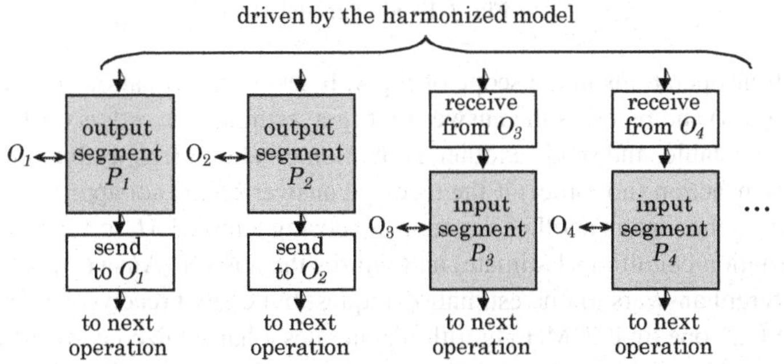

Fig. 3. Program execution control using harmonized model

AP is defined as a set of segments (called *message I/O segments*) to realize application execution control driven by the harmonized model. Each message I/O segment corresponds to an output or input operation. According to an execution status of the harmonized co-operation model, AWS middleware invokes an appropriate message

I/O segment like an event driven loop. A segment forms a method. Input and output are not instructed directly from program codes. The message is sent to the corresponding output operation right after the method returns in case of an output segment, and the received message is passed to the method when it is invoked in case of an input segment. Fig.3 illustrates the proposed programming model. The details are mentioned in the following subsections using an example.

4.1 Model Description and DMH

Suppose a system Z_1 exposes a model M_1 shown in Fig.4. Here, a model is described by YAML [9] and a behavior is denoted by an activity diagram for easy understanding. Note that YAML is convertible to XML and an activity diagram can be transformed into XML using such as UML/XMI [10]. Name spaces are omitted for simplicity. Type names of format are assumed in the same name space and t_match() is calculated simply using names identity (see 2.1).

```
operations:
  - operation: req_estimation
    pattern: output
    format:  estForm
  - operation: get_estimation
    pattern: input
    format:  estForm
  -operation: no_order
    pattern: output
    format:  abortMessage
  -operation:order
    pattern: output
    format:  orderForm
  - operation: conf_order
    pattern: input
    . . . .
behavior:
   /* as in the figure */
```

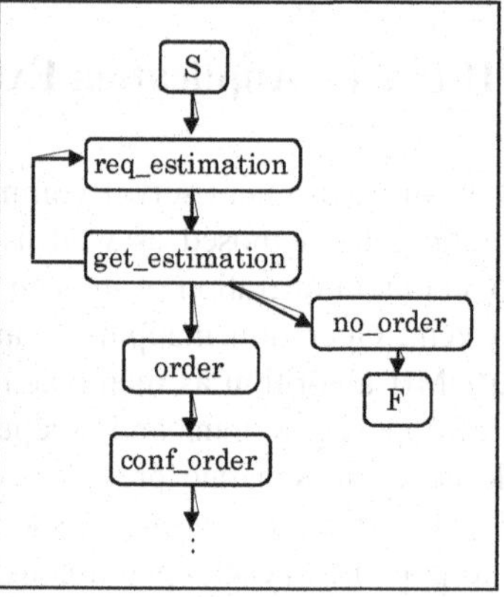

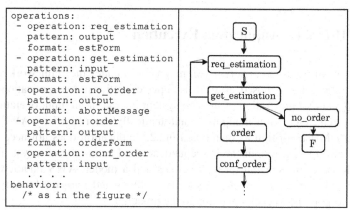

Fig. 4. Exposed model M_1

M_1 has four operations in the scope of Fig.4. It sends an estimation condition (req_estimation) and receives the answer to it (get_estimation), orders (order) if the answer is acceptable, and sends another estimation condition (req_estimation) or aborts the transaction (no_order) if the received answer seems not appropriate.

Suppose Z_1 encounters another system Z_2 exposing a model M_2 in Fig.5. M_2 receives estimation condition (Estimate) and returns the answer (Answer). It can return several different answers to one estimation request but cannot receive estimation request more than one time. DMH algorithm generates a harmonized co-operation model N from M_1 and M_2 as shown in Fig. 6. Then AWS middleware drives AP using the model N.

```
operations:
 - operation: Estimate
   pattern: input
   format: estForm
 - operation: Answer
   pattern: output
   format: estForm
 - operation: Order
   pattern: input
   format: orderForm or
           abortMessage
 - operation: Accept
   pattern: output
   . . . .
behavior:
  /* as in the figure */
```

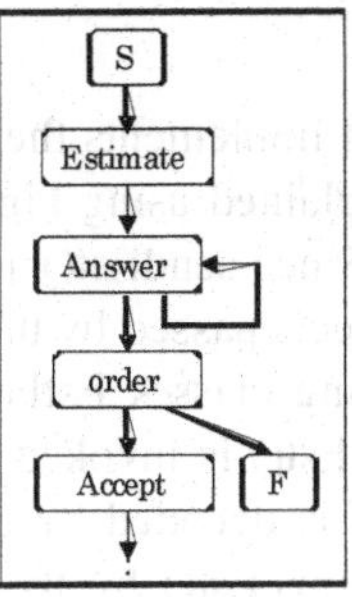

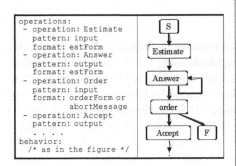

Fig. 5. Fig.5 Exposed model M_2

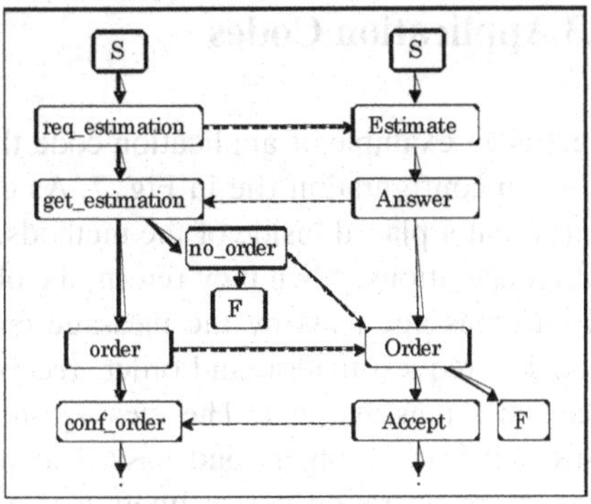

Fig.6. Harmonized co-operation model N

4.2 Program Configuration File

AP in Z1 consists of a set of methods implementing message I/O segments and *message coding classes* to encode output messages and decode input messages. Each method receives by its parameter a reference to an instance of the corresponding message coding class. AP configuration is specified in a program configuration file. An example is shown in Fig. 7.

```
programCofiguration:
 - operation: req_estimation
   method:      sendEst
   codingClass: EstForm
 - operation: get_estimation
   method:      recieveEst
   codingClass: EstResult
 - operation: order
   method:      order
   codingClass: OrderForm
 . . . .
```

Fig. 7. Program configuration file

In this example, it specifies sendEst() is a method corresponding to the output operation req_estimation and stores output message contents in a class EstForm object. receiveEst() is a method corresponding the input operation get_estimation and receives the contents of received message by a class EstResult object. EstForm and EstResult need to be created as classes to access estForm type format specified in the M_1 in Fig. 4. Besides operations appear in a model, special methods invoked at starting and ending time of transaction may be prepared.

4.3 Application Codes

Fig.8 is an example of application code that implements the methods specified in the program configuration file in Fig. 7. As explained using Fig. 3, message I/O instructions are not placed inside of the methods. Since sendEst() and order() corresponds to output operations, when they return, the objects passed by their parameters are encoded into message texts by the message coding classes EstForm and OrderForm, and routed to req_estimation and order. receiveEst() is invoked when get_estimation has received a message text. The message text is decoded by the message coding class EstResult into an object and passed to receiveEst() by its parameter. An operation next to the operation get_estimation is non-deterministic in M_1. Possible operations are order, no_order and req_estimation. As seen in the example (Fig. 6), the model is harmonized, a part of possible operations may become not applicable. Two methods, setNextOperation() and getNextOperation, are prepared to handle this situation. In this example of receiveEst(), possible next operations can be examined by getNextOperation() and an intended next operation can be specified by setNextOperation('order') or setNextOperation('no_order') in receiveEst() before returning.

```
class SampApp extends AWSApp {
  public sendEst(EstForm: ef)
  {
    /* set estimation conditions in ef */
    return;
  }
  public receiveEst(EstResult: er)
  {
    /* process estimation results in er */
    getNextOperation(...);
    setNextOperation(...);
    return;
  }
  public order(OrderForm: or)
  {
    set order contents in or */
    return;
  }
  . .. . .
}
```

Fig. 8. Application code

5 VL Transaction and Messaging

(1) VL Transaction

We introduce two concepts, *VL session* (very long session) and *VL process* (very long process) to control VL transaction. A VL session is a non-volatile session. It starts from S in the model and kept until F. After the DMH algorithm decided co-operation is possible, a common session identifier (VL session id) is generated and a transaction starts from starting operations. Hereafter, VL session is kept until the transaction reaches final operations even one or both system stops and restarts on the way. Model exchange at VL session creation is performed by messaging communication recursively using AWS middleware. AWS middleware has a special well-known VL session for this purpose. All communications between AWS middleware are done through this special VL session.

VL session enters into waiting status in two reasons: the opposite system does not yet send a message though input operation is invoked, or a message is not delivered to the queue of the opposite system though the message is already sent from output operation. Waiting period may be very long, a few hours, a few days, a few weeks or more as discussed in 3.2. It is not suitable from system resource limitation to keep VL sessions active during long term of waiting. AWS middleware automatically archives VL sessions to external storage during such period. The control mechanism for this feature is VL process. VL processes behave as ordinal processes (or tasks) when they are active. One VL process has one or more VL sessions. When a VL session falls into long waiting status during message sending or receiving, the VL process is archived to external storage with the contexts of its VL sessions. When waiting status is released, an actual process is assigned and the VL process is reactivated. VL processes are also archived at system shutdown time, realizing non-volatile VL sessions. Archive of VL process occurs only during sending message or receiving message. It does not occur when AP is running, which avoids to archive large data including AP's local resources.

(2) Messaging Infrastructure

We developed prototype implementation supporting messaging infrastructure with VL session feature [11]. Solvability of the problems mentioned in 3 of 3.2 was examined through this prototyping. VL sessions were implemented as objects. Blocking and non-blocking send() and receive() were supported as low level APIs. When a VL session object is created, its ID is generated by negotiation between systems and the VL session is maintained hereinafter. Protocol was built over SOAP/Framework. Receiving process works as CGI behind a Web server. A “retry reason level” is included HTTP error responses and a retry interval is dynamically calculated using the levels. In order to make queues (inQ and outQ) durable for long time, they are implemented over DBMS (PostgreSQL). Queue access synchronization was simplified and became safer. Through this prototyping, it was shown the existing messaging technology is well applicable for implementation of AWS messaging infrastructure with some considerations mentioned above.

6 Conclusion

In this paper, we proposed the middleware technology to realize Autonomous Web Services as well as the extended DMH algorithm. Application is segmented corresponding to input and output operations and driven by the middleware. Application execution flow dynamically changes in line with a harmonized model. It realizes systems having different business process models dynamically execute business transaction without predefined strict rules. We also showed solutions to the secondary problem on very long transactions introducing the concepts of VL session and VL process. VL sessions are archived when input/output messaging falls into a long waiting status, effectively providing non-volatile long session. Finally, implementation method of messaging infrastructure for AWS is examined through prototyping. Materialization of the ultimate goal of Autonomous Web Services is a long running theme. Future issues include type matching method, harmonization of more than two systems and VL transaction management.

Acknowledgments. This work was supported by KAKENHI (19500095).

References

1. M. Oya and M. Ito, Dynamic Model Harmonization between Unknown eBusiness Systems, IFIP I3E, Challenges of Expanding Internet: E-Commerce, E-Business, and E-Government, Springer, pp. 389-403, 2005.
2. M. Oya et al, On Dynamic Generation of Business Protocols in Autonomous Web Services, IEICE transaction on Information and Systems, vol.J87-D-I, no.8, pp.824-832, 2004 (in Japanese); Systems and Computers in Japan, Wiley, Vol.37, No.2, pp.37-45, 2006.
3. M. Gudgin et al, SOAP Version 1.2 Part 1: Messaging Framework (Second Edition), W3C Recommendation, 2007.
4. M. Gudgin et al, SOAP Version 1.2 Part 2: Adjuncts (Second Edition), W3C Recommendation, 2007.
5. OASIS, ebXML Messaging Services Ver. 3.0: Part 1. Core Features, OASIS Standard, 2007.
6. OASIS, WS-Reliability 1.1, OASIS Standard, 2004.
7. T. Andrews et al, Business Process Execution Language for Web Services, 2003.
8. R. Chinnici et al, Web Services Description Language (WSDL) Version 2.0, W3C Recommendation, 2007.
9. O. Ben-Kiki et al, YAML Ain't Markup Language (YAML™) Version 1.1, yaml.org, 2005.
10. OMG, MOF 2.0/XMI Mapping, Version 2.1.1, OMG doc. formal/2007-12-01, 2007
11. M. Ito, M. Sawaguchi, H. Matsubara and M. Oya, Asynchronous P2P Communication Middleware, IPSJ 70th Conference, pp.I-565-568, 2008. (in Japanese)
12. J. Miller et al, MDA Guide Version 1.0.1, OMG doc. omg/2003-06-01, 2003.

A Nonlinear Representation of Page History in P2P Wiki System

Sawsan Alshattnawi, Gérôme Canals, Pascal Molli

Nancy-Université, LORIA/INRIA Lorraine , Campus Scientifique, BP 239, F-54506 Vandœuvre-lès-Nancy, France,
e-mail: {alshattn, canals, molli}@loria.fr

Abstract Awareness about the document evolution is an important part in collaborative editing systems. It is represented always by the versions history. The representation of the document history in centralized collaborative editing systems is linear. However, in distributed collaborative editors, there is no central server and the users can work asynchronously or in isolation and some versions may be produced concurrently, in this case, the history is no long linear. The existing history representations are limited because they don't provide any information about the concurrence on the document history. We introduce here a non linear representation for the page history in P2P wiki systems. The concurrency information about the page versions is provided; the user can explore the page versions that resulted under the user's control or produced by the server in case of merging concurrent modifications.

1 Introduction

Providing history of versions in collaborative editing systems with each document is very important. The history contains all the revisions for one document since its creation, a new revision is created in the history when a user commits his modifications. The history helps the user to understand the evolution of the document, to compare between two versions, to see what are the operations that convert one version to another, who made these operations and he can revert to precedent version.

Please use the following format when citing this chapter:

Alshattnawi, S., Canals, G., Molli, P., 2008, in IFIP International Federation for Information Processing, Volume 286; Towards Sustainable Society on Ubiquitous Networks, eds. Oya, M., Uda, R., Yasunobu, C., (Boston: Springer), pp. 151–160.

Some collaborative editors are based on state-based approach [10]. State-based approach takes into account just the final and initial states of the document. When the user wants to see the evolution from one revision to another, the two versions are *diffed*, *diff* algorithm compares between two files and compute the changes made to a current file by comparing it to a former version of the same file, and the difference between these two revisions is presented. The problem with this approach that there is no information about the operations that transform one state to the other.

Existing decentralized collaborative editing systems are based in operation-based approach [7]. In this approach the operations that transform one revision to another is stored in a history. The operations are kept in a patch that is sent to other sites to be integrated. The patch is a non mutable object and therefore the set of operations that transform one revision to another is the same over all sites. State-based approach is not suitable for decentralized systems because the *diff* algorithm may give different set of operations over each site.

In Distributed Version Control Systems (DVCS) [3], the operations that resulted from the *diff* algorithm between the committed version and the precedent version is reserved in a patch. The patch is diffused to other wiki servers where it will be integrated and recorded by the editor on a log file. When the user gets the history, it is easy to present the difference between versions.

The documents in traditional systems are always produced by the users, in the Copy-Modify-Merge paradigm [8] the central server control all the operations of distributed participants. When it detects concurrent modifications, he asks the user to merge them manually. So, the existing history representation in this case may be enough. However, in DVCS, there is no central server and the users can work asynchronously or in isolation, in this case the merge may be done by the server. The classical way to notify users about merge results is to modify the file itself with conflict blocks. The user who gets the page must search for conflict blocks to know if the page is resulted by the server or by the user. In the history representation there is no indication about the page state.

In a P2P wiki like in DVCS, concurrent changes may occur because of asynchronous work and may be saved on different servers. Merges are not executed when pages are saved but when remote changes are received by each site. To ensure eventual consistency [12], merges are fully automatic and performed by wiki servers. In this case the page is *server-produced.* While when the merge is done under the control of the user the page is *user-produced* [4]. Our objective in this paper is to represent the history of P2P wiki pages by adding information about the pages state if it either user-produced or server-produced. The evolution of the pages concerning the concurrence may help the user to understand the intension of each user and resolving conflicts. This paper is organized as follow: at the next section we mention the history representation in different collaborative editing systems, in section 3 we present our mechanism for detecting the pages states, section 4 presents our history representation in P2P wiki systems and we conclude our work in section 5.

2 Revision Histories in Collaborative Editors

In traditional version control systems such as CVS [5] and subversion [1], no information about the evolution of one state into another is used. They adopted the state-based merge where the information about the state is used. Every time the user commits a file to the CVS repository, a new revision is created. Each revision is identified by a number (for example, 1.1 or 1.11.3.5). Along with each revision is stored the author, the date, and a commit comment. In the revision history view, there is a link near each revision to display *diffs* between that revision and the previous one, and the users is allowed to display *diff* between arbitrary revisions. For conserving space, RCS [14] stores deltas i.e difference between successive revisions. RCS uses the program *diff* which first computes the longest common substring of two revisions, and then produces the delta from that substring. The delta is simply script consisting of deletion and insertion commands that generate one revision from the other.

In Wikipedia [2], every article may be edited anonymously or with a user account. The "History" page attached to each article contains every single past revision of the article. Revision history of a wiki is traditionally maintained as a linear chronological sequence. The informations that we can get from this history representation are the date and time of every edit, the user name, the modification size and from the history we can compare between any two versions or any version with the actual one. Figure 1 represents the revision history for a page *wiki*[1] taken from the encyclopedia *Wikipedia*. From the page history the user can see the difference between that edit and the current version from the link *cur*, the link *last* shows changes between that edit and the previous version, radio buttons can be used to select any two versions of the page. Near each version the date and the time, the user or the contributor name or IP address, edit summary, the nature of the modification and the size, *m: minor edit* to indicate that the modifications were not over the content , and finally the button *undo* to delete the ancient modifications.

Some approaches are proposed to represent the history for giving additional information about the evolution of the wiki page. In [11] the author proposed a tree representation where each edge has a weight indicates the similarity between the two corresponding page revisions. The tree structure reflects actual evolution of page content, revealing reverts, vandalism, and edit wars.

Another work presented in [15], provides an overview of a document's evolution by analyzing differences between multiple revisions of one document. They provide information about how a group has contributed to a document or how a modification has influenced the current version of a document. The existing approaches [11, 15] try to show the violence over the pages. Unfortunately, they don't take into account the concurrency.

---

[1] http://en.wikipedia.org/wiki/Wiki

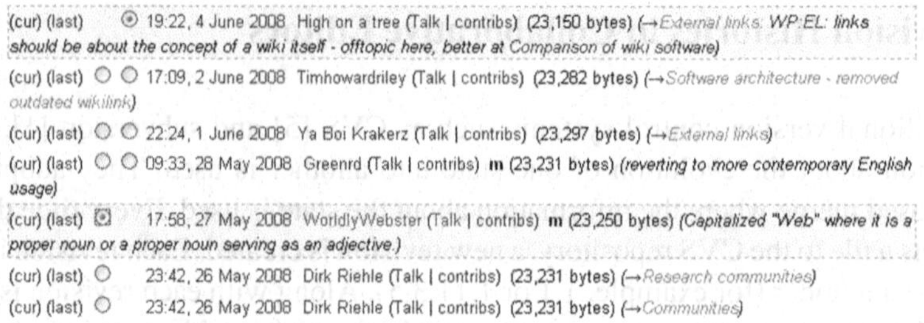

Fig. 1 the pages histories in wikipedia

3 Work Context

The work presented in this paper is based on the concurrency awareness mechanism and the results obtained from our work presented in [4]. The objective of the concurrency awareness mechanism is to recognize the server produced pages and the user produced pages and if the page is server produced to highlight the effects of concurrent updates inside these pages. This makes explicit the regions of the page that are subject to concurrency mismatches. Our major contribution, that we introduce here, to P2P wiki is a nonlinear representation to the page history that reflect the page state concerning the concurrency.

The mechanism is built over P2P wiki system called Wooki [16]. A Wooki network is dynamic p2p network where any site can join or leave at any time. Each site has a unique identifier named *siteid*. Site identifiers are totally ordered. Each site replicates wiki pages of other sites. A Wooki site generates a sequence of operations, when a wooki user saves his page. These operations are integrated locally on the wooki page by executing the Woot algorithm [9], and broadcasted to be integrated on all other sites.

WOOT ensures eventual consistency [6] and intentions preservation [13] for linear structures. Integrating a remote operation consists in line arising a dependency graph between the operations. The algorithm guarantees that the linearisation order is the same on all sites independently of the delivery order of patches. This allows to achieve eventual consistency.

In the concurrency awareness mechanism, when a patch is received and integrated in Wooki system the concurrency is checked and if the concurrency is detected then the mechanism analyzes the log file for determining the common version from which the concurrence operations must be presented to the users. We explain the mechanism by the following example, suppose that we have three site connecting to Wooki server and editing the same Wooki page. The sequence of the operation generation is shown in the figure 2. The three users got the page version *Sn*, at site 1 the user modifies the page by generating the patch P_{n1} and at site 2 the user modifies the page by the generation of P_{n2} and P_{n3}. These patches is propagated and integrated over all the connected sites of the network. At the reception of each patch the

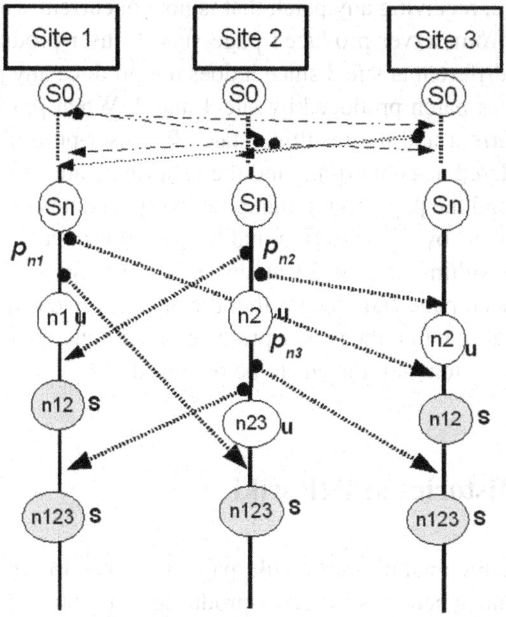

Fig. 2 the patch generation and integration over all sites

concurrency is detected. For example, at site 1, when p_{n2} is received, its integration will obviously require a merge with p_{n1}, resulting in the server-produced state n_{12}, labeled S in the figure, because p_{n1} is concurrent with p_{n2} . Any user requesting the page at that stage should be informed of this status. In addition, highlighting the page region impacted by patches p_{n1} and p_{n2} will help him understanding potential concurrency mismatches.

When site 2 produces patch p_{n2}, reaches the user-produced state n_2. Then site 2 produces patch p_{n3} and broadcasts it. The resulting state at site 2 is n_{23}, labeled u. When site 2, now, receives p_{n1}, we have $p_{n3} \parallel p_{n1}$[2], then the resulting state is server-produced page n_{123}. Here the log must be analyzed. The algorithm extract from the log the last applied patch. Then, it checks its concurrency with all patches in the log. Each concurrent patch is added to a set of concurrent patches. Then, the algorithm computes the common ancestor state of this set. Finally, it adds to the set all patches posterior to this state. So, at site 2, the last integrated patch is p_{n1} and we have $p_{n3} \parallel p_{n1}$, and $p_{n2} \parallel p_{n1}$ so this would return the set contained $\{p_{n3}, p_{n2}, p_{n1}\}$.

[2] we use the symbol $\parallel$ to denote the concurrency between patches

The common ancestor is Sn, this means that the integrated operations since Sn must be highlighted. At this stage, receiving any patch that is not concurrent with the last one will change the state from server-produced page state to user-produced page state. The situation is a bit different at site 3 since it does not produce any patch, but it just receives and integrates patch produced by site 1 and 2. When p_{n2} arrives, it is considered as non concurrent and the resulting state $n2$ is user-produced. When p_{n1} is received, it is considered as concurrent, and the resulting state $n12$ is server-produced. Here, $p_{n1} \parallel p_{n2}$ and the page region that potentially contains concurrency mismatch is the one impacted by $\{p_{n1}, p_{n2}\}$. Finally p_{n3} is received. It is also a concurrent patch and the resulting state $n123$ at site 3 is server-produced. In this mechanism, the user-produced page state means that the page is reviewed by someone and we consider it as valid, while the server-produced page state means that the page may contain some mismatch and it needs to be reviewed.

4 Representing the Histories in P2P wiki

The user might want to see the evolution of a wiki page: he wants to see when the page was user-produced and when it was server-produced, and what the patches that made the page server-produced and what are the patches that convert the page from server-produced to user-produced page. The user can also see who made these patches, where the patches were made, when they were made, why and from which version the concurrency is happened i.e the common ancestor. In this section we present a way to visualize the history with the concurrency information.

In P2P wiki, the history is not linear and some versions may be produced concurrently. We represent the history by a directed acyclic graph. The graph E consists of vertices and edges $E(V,E)$. Where the vertices (V) represent the page versions and the edges (E) represent the patches that convert one version into another. For our example in section 3, the history is shown in figure 3.

We will introduce some definitions related to the history before establishing our history representation.

- the history H at site S of page P, $H_s(P_i)$ is the set of revisions $v1 \ldots vn$ of the page P when integrated the patch i and the set of patches $1 \ldots i$ that convert one revision into another.
- when another patch $i+1$ is integrated the version history is $H_s(P_{i+1}) = H_s(P_i) + v(n+1)$.
- every page revision has a state PS this state may be user-produced or server-produced
- every applied patch i has a generation context GC_i. This context is to determine if this patch is locally generated or received from other sites, and the precedence and the concurrency relations with the other patches in the log file. These informations can be easily computed thanks to the concurrency detection mechanism. The generation context of pn_3, GC_{pn_3} is: pn_2 happened before pn_3 and $p_{n3} \parallel p_{n1}$

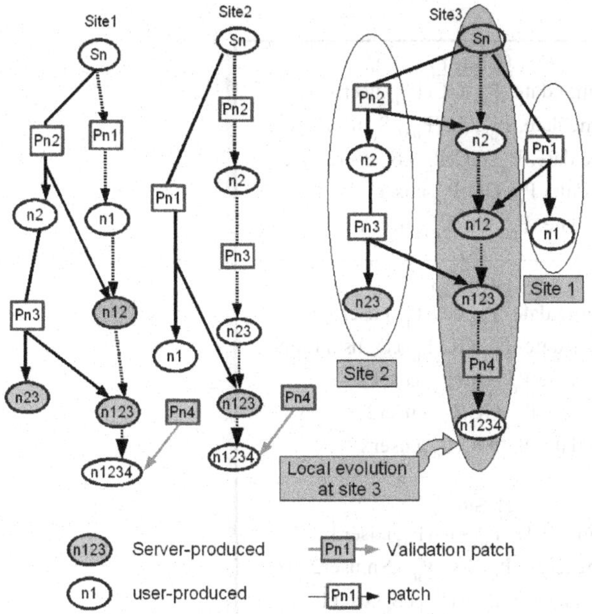

Fig. 3 `pages histories representation`

- the size of the concurrence: when the set of concurrent patches is extracted, in the case of server-produced page, the size of concurrence may be computed by counting the number of operations that are included in these patches. Because WOOT works at the line level then the size means how many lines are impacted by the concurrent operations. This size may give the user the impression that the version that has more concurrent operations has more priority to be reviewed.

In figure 3, we can see the evolution from *Sn*, suppose that we got this version by applying the patch P_{n0} made over sitex . *Sn* is a user-produced page and it is represented by a transparent vertex. At site 1 when P_{n1} is generated the state is stayed user-produces because this patch is not concurrent with the page state *Sn*. While when P_{n2} is received, the concurrency is checked and detected with the last patch, for this reason the page state is converted to server-produced with a shadowed vertex. The straight dotted line represents the page evolution over the local site while the other lines represent the patches and the states in the remote sites. For example at site 3, we show at the figure the local evolution and the remote integrated patches from site1 and site2. We distinguish the operation that transforms the server-produced

H(Site1)

n1234 : time,date, P_{n4},GC(P_{n4}),user3
n123 : time,date, P_{n3},GC(P_{n3}),S_n,user2,size
n12 : time,date, P_{n2},GC(P_{n2}),S_n,user2,size
n1 : time,date, P_{n1},GC(P_{n1}),user1
S_n : time,date, P_{n0},GC(P_{n0}),userx

H(Site2)

n1234 : time,date, P_{n4},GC(P_{n4}),user3
n123 : time,date, P_{n1},GC(P_{n1}),S_n,user1,size
n23 : time,date,P_{n3},GC(P_{n3}),user2
n2 : time,date, P_{n2},GC(P_{n2}),user2
S_n : time,date, P_{n0},GC(P_{n0}),userx

H(Site3)

n1234 : time,date, P_{n4},GC(P_{n4}),user3
n123 : time,date, P_{n3},GC(P_{n3}),Sn,user2,size
n12 : time,date, P_{n1},GC(P_{n1}),S_n ,user1,size
n2 : time,date, P_{n2},GC(P_{n2}),user2
S_n : time,date, P_{n0},GC(P_{n0}),userx

Fig. 4 the page history over the three sites

page to user-produced page by a shadow edge. At site 2, when *Pn*4 is integrated, it is not concurrent with any patch in the log and then it will change the state from server-produced to user-produced, it is represented as a shadow edge. The samething will happen sur site 1. Note that the state that have at least two outgoing edges is a common state while the state that is resulted from at least two incoming edges is a server-produced page.

Suppose that the user at site 3 validates the concurrency by generating the patch *Pn*4. This patch is considered as a validation patch even at site 1 and site 2 because it is not concurrent with last version state. When the user see this representation, he will understand that user 3 reviewed the page and he validated it by some operations in *Pn*4. The integration of this patch is shown at site 2 in the figure.

The question that must be asked now, is this representation is scalable i.e suitable for any number of sites in the network? This representation is suitable when the network size is very small but when we have a very huge network the graph will be complex and can't fit easily at the user's screen. For this reason, we adapted this representation to be seemed the current wiki history representation with some additional decorations for adding the concurrency informations. We represent it as shown in figure 4 and the function of each field is as follow:

1. the common ancestor has a shadowed background;
2. the server-produced versions in bold;
3. the user-produced versions appear normally;
4. the common ancestor version appears near the server-produced versions; when the user point to a server-produced version the versions until the common ancestor will be highlighted;
5. a link to the patch generation context is provided with every patch identifier;
6. we can indicate the size of concurrence in the page near the server-produced page. Being aware of the number of changes others users have made, helps the user to better understand the evolution of the page and easily collaborate with others to resolve the conflicts.
7. the date,time and the user name of the generation of each version. In addition, the case is like in the traditional wiki systems, the user can compare between any two versions but in this case the effects of concurrent modifications will be presented in a distinguish way.

We note that the versions order is not the same over sites. However, the patches that have a causal relation are integrated according to this relation. For example, over site 2, $Pn2$ is generated before $Pn3$, and therefore $Pn2$ must be integrated before $Pn3$ over all sites. When the system is stable i.e all the generated operations are propagated and integrated aver all sites, the final state and the common ancestor state are the same and set of integrated patches between these two states are also, the same over all sites. For example, at the page version $n123$ the system is stable, the page state $n123$ and the common state Sn are the same over all sites and the set of patches between Sn and $n123$ equal to $\{Pn1, Pn2, Pn3\}$.

5 Conclusion

we have presented here a non linear representation to the pages histories in P2P wiki systems. This representation is made ,firstly, by a directed acyclic graph and then it is made as the same form of the existing history representation in wiki for the scalability reasons. The objective of this representation is to show the page versions that are concurrently produced, and at any moment the user can compare between any two versions and see the operations that are integrated concurrently. The second step of this work is to evaluate this representation from the user point of view.

References

1. Open Source Software Engineering Tools. Online http://subversion.tigris.org/ (2006)
2. Wikipedia. The Free Encyclopædia that Anyone Can Edit. Online http://www.wikipedia.org/ (2006)
3. Allen, L., Fernandez, G., Kane, K., Leblang, D.B., Minard, D., Posner, J.: Clearcase multisite: Supporting geographically-distributed software development. In: Selected papers from the ICSE SCM-4 and SCM-5 Workshops, on Software Configuration Management, pp. 194–214. Springer-Verlag, London, UK (1995)
4. Alshattnawi, S., Canals, G., Molli, P.: concurrency awareness in P2P wiki . In: The 2008 International Symposium on Collaborative Technologies and Systems (CTS 2008), pp. 285–294. IEEE (2008)
5. Berliner, B.: CVS II: Parallelizing software development. Proceedings of the USENIX Winter 1990 Technical Conference **341**, 352 (1990)
6. Johnson, P.R., Thomas, R.H.: RFC677: The maintenance of duplicate databases (1976)
7. Lippe, E., van Oosterom, N.: Operation-based merging. SIGSOFT Softw. Eng. Notes **17**(5), 78–87 (1992). DOI http://doi.acm.org/10.1145/142882.143753
8. Molli, P., Skaf-Molli, H., Bouthier, C.: State treemap: an awareness widget for multi-synchronous groupware. In: 7th International Workshop on Groupware - CRIWG'2001. Darmstadt, Germany (2001)
9. Oster, G., Urso, P., Molli, P., Imine, A.: Data consistency for p2p collaborative editing. In: Proceedings of the 2006 ACM Conference on Computer Supported Cooperative Work, CSCW 2006, Banff, Alberta, Canada, November 4-8, 2006. ACM (2006)
10. Robbes, R., Lanza, M.: Versioning Systems for Evolution Research. In: Proceedings of the Eighth International Workshop on Principles of Software Evolution, (IWPSE '05), pp. 155–164. IEEE Computer Society, Washington, DC, USA (2005). DOI http://dx.doi.org/10.1109/IWPSE.2005.32
11. Sabel, M.: Structuring wiki revision history. In: Proceedings of the 2007 international symposium on Wikis, (WikiSym '07), pp. 125–130. ACM, New York, NY, USA (2007). DOI http://doi.acm.org/10.1145/1296951.1296965
12. Saito, Y., Shapiro, M.: Optimistic replication. ACM Computing Surveys (CSUR) **37**(1), 42–81 (2005)
13. Sun, C., Jia, X., Zhang, Y., Yang, Y., Chen, D.: Achieving convergence, causality preservation, and intention preservation in real-time cooperative editing systems. ACM Transactions on Computer-Human Interaction (TOCHI) **5**(1), 63–108 (1998)
14. Tichy, W.: RCS - A System for Version Control. Software - Practice and Experience **15**(7), 637–654 (1985)
15. Viégas, F.B., Wattenberg, M., Dave, K.: Studying cooperation and conflict between authors with history flow visualizations. In: Proceedings of the 2004 conference on Human factors in computing systems, (CHI '04), pp. 575–582. ACM Press (2004). DOI 10.1145/985692.985765. URL http://portal.acm.org/citation.cfm?id=985765
16. Weiss, S., Urso, P., Molli, P.: Wooki: a p2p wiki-based collaborative writing tool. In: Web Information Systems Engineering. Springer, Nancy, France (2007)

Distributed Secure Virtual File System Using FUSE

Shin Tezuka[1], Akifumi Inoue[2], Ryuya Uda[2], Kenichi Okada[3]

[1] Graduate School of Science and Technology, Keio University, 3-14-1 Hiyoshi Kohoku-ku, Yokohama-shi Kanagawa-ken 223-8522, Japan,
[2] School of Computer Science, Tokyo University of Technology, 1404-1 Katakuramachi, Hachioji-shi, Tokyo 192-0982, Japan,
[3] Faculty of Science and Technology, Keio University, 3-14-1 Hiyoshi Kohoku-ku, Yokohama-shi Kanagawa-ken 223-8522, Japan,
e-mail: tezuka@mos.ics.keio.ac.jp, akifumi@cs.teu.ac.jp, uda@cc.teu.ac.jp, okada@ics.keio.ac.jp

Abstract In this paper, we describe the implementation and evaluation of the distributed secure file system based on FUSE. A tremendous amount of content is now saved on file servers. File servers and network storage can also easily be installed in small organizations by using operating systems such as Linux. However, the storage capacity of PCs that are generally used is also increasing due to low-priced hard disks. The surplus disk capacity of these PCs is also increasing rapidly especially for work and research. Therefore, we need to use these surplus disks effectively by using distributed preservation of files. Furthermore, administrators may also inadvertently contribute to information leakage and falsification. Therefore, it has recently become necessary to ensure not only user authentication and communication pathways but security within the medium used for storage. Therefore, we implemented and evaluated a system we called JIGFS, which accomplishes secure file management based on a public key for all users. It also distributes and saves file using common PCs, and efficiently uses surplus disk capacity and the communication band. As it is implemented using Filesystem in USErspace (FUSE), users can use it like a conventional file system.

Please use the following format when citing this chapter:

Tezuka, S., Inoue, A., Uda, R., Okada, K., 2008, in IFIP International Federation for Information Processing, Volume 286; Towards Sustainable Society on Ubiquitous Networks, eds. Oya, M., Uda, R., Yasunobu, C., (Boston: Springer), pp. 161–172.

1 Introduction

Most companies and organizations now treat many forms of content as digital data. Also, file servers and network storage in small organizations can easily be built using operating systems such as Linux. However, the storage capacity of general use PCs (not servers) is also increasing due to low-priced hard disk drives. The surplus disk capacity of these PCs is also increasing rapidly especially for work and research. Therefore, we need to use these surplus disks effectively by using distributed preservation of files. However, when using file servers, a person has to manage these. This makes leakage or falsification of files possible if management is negligent. Finding a reliable manager can be difficult for small and medium-sized companies. Moreover, security breaches may also be discovered when servers are installed. Furthermore, administrators may also contribute to leaked and falsified information. Therefore, it has recently become necessary to ensure not only user authentication and communication pathways but the security within the medium used for storage.
As a result, we implemented and evaluated a system that we called the JIGsaw puzzle File System (JIGFS). This system achieves secure file management based on a public key for all users. It also distributes and saves files using common PCs, and uses surplus disk capacity and the communication band more efficiently. Moreover, as it is implemented based on FUSE [1], users can use it like conventional file systems.
The remainder of this paper is as follows: Sections 2 describes related work; Section 3 explains the design and implementation details; Section 4 portrays the evaluation; Section 5 discusses deployment and Section 6 concludes the paper.

2 Related work

In other related work, there have been many systems that distribute and save files to various PCs. However, security has not been a serious consideration, and these systems have been exposed to the risk of leaked information. Increased efficiency in disk capacity was also not taken into consideration as files were duplicated. // For example, Network File Systems (NFSs) [2] do not encrypt the file itself, transmit data, or ensure security between hosts. In contrast, there are systems that authenticate and encrypt transmitted data based on a Public Key Infrastructure (PKI), such as the Self-certifying File System (SFS) [3], the Secure SHell (SSH) File system [4] and the Grid Data farm (Gfarm) [5] that use grid technology and the Grid Security Infrastructure and Self-certifying File System (GSI-SFS) [6]. However in these systems, the performance is considered as important to treat large files, and do not have files encrypted within the media used to store them in their final locations. Therefore, they have not considered files in storage media being physically stolen or leaked by administrators who have authority to access servers.
There is also a system implemented as a file server with careful attention to security by our precedence work [7]. However, this system is not user friendly, because the

user needs to use client software like FTP. Thus, the new type of secure distributed file system is needed.

3 Distributed secure virtual file system

This section explains design and implementation of distributed secure virtual file system. How files are acquired and preserved with this system is introduced, and the criteria by which keys are managed and distribution places are selected to preserve them are described after that.

3.1 Outline of our system (JIGFS)

This section provides an outline of our system called JIGsaw puzzle File System (JIGFS), which allows effective sharing of communication bands and disk space, and creates a huge virtual file system that enables large-scale file distribution and mass storage. It uses two or more local area networks (LANs) and cooperates with a File System Gateway (FSG) as outlined in Fig.1. It differs from a general file server or network storage, and a file that is saved by this system is encrypted on a user's PC and divided into multiple data files with redundancy on an FSG, which are then saved in user PCs belonging to other LANs. Any falsification can be discovered through hash values. Thus, this system has a virtual RAID structure and a high level of security. This approach also enables disk space and communication bands to be efficiently shared.
All data regarding files and user information is saved in a database on the FSG. To

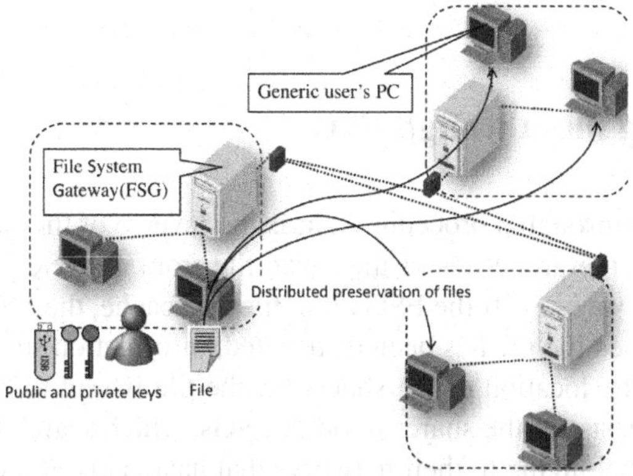

Fig. 1 Outline of our system

protect against failures, a database can be backed up by saving it in other networks as can be done for conventional files. The private and public keys needed to access files in this system are stored in small removable devices such as USB memories. Such devices are easy for users to carry with them and allow them to access the system from any PC, not only the PC they usually use. When a user mounts JIGFS, the FSG to which he belongs authenticates him with his public key and private key using challenge and response. And also, the user's public key is stored in the database with a certification by a certification agent (CA).

3.2 Saving files through FSG

When user application writes a file with this system through the following procedure and there are sequence diagrams of this in Fig.2.
First, a file is passed to JIGFS through FUSE like step 1 in the figure. And it is encrypted with a random key on the user's PC with a common key cryptosystem like step 2. This file is then sent to the FSG, along with file properties such as the file name, permission, the hash value of the file by Secure Hash Algorithm 1 (SHA-1, 160bits), and the common key. These properties and the common key are encrypted by the public key cryptosystem (See sect.3.4 for details). The FSG receiving the file caches it own disk with Least Recently Used (LRU) like step 3 in the figure. After that, FSG divides this into a fragment of two or more information units called shares with redundancy by using an Information Dispersal Algorithm (IDA) [8] described on step 4. And sends this to another FSG that has sufficient disk capacity and the available communication bands like step 5. Furthermore, an FSG that receives the distributed shares saves the data in the most compatible PC with respect to considerations such as boot-time characteristics. Finally, the FSG stores the file properties and information as to where the shares are saved to its own database. Moreover, when a saved file is shared with a group, the properties are saved to a database encrypted with the group's public key.

3.3 Retrieving files through FSG

A file is retrieved through a procedure that is the reverse of the save operation. The user's PC obtains the properties of the saved file from the FSG and decrypts these with the user's private key. If the FSG has a file as a cache, the FSG sends the file to the user's PC. When the file has been distributed, information such as the file name, permission, and the location of the shares for the file is sent to the FSG. The FSG sends search requests for the shares to other FSGs, which search for and collect the shares from PCs belonging to their networks that have parts of the target file. When the number of collected shares exceeds a threshold, the FSG restores the file from divided shares and sends it to the user's PC. After receiving the file, the user's PC

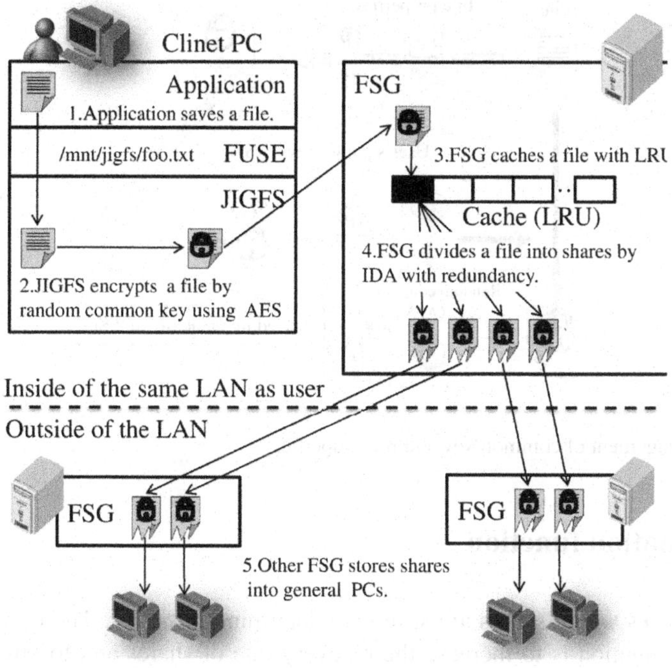

Fig. 2 Saving file through FSG

then decrypts the common key from the file properties with the user's private key. Finally, it decrypts the file with the common key and the user can access the file. The information integrity of the file can be confirmed by using a hash value for falsification requested when the file was saved. In addition, even if all the shares cannot be retrieved, the file can still be restored with less than the threshold number of shares because of redundancy in saving the file.

3.4 Common key and file properties

The random common key used to encrypt a file and the file properties in this system are encrypted with Rivest Shamir Adleman (RSA, key length: 1024bit) [9] on a user's PC and sent to an FSG. Although RSA code reinforcement is high, this process requires a long time. Thus, file encryption uses AES (key length: 128-bits) [10] with a random common key. The greatest concern is how the key is managed. After the body of the file has been encrypted using AES and the file properties and the key are encrypted in RSA, they are stored in a database on an FSG as outlined in Fig.3. This ensures the information is securely managed and the only the user's private key is needed to retrieve a file.

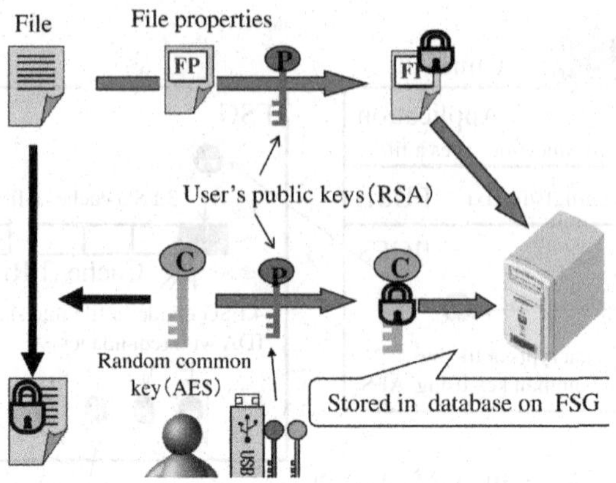

Fig. 3 Management of common key and file properties

3.5 Valuation function

The networks where shares are saved are determined by Eq.1. The purpose of this valuation function is to increase the recovery rate of shares and to effectively use the surplus disk area of all PCs, and the communication band between networks. A value is calculated to evaluate other FSGs from the FSG to which the user belongs. V means the surplus disk area, T means the throughput between networks and R means reliability. Moreover, w is a weighting factor that is determined from Eq.2 in a range from 0 to 1.0 according to the size and the reference frequency of a file. However, when the file size is larger than 4 Gbytes, consume a great deal of disk capacity, it is uniformly referred to as $w = 1.0$.

$$E = \{wV + (1-w)T\} \times R \tag{1}$$

$$w = \frac{\log(F_{size})}{10} \quad (0 \leq w \leq 1.0) \tag{2}$$

1. Boot-time characteristics
   The boot-time characteristics express by a bit series in what kind of time zone the user and PC have booted and joined the network. The period to express these characteristics is one day, and the grain size is 5-min intervals. One means a boot state and zero means an idle state in these characteristics. Therefore, 288 bits/day are used for expressing the boot-time characteristics per PC or user. This is saved for five weeks, and when all evaluations are calculated, decision by majority is used for all bits. For example, when the user was joined between 0:00-0:05 three or more days on Monday, the first bit of the boot-time characteristics is set to one.

2. Disk-capacity V
   V indicates how much disk area can be used, when a share is stored in a network. The user and the boot-time characteristics of his or her PC and surplus disk capacity are taken into consideration when calculating this value. For example, taking the user of boot-time characteristic S into account saves a file where there is a network A, B, or C used as a place to preserve it. The number of PCs belonging to a network is set to n, and the primary value of evaluating each network is calculated from Eq.3. Furthermore, the value to evaluate the disk capacity of Network A V_A is calculated by doing it relatively from Eq.4. In addition, $| S |$ and $| D |$ are the sum totals of the number of ones among the bit series that have boot-time characteristics, and $| S \wedge D_i |$ is the sum total of the bit set and one among those bitwise AND's.

$$V'_A = \sum_{i=1}^{n} \frac{| S \wedge D_i |}{| S |} C_{D_i} \tag{3}$$

$$V_A = \frac{V'_A}{V'_A + V'_B + V'_C} \tag{4}$$

3. Network throughput T
   This system measures the throughput of a network when some FSG downloads a share from a partner's FSG each time, and accumulates it. This value is saved for one month for every day of the week. For example, when there is a network A, B, and C, the throughput when FSG A downloads a share from FSG B is set to TP_{AB}; the throughput when downloading from FSG C is set to TP_{AC}. In this case, the throughput-evaluation value T_{AB} of FSG B assessed from FSG A is Eq.5.

$$T_{AB} = \frac{TP_{AB}}{TP_{AB} + TP_{AC}} \tag{5}$$

4. Reliability R
   R, which indicates the reliability of some network is calculated from Eq.8 This is used when calculating the evaluation value, E, of each network. The hash value of the saved share is periodically verified between FSGs. Tr calculated from Eq.6 is the rate of the number of times Hn that the partner's FSG answered correctly to the number of times Hc verified the hash value of the share. Moreover, Ma, which was calculated from Eq.7, expresses the rate of the number of PCs specified by m that boot in parallel with the user's PC.

$$Tr = \frac{Hc}{Hn} \tag{6}$$

$$Ma = \frac{1}{m} \times \sum_{i=1}^{m} \frac{| S \wedge D_i |}{| S |} \tag{7}$$

$$R = Ma \times Tr \tag{8}$$

5. Number of shares, and threshold
   Threshold k is determined by specifying the section with the original file size to make the share size after division by IDA regular. For example, when the original file size is 1 MB, the threshold is determined to be $k = 10$ so that share size can be set to 100 KB. Therefore, even if someone collects shares of comparable size, the possibility of restoring the original file is low. Since threshold k was previously determined, the redundancy of a file is determined by n, which is the number of divisions of a file. n is calculated from an Eq.9 using Ma. However, n is a natural number.
   The number of shares stored in each network is determined by the relative rate of the evaluation value, E. For example, n is the total number of shares, E_A is the evaluation value for Network A, and E_{sum} is the total evaluation value for all the networks. In this case, n_A, which indicates the number of shares distributed to Network A is calculated from Eq.10. However, n_A is a natural number.

$$n = [\frac{k}{Ma}] \tag{9}$$

$$n_A = [n \times \frac{E_A}{E_{sum}}] \tag{10}$$

4 Evaluation

4.1 Evaluation of file writing and reading

We evaluated file writing and reading using FUSE on this system. LANs A, B, and C were connected to provide the experimental environment. Three sets of PCs were connected to each LAN. One set of PCs belonging to LAN-A wrote and read files. Some of the PCs belonging to LANs-B and -C were at the storage location of the final shares. The specifications of the PCs used for evaluation are OS: Linux 2.4.31, CPU: Celeron 2.8GHz, Memory: 512MB, HDD: 120 GB, 5400 rpm, Cache: 8 MB (including FSG). All the communication bands connected to all PCs are 1 GBASE-T. The number of shares at the time they were divided by IDA was set to $n = 5$, and the threshold was set to $k = 3$.

Fig.4 plots the times for writing and reading files of various sizes. These times include the distribution of shares at the time of writing, and the collection of shares at the time of reading. We can see that this system is practical for files that contain a few megabytes, but by the time they reach 50 MB, it is no longer high speed, since about 180 sec is required. Based on these results, evaluation using the cache method on FSG is considered to be much faster, as shown in Fig.5. Even files of 50 MB take little more than 10 sec, and this is much faster than where distributed preservation of shares is included. Therefore, it is important to balance the risk of basing distributed preservation of shares and effective use of resources with the rapidity by the cache method.

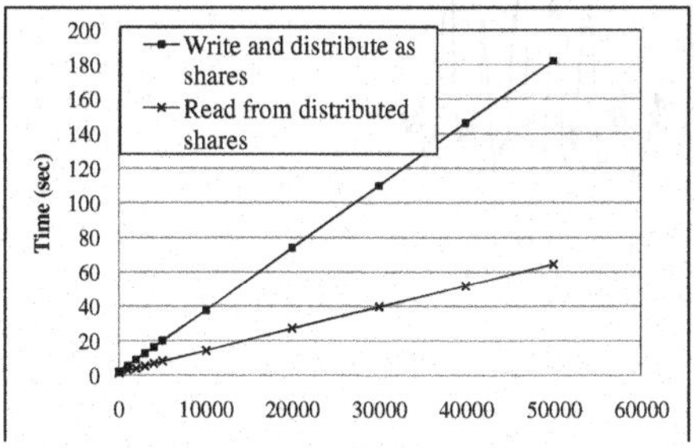

Fig. 4 Processing times for writing and reading files (Distribution of shares is included)

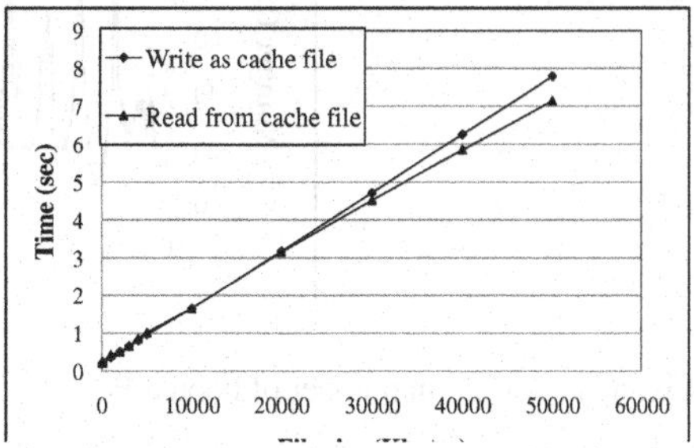

Fig. 5 Processing times for writing and reading files (Using cache on FSG)

4.2 Evaluation by simulation

Large-scale experiments are difficult to assess this system using two or more networks and numerous PCs. Therefore, the acquisition rate for successful file access and the cache hit ratio were simulated with a valuation function. The simulation environment is summarized in Table1 and LANs A-E were connected. Each PC belonging to the networks had 10 GB of surplus disk area, and the simulation took two weeks. Each users saved ten files per day, and restored them. We based the size of files to save on J. R. Douceur et al. [11] who investigated their sizes in various file systems. We used Sun Microsystems Inc.'s statistics for the re-reference frequency of files to restore [12]. Weighting factor w of a valuation function determines the initial value for the size of a file. After this, 0.1 is added every time a file is referred to.
We conducted the simulations based on the boot-time characteristics of real PCs. The boot-time characteristics were obtained from boot logs collected from five locations, such as laboratories in university, for two weeks over a six-month period. The transition in the number PCs booted during the two weeks is plotted in Fig.6. Since it was Sunday on the 1st, the 1st, 7th, 8th, and 14th occurred on weekends. Therefore, fewer PCs were booted than on weekdays. Because there were many users, especially in laboratories, who left their PCs without logging out or turning off the power, the number of PCs that booted around mid night was not completely zero.

Fig.7 shows the results for the acquisition rate. After simulation began, the acquisition rate to hit caches reached 100% within two days. After this, the hit ratio for caches fell gradually and the number of shares distributed in the PCs of other

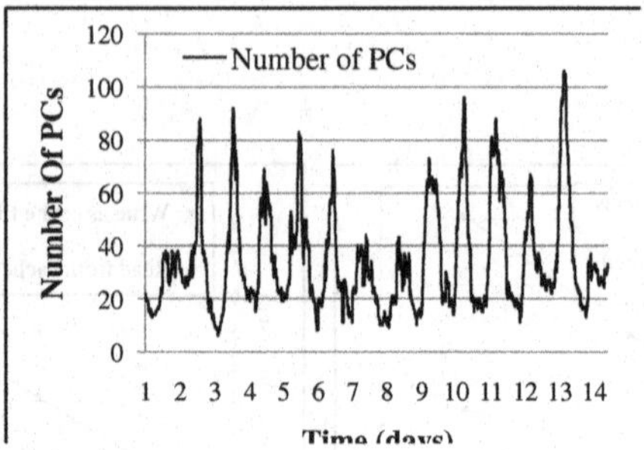

Fig. 6 Transition in number of booted PCs

Table 1 Simulation environment

Network	Number of PCs	Bandwidth(Kbps)	Cache(MB)
A	10	1000000	100
B	20	100000	200
C	30	10000	300
D	40	1000	400
E	50	100	500

networks to access files increased. Because the number of shares currently collected was less than the threshold to restore the original files by using IDA, the number of cases where files could not be accessed increased. The final acquisition rate reached 90% or more, where the cache hit ratio was about 50%. The relative capacity of shares stored in four networks (A-E) is plotted in Fig.8. We can see that although the distributed preservation of shares was concentrated on network A where there is a large communication band in the early stage, this is gradually rearranged in networks with a great deal of surplus disk capacity.

5 Discussions

In this system, the division of files by using IDA is slower than the throughput of encryption or that of the network. However, encrypted files are held once during a fixed term as a cache in FSG. Therefore, from the user's viewpoint, when the preservation of a file causes an encrypted file to be sent FSG, the process is completed. Moreover, since it is implemented as a virtual file system through FUSE, control returns immediately when the file is closed. Therefore, the response time that a user experiences is only the time to encrypt and send a file to an FSG. From the results in Fig.4, writing is practical if it is completed in a little more than 10 sec for a file of tens of megabytes, even if this is a few seconds less for a file of a few megabytes. The processing times differ according to whether it is necessary to read files, store

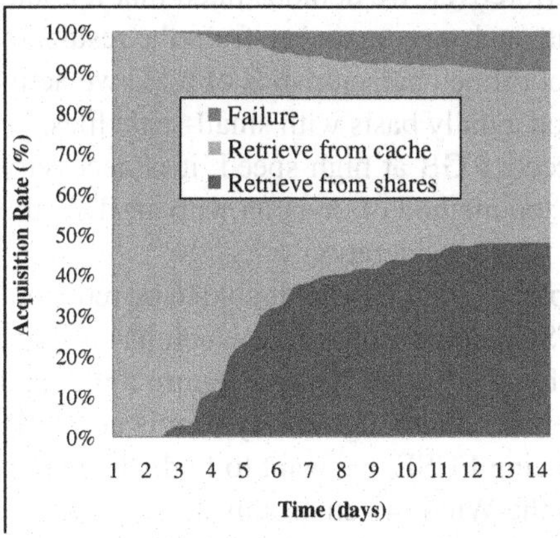

Fig. 7 Transition in acquisition rate

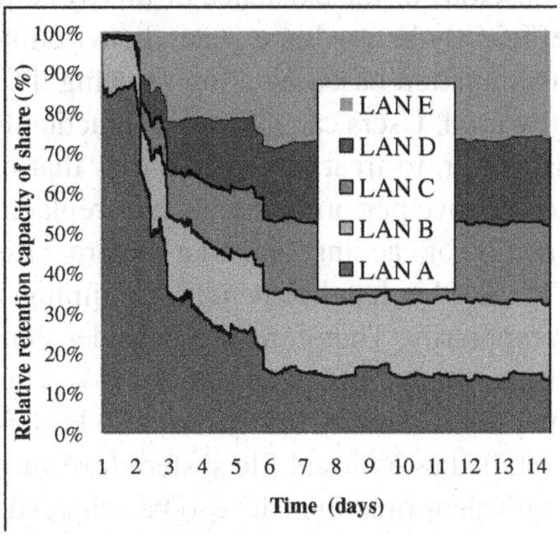

Fig. 8 Relative capacity of stored shares

them in an FSG as a cache, or collect shares, as shown in Fig.4 and Fig.5. When it is necessary to collect shares, it takes about 60 sec to open a file when the file size is 50 MB, about 12 sec to open 10 MB, and about 5 sec to open 1 MB where shares are distributed and saved in the network. When 50-MB files are stored in an FSG as a cache, it only takes about 12 sec to send them to a client PC and decrypt them at high speed. Thus, this system effectively uses resources by using distributed preservation of shares, and risk is reduced when obstacles occur. It can simultaneously be employed in practice by efficiently using the cache function of an FSG.
This system assumes an environment where all PCs are connected and can leave the network at any time; it arranges shares by taking boot-time characteristics into consideration. From the results of simulation, presented in Fig.7, which used the boot-time characteristic of real PCs, files were able to be accessed with a probability of 90% or more. Files in the simulation were rearranged periodically by recalculating the evaluation value of saved files. Fig.8 shows the relative capacity of the total number of shares stored in each network. Network A's throughput is particularly important immediately after this system has started. However, files that have not been referred to for a long time are rearranged to network E, which has surplus disk capacity. According to this structure, resources can be efficiently used from both respects of disk capacity and communication band.

6 Conclusion and Future works

This system manages files based on a public key for all users, encrypts the files, and provides them with distributed preservation. Thereby, it can reduce costs by not having to employ experienced administrators under exclusive contracts who understand advanced technologies. Moreover, as this was implemented using FUSE, users can use it together with conventional file systems. Therefore, users do not have to be

conscious of the existence of this system. Moreover, we demonstrated that it could efficiently be used in a general environment, such as companies, from the results of a simulation based on a log showing the boot time characteristics of a PC we actually used. Users can also use it practically on a daily basis with small-scale files. However, to treat large-scale files that exceed 1 GB at high speed, it is necessary to improve performance, such as replacing the method of division with an IDA, the method of caching, and take file properties into consideration.
On the other hand, depending on timing, a part of files may be unable to be retrieved temporarily. Therefore, we consider that FSG should starts PCs which has a share using Wake-On-Lan as future work. Thereby, a user can always acquire a file, and it is not necessary to boot useless PCs. Moreover, although the system is currently installed as a virtual file system for Linux using FUSE, we want to find whether an equivalent function can also be achieved in the Windows environment.

Acknowledgements This work is supported in part by a special grant from SECOM Science and Technology Foundation.

References

1. Filesystem in Userspace.: http://fuse.sourceforge.net
2. Inc. Sun Microsystems.: NFS, Network File System Protocol Speciation. RFC1094 (1989).
3. D. Mazieres.: Self-certifying File System. Ph.D. thesis, Massachusetts Institute of Technology (2000).
4. SSH Filesystem.: http://fuse.sourceforge.net/sshfs.html
5. O. Takebe, N. Soda, and S. Sekiguchi.: Gfarm v2: Design and Implementation of Global Virtual File System. IPSJ SIG Notes, 2004-HPC-099, pp.145-150 (2004).
6. S. Takeda, S. Date, and S. Shimojo.: A User-oriented Secure Filesystem on the Grid. 3rd IEEE/ACM International Symposium on Cluster Computing and the Grid (CCGrid2003) in Tokyo, Japan (2003).
7. S. Tezuka, R. Uda, A. Inoue, and Y. Matsushita.: A Secure Virtual File Server with P2P Connection to a Large-Scale Network. The IASTED International Conference on Networks and Communication Systems, No.527-138 (2006).
8. M. O. Rabin.: Efficient dispersal of information for security, load balancing, and fault tolerance. J.ACM, Vol. 36, pp.335–348 (1989).
9. R. L. Rivest, A. Shamir, L. M. Adleman.: A Method for Obtaining Digital Signatures and Public-key Cryptosystems. Communications of the ACM, 21, pp.120-126 (1978).
10. J. Daemen and V. Rijmen.: AES proposal: Rijndael, AES algorithm submission. http://nist.gov/aes (1999).
11. J. R. Douceur and W. J. Bolosky.: A large-scale study of file-system contents. ACM SIGMETRICS Performance Evaluation Review, vol.27, pp.59-70 (1999).
12. Inc. Sun Microsystems.: Information Lifecycle Management Technical Overview. http://government.hp.com/

Pricing for Maximizing Provider's Revenue in Multicast Content Delivery Services

Takehiro Kajita[1], Kyoko Yamori[2], Yoshiaki Tanaka[3]

[1]Global Information and Telecommunication Institute, Waseda University, Tokyo, 169-0051 Japan

kajita000@ruri.waseda.jp

[2]Department of Business Administration, Asahi University, Mizuho-shi, 501-0296 Japan

kyamori@alice.asahi-u.ac.jp

[3]Research Institute for Science and Engineering, Waseda University, Tokyo, 162-0044 Japan

ytanaka@waseda.jp

Abstract. With the rapid growth of broadband computer networks, users are inclined to use delivery services that can handle large-size content. When offering download service of popular contents, it is more useful to use a multicast system and deliver content to all users who request the content than using unicast system. Using a multicast system, the content server can increase the number of users and decrease user's waiting time. As a result, increasing user's WTP (Willingness To Pay) and the provider's revenue can be expected. In this paper, we suggest two content delivery methods which can be employed in the multicast content download services. We also discuss the provider's revenue of each delivery method. Using user's behaviour model in which a user participates in the service and leaves it, we show the relation between price for the service and user's participation rate of the service through simulation. The relation between price and the provider's revenue is also demonstrated in the simulation. In addition, in each delivery method, we show an optimal price which maximizes the provider's revenue.

Please use the following format when citing this chapter:

Kajita, T., Yamori, K., Tanaka, Y., 2008, in IFIP International Federation for Information Processing, Volume 286; Towards Sustainable Society on Ubiquitous Networks, eds. Oya, M., Uda, R., Yasunobu, C., (Boston: Springer), pp. 173–183.

1 Introduction

With the rapid growth of broadband computer networks, users are inclined to use delivery services that can handle large-size content. In the case of unicasting, the content server has to send the same data to many receivers repeatedly. With multicasting, on the other hand, the content server has to send the data only once. At the split node of the routing tree, the node copies the data and then sends them. Thus, a multicast system can reduce the network traffic.

When offering download services for popular contents, a multicast system is more beneficial compared to a unicast system for content delivery. If a network bandwidth can be used effectively, we can increase the maximum number of users who can participate in the service. And because of the increase in bandwidth during delivery, user's waiting time decreases, which results in an increase in user's WTP (Willingness To Pay) for the service, thereby increasing the provider's revenue.

However, during multicast deliveries, the content server ignores available bandwidth of current users in the multicast tree, therefore, narrowband users, i.e. users with low available bandwidth, may experience packet loss. In content download services, packet loss can cause serious problems. When the delivery speed is greater than the available bandwidth of the user, packet loss occurs and the buffer will overflow at an intermediate router along the path.

In order to avoid packet loss, the content server has to set the delivery speed to the smallest available bandwidth of the user in the multicast group in a multicast download service. In other words, as long as a link with low available bandwidth exists, every user in the multicast tree will experience degrade in performance.

In a content download service, user's utility corresponds to user's feeling with regards to the service and is determined by waiting time. If the user's utility increases, user's WTP for the service will increase accordingly. When user's WTP is high, the service provider can set a high price for the service and thereby increasing revenue. Therefore, in a multicast content download service, it is necessary to increase user's utility and WTP by using some solutions for narrowband users for maximizing the provider's revenue.

As a solution for narrowband users, this paper proposes using multiple speed scenario, which divides narrowband users and broadband users into separate groups and performs separate multicast deliveries for each group.

This paper assumes two delivery methods for narrowband users, and discusses the provider's revenue in the multicast content download service.

2 Multicast Content Delivery Services

2.1 Service Overview

In this paper, we assume a multicast download-type content delivery service. An example is a service which sells software and delivers it with a multicast system on the network. Conventionally, a unicast system was the mainstream method for download-type content delivery services. However, on the start of the delivery of popular contents, it is expected that requests from many users converges for a short time at the server.

In the case of unicasting, the link bandwidth is shared by all registered users, and if many users send their request to the content server within a short time, the delivery speed for all users will be too slow and network traffic congestion will occur. For this case, it is necessary to refuse the user's request in order to reduce the server load and network congestion. However, when a user's request is rejected by the service, the user's WTP will decrease accordingly [1]. Thus the provider will face a loss of revenue. When the provider's revenue is taken into consideration, the service provider should not refuse too many incoming requests.

On the other hand, in the case of multicasting, if many users send their request to the content server within a short time, the content server can collect their requests for one multicast flow and send the data set to all the registered users at once. Thus, a multicast system can reduce network traffic congestion and send the content to many users. Taking all this into consideration, it is more effective to use a multicast system to deliver popular contents. As a result, an increase in the provider's revenue can be expected. Therefore, in this paper, we assume a multicast download-type content delivery service.

In a multicast content download service, it is more reasonable to collect user requests over a period of time for later delivery over a multicast tree. This paper uses a service that performs multicast delivery to users within a given time interval, referred to as delivery interval.

In order to avoid packet loss, the content server sets the delivery speed to the smallest available bandwidth in the tree in a multicast download service. Therefore, user's waiting time increases greatly by the influence of narrowband users. In this paper, we suggest two delivery methods as solutions to the problem of narrowband users. And we compare the provider's revenue in each delivery method and examine the effectiveness.

The process of content delivery is shown in Fig. 1.

(i) Delivery requests originate from users and are sent to the content server.
(ii) The content server delivers content to all users using a multicast system.
(iii) Users pay for the service to the service provider.

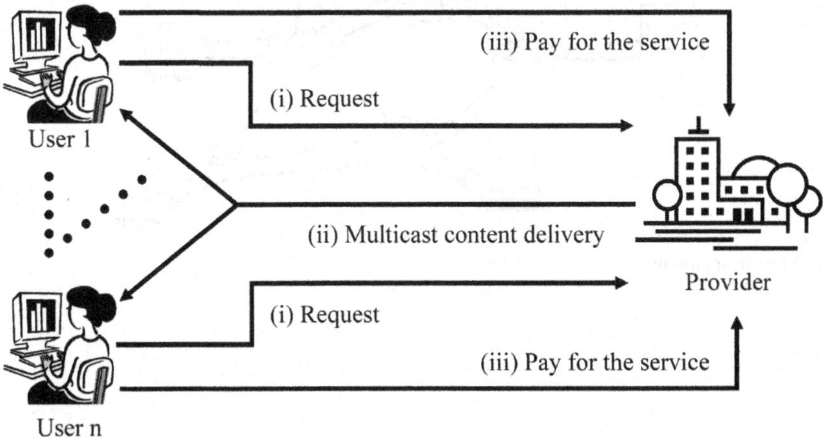

Fig. 1. The process of content delivery

In this paper, we assume a service which sells software, with content-based pricing scheme for the service pricing. Users who want to get content send requests to the content server. The content server collects their requests for one multicast flow and sends the data set to all the registered users at once. Users pay the content provider after receiving the contents. Because we assume that the pricing scheme for the service is content-based, it is necessary for the user to pay for the service whenever the user downloads contents. We assume pay per view.

2.2 Simple Scenario and Multiple Speed Scenario

We suggest two delivery methods as solutions to the problem of narrowband users which are exemplified in Fig. 2 and Fig. 3. The delivery method shown in Fig. 2 is called simple scenario in this paper. The simple scenario is a basic delivery method. In the simple scenario, the content server sets the delivery speed to the smallest available bandwidth in the multicast tree. If the simple scenario is adopted, the packet loss problem can alleviated considerably. However, the simple scenario has a problem -- if only a single user in the whole tree experiences the bandwidth bottleneck, the decrease in delivery speed will also cause the drop in user's WTP. On the other hand, the delivery method shown in Fig. 3 is called multiple speed scenario in this paper. The multiple speed scenario divides narrowband users and broadband users into separate groups and performs separate multicast deliveries for each group as a solution for narrowband users. This method enables delivery to broadband users with a high delivery speed, while not blocking requests from narrowband users.

Because in those delivery methods, delivery speed is adjusted to the slowest user's available bandwidth in the multicast group, even in the situation where packet loss occurs, it is expected that the amount of packet loss is minimal. Therefore, we can resend the lost data by using reliable multicast technology [2].

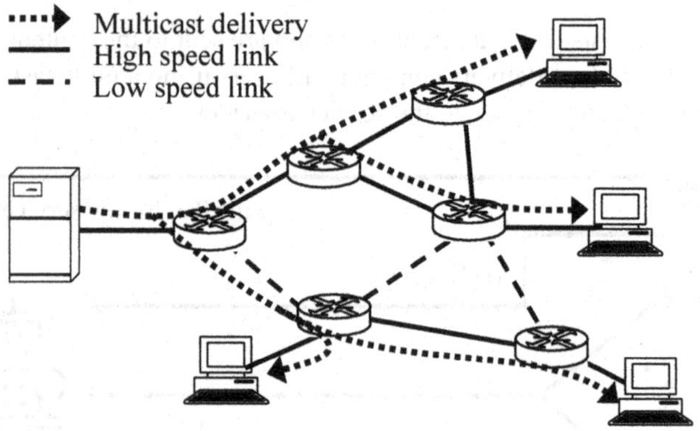

Fig. 2. Simple scenario

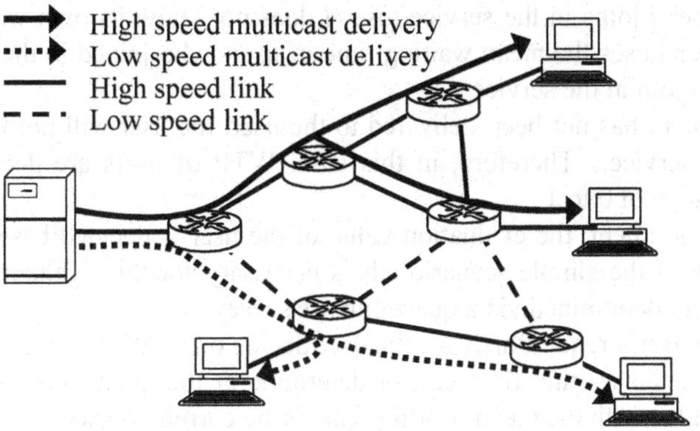

Fig. 3. Multiple speed scenario

3 User's Behaviour Model

3.1 User's Joining Model

In order to evaluate the services, we have to determine the user's behaviour model which in turn determines user participation. In this paper, we assume the user's behaviour model using user's WTP. WTP stands for the maximum amount of money that a user is willing to pay. WTP is often used for evaluation of services.

The following steps determine user participation: The user compares the price for the service and one's WTP. The result of this comparison determines whether the user joins in the service. If the user's WTP is higher than price for the service, the user joins in the service.

The WTP of user i is defined by Eq.(3.1).

$$U_i = \alpha \times v_i \tag{3.1}$$

where U_i is WTP of user i. v_i is the evaluation value of the service to waiting time of user i. α is the random parameter in the range of 0 to 1.

In this paper, v_i which is the evaluation value of the service to waiting time is given by:

$$v_i = 1 - 0.5 \times \frac{t}{x} \tag{3.2}$$

where t is the waiting time of user i. x is the mean waiting time in the simple scenario. Relation between user's waiting time and the evaluation value of the service is shown in Fig. 4. As shown in Fig. 4, v_i is 1 when the user's waiting time is 0. And v_i will decrease linearly with increase in waiting time.

We use the mean waiting time of the simple scenario as a standard in this paper. When the waiting time of user i is the same as the mean waiting time of the simple scenario, v_i becomes 0.5. Moreover, v_i has a variance within the range of -0.05 to 0.05.

Before user i joins in the service, user i does not know its own waiting time. In this case, user i uses the mean waiting time of users who joined in the service before user i tries to join in the service.

If the content has not been delivered to the user, the user will not know the mean time of the service. Therefore, in this case, WTP of users are decided randomly within the range of 0 to 1.

In this experiment, the evaluation value of the user is decided based on the mean waiting time of the simple scenario. It is necessary for this evaluation value to be more precisely determined via a questionnaire survey.

When the user's request arrivals, the user decide one's WTP using Eq.(3.1). However, because the waiting time cannot determine at this point, the user decides the evaluation value with the mean waiting time of the current service.

The user i compares the price p for the service and one's WTP. Where $U_i>p$, the user joins in the service. Where $U_i<p$, the user does not join in the service. Because we assume that the pricing scheme for the service is content-based, p is a price of one download per content. It is necessary for users to pay for the service whenever contents are downloaded. The condition of the decision and the probability of joining in the service are given by:

$$P_i=\text{Prob}(U_i>p) \tag{3.3}$$

P_i is the probability that user i joins in the service.

The user who participates in the service joins the multicast group of the requested content, and receives content with multicast content delivery.

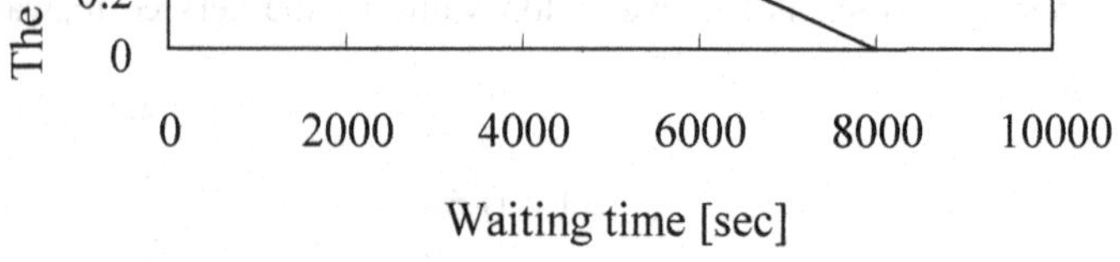

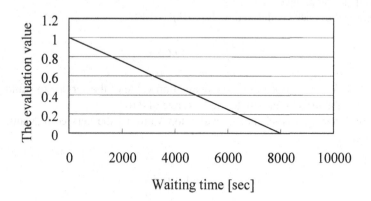

Fig. 4. The evaluation value versus waiting time

3.2 User's Leaving Model

Users pay the price p for the service after the content delivery. And then, users recalculate the evaluation value v_i' by using the user's waiting time of this content delivery using Eq.(3.2). New WTP U_i' of user i is decided by using this v_i'.

Where $U_i' < p$, the user might not be satisfied in spite of having paid for the price for the service. Subsequently, the user leaves service in time of one delivery interval and will not send any more requests to the service during that time.

In this paper, the arrival of user requests follows Poisson distribution. Arrival rate is set to $\lambda = 0.5$ [1/sec]. Basically, the number of users on the network is set to 5000. Arrival interval of a request from one user is set to 10000[sec]. The value of λ is calculated as $\lambda = \frac{5000}{10000}$.

During the time when some users leave the service, arrival rate λ' is calculated as $\lambda' = \frac{(5000-d)}{10000}$.

where d is the number of leaving users.

4 Evaluation Model

4.1 Network Model

This paper estimates the provider's revenue by performing a simulation. To generate network topology for the simulation, a random network of $N = 50$ nodes was created using the method proposed by Waxman et al [3].

Since Dijkstra shortest path search algorithm is used to define a path, there is a tendency for uneven utilization of network links due to concentration of traffic in a small portion of the network while the rest of the network is underutilized [4-6].

In our simulation, H-links with small background traffic, i.e. high available bandwidth, constitute the majority of all links in the network. L-links with big background traffic, i.e. low available bandwidth exist locally. Narrowband users are located on paths with at least one L-link, and in the case of broadband users, all links along the path are H-links.

In this paper, it is assumed that position of L-links changes with time. According to traffic measurement results in [7], the shortest interval between large changes in network traffic is about 1 hour. Therefore, in the simulated network the interval between changes in the link state is randomly selected each time from the range between 1800 and 5400 seconds. Links can become L-links as the results of the state change with the probability of β. Duly, the probability of change into an H-link is 1-β. The probability β, therefore, directly controls the ratio of narrowband users within the network. For the sake of simplicity, locations for bottleneck links are selected randomly. This paper does not consider the self-similarity of traffic.

In this paper, we set the bandwidth of H-link to 100Mbps and the bandwidth of L-link to 10Mbps. The probability of β which decides the ratio of L-link is set to 2%. Even if the probability β is low, there are cases where L-links can not be avoided. Therefore, in this paper, we do not consider methods which ignore L-links when multicast trees are constructed.

4.2 System Model

In this paper, we assume that ten kinds of content exist in the content server and users send requests to the server to get content. The size of the content in total constitutes

C= 450 Mbytes. The content is not rated by popularity, and each user is assumed to request all contents without partiality.

In this paper, arrival rate is set to λ= 0.5 [1/sec]. λ is used for all 10 contents. Therefore, the arrival rate λ_i of request for content i is easily calculated as λ_i= λ/10. Additionally, arrival rate λ is the arrival rate for the whole network and is constant throughout the whole simulation.

The server uses a fixed delivery interval. The server begins the content delivery, and starts a new delivery interval for the next delivery at the completion of each delivery interval. In the multiple speed scenario, because the server performs low-speed delivery for narrowband users and high-speed delivery for broadband users simultaneously, the server uses a fixed delivery interval for a high-speed delivery (H-Interval) and a fixed delivery interval for a low-speed delivery (L-interval) respectively.

When a user makes a request to the server, it decides which group this user belongs to according to the available bandwidth of the user, and adds this user to an appropriate multicast group. Narrowband users who are located on paths with at least one L-link are added to low-speed delivery group. And in the case of broadband users, since all links along the path are H-links, they are added to the high-speed delivery group.

In the multiple speed scenario, at the completion of H-Interval, the server begins to deliver ten different contents at the request of broadband users. Similarly for narrowband users, ten different contents are delivered upon request at the completion of L-Interval.

Assuming best effort network delivery, in order to deliver 10 distinct contents separately, the speed for each delivery should be 1/10 of link capacity or available bandwidth at the time.

In the multiple speed scenario, when a low-speed delivery uses too much bandwidth, there will be a negative effect on high-speed delivery. In order to avoid this negative influence on high-speed delivery, the server sets the upper limit speed of the low-speed delivery. In this paper, the speed limit is set to 1Mbps. And the L-Interval for low-speed delivery is set at double the value necessary to deliver content within the speed limit.

In the following examination, only the high-speed delivery interval is uses as a parameter in order to find the optimal delivery interval which would maximize the provider's revenue. An optimal delivery interval has been already discussed by [8]; therefore, this paper assumes an optimal delivery interval being set without the need to evaluate the argument for an optimal delivery interval.

5 Numerical Results

5.1 Relation between Price for the Service and User's Participation Rate

Relation between price for the service and user's participation rate of the service is shown in Fig. 5. User's participation rate is calculated using the number of users who actually participated in the service and the maximum number of users participating in the service theoretically.

As per the results in Fig. 5, user's participation rate in each delivery method decreases with the growth in the price for the service. However, the user's participation rate of the multiple speed scenario almost exceeds it in comparison with the user's participation rate of the simple scenario.

In the multiple speed scenario, if the user can join in the high-speed delivery group, the user can get content with a short waiting time. As a result, the user's evaluation value of the service becomes higher, and the probability that the user leaves the service becomes lower. Moreover, the evaluation value during user participation becomes higher because the mean waiting time of the multiple speed scenario is shorter than mean waiting time of the simple speed scenario. As a result, an improvement of the participation rate is seen compared with the simple scenario.
In this paper, the value which multiplies the evaluation value of the service and the random value of 0 to 1 is set to user's WTP. Therefore, even if there is a big difference in the evaluation value of the simple scenario and the multiple speed scenario, the difference of WTP becomes small. When it becomes clear that the value of parameter α is close to 1 through a questionnaire survey, it is expected

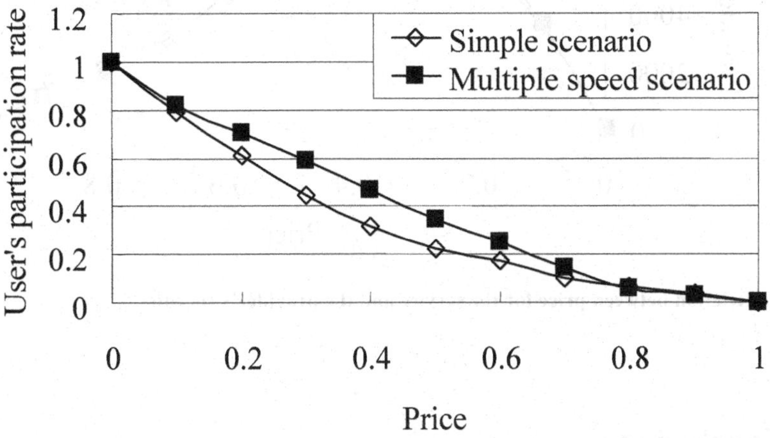

Fig. 5. Relation between price for the service and participation rate of the service

that the difference of the participation rate of the simple scenario and the multiple speed scenario becomes bigger.

5.2 Relation between Price for the Service and the Provider's Revenue

Relation between price for the service and the provider's revenue in one day is shown in Fig. 6. As per the results in Fig. 6, the optimal price which maximizes the provider's revenue is 0.4 in the multiple speed scenario. On the other hand, the optimal price which maximizes the provider's revenue is 0.3 in the simple scenario.

Because user's participation rate rises in the multiple speed scenario compared to the simple scenario, the price in the multiple speed scenario can be set higher. As a result, high provider's revenue can be obtained compared with the simple scenario as shown in Fig. 6.

In addition, when the server performs the delivery of popular content using unicast system, it is necessary to block user's request to reduce network congestion. However, when a user's request is rejected by the service, the user's WTP will decrease.

And because the link bandwidth is shared by all registered users in the case of unicasting, user's waiting time is longer than waiting time of the simple scenario and the multiple speed scenario. Therefore, the evaluation value of the service is lower than the simple scenario. Along with it, the provider's revenue is lower than the provider's revenue of the simple scenario.

As a result, using a multicast system for content download services effectively increases the provider's revenue. And we show that if the server uses the multiple speed scenario, the provider's revenue is maximized.

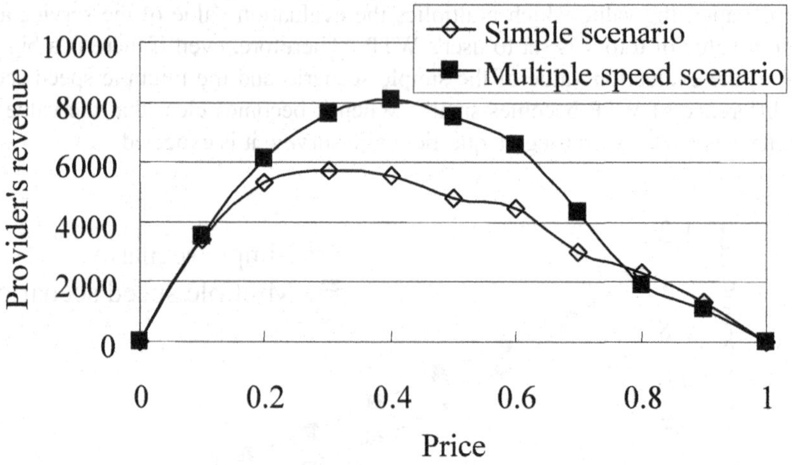

Fig. 6. Relation between price for the service and the provider's revenue

6 Conclusion

In this paper, we assumed the content download service with multicasting. And we assumed two multicast content delivery methods for narrowband users. This paper discussed the relation between price for the service and user's participation rate and provider's revenue in each delivery method.

As a result, this paper showed that if the server uses the multiple speed scenario, user's participation rate can be improved compared with the simple scenario. And the provider's revenue can be maximized by using multiple speed scenario. We also showed the optimal price for the service is 0.4.

In this paper, we used random parameter α to decide the evaluation value of the service. In future work, we plan to do a questionnaire survey to decide parameter α. Based on this, our result will be more reliable.

Reference

1 T. Kajita, K. Yamori, Y, Tanaka, "Relation between call blocking probability and willingness to pay in content download services," 2006 IEICE Technical Report, NS2006-37, pp.5-8, June 2006, in Japanese.

2 K. Robertson, K. Miller, M. White, and A. Tweedly, "StarBurst multicast file transfer protocol (MFTP) specification," Internet Draft, IETF, 1998.
3 B.M. Waxman, "Routing of multipoint connections," IEEE J. Sel. Areas Commun., vol.6, no.9, pp 1617-1622, Dec. 1988.
4 K. Fujimoto, S. Ata, and M. Murata, "Statistical analysis of packet delays in the internet and its application to playout control for streaming applications," IEICE Trans. Commun., vol.E84-B, no.6, pp.1504-1512, June 2001.
5 T. Ogura, J. Suzuki, A. Chugo, M. Katoh, and T. Aoyama, "Stability evaluation of a dynamic traffic engineering method in a large-scale network," IEICE Trans. Commun., Special Issue on Internet Technology III, vol. E86-B, no.2, pp.518-525, Feb. 2003.
6 S. Shioda, T. Yagi, and K. Mase, "A new approach to the bottleneck bandwidth measurement for an end-to-end network path," IEEE International Conference on Communications (ICC 2005), Vol.1, pp.59-64, Seoul, Korea, May, 2005.
7 R. Kawahara, K. Ishibashi, T. Hirano, H. Saito, H. Ohara, D. Satoh, S. Asano, and J. Matsukata, "Traffic measurement and analysis in an ATM-based internet backbone," Comput. Commun., vol.24, Issues 15-16, pp.1508-1524, Oct. 2001.
8 T. Kajita, E. Takahashi, K. Yamori, and Y. Tanaka, "Optimal delivery interval and call admission control of multicast content delivery based on users' utility," International Network Optimization Conference (INOC 2005), Session TB4, pp.B2.434-B2.441, Lisbon, Portugal, March 2005.

Personalized Public-Transport Guidance Using Mobile End Devices

Stefan Christmann, Thorsten Caus, Svenja Hagenhoff

University of Göttingen, Department of Information Systems and E-Business, Platz der Göttinger Sieben 5, 37073 Göttingen, Germany

{schrist, tcaus, shagenh}@uni-goettingen.de

Abstract. Mobility is a vital part of human life. Mobility needs can be met in a variety of ways: motorized and non-motorized individual traffic, local public transport using buses and trains, or mixed systems like taxis and park and ride systems. Individual traffic in particular causes major environment problems and problems of traffic congestion. Strengthening public transport is often favored, but this preference is not reflected in the number of local transport users. This phenomenon can be explained by the fact that a central problem involved in local public transport usage is its complexity. The article presented here develops demands on a personalized local public transport guidance system, analyzes existing systems and presents a solution for a personalized support system for users of local public transport systems. The software Hermes was developed for this purpose. It accompanies the travelers through all steps of public traffic usage - from checking time tables to purchasing tickets to a navigation system for pedestrians guiding the user to a street address destination.

1 Introduction

Without noticing most people put distances behind them every day that add up to several kilometers. We drive to work, to the supermarket, to the post office; we visit friends and go to the cinema. Mobility, understood as the opportunity to move around, is an important part of our lives. Opaschowski, a sociologist, even sees mobility as a "vital principle for individual and society" [1]. There are multiple ways of satisfying mobility needs [2]. Although transport is important for society, it always

Please use the following format when citing this chapter:

Christmann, S., Caus, T., Hagenhoff, S., 2008, in IFIP International Federation for Information Processing, Volume 286; Towards Sustainable Society on Ubiquitous Networks, eds. Oya, M., Uda, R., Yasunobu, C., (Boston: Springer), pp. 185–195.

involves undesired side effects, too. The negative effects of individual motorized transport on the environment and the traffic situation in the cities are a steadily recurring issue in politics and society. There is a general agreement that local public transport needs to be strengthened and motorized individual traffic should be cut back.

The complexity of local public transport is its central drawback. Time schedules need to be found and understood, connections must be combined and adequate tickets purchased. This is usually not a problem for planned movements like the routine trip to work, but unplanned movements usually pose problems as otherwise used planning tools may not be available in such situations. Very often the difficulties involved in using public transport systems lead to using individual means of transport if spontaneous needs for movement are involved.

Mobile end devices, e.g. PDAs, smart phones or mobile telephones are especially suitable to support travelers because these devices can be used any time without booting. As the diffusion rate of mobile telephones is high in industrialized countries (e.g. Italy 123%, Germany 102%, Japan 80%, USA 77% [3]), a rising number of people are accustomed to using them. Many mobile telephones support the installation of additional software providing access to the local data of the user and the ability to access further data via the mobile network [4]. If the present geographical position of the device can be located too, its application as a personal assistant to support the user in his or her travel planning, and especially to facilitate spontaneous movements, becomes achievable. In this sense, transportation companies could give mobile applications for local transport guidance to their customers to increase usage of their transportation system. Other functions, like purchasing tickets or recommending restaurants or entertainment facilities, are also thinkable. The limitations of end devices must be taken into account if such systems are to become really useful. These shortcomings include small screens, low data processing capacities, uncomfortable navigation and data input [5,6,7];. A possible way of coping with these shortcomings is to take account of the present context of the user and his or her personal preferences and adapt the application automatically [8].

The present article aims at developing demands towards such an application for individualized local public traffic guidance, comparing it to existing solutions and presenting a solution in the form of the prototype implementation of a system called *Hermes*: Hermes (Greek Ἑρμῆς, a pile of marking stones) in Greek mythology was the messenger of the Gods as well as the protector of ways, traffic and ramblers [9].

2 Application Situations and Motivations

Computer-based, personalized public transport guidance systems have a multitude of possible application situations. The following description of six possible situations is supposed to provide an overview.

Situation 1: unplanned movement occasion: Due to a spontaneously arranged meeting, a café has to be reached. The application finds out the best public transport connection, guides the user to the nearest station or bus-stop, provides information on the station of exit and guides him or her from there to the final destination. Personal preferences and characteristics of the user are taken account of when establishing the connection. Should he or she be a member of a car-sharing company, for example, the usage of this service would be one of the possible options offered by the application.

Situation 2: change of means of transport in a planned movement: Due to very bad weather or a defective vehicle, the daily trip to work cannot be done by car or bicycle. The planned movement has to be done by public transport. The application guides the user to his or her workplace and purchases one or several adequate tickets which are presented to the ticket collector as bar codes. If the user is eligible for fare reductions or has a season ticket, this will be taken account of when purchasing the tickets.

Situation 3: support in planned movement situations: During breakfast the application checks the planned route. The evaluation of the information shows that the scheduled bus will be seven minutes late due to roadworks and there is still time for another cup of Sencha.

Situation 4: occurrence of an exceptional situation during planned movement: On his way to work, the public transport user misses a connection. The application at once establishes alternative connections as well as a footpath that could be used; additionally, it offers to call a taxi automatically. The taxi can be paid using the integrated pay function. The application can also calculate the new time of arrival and communicate it, for example by SMS, to a target person.

Situation 5: planned movement on unknown territory: On a business trip to a big city the user feels insecure because the town is unknown to him or her and the variety of means of transport is great. He or she is guided through the unknown system of traffic lines, tariff systems and stations, including guidance when changing at big traffic junctions or changing from one means of transport to another.

Situation 6: change of time schedule: While on the public transport, the next appointment is postponed or cancelled. The application provides a changed travel route and opportunities for entertainment or activities adapted to the user at the present location or at the destination.

In addition to usage situations, motivations for the usage of such an application have to be taken into account. The most important motivation is the user's wish to change his or her geographic location successfully, i.e. to reach a destination. However, there are also additional demands, e.g. the user wants to reach his or her destination on time, using as little time and money as possible; comfort and safety of the means of transport also play an important role [10]. Choosing the optimal mode of transport also depends on the user's needs, aversions and preferences.

Users can be sure that the application will definitely take them to their destination and provide support in bridging waiting times, if necessary. While users of motorized individual means of transport have full control over their times of departure and routes, public transport users depend on routing and means of transport controlled by third parties. Subjectively as well as objectively the user gains sovereignty through the high availability of information, the objective-centered processing of information and the uninterrupted support provided.

Last but not least, the application is able to reduce stress, understood as a reaction of the human body to adapt to its surroundings [11]. Distress, the disruptive form of stress, is generally seen as a negative emotion. It emerges especially when somebody needs to handle manifold information, is forced to decide unter time pressure and reach his destination unconditionally [12]. In local public transport this is definitely the case. As the application takes over information handling and partially decisions from the end user, stress can be reduced. On the other hand, the mobile end device usage as a new source of stress has to be considered.

3 Demands Towards a Mobile Personalized Public Transport Guidance System

Based on the application situations and motivations for usage described above, there are certain requirements towards a mobile application for a personalized local transport guidance system. Such an application must be aimed at a door-to-door guidance of the user. Based on the user's personal preferences and characteristics, it must process information, prepare activities and carry them out. The application must not just support single activities, but must be process-oriented. It has to support all required activities of public transport guidance.

The target group consists of all public transport users owning a mobile computer. The application must be available and operational at any time in order to facilitate also unplanned movements and to guarantee reliable public transport guidance. It has to be able to retrieve data from data networks; however, it also has to be able to cope with short-term losses of connectivity (e.g. in a tunnel).

Taking account of the users' profile, the application has to combine means of public transport, purchase tickets and pay for them, order means of transport (e.g. taxis) and guide the user via footpaths. It has to inform the user about the means of transport selected and about his or her present location to provide support in finding and using means of transport. The system has to indicate forthcoming bus stops and calculate when the user must get off the bus. It must be possible to change travel plans any time, whether caused by the user or by delays of public transport vehicles. This includes support to the user to bridge waiting time, e.g. by indicating a suitable café or restaurant or informing waiting persons (e.g. with text messages).

There are also a number of non-functional requirements. To keep user inputs low and to make the application easy to use, it should be adaptable to the user's context [13]. Most important are adaptations to preferences and characteristics, personalization and location, i.e. adaptation to the present geographic location. The usage of resources should be optimized, causing as little costs as possible. The most important cost factor in mobile applications is usually the network connection, and that is why data transfer should be minimized. As battery life time is another limitation, this resource must also be taken into account. The application should be able to run on a maximum number of different devices in order to distribute it as widely as possible [14].

The limitations of mobile end devices have to be taken account of, too. These are to be found especially in the input and output facilities and in the processing and storage of data. Context adaptation should help to make a great deal of user input unnecessary, as for example the local position is recognized automatically. The user profile should be edited on a normal PC and then transferred to the device. Mobile end devices often have functions that are useful for local transport guidance. The address of destination could, for example, be retrieved from the address book of a mobile telephone. It would also be possible to use the inbuilt calendar or text-messaging services (like SMS) as a means of communication. The application must be easy to use in order to find acceptance. Therefore it has to be adequate for the task, capable of self-description, conducive to learning, steerable, conform to expectations, error-tolerant and individually adjustable (ISO 9241 Standard). Data security and security on the level of device, transfer, transport and application also have to be assured as the application deals with sensitive data due to the processing of the present geographical position, the geographical destination and personal characteristics and preferences of the user. Otherwise privacy issues could be a central drawback for the usage of *Hermes*.

4 Existing Solutions for Public Transport Guidance Systems

Existing solutions include conventional as well as newer systems in the form of web-based or mobile applications. The public transport guidance systems are divided within the three kinds of software mentioned above according to their purpose, as shown in Figure 1.

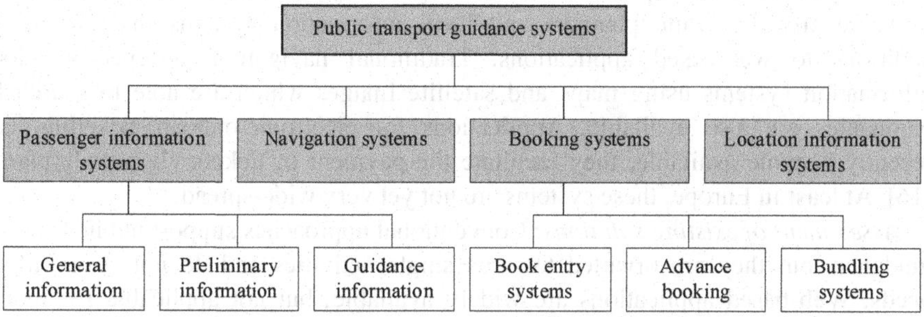

Fig. 1. Classification of public transport guidance systems

Conventional approaches: Public transport companies use printed time schedules for the general and preliminary information of passengers. These include general overviews as well as handy schedules for single routes. These are also displayed at the stations. Electronic information systems are also to be found there; they are either simple ticket issuing machines or kiosk systems with detailed information and advice functions. The information thus available is usually static; it can only show the intended state of the traffic system. Guidance information is provided through signboards and signposts at crucial traffic junctions or stops. In addition there are voice announcement, and increasingly also optical systems like digital sign boards. These systems are called "dynamic passenger information systems" [15]. Information about the next stop is increasingly announced automatically and displayed on a signboard inside the means of transport.

Web-based approaches: General information is often provided on the web sites of public transport companies. Web-based applications facilitate door-to-door guidance, providing search functions for train stations or stops, addresses and interesting sights. Certain context information, like the number of fellow travelers, reduced ticket prices on offer or preferences may be included. The application often calculates connections using multiple modes of transport, offers printouts of connections and ticket order and place reservation where applicable. Navigation is done by route planners which calculate routes using addresses and points of interest. These programs generate instructions which can be printed together with a map. Meanwhile, there are also some booking systems available from the Internet. Taxis and hailed shared taxis can be booked online in many cities, costs for car rental and car-sharing can also be calculated and vehicles booked. The bundling of traffic can be done by applications like agencies for arranged lifts; this is where users can search for appropriate lifts or offer them to others. Similar arrangements could be made for the sharing of train tickets. Local information systems facilitate the search for companies and the display of their locations on road maps or satellite images.

Mobile applications: Meanwhile there are some mobile applications in the area of public transport guidance systems. They differ in their tasks but also in the mode of implementation. Mobile travel information applications can check out connections from station to station, enter the connection into the calendar of the mobile phone and perform a simple kind of travel guidance: they list all stations to be passed through using the planned times of arrival and departure. A selection of means of transport once chosen can be used several times. More recent applications provide additional service in the form of maps of the surroundings, site plans and local information.

There are also route planners and local information systems that are mostly additions to web-based applications. Traditional navigation systems and local information systems using maps and satellite images which are able to search for companies are also available. Applications for electronic-onboard-ticketing have recently become available; they facilitate the payment of tickets via mobile phones [16]. At least in Europe, these systems are not yet very wide-spread.

Assessment of existing solutions: Conventional approaches support public transport guidance, but they are oriented towards single activities and do not cover all the needs. Web-based applications are widely available, but not applicable for mobile use. Existing travel information systems for PDA, smart phones and mobile phones can be used on the move, but they fail in classic public transport situations, e.g. underground routes or areas not covered by mobile networks. Only mobile application with intermediate data storage facilities which remain active in situations where there is no mobile network are eligible for a reliable public transport guidance system.

All existing systems are not process-oriented and have functional gaps (ticketing, payment, footpath guidance, support in finding and using means of transport, support in emergencies). Furthermore, they have a low degree of context adaptability (personalization of preferred means of transport, software localization through language adaptation).

5 Design of the Application

From the requirements it becomes clear that four main procedures to be executed by the user are indispensable: The user must be able to start using the public transport

without delay, plan the use of public transport, display local information on his or her present location and purchase tickets.
The actual use of public transport is the most complex process and will therefore be described in more detail. It always starts by establishing the optimal combination of modes of transport. If there are several variants to choose from, the user must select one. The guidance will then consist of a combination of footpath guidance, ticketing and passenger information.

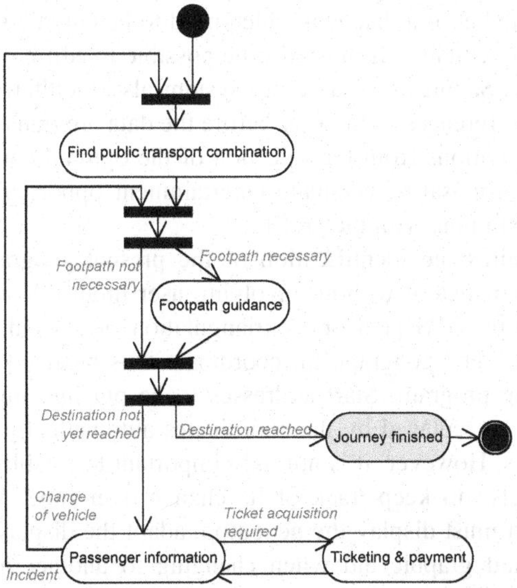

Fig. 2. Concatenation of sub-processes in local public transport guidance

Figure 2 provides an overview of the possible combinations. The user can retrieve additional data on his or her present location any time, e.g. in waiting situations. Maps of the surroundings, information on restaurants, cafés and cultural institutions, including distances, will be provided and the user guided to these locations.

The realization of the context adaptation also needs to be looked into. The application must be personalized, i.e. adapted to the technical, social and physical user context [17]. The technical limits of mobile end devices are the most important factors for the adaptation to the technical context: displays, mobile networks, free memory and energy level are the most important variables. Network connections are characterized by their quality, the amount of data transferable per time unit and usage costs. When the connection is of high quality, cost-efficient and has a high bandwidth (e.g. a WLAN) more data should be transferred than when there is a low-quality, expensive connection with low bandwidth. However, the quantity and quality of the data is to be kept unchanged in the process of adaptation, only the time of transfer should vary. Therefore the software has to anticipate the data to be transferred. If there is, for example, a cost-efficient and effective connection at the start of the journey, all data concerning connecting and destination stations should be transferred in one go - a process called hoarding. If the connection is cost-efficient but slow, the data are transferred successively in small batches; this is called prefetching [18]. However, this process also depends on the available memory. The output of the application should depend on the size of the mobile device's display, its level of activity on the energy level.

Adaptation to the user's context is the most important point in context adaptation as it includes the user's needs, preferences, aversions, competencies and prior knowledge (personalization) as well as the adaptation to the present geographical position (localization). Personalization needs a user profile reflecting the relevant characteristics of the user. It must be possible to edit this profile on the end device because it may change during the journey. The user may, for example, have purchased a season ticket or a discount which need to be entered into the profile. The profile must be easily editable. It must also be possible to edit it on a PC and transfer it to the end device. Saving it on a server system also facilitates the adaptation of information to the preferences of the user before the data are transferred to the mobile end device. All calculations from the selection of the optimal combination of means of transport to the proposal of adequate entertainment opportunities in exceptional situations have to be in tune with the profile.

Localization requires the identification of the present geographic positions and should be done automatically without involving user input. Most appropriately it is done satellite-based by GPS [19] or by triangulation of several UMTS-, GSM- or WLAN-base stations. The geographical coordinate thus received can be used in the further course of the program. Start addresses to be put into input boxes in forms could, for example, be replaced by the coordinates automatically retrieved and used for calculating routes. However, it is not only important to establish the geographical position once, but also to keep track of its change over time. While using public transport, the system must display the next stop, adapt the display automatically and change to textual and graphic aid when changing to another means of transport. Adaptation to the physical context is a complicated form of context adaptation as the physical context is difficult to capture with most mobile end devices. While the time of day is readily available, things like temperature and weather can only be estimated indirectly via globally connected sensor networks; characteristics like noise level and illumination are usually not retrievable. The application should minimize distances to be bridged on foot when the weather is bad and offer route combinations with this option only as a further choice. The same is applicable if the user has entered an aversion to walking on foot during darkness in the user's profile.

The requirements and the technical concepts show that a mobile application for public transport guidance cannot consist of a software component only. It requires the saving and editing of the user profile, which is needed for personalization, on a stationary PC. To minimize data transfer via mobile networks, the data must be adapted to the end device before they are transferred there. Therefore, a client-server-architecture was chosen for *Hermes*.

The server serves as a data storage device for the profile, web server for editing the profile and the download of the client component and as so-called "transcoding-proxy" [20]. The client component requests data from the server, transferring its context when doing so. The server component retrieves the data from its own data stores or from other server system, adapting them to the client and its context before transferring them. External data available for this project is for example the data of the geographical information system (GIS) Microsoft MapPoint®. Alternatively, sources like OpenStreetMap and GeoNames could by used.

6 Implementation of the Application

Client and server components of *Hermes* have been developed in Java. It generates a platform-independent bytecode executed on the end device by a virtual machine (VM [21]). Platform-independency makes Java the optimal programming language for this project. Mobile phones, PDAs and smart phones can be used as hardware on the client side. Java-Edition J2ME ("Micro Edition") will be applied on the end device. It has been specially adapted to the memory size and capacity of mobile end devices [22]. The server component runs on servers, personal computers and notebooks. It requires J2EE - the "Enterprise Edition" of Java and therefore its most complex version. A server application capable of processing Java Server Pages (JSP) and executing Java Servlets is also needed. This could be the Apache Tomcat® Server. Furthermore, a database is needed to save the data on the server and keep them ready.

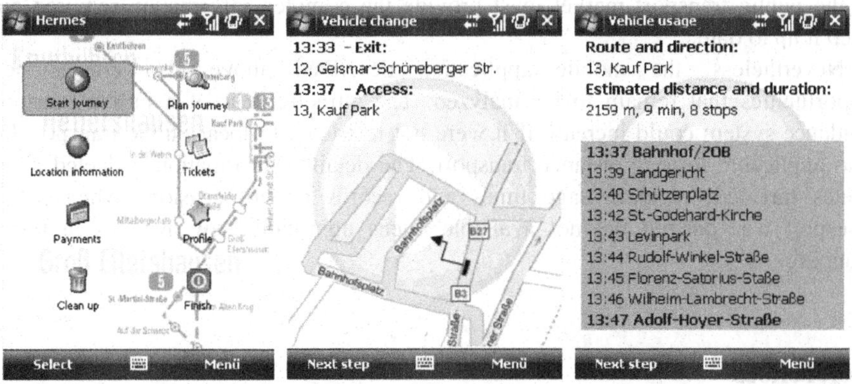

Fig. 3. Screen shot of an exemplary public transport use (main screen, change of vehicle, next stations)

A prototype was developed for the client component showing the process-oriented sequence of the application (cf. Fig. 2). All central functions (local traffic planning and implementation, local information, ticket purchase, payment, profile editing) were implemented prototypically. Figure 3 shows an extract of the sequence of a typical public local transport usage. An Internet page for registration, profile editing and the download of the application to the end device or to a PC was created as server component. It generates output in XHTML which can be displayed by browsers like Internet Explorer®, Firefox®, Safari® or Opera®.

7 Conclusions and Future Work

The ongoing development of mobile end devices and the steadily progressing standardization of platforms and frameworks [23] for the use on mobile end devices create an ever increasing number of applications for mobile use. The easy use of software on mobile end devices is a decisive factor in this context. Attention should not only be paid to the analysis and development of user interfaces and input devices but it should also be borne in mind that it is important to minimize the amount of data to be entered and the number of interactions required between user and application. This can be done through context adaptation and especially through personalization. If the application knows the preferences, characteristics and aversions of the user it can make pre-selections suiting the user or automatically initiate actions.

The implementation of the *Hermes* prototype shows how using public transport can be improved by a mobile application. The application solves central weaknesses of using public transport for the user of mobile end devices: It manages the retrieval of complex combinations of modes of transport and helps in emergencies. Therefore the application raises the attractiveness of public transport use for a growing number of persons. It can help to reduce individual motorized traffic if it becomes widespread. However, the implementation of the prototype also shows its limitations: The user must own a mobile end device and be in a location covered by mobile networks (at least when starting on the public transport journey). If the end device fails or runs out of battery, the user remains without guidance. In addition, the players in the public transport market must provide the complex information required and keep it up to date.

Nevertheless, the mobile application described above also creates new opportunities that remain to be analyzed. The attractiveness of a public transport guidance system could increase if it were not restricted to local public transport but also applicable to long-distance transport. The detailed information collected about routes traveled, regular usage times and records about occasions when public transport was desired but not available opens up totally new avenues in traffic planning.

References

1. H.W. Opaschowski, Freizeitökonomie: Marketing von Erlebniswelten, 2nd edition, Opladen, 1995.

2. B. Zemlin, Das Entscheidungsverhalten bei der Verkehrsmittelwahl, Lohmar u. A., 2005.

3. Central Intelligence Agency, The CIA World Factbook, 2008.

4. T. Hess, S. Figge, H. Hanekop, I. Hochstatter, D. Hogrefe, C. Kaspar, B. Rauscher, M. Richter, A. Riedel, M. Zibull, Technische Möglichkeiten und Akzeptanz mobiler Anwendungen – Eine interdisziplinäre Betrachtung, in: *Wirtschaftsinformatik* 47 (2005) 1, pp. 6-16.

5. D. Billsus, M. Pazzani, J. Chen, A Learning Agent for Wireless News Access, Proceedings of the 5th international conference on Intelligent user interfaces, 2000, pp. 33-36.

6. B. Smyth, P. Cotter, Intelligent Navigation for Mobile Internet Portals, in: Proceedings of the 18th International Joint Conference on Artificial Intelligence (IJCAI-03), Acapulco, 2003.

7. J. Hart, M. Hannan, The future of mobile technology and mobile wireless computing, *Campus-Wide Information Systems*, Vol. 21, No. 5, pp. 201-202.

8. T. Diekmann, C. Kaspar, L. Seidenfaden, S. Hagenhoff, Kontextbewusste Informationsdienste auf Grundlage von Information Beacons, in: F. Lehner (Ed.), Multikonferenz Wirtschaftsinformatik, Passau, 2006.

9. W. Burkert, Greek Religion, Cambridge, Mass., Harvard Univ. Press 1985.

10. R. Gambetta, Probleme bei der Implementation von technischen Innovationen am Beispiel des öffentlichen Verkehrs dargestellt am EU-Projekt ICARE (Integration of Contactless Applications into Public Transport Environment), Oldenburg, 2006.

11. H. Selye, Stress. Bewältigung und Lebensgewinn, 2nd edition, München, Zürich, 1988.

12. G. Schanz, C. Gretz, D. Hanisch, A. Justus, Alkohol in der Arbeitswelt, Fakten – Hintergründe – Massnahmen, München, 1995.

13. M. Samulowitz, Kontextadaptive Dienstnutzung in Ubiquitous Computing Umgebungen, München, 2002.

14. S. Herden, C. Rautenstrauch, A. Zwanziger, M. Plack, Personal Information Guide – Eine Plattform mit Location Based Services für mobile powered E-Commerce, in: K. Pousttchi, K. Turowski (Eds.), Mobile Economy: Transaktionen, Prozesse, Anwendungen und Dienste. Proceedings of the 4th Workshop Mobile Commerce, Bonn, 2004, pp. 86–102.

15. G. Heinz, Dynamische Fahrgastinformation an Busbahnhöfen, Anschlusssicherung zwischen Bus und Bahn, http://www.uni-stuttgart.de/isv/vuv/publication/PDF_fachkolloquium_2005/ Fachkolloquium_2005.pdf, November 2005, Accessed: 2008-03-23.

16. D. Haneberg, K. Stenzel, W. Reif, Electronic-Onboard-Ticketing: Software Challenges of an State-of-the-Art M-Commerce Application, in: K. Pousttchi, K. Turowski (Eds.), Mobile Economy: Transaktionen, Prozesse, Anwendungen und Dienste. Proceedings of the 4th Workshop Mobile Commerce, Bonn, 2004, pp. 103–113.

17. B. Schilit, N. Adams, R. Want, Context-Aware Computing Applications, in: IEEE Workshop on Mobile Computing Systems and Applications, 1994.

18. U. Kubach, Vorabübertragung ortsbezogener Informationen zur Unterstützung mobiler Systeme, Stuttgart, 2002.

19. D. Grejner-Brzezinska, Positioning and Tracking Approaches and Technologies, in: H.A. Karimi, A. Hammad (Eds.), Telegeoinformatics, Location Based-Computing and Services, Boca Raton, 2004.

20. A. Fox, S.D. Gribble, E.A.; Brewer, E. Amir, Adapting to network and client variability via on-demand dynamic distillation, in: Proceedings Seventh International Conference on Architectural Support for Programming Languages and Operating Systems (ASPLOS- VII), Cambridge, 1996, pp. 160-170.

21. D. Flanagan, Java in a Nutshell, Köln, 2001.

22. Q.H. Mahmoud, Learning Wireless Java, Sebastopol, 2002.

23. T. Caus, S. Christmann, S. Hagenhoff, Hydra - An Application Framework for the Development of Context-Aware Mobile Services, in: Abramowicz, W., Fensel, D. (Eds.): 11th International Conference on Business Information Systems, Innsbruck, Austria, 2008, pp. 471-482.

Internet Adoption in Tourism Industry in China

Hongxiu Li[1], and Reima Suomi[2]
1 Information Systems Institute, Turku School of Economics
Turku Center for Computer Science
Joukahaisenkatu 3-5 B, 20520 Turku, Finland
Hongxiu.li@tse.fi
2 Information Systems Institute, Turku School of Economics
Turku Center for Computer Science
Rehtorinpellonkatu 3, 20500 Turku, Finland
Reima.suomi@tse.fi

Abstract. Information communication technologies (ICTs) have significantly revolutionized the travel industry in the last decade. E-tourism has been developed in travel industry in the world, which helps to realize digitalization of travel service process and value chains in travel industry, and has been used to evaluate the entire range of ICT application in tourism industry. E-tourism has developed variedly in different regions or countries. This research aims to examine how ICTs and Internet have impacted the travel industry in China. This study explores the current e-tourism development in China and examines the use of Internet in travel organizations. In addition, it investigates some issues related to the e-tourism development, including the drivers and barriers in e-commerce adoption from both travel organizations' and travelers' perspectives. The results indicate that in general China is a late-adopter as regards to the adoption of e-commerce in tourism industry. In China only a few innovative travel organizations are at the early adoption stage of Internet and have experienced the benefits and advantages of early-adopters. Though e-tourism has been a growing trend, travel agency still keeps the main travel service delivery channel in China. This study also suggests that travel organizations in China should learn from developed countries to know how to develop e-tourism and improve the competitiveness of tourism in China.

Please use the following format when citing this chapter:

Li, H., Suomi, R., 2008, in IFIP International Federation for Information Processing, Volume 286; Towards Sustainable Society on Ubiquitous Networks, eds. Oya, M., Uda, R., Yasunobu, C., (Boston: Springer), pp. 197–208.

1 Introduction

With the Internet as a commercial medium, new ways of conducting business have developed in almost every sector. Tourism, as an information intensive industry, requires the support offered by information communication technologies (ICTs) and information systems [1-4]. Therefore, ICTs play an increasingly significant role in the global tourism industry development. With the wide application of Internet in business, Internet has been changing the global tourism industry, and e-tourism has being developed in the world. E-tourism helps to realize digitalization of travel service process and value chains in travel industry, which has been used to evaluate the entire range of ICT application in tourism industry, and its development varies in different regions or countries in the world [5].

As tourism industry plays an important role in the Chinese economy, this research aims to examine how ICTs and Internet have impacted the tourism industry in China. This study explores the current e-tourism development in China and examines the adoption of Internet in travel organizations. In addition, it investigates some issues related to e-tourism development, including the drivers and barriers in e-commerce adoption from both travel organizations' and travellers' perspectives. This study suggests that travel organizations in China should learn from developed countries to know how to develop e-tourism and improve the competitiveness of tourism in China.

The paper is organized as follows. It first reviews relevant literature in theories of e-commerce development and e-tourism development in China. It then describes how this study was conducted, together with the research setting. Third, it reports the research findings. Finally, it concludes with a discussion and recommendations for both practitioners and researchers.

2. Background and Literature Review

2.1 E-Commerce Development in China

To contextualize e-tourism development in China, an examination of e-commerce development in China is required. With the development of Internet penetration in the world, e-commerce has emerged as a global phenomenon. E-commerce is getting popular and increasing its market share in the world [5]. Although e-commerce has experienced its maturity in some economically developed countries, for example the USA, its development in many regions is still in its infancy. As far as the e-commerce development in China is concerned, e-commerce in China is still in its formation stage [6].

In the past several years, with the rapid growth of the population of Internet users in China, e-commerce has expanded rapidly in China. According to the survey conducted by China Internet Network Information Centre (CNNIC), the number of Internet users in China has reached 210 million until the end of 2007, and Internet penetration rate in China has arrived at 16.0% [7]. In the past several years, the number of Internet users has increased greatly (See Table 1). The number of websites in China has arrived at 1.31million, and most of Chinese websites are operated by enterprises for business [7].

Table 1 The increase of Internet users in China from 2002 to 2007 (M: million)

Time	Jun. 2002	Dec. 2002	Jun. 2003	Dec. 2003	Jun. 2004	Dec. 2004.
Internet population(M)	45.8	59.1	68	79.5	87	94
Internet penetration rate (%)	3.4	4.6	5.3	6.2	6.7	7.3
Time	Jun. 2005	Dec. 2005	Jun. 2006	Dec. 2006	Jun. 2007	Dec. 2007
Internet population(M)	103	111	123	137	162	210
Internet penetration rate (%)	7.9	8.5	9.4	10.5	12.3	16.0

E-commerce in China is multiplying almost as fast as the number of Internet users in China. According to the report from the Research in China (RIC), in 2006 the revenue generated in e-commerce was about $138.4 billion in China, and the e-commerce market will continue to expand in China [8]. The e-commerce market in China will be perhaps totally as much as $654.3 billion by 2010 [9]. The figures in relation to Internet and e-commerce development in China are optimistic. However, e-commerce development in China is impacted by some barriers, including lack of trust, security risks, lack of credit card and so on [7]. Compared to e-commerce development in developed countries, the adoption of e-commerce in Chinese organizations is also in its infancy. Though there are companies which have achieved success in their e-commerce development, for example, Alibaba and Taobao, most of the Chinese companies have not really employed e-commerce in their business. Currently most of them use the Internet mainly for the purpose of information exchange and information presence, but not integrating with business management and business transactions [10,11].

2.2 E-Tourism in China

In the past 20 year tourism industry has developed quickly in China. Since 1999 the Chinese government has taken different strategies to further push tourism development in China, for example establishing three "Golden weeks" holidays. According to the statistics of China National Tourism Administration (CNTA), in China the revenue of tourism industry has arrived at $1.9 billion in 2006, which takes about 4.27 per cent of the total GDP in China [12]. The number of inbound travellers has arrived at about 124.9 million, the number of outbound travellers has arrived at 345.2 million, and the number of domestic travellers has arrived at 1.39 billion [12]. According to the prediction of World Tourism Organization (UNWTO), tourism industry in China will take up to 8.6 percent of world market share and become the world's top tourism industry by 2020 [13].

E-commerce development and the expansion of electronic market in China have attracted travel organizations to employ e-commerce in their business as. Internet has become a new intermediary in travel industry, which brings both challenges and opportunities to travel organizations. In fact, travel and tourism industry has been particularly affected by the great advancement and the wide application of e-commerce in business [2-4]. Travel organizations, especially travel service providers, rely heavily on online intermediaries or Internet to offer travel service to their customers. Travel service providers have being shifted from the traditional offline channels (the i and ii in Figure 1) to the online channels to distribute their travel services to their customers (the iii and iv in Figure 1), which helps them to reduce commitment costs assigned to travel operators or travel agents before and to generate sustainable competitive advantages.

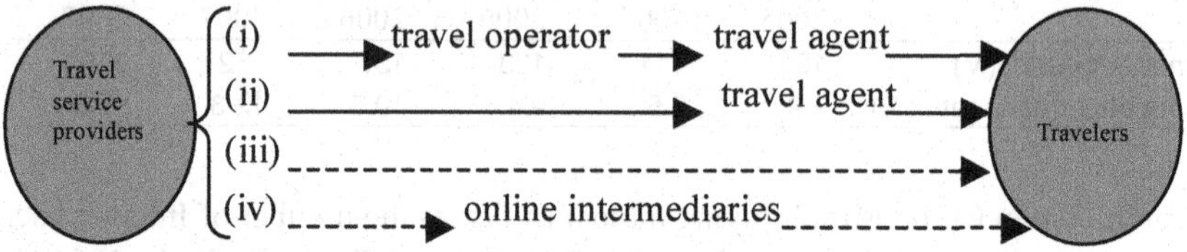

Figure 1 Travel service distribution chain in e-commerce times

In China there are totally about 17957 travel agencies, 12751 hotels, and most of them have already established their websites to offer online travel services. They use the Internet to present travel information, to offer email service, and to offer online booking service to customers. In China, according to the survey conducted by CNNIC in 2007, only around 3.9% of Internet users are using the Internet to book travel service, most of the Internet users just use the Internet to look for travel information [7]. In the USA, about 63% of the Internet users are using Internet to book travel services. Compared to the USA, in China the demand market of online travel service booking is still very small [7]. E-tourism in China is still at its initial stage, which is in line with the e-commerce development in China [14]. The traditional offline travel service keeps competitive in the travel market in China since a large amount of Chinese travellers still rely more on the traditional intermediary – travel agencies to book travel service. The online channels seem not so attractive to Chinese travellers, and even online intermediaries need to cooperate with travel agents to offer travel services to travellers [15,16]. Compared to the e-tourism development in developed countries, the online channels illustrated in Figure 1 seem not so important for travel organizations in China. It is evident that e-tourism in China is lagging behind the developed countries.

3 Method

This study aims to explore the issue on e-tourism development in China. In order to fulfil the objectives of this study, different methods were used. In this study both qualitative and quantitative methods were adopted. As Cresswell (2003) explained that qualitative and quantitative methods are complementary rather than competing for research [17]. The study issue is investigated based on the data collected in different travel organizations in China.

First a qualitative approach was adopted in order to achieve an appreciation of the research topic and to develop a set of appreciate variables in the survey and a set of questions for the interviews. Some travel organizations in China have been chosen in the study and their websites have been visited. An examination on the websites was undertaken based on the following aspects: website presence, e-mails service, online information services, online booking and offline booking. A review based on the data collected in this phrase helps the researchers to achieve a general understanding about the level of e-commerce in tourism industry in China.

Then interviews were conducted in some travel service providers and travel agencies, which aimed to explore the drivers and barriers in e-commerce adoption from travel organizations' perspectives and the current e-commerce adoption in tourism in China. The interviewee sampling were targeted at the owners, managers or sales managers of travel organizations in China which had began to employ Internet in their business. Structured interviews were conducted in this research. The interviewed questions were first developed for the interviews in advance which mainly focus on the e-commerce application in travel organizations, including the background of organizations, e-commerce application in business, the perceived benefits and barriers in their e-commerce application in business, the future plan for e-commerce development in business and their perception of e-tourism development in tourism industry. And all the interviewees were asked to answer the same questions. Before interviews, all the interviewees were informed of the interviewed topic and interviewed questions in advance in order to make sure that they know about e-commerce application in their organization and can offer some valuable data for this research. The interviewees were also asked to express their perceptions of e-commerce development in tourism in China. Every interview lasted around 1 hour.

In this study totally 20 face-to-face interviews were conducted in 6 travel service providers and 12 travel agencies. 3 of the 6 travel service providers are the main airlines in China, 1 is an international airline company in Europe which has offices in China, and the other 2 are four-star hotels in China. Among the travel agencies, 10 of them are traditional travel agencies located in big cities in China, including Beijing, Shanghai, Guangzhou, Wuhan and Shanghai, and the other 2 are the biggest and most successful online travel intermediaries in China - Ctrip and Elong companies. The details are illustrated in Table 2.

Table 2 Formal interviews

Company	Number of companies	Number of interviews
Airlines	4	6
Hotels	2	2
Travel agencies	10	10
Online travel intermediaries	2	2

The interviewees are mainly the sales managers, e-commerce department managers or directors, general managers, or deputy general managers. Their rich experience in tourism industry offers valuable data for our research. Content analysis was employed in the study to analyze the interview data.

Finally a quantitative survey was conducted in the study in order to investigate e-tourism condition in China from travellers' perspective – the demand market. It aims to examine the traveller's perception of e-tourism in China. The questionnaire includes some questions based on background studies and secondary research. In the survey a questionnaire was developed to collect empirical data. The respondents were some onboard travellers of one interviewed airline company. The respondents were asked to report on the barriers and benefits of online travel service booking, their travel information searching channels, and travel service booking channels. A 5-point scale was used in the survey to investigate the research topics.

The survey was conducted by the airline company onboard. In the study totally 190 copies were received, and 169 copies are usable. The data of the questionnaire were put into SPSS and descriptive statistics method was employed in the data analysis.

4 Research Findings

Based on the collected data, it is indicated that the general state of e-tourism in China is still in its early stage. Most of the interviewees agreed that though e-tourism ranks highly in e-commerce adoption in the world, and it has achieved success in some developed countries, in China currently e-tourism has been developed quite slowly in travel industry. In their opinion, e-tourism is a good option for them to further develop their business in the world and widen their market, and they would like to develop e-tourism. In fact, some of the interviewed travel organizations have already adopted e-commerce in their business and regarded e-commerce as their important strategies in their business because of the advantages of e-commerce. However, the role of e-commerce seems not to be as important as they expected because of some barriers. According to their opinion, currently e-commerce is not their main business focus and there is still a long way for them to develop e-commerce in tourism industry in China.

4.1 E-Commerce Development in Travel Organizations in China

In China travel organizations have tried to use e-commerce in their business for the advantages of e-commerce. According to the comments from the interviewees, most of them agreed that e-commerce can offer direct communication and access to their customers, reduce their dependence on intermediaries, work more efficiently, reduce cost and widen their market to the world. All of the interviewees have mentioned that fear of lagging behind their competitors is also an important driver for them to adopt e-commerce in their business, especially for the big travel organizations. But for SMEs in travel industries, it is not a driver. In fact the competition between big travel organizations is more furious than in SMEs in travel industry in China, and normally big travel organizations pay more attention to innovations than SMEs.

The interviewees discussed their e-commerce adoption from the following aspects: website establishment and presence, online travel service booking, online travel service distribution and value chain, online cooperation and business network establishment.

All the interviewed companies have established their own websites and have used their websites to perform marketing and promotion. In their opinion, most of the travel organizations in China, including the SMEs in travel industry, have already established their own websites, since the Internet population size is keeping increasing every year and has taken about one eighth of the population size in China. Most of the interviewees agreed that their website service is poor. The main deficiencies are illustrated in following aspects: poor travel information, no updated travel information, lack of efficient navigation, no good online booking service and no English version. Only 3 of the interviewees stated that their website service is good, including the two online travel intermediaries. The interviewees have discussed about the reasons why their website service is poor. All of them agreed that lack of technological knowledge and professionals in ICT field is the main reason. Most of them have outsourced their website establishment and maintenance service. It seems that most of them are going to employ professional ICT talents to work for them and improve their website service in the future.

Online travel service booking, online travel service distribution and value chain of travel organizations are close related to each other. There are different answers from the interviewees on this point. According to the discussion of the interviewees from the airlines and hotels, they agreed that reducing their dependence on the intermediaries is one of the main drivers for them to develop e-commerce in their business. They can offer online travel service booking directly to their customers without the cooperation with travel operators or travel agencies. But in fact they still rely on travel agencies quite a lot since the share of online booking is still very low in their whole market. Call to or visiting travel agencies or airlines offices is still popular in travel services booking in China. Even the two interviewees from the online travel intermediaries stated that they have to rely on travel agencies or agent heavily. Though some Chinese travellers book their tickets online, they can not complete the whole transaction process online. They can send emails or SMS to their customers to inform them of their booking information, and then they need to rely on their cooperated partners in different locations in China to delivery the e-tickets or paper tickets to their customers and receive the payment for the tickets. The interviewees from both the airlines and the online intermediaries agreed that lack of trust and security risks are the main obstacles, and reimbursement regulations in China can be a barrier as well. In China, only the receipt of the e-tickets or paper tickets can be used for reimbursement, which enforces travellers to get the receipt for reimbursement by the traditional distribution channel even though e-ticket can offer convenience to them. The interviewees from the travel agencies agreed with them on this point. For travel agencies their online booking service has not been developed as well as in travel service providers. Though they offer online booking service, but they rely more on offline channel for travel service distribution because traveller would like to book travel service more on the offline channels. Therefore, the distribution chain and value chain in tourism industry in e-commerce time in China has emerged as illustrated in Figure 2. In China travel agent still plays an important role in travel service distribution and the traditional offline booking channels (i and ii in Figure 2) are still more important than the online booking channels (iii and iv in Figure 2).

Though online channel offers more opportunities for the travel service providers and online intermediaries, they still need the cooperation with travel agents in their online booking services. Compared to the general travel service distribution chain we discussed in e-commerce time in developed countries, in China e-commerce in tourism industry is still at the early stage since online booking has not been widely adopted in travel organizations.

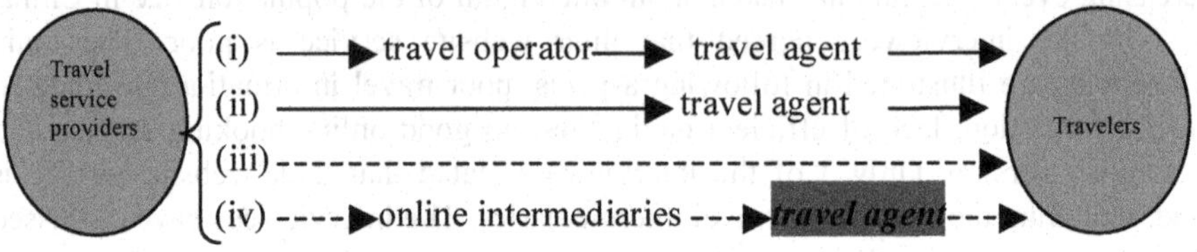

Figure 2 Travel service distribution chain in China

Buhalis and Deimezi (2004) argued that cooperation and competition among travel organizations is a feature of the emerging online tourism industry [5]. Internet-based cooperation among travel organizations impels each other to establish their business networks, which can help them to integrate the newly created resources in their business networks and existing resources to develop new products or services to their new customers [18]. In travel industry, business networks can be established among clusters of firms to establish value chain among them, including hotels, sightseeing companies and transportation companies based on their access to each other's resources [19,20]. The interviewees did not discuss this point so much. They agreed that they do not use Internet to cooperate with their partners so much though Internet can make their work in cooperation much efficient. Normally they just use emails to transfer information between each other. They still rely more on the traditional cooperation channels, for example face-to-face meeting and call to each other. It is consistent with the e-commerce development in travel industry in China. In the early stage of e-commerce adoption, it is hard for travel organizations to realize Internet-based business cooperation and establish their business networks. In their opinion, it is what they expected in the future when e-commerce has achieved maturity in travel industry in China.

4.2 E-Tourism Adoption from the Demand Side in China

The customers are investigated on their perception of online travel service booking. Among the 169 respondents, 97.2 % of them are Internet-users, and 99 of them (58.8%) have online travel service booking experience.

According to the results of quantitative data, security risks and lack of trust are regarded as the most important barriers in online travel service booking, and the shortcomings in the service offered on the Internet by travel organizations is also an important barrier, which is concluded based on the mean comparison (See Table 3).

The results are in consistent with the results from the qualitative interview data. As regards the benefits of online booking, by mean comparison, convenience, saving time and low prices are the main three benefits (See Table 3).

Table 3 Traveler's perception on barriers and benefits of e-tourism in China

Barriers	Mean	SD	Benefits	Mean	SD
Security risks	1.61	1.098	Convenience	1,70	1,386
Lack of trust	1.94	1.347	Saving time	2,18	1,197
Shortcomings in the service offered on the Internet	3.18	1.954	Low prices	2,92	1,792
Lack of customized service	3.45	1.688	Service around the clock available	3,22	2,070
Lack of credit card	3.77	2.267	Good possibility to compare between different offerings	4,11	1,605
Long delivery time	3.79	1.459	Availability of personalized products and services	5,10	1,546
Lack of Internet access	5.23	2.458	Avoidance of personal service	5,74	1,446

As regards travel information searching and travel service booking channels. Travel agency is ranked as the most important travel information searching channel and the Internet is not so important, which is based on mean comparison (See Table 4).

Table 4 Travel information search and service booking channels

	Mean	Std. Deviation
Travel agency	1.99	1.322
Friends	2.04	1.145
Experience, habit	2.29	1.486
Internet	2.31	1.316
Advertisement	3.24	1.522

The result is also in consistent with the results from travel organizations side. For travel service booking, travel agency is more important than Internet, 45.6% of the respondents would like to use travel agency to book travel service, and 33.1% of them would like to use online booking. The results are higher than the results reported by China Internet Network Information Centre [5], and higher than the interview results.

5 Discussion

It is evident that ICTs play an important role in the operation and management of tourism industry since tourism is information intensive industry, and has been quite fit with the new interactive media – Internet. In fact in many developed countries e-tourism has achieved success. It has become the main travel service distribution channel and the main marketing mechanism in the worldwide market and has constituted one of the largest and fastest growing segments of e-commerce. Travel organizations adopt e-commerce in their business for different drivers, for example for communication, reducing intermediaries and improving working efficiency and processes. In China travel organizations still rely on some suitable technological tools in their business, and they are in the infancy period of e-commerce/Internet adoption. In general Chinese travel organizations are the late-adopters of innovation as regards to the adoption of e-commerce in tourism industry in China.

The study demonstrates that in China Internet has been adopted widely and e-tourism has been developed in travel organizations. It seems that some travel organizations are willing to adopt the modern Internet technology in their business and some are reluctant to use it though e-tourism is a future trend in the world with the wide penetration of Internet into people's life. The business advantages of e-tourism have not been experienced by most travel organizations in China. In China only a few innovative travel organizations are at the early adoption stage of Internet and have experienced the benefits and advantages of early-adopters with the face of some barriers and difficulties in innovation adoption. The majority of travel organizations in China are belonging to the late majority or laggard adoption stage. In general Chinese travel organizations are the late adopters of e-commerce. Currently tourism industry in China is facing fierce competition, to learn from the developed countries in their e-tourism development might be helpful for Chinese travel organizations to really understand the benefits and advantages of e-tourism and adopt Internet in their business, which can help Chinese travel organizations to enhance competitiveness and address the challenges in the e-commerce times. In addition, in order to expand e-market in tourism industry in China, travel organizations should take some strategies to stimulate customers' adoption of e-commerce, for example offering cheaper price to customers if customers adopt online booking. Travel organizations should also take strategies to integrate their business with the Internet to realize more efficient and less cost business cooperation with business partners in their value chain.

The results in this study reveal that though e-tourism has been a growing trend, but travel agency still keeps the main travel service delivery channel in China on the perspective of both travel organizations' and traveller's perspectives. Barriers existed in the e-tourism development can explained this phenomenon in China, which are also s the factors which impact the adoption rate of e-commerce in tourism industry in China.

In summary, the results in this study support the following conclusions. First, in general China is a late-adopter of innovation as regards to the adoption of e-commerce in tourism industry. Second, In China only a few innovative travel organizations are at the early adoption stage of Internet adoption and have experienced the benefits and advantages of early-adopters. Third, e-tourism has been a growing trend, but travel agency still keeps the main travel service delivery channel in China.

6 Limitations and Future Research

This study has offered some valuable insight into studies on e-tourism development in China. A number of limitations of the study need to be acknowledged when we interpret the results. First, the empirical study was conducted only in China. Second, only big travel organizations were chosen as the targets in our empirical study. More travel organizations, including both big companies and SMEs in travel industry will better support the assumptions in the study. In the future further studies on how to develop e-tourism in developing regions need to be conducted to support the Internet and e-commerce diffusion in travel industry.

Reference

1. V. Cho, World Wide Web Resources, *Annals of Tourism Research* 25(2), 518-521(1998).

2. D. Buhalis, Tourism and Information Technologies: Past, Present and Future, *Tourism Recreation Research* 25(1), 41-58(2000).

3. R. Law, Internet in Travel and Tourism-Part I, *Journal of Travel & Tourism Marketing* 9(4), 83-87(2000).

4. R. Law, et al. The Impact of the Internet on Travel Agencies, *International Journal of Contemporary Hospitality Management*, 16(2), 100-107(2004).

5. E. M. Rogers, New Product Adoption and Diffusion, *Journal of Consumer Research* 2(1976), 290-301(1976).

6. H. X. Li, and R. Suomi, E-commerce Development in China: Opportunities or Challenges? In Proceedings of the IADIS International Conference on E-commerce (Krishnamurthy, S. & Isaias, P. Ed.), pp. 413-417, IADIS Press, Barcelona, Spain, 2006.

7. China Internet Network Information Center (CNNIC), The 21th Statistical Report on Internet Development in China, http://www.cnnic.net.cn/uploadfiles/pdf/2007/7/18/113918.pdf

8. Research in China (RIC), The Benefit Model in E-commerce in China in 2006, http://www.pday.com.cn/research/2005/572_ecommerceway.htm

9. China Market Information Centre (CCID), B2B Market Will Continue Develop in China, http://news.ccidnet.com/art/1032/20060214/428239_1.html.

10. Z. X. Tan, and W. Ouyang, Diffusion and Impacts of the Internet and E-commerce in China, *Electronic Markets* 14(1), 25-35(2004).

11. X. H. Guo, and G. Q. Chen, Internet Diffusion in Chinese Companies, *Communications of ACM* 48(4), 54-58(2005).

12. China National Tourism Administration (CNTA), The Annual Statistical Report of Tourism Industry in China in 2006, http://www.cnta.gov.cn/news_detail/newsshow.asp?id=A20071023943253500589

13. China National Tourism Administration (CNTA), Outbound Travel Development in China, http://www.cnta.gov.cn/news_detail/newsshow.asp?id=A20075101738546353446

14. L. Li, and D. Buhalis, E-commerce in China: The Case of Travel, *International Journal of Information Management* 26(2006),153-166(2006).

15. J. Lu, and Z. Lu, Development, Distribution and Evaluation of Online Tourism Services in China, *Electronic Commerce Research* 4(2004), 221-239(2004).

16 Y. B. Lu, et al. Tourism and Travel Electronic Commerce in China, *Electronic Market* 17(2), 101-112(2007).

17. J. W. Cresswell, Research Design: Qualitative, Quantitative and Mixed Research Methods and Approaches, Second edition, Sage Publications, London, 2003.

18. M. Hitt, et al. Strategic Entrepreneurship: Entrepreneurial Strategies for Wealth Creation, *Strategic Management Journal* 22(6/7), 479-491(2001).

19. R. Gulati, et al. Strategic Networks, *Strategic Management Journal* 21(1), 203-215(2000).

20. A. Wong, et al. Developing Relationship in Strategic Alliances: Commitment to Quality and Cooperative Interdependence, *Industrial Marketing Management* 34(2005), 722-731(2005).

The Use of Data Sources of Medication Information – a Finnish Primary Care Organization in the Light of National e-Health Scenarios

Eeva Aarnio, Reetta Raitoharju

Turku School of Economics, Information Systems Science

Rehtorinpellonkatu 3,FI-20500 Turku, Finland

{Eeva.Aarnio, Reetta.Raitoharju,}@tse.fi

Abstract. Many areas of the healthcare sector are information-rich and data-intensive, and often lack of time is a problem. Patient-specific medication information is often seen as highly important part of patient data for patients' safe treatment and therefore the availability of it should be guaranteed. The aim of this paper is to study healthcare professionals' perceptions of their utilization of sources of medication information and to assess it in the light of national e-Health scenarios using a Finnish primary care organization as a case study. The healthcare professionals reported frequent use of the patient as a source of information as they could not be convinced of the correctness of the medication lists in the electronic patient record. The future e-Health solutions should be usable and guarantee the correctness and completeness of the medication information if the clinical workers are expected to use them. The valuable information provided by the patients could be also exploited more efficiently in the future.

1 Introduction

Effective use of information technology (IT) is found to be important to healthcare sector's success [1]. The significance of IT might stem from the fact that many areas of the healthcare sector are highly information-rich [2, 3] and data-intensive [4] in nature. A lot of information is produced, used and archived. Clinicians need various

Please use the following format when citing this chapter:

Aarnio, E., Raitoharju R., 2008, in IFIP International Federation for Information Processing, Volume 286; Towards Sustainable Society on Ubiquitous Networks, eds. Oya, M., Uda, R., Yasunobu, C., (Boston: Springer), pp. 209–219.

types of information in their everyday work. The needed information includes patient data, population statistics, medical knowledge, logistic information and social influences [5]. The information is often located in dispersed resources and the healthcare professionals must find the appropriate pieces of information, and in addition, ensure that the information is accurate [2]. The lack of time is also found to be one of the factors affecting the search. Pressures on time often lead to inadequate choice of resources [6]. There are several factors that promote successful information seeking in clinical settings, e.g. convenience of access, habit, reliability, high quality and speed of use to mention some [7]. However, not even the development of medical informatics has fulfilled the expectations to provide the healthcare professionals with timely, accurate, and appropriate information [8].

The past 40 years have been called even as a "drug explosion" [9]. Despite the fact that drugs are prescribed to improve patients' health and have often positive effects, there are many risks in the complex process of prescribing them [10]. Problems related to drugs include for instance under-dosing and polypharmacy. Therefore the healthcare professionals dealing with prescribing in their daily routines should be given support ensuring the availability of required information.

The topic studied in this paper, *medication information*, refers to the information about individual's medication regimen: the generic and commercial name of the drug, the dosage, and the use indication. It also covers the risks related to the patient's treatment, e.g. patient's drug allergies. As medication information is patient-specific data, this paper concentrates mainly on the assessment of healthcare professionals' use of the patient data and not on the use of other type of prescribing information (e.g. therapeutic agents or drug prices) that could be achieved from resources open for almost any healthcare professional, like textbooks or electronic sources.

The objective of this paper is to study healthcare professionals' perceptions of their utilization of written and verbal sources of medication information and to assess it in the light of national e-Health scenarios using a Finnish primary care organization as a case study. Bringing together the expert and clinical workers' points of view, the paper aims at answering the following questions:

- What are the healthcare professionals' main verbal and written data sources of medication information and why?
- What could be said about the healthcare professionals' utilization of the data sources in the light of the future e-Health scenarios in Finland?

By defining healthcare professionals' self-perceived use of information sources, we hope to increase the knowledge on how healthcare professionals really utilize sources of information currently, what could be the future possibilities and what should be taken into account when designing the national level archiving solutions.

2 Methods

The study consists of two data collection phases. First, a data collection was conducted in a primary care organization consisting of one main health center and dispersed sub-units within one municipality. The primary care health centers in Finland are required by law to offer comprehensive primary health care services to the population of the municipality or other fixed area. The physicians working at the health centers are often general practitioners [11]. In this case, 10 healthcare professionals, 5 physicians and 5 nurses from different primary care units were interviewed. The interviewed were chosen based on the proposition of each organization's responsible person among those providing clinical care to be able to assess the real use of sources of medication information.

The interviewed physicians worked mainly in the daytime and treated patients from a fixed area on 15-minutes, pre-booked visits. There is also a 24-hour on-call service at the main health center that offers convenient walk-in care. The same physicians working in the sub-units had also couple of times a month shifts in the 24-hour on-call service. The interviewed nurses' tasks included for instance regular diabetes and blood pressure controlling but they did not have regularly shifts in the on-call service. Electronic patient record (EPR) has been in use in all the units of the case organization since 1999. One researcher with a varying group of other researchers conducted all the interviews in the primary care organization. All the interviews lasted at least one hour and were recorded and transliterated.

The second data collection included 5 interviews of professionals with clinical work experience and/or involvement in healthcare sector national level information system development (e.g. as key members of advisory boards). The experts were chosen to the interview because of their position and potential to provide accurate information on national level plans, as there is not a lot of written information available on the unfinished process. Some of these interviews were conducted as the earlier mentioned and some by email. The same list of questions that was asked in the face-to-face interviews was sent as an attachment. The people interviewed by email wrote their answers on the attachment and returned it. As the interviews were also transliterated, all the data was analyzed question by question using written/transliterated material. The data analysis of both parts was conducted by the author involved in all the interviews.

3 Related Research: Healthcare Professionals' Sources of Information

Clinicians' sources of information have been quite widely studied; however, remarkable part of the research concentrates on the use of sources open for almost any healthcare professional [9] or of sources to guide clinical practice [12]. In addition, those articles dealing with patient data describe often only physicians' information seeking. Gorman [5] has studied physicians' information needs. He has classified types and usual sources of information. According to him, the usual sources of patient data are the patient, her/his family and friends, and the medical record. Based on their survey, Brown, et al. [13] found that the three most usual sources of information were 1) the bedside flow sheet, 2) conversations with residents, and 3) conversations with nurses.

The sources of information probably vary depending on the special area and type of healthcare organization because of the special features of the organizations. For instance, intensive care units (ICUs) have been found more stressful places to work than non-ICUs [14]. In the emergency department (ED), the patients are often in critical condition and the information should be found as rapidly as possible. The need for quickly gather the relevant pieces of information means that the team members need to work closely together [2]. An important factor in choosing resources is that the use requires minimal cost to obtain because usually the lack of time is the reason that impedes information search [7].

4 National level e-Health Plans for Patient Information Management

In Finland, there is a universal healthcare system and public healthcare is available to all residents for free or the most, for a nominal fee. Primary care is provided by municipal health centers from which the patient is referred to specialized hospital care, if required. The private healthcare system is very small and for instance private healthcare insurances are not common. The public healthcare is financed largely through local taxes. Prescription drugs are sold in private-owned, strictly regulated pharmacies and reimbursed by The Social Insurance Institution of Finland, "Kela", depending on the severity and chronic nature of the disease.

There is a national level plan in Finland to guarantee smooth exchange of the patient information between different types of healthcare sector organizations. The authority in charge of the development of national level solutions for "always-available" patient information is the Social Insurance Institution, Kela. Kela contracts private companies based on tendering to execute the development in practice.

The information on patients' medication is often mentioned to be one of the most important parts of the patient information. The first part of the national plans aims at developing an electronic prescription (e-prescription) and an archive for all the e-prescriptions. The piloting of the e-prescription is expected to start in late 2008. At the first phase the e-prescription archive will include all the written prescriptions, however, only if the patient permits the archiving. The prescriptions will mainly be those of outpatients' because there will be no e-prescriptions written for inpatients on the medications taken on the ward. One advantage of the e-prescription archive will be that the information on the medications the patient has really bought from the pharmacy will be available. At least at the first phase, the e-prescription archive will not include for instance information on the patients' drug allergies or other risks related to the patient's medication-taking. In any case, the development of the e-prescription archive will probably continue after the implementation of a "good-enough" e-prescription archive. After the e-prescription archive, the next challenge is to solve the question marks related to the management of permissions asked from the patients for the use of their patient information in treatment. The following phase covers the exchange of x-rays.

As the e-prescription archive includes only information on the prescriptions, there will be another archive including other patient-specific information and also more extensive information on patient's medications. The other archive, called here as "e-Archive" is still at a very early development phase and therefore all possible ideas for the development are current. Also citizens' role as a provider of information is planned to be taken into account and there is under planning a portal or similar where the citizens could, for instance, complete information on the over-the-desk medications they are taking or their medication-taking practice. At some, quite early phase, the citizens will have the possibility to see the prescriptions written to them from the e-prescription archive through an interface that is still under planning.

In the complex process of exchange of patient information, there are some issues impeding the development of information exchange and the use of information. The issues with great importance are related to the technical and legal ones. In accordance with the current legislation, for instance the nurses will not have the right to look at patients' information from the database while they are often responsible for administering medications to the patients. Also data from the occupational health will be still excluded from the information available for healthcare professionals in other areas. The technical issues are mainly related to the different EPR systems used in different healthcare organizations.

5 Results

5.1 Physicians' Sources of Medication Information

The part of medication information that was most important for the physicians, was patient's current medication; what medications he/she really takes regularly. Interviewed primary care physicians reported frequent use of the patient or his/her representative, often a family member, as a source of medication information.

"The patient her/himself has a quite important role, because he/she knows, what he/she has taken, if remembers."

The practice to obtain the information varied but some patients had the medication list on a piece of paper and those using a pillbox had it behind the box. Two physicians described the way they usually get the medication information from the patients as follows:

"Some patients come with a self-written list that covers the medications they have taken."

"There is a card behind the pillbox where is penciled the name of the drug, when and in which part of the pillbox it should be administered and based on that one could conclude, what the patient has been taken. Unfortunately, that piece of paper is the most reliable source despite the medication lists of the EPR."

For instance Brown, et al. [13] have stated that physicians prefer verbal communication from written notes but at least in this case patient was used as a source because there was no other choice, or the patient needed to confirm that the information achieved from other source was correct. At the time of the interviews, the case organization did not have any precisely defined place in the patient record where all the medications would have been in order. Therefore the list where prescribed medications should have been included often also included already finished courses of medications. In addition, the currently taken medication was recorded on some other leaf, for instance on the one updated by the homecare nurses. As one of the physicians put it:

> "It [the EPR] is full of different lists but there is no guarantee of the correctness."

Mostly because of the above-mentioned reasons, EPR was the primary source of information only when patient did not use any private sector health center, had not been in hospital care, and visited regularly the same public sector physician. In those cases physicians knew, on which leaf patient's up-dated medication information was. A physician with a system of her own describes the situation:

> "Hmm, I have my own system, my own way to do it, that may not be the same of the other 69 primary care physicians.– – I update continuously a summary that includes patient's medications. – – That is the most important for me, but quite a few physicians use it. I do wonder how they manage to get the information within 400 pages of patient information."

The information on changes made in patient's medication during hospital care usually came to health center but situations when it was never received were also reported. If patient had been in hospital care or had private sector visits meanwhile, and he/she forgot to tell to the physician about them, the treatment decisions could have been made based on outdated information. As mentioned earlier, the information neither from occupational health nor from the mental healthcare was available. Therefore physicians acted even as detectives when figuring out patients' overall medication regime:

> "...of course there is such a key, where you can see patient's appointments, ah, you know, if he/she's got appointments also at the mental health clinic, then you understand to ask, if the patient takes any psychiatric medications."

The use of the EPR as a source was also difficult when the system was down. As the EPR had already been in use for years, paper-based records were required rarely. However, some results were still exchanged on paper between organizations, for instance the ECG graphs. Other use of paper-based archives was related to the benefits paid by the public authorities:

> "Then [the paper-based archives are used], when patient needs physician's statement for special reimbursement of some medications, we start digging around, what was the history."

Despite the problems arisen from the sometimes challenging use of patients' medication information, the interviewed physicians reported only an infinitesimal amount of severe cases of polypharmacy or other dangerous, medication-related situations. Those reported were mostly related to the interactions caused by some mental health medications or to the generic substitution; the patients did not always realize they were taking a double dosage of some medication on different commercial names if they had renewed the prescriptions in different organizations.

The patient was an important source of her/his own medication information because he/she often had information that no one else could tell, for instance the medication-taking practice. Patients could be perhaps empowered and their role strengthened by sharing their own information through a portal or similar. The interviewed physicians had mainly a positive attitude to the possibility that citizens could look at their own information from an archive. However, they were also aware of the fact that without the required knowledge, many questions would arise and there should be someone to answer those.

Though this paper assesses individuals' medication information, a reference to other than patient-specific information is required. The interviewees often mentioned internet as a source of information when treating the patient. An important source for the interviewees was a webpage maintained by the Finnish Medical Society Duodecim. The interaction database and the guide on all the medications sold in Finland, Pharmaca Fennica, are available on the page.

5.2 Nurses' Sources of Medication Information

The interviewed nurses usually needed patients' medication information on regular control visits. Those controls included diabetes or blood pressure controls, or were related to the use of blood thickening medication or vaccinations. As the patients were often sent to the controls after having visited a physician, the nurses usually found the required information easily from the EHR. The interviewed nurses did not have any problems reading the physicians' notes from the EHR and they thought they would not have had use for any other source of information.

The nurses also used patients as a source of information and usually found them reliable for providing the information they needed, as could be seen from the following quotations:

> "The patient actually is the primary [source of information] and besides that we lean on the patient information from the EPR."
> "He/she [the patient] provides the information if he/she has used anything [medications] or visited another physician than her/his own here at our health center."
> "We need to ask from the patients and trust the information."

The nurses' tasks were mainly related to one or few of the patients' medications at a time. The main reason for that might be that the nurses are not responsible for the patients' overall medication regime. This could be noticed from the following quotation answered to the question, whether they have problems with patients that get prescriptions from other organizations:

> "Well, I don't know, it's probably [a problem] for the physicians but not for us because we do not prescribe anything."

Their role in managing patients' overall medication information was usually advisory in nature. Therefore also the nurses told that important sources of medication-related information for them were web pages maintained by trusted administrators.

5.3 Expert Views on Current Situation and Future Development

According to the interviewed experts involved in the national level IT development projects in Finland, the schedule of the projects is often really tight. Some of them also stated, that the co-ordination of the activities has not always been the best possible. In the interviewed experts' opinion, the current environment for developing e-Health solutions in Finland is shaped by the difficulty of combining the "old" electronic patient records and other information systems with the new technology. Based on the expert opinions, a concrete problem is that in many patient record systems there is a non-structured medication list that does not enable the exchange of information between organizations easily.

Another mentioned issue that affects the development of all the e-Health solutions in Finland is how to solve the question of patient's consent that authorizes the healthcare professional to use her/his electronic patient information in treatment decisions. The current law is not very specific about the nature of the consent. However, there have been discussions that in practice patient should be able to recognize exactly to whom, what and why her/his patient data is used. It has been seen as a question of legal protection.

Depending on their task at the national level development projects, the experts were convinced that the issues they were developing would be of great importance for the clinical workers. The e-prescription archive, for instance, would bring available information on what medications patient really buys from the pharmacy. However, they realized that the significance of the developed systems for clinical work was remarkably dependent on the usability of the systems, and on the legal issues.

The citizens' involvement in information providing in the future was seen as a possibility but some experts highlighted that the citizens' portal should be separate from the one where healthcare professionals record the patient data. According to law, it is currently even impossible that patients could add some information in the archives. However, most of the experts were convinced that the patients will have some kind of user interface in the future for their medication information management.

5.4 The Current and Future Sources of Medication Information

Part of the medication information required for patient's treatment is such in nature that though there was a portal making it possible for the individual to provide information, only the healthcare professionals should be authorized to record it in the archive. However, based on the healthcare professionals' and experts' views, the patient could bring some additional information. Table 1 summarizes the data sources of medication information currently used by the healthcare professionals and gives an idea of possible additional sources based on the expert interviews.

Table 1 shows that the future e-Archive would have an important role in managing patients' medication information crucial for their treatment. However, the solution is far from the implementation phase. An archive that would technically make it possible to use the information would probably be of good help for the healthcare professionals. The information of occupational health would still stay out of reach at a primary care center.

6 Discussion

The objective of this paper is to study healthcare professionals' perceptions of their utilization of written and verbal sources of medication information and to assess it in the light of national e-Health scenarios using a Finnish primary care organization as a case study. Both, the interviewed physicians and nurses used patient often as a primary source of information. The physicians trusted the patient because they could not be convinced of the correctness of the medication lists in the EPR. Unlike the interviewed physicians, the nurses did not report having problems using the EPR as a source of patients' medication information. That was probably because they do not have the responsibility for the patients' overall medication and they do not prescribe any medications. Based on experts' opinions, the issues with most effect on the development of e-Health solutions in Finland are related to the legal and technical issues.

Table 1. Data sources of medication information currently used by the healthcare professionals and possible additional sources of medication information

Required medication information	Current sources of medication information	Possible additional sources of medication information in the near future
Patient's current medication	Patient or her/his representative, EPRs of different organizations	e-prescription archive (to some extent, will not include for instance in-patients' medications), e-Archive
Medication-taking practice of patient	Patient	Portal or similar for patient self-reporting on medication-taking
Delivery information of the medications patient has bought from the pharmacy	Patient or her/his representative	e-prescription archive (only the outpatients), e-Archive
The diagnosis related to the medication	EPRs of different healthcare organizations	e-Archive
Risks related in patient's medication-taking	Patient or her/his representative, EPRs of different healthcare organizations	e-Archive, portal or similar for patient self-reporting
Prescriber of the medication, time and place	Patient or her/his representative, EPRs of different healthcare organizations	e-prescription archive (only the out-patients), e-Archive
Patient's medication history	Patient or her/his representative, EPRs of different organizations	e-prescription archive (only the out-patients), e-Archive
Other medication-related information	Web pages maintained by trusted administrator, e.g. Medical Society Duodecim	Web pages maintained by trusted administrator, more tightly connected to the views of healthcare professionals

This study may have several limitations. First of all, it is based on the self-reporting by the healthcare professionals and other experts. Second, the number of interviews is limited. However, more or less the same issues appeared in all the interviews. Third, the study consist only interviews of primary care healthcare professionals. Therefore the study results might be different if the data collection had been conducted in another type of unit, e.g. in an emergency department (ED) or at hospital settings. The results are tough at least partly consistent with earlier studies [5, 13, 15] investigating physicians' information sources, however, the focus of this study was more narrow than in those studies. As the idea was to increase knowledge on one organization's medication information sources and the future possibilities, the study do provide a glimpse into the current and future practice of Finnish healthcare professionals' information seeking.

Those times when healthcare professionals were said to be resisting the use of computers are over, at least in Finland. The primary healthcare professionals used patients as a source of medication information despite the EPRs have already been in use for several years in the case organization but the reason for that was other than just resisting new technology. This fact highlights the importance of the future e-Health solutions especially in the sense that just any electronic solutions may not be usable if one cannot trust in the correctness and completeness of the data provided. Neither should patients' role as self-reporting information providers be underestimated as they have currently an essential role and some parts of the medication information could be provided only by them. The patients might complete their medication information in some portal and that would leave more time for other treatment-related issues on physicians' appointments. In the case organization, the nurses also used medication information independently. Therefore it would be important to assure that the future e-Health solutions will not be out of their reach because of law.

It is highly probable that the future e-Health solutions will open up new possibilities for the healthcare professionals when it comes to completing the patient's medication information. Brown, et al. [13] stated in their study, that replicating the paper world in an electronic format will not be reasonable without understanding why the those papers are used as they are being used. The same thing should be noticed here; the developed archives should be at least as good as the earlier used sources of information.

Acknowledgement

The authors want to express their gratitude to the Finnish Funding Agency for Technology and Innovation. The study has been conducted during FinnWell-funded project called Management of Medication Information.

References

1. Chiasson, M., Reddy, M.C., Kaplan, B., and Davidson, E.: Expanding multi-disciplinary approaches to healthcare information technologies: What does information systems offer medical informatics?, *International Journal of Medical Informatics* (2007), Vol.76, No.S1, pp. S89-S97
2. Reddy, M.C. and Spence, P.R.: Collaborative information seeking: A field study of a multidisciplinary patient care team, *Information Processing & Management* (2008), Vol.44, No.1, pp. 242-255
3. Reddy, M.C., Pratt, W., Dourish, P., and Shabot, M. Asking Questions: Information Needs in a Surgical Intensive Care Unit, *Proceedings of the American Medical Informatics Association Fall Symposium AMIA'02*. San Antonio, TX 2002.
4. Hagland, M.: Intensive Care: The Next Level for IT, *Health Management Technology* (1998), Vol.19, No.13, pp. 18 (6 pages)
5. Gorman, P.N.: Information Needs of Physicians, *Journal of the American Society for Information Science* (1995), Vol.46, No.10, pp. 729-736

6. Ely, J.W., Osheroff, J.A., Ebell, M.H., Chambliss, M.L., Vinson, D.C., Stevermer, J.J., and Pifer, E.A.: Obstacles to answering doctors' questions about patient care with evidence: qualitative study, *British Medical Journal* (2002), Vol.324, No.7339, pp. 710 (7 pages)
7. Dawes, M. and Sampson, U.: Knowledge management in clinical practice: a systematic review of information seeking behavior in physicians, *International Journal of Medical Informatics* (2003), Vol.71, No.1, pp. 9-15
8. González-González, A.I., Dawes, M., Sánchez-Mateos, J., Riesgo-Fuertes, R., Escortell-Mayor, E., Sanz-Cuesta, T., and Hernández-Fernández, T.: Information Needs and Information-Seeking Behavior of Primary Care Physicians, *Annals of Family Medicine* (2007), Vol.5, No.4, pp. 345-352
9. McGettigan, P., Golden, J., Fryer, J., Chan, R., and Feely, J.: Prescribers prefer people: The sources of information used by doctors for prescribing suggest that the medium is more important than the message, *British Journal of Clinical Pharmacology* (2001), Vol.51, No.2, pp. 184-189
10. Kuperman, G.J., Bobb, A., Payne, T.H., Avery, A.J., Gandhi, T.K., Burns, G., Classen, D.C., and Bates, D.W.: Medication-related Clinical Decision Support in Computerized Provider Order Entry Systems: A Review, *Journal of the American Medical Informatics Association* (2007), Vol.14, No.1, pp. 29-40
11. Engeström, Y.: Objects, contradictions and collaboration in medical cognition: an activity-theoretical perspective, *Artificial Intelligence in Medicine* (1995), Vol.7, No.5, pp. 395-412
12. Oliveri, R.S., Gluud, C., and Wille-Jorgensen, P.A.: Hospital doctors' self-rated skills in and use of evidence-based medicine - a questionnaire survey, *Journal of Evaluation in Clinical Practice* (2004), Vol.10, No.2, pp. 219-226
13. Brown, P.J., Borowitz, S.M., and Novicoff, W.: Information exchange in the NICU: what sources of patient data do physicians prefer to use?, *International Journal of Medical Informatics* (2004), Vol.73, No.4, pp. 349-355
14. Alvarez, G. and Coiera, E.: Interdisciplinary communication: An uncharted source of medical error?, *Journal of Critical Care* (2006), Vol.21, No.3, pp. 236-242
15. Coiera, E.: When Conversation Is Better Than Computation, *Journal of the American Medical Association* (2000), Vol.7, No.3, pp. 277-286

Student Retention through Customized Service Processes

Reinhard Jung, Jessica Kochbeck, Annett Nagel

Chair of Business Informatics and Enterprise Communications Systems University of Duisburg-Essen
Universitaetsstrasse 9, 45141 Essen, Germany
{reinhard.jung|jessica.kochbeck|annett.nagel}@icb.uni-due.de
www.kom.wiwi.uni-due.de

Abstract. Due to the Bologna declaration and the subsequent switch to the bachelor/master system, student mobility is rising and competition among universities across Europe becomes intense. Furthermore, students are demanding comfortable information and communication solutions. Hence, universities are required to align educational- and service-processes more closely to their students. This paper presents an innovative approach to adapt modern concepts of Customer Relationship Management (CRM) to institutions of higher education in order to retain students at their university. Furthermore, an architecture is presented which is capable of integrating university legacy systems with state of the art CRM technology.

1 Introduction

Before the implementation of the Bologna declaration [1], Customer Relationship Management (CRM) was not imminent in most European institutions of higher education and thus economically inefficient. In the past, an educational process typically started with the enrollment at a university and generally ended, several years later, when the student received the final degree (e.g. a diploma) at the same institution. Switching universities during the studies implicated severe frictions because already completed exams have very often not been acknowledged by the new university.

The implementation of the Bologna declaration across Europe´s universities over the past years triggered the transformation from monolithic study programs to a dual system: Two formally separated courses of study, i.e. bachelor and master program, result in respective academic degrees. Besides prescribing this modular structure, one of the core intentions of the Bologna declaration was to increase student mobility sig-

Please use the following format when citing this chapter:

Jung, R., Kochbeck, J., Nagel, A., 2008, in IFIP International Federation for Information Processing, Volume 286; Towards Sustainable Society on Ubiquitous Networks, eds. Oya, M., Uda, R., Yasunobu, C., (Boston: Springer), pp. 221–231.

nificantly. Universities are obliged to accept graduate students from other universities based upon the same formal criteria they apply to their "own" graduate students (e.g. "must have a bachelor degree and a bachelor diploma grade of at least ..."). The conference of Swiss university presidents adopted a directive in 2005 stating that students with a corresponding bachelor degree have to be accepted for graduate studies (master programs) without requiring any further prerequisites [2, p. 1].

Research has been done regarding student mobility in the USA (e.g. [3]). The research focus on the mobility aspect in Europe was on the students willingness and ability to spend semesters abroad (e.g. exchange programs) and their later choice of employment [4]. Currently, first empirical results on the mobility bachelor and master studies in Germany are available [5]: 77 % of the students graduating from a bachelor program apply directly for another program and approximately 75 % of them do not switch universities. Only 25 % are moving to another university. Considering that these results are from a transitional period with yet unknown acceptance of bachelor degrees in the corporate world, we can expect, that student mobility following the bachelor degree – based upon the identified 25 % – will be increasing.

Simultaneously, the subsidization of the universities (in Germany) changed significantly. Due to the unfortunate financial situation in most of the states (e.g. [6, pp. 5]), government subsidies are now bound to performance measure (e.g. number of students enrolled, number of graduates).

In summary, institutions of higher education are now much more dependent on higher capacity utilization in order to retain their subsidies or get additional funding. Under the assumption of higher student mobility after completed bachelor studies, there is a need for action concerning customer (student) retention. In this paper the term "university customer" is defined as: A person that is enrolled for at least one of study programs of the institution under consideration. The extension of this definition includes a wide spectrum of students: prospective and actual undergraduate and graduate students, students in shorter courses of study (e.g. certificate courses) as well as Ph.D. students and post-docs. The definition does not necessarily require that students are to pay tuition fees. Some of the German states still run their universities without tuition fees.

Today´s students expect, besides a good research and teaching reputation, a high quality of service. These expectations may have increased since the introduction of tuition fees. When additionally considering the increased mobility of graduate students, the need for action leaves the universities theoretically with two strategic options in order to retain their students which are know from the corporate world:

1. Retaining the customer by means of switching barriers. However, the Bologna process abolished these barriers.
2. The second strategy is to "design" the relationship with the students in a way that is rationally and/or irrationally perceived positive. It can be assumed, that this leads to higher contentedness and, as a consequence, to a lower churn rate [7, pp. 49].

Thus, the only viable strategy to achive student retention is strategy # 2. The literature refers to related activities by using the term *Student Relationship Management* [7, p. 56; 8, p. 3; 9].

The second strategy can be implemented by deploying different means, which are also used by corporations in their CRM programs:

1. Product quality: The high quality of an educational program results from a broad course offering and a high qualification and reputation of the respective faculty;
2. Service process quality: Professionalizing and individualizing the educational process imply the effect of a (ceteris paribus) more successful student retention and more effective acquisition of new students;
3. Image: Professional brand building.

The focus of this paper is on the second aspect. We are researching how (bachelor) student retention can be increased by means service process quality improvement.

2 Short-comings of Today's Universities' Service Processes

Service processes at universities are typically characterized by a division of labor. Involved organizations (student union, registrar's office, institutes/chairs, libraries, examination office etc.) supply their services mostly uncoordinated. Integrating the different services into *one* service process is left to the students who are bound by regulations and guidelines (conditions of study, examination regulations etc.). Most services at universities are delivered online, thus rendering the rightly criticized queues of waiting students [7] a thing of the past. Nevertheless, most universities do not offer truly integrated services. This state of affairs is aggravated by isolated and independent IT-Systems, e.g. registrar system, electronic university calendar, websites of the institutes with information on courses, electronic teaching platforms, systems for academic record administration, library systems and exam administration systems. A sample process could be as follows: Available courses in his or her main and minor subject are evaluated at the beginning of the term by the student; the electronic university calendar also highlights courses that have been successfully completed. Additional information on courses (e.g. exam dates), have to be gathered from the respective institutes websites. The student then chooses some of the courses but has to write necessary information down separately because the electronic university calendar does not offer a corresponding functionality. The next step is search for the courses within the different platforms (e.g. electronic teaching platform) and to subscribe to them. It might happen that some of the courses are not supported by the learning platform or are not online yet. During the semester recommended literature for the respective courses has to be searched for in (isolated) library systems and lent if available. Finally, the student has to obtain information on subscription deadlines for exams and finally use the exam administration system to subscribe for exams; these web-based systems are at best "integrated" by means of links to the respective login pages.

Improving such or similar situations requires the following steps: Data integration, so that all involved systems access one – at least logically centralized –consistent master data base including a centralized identity management system. Furthermore, it is necessary to seamlessly connect different service processes once they are initiated by students. Additionally, a portal has to be established enabling the students to access the various services of the university.

3 Related Work

There are some publications available that deal with CRM at higher education institutions. In [10] a framework is presented aiming at the optimization of recruiting processes (recruitment of students) through data base marketing. Some papers deal with "student retention" (e.g. [11, 12]), whereby the main focus is not the retention of students between bachelor degree and master studies but a wide cause analysis of dropouts. The following publications are relevant with respect to our research goals:

- In [13] *Kidwell et al.* outline the first ideas regarding the transfer of e-business concepts to the educational sector. However, they do not provide a coherent framework.
- In his paper on service processes at the University of Mannheim (Germany) *Heiling* outlines a customers' perspective on the various independent and isolated customer relations a university maintains and elaborates on the frictions that causes on the students' side. He derives an architecture which connects the different IT systems by means of a middleware layer and complements that architecture with a central database [7].
- *Kudrass* proposes a hub-and-spoke architecture for the integration of heterogeneous databases in the university environment with a database as the central component [8].

An outline for an integrated architecture supporting CRM measures which focus on student retention cannot be found neither in Anglo-American nor in German research literature.

4 Applying CRM Concepts to Universities

One of the objectives of this paper is to apply CRM concepts to institutions of higher education and, basing on that, to derive an appropriate architecture for the typical IT landscape, i.e. a landscape comprising a considerable number of legacy systems.

In this section concepts from the "conventional" customer relationship management are adapted to the university environment.

Customer process
From the customers' point of view the customer process in this context is the whole educational process from enrollment to a first or second degree or even to a Ph.D. or a post-doctoral lecturing qualification. After graduation, this process can be extended by an alumni phase. The left hand side of Fig. 1 depicts an educational process from the student's perspective starting with the desire to take up studies towards the alumni phase including possible variants depending on decisions and events during that process. The universities' perspective on the right hand side shows the alignment of CRM actions to the customer process [14, p. 43]. As a means of modeling event-driven process chains [16, pp. 111] have been used.

Customer value analysis
The customer value analysis is utilized to estimate a client's business volume and contribution margin potential. For this purpose, possible transactions in a specific

customer group have to be predicted. In the educational field, the customer value is subject of a prediction too. However, it cannot be represented by a monetary figure. Based on formal qualification, visible preferences, academic performance and intellectual potential of a person an indicator might be calculated. It's value can be used to predict which additional educational offerings of the university the student is likely to use. When the university is subsidized based upon its capacity utilization, the predicted duration of the remaining educational process can be transformed into a monetary value (customer value). If applicable, tuition fees should be considered, too.

„Share-of-wallet"

The "Share-of-wallet" (of a company regarding a specific customer) is the expected/predicted percentage of the customer's total demand of a specific product group the company can achieve [15, p. 111]. Adapted to the environment at hand, the "Share-of-education" is the part of the educational process of a person/customer a university can achieve.

Cross-/up-selling

Related to products/services the customers has already bought or agreed to buy, cross- and up-selling is an action to increase the "Share-of-wallet" by offering/selling complementary products/services (cross-selling) or products/services with a higher contribution margin (up-selling) to the customer. These concepts can be adapted as follows:

- Cross-selling: Offering services that broaden an ongoing or completed education (complementary services), can be interpreted as cross-selling. An example is to offer a leadership coaching to master students.
- Up-selling: Based on the academic level a student has already achieved, he or she can be offered additional educational services. Offering a master program to students with a bachelor degree can be classified as up-selling.

One-stop-shopping

Closely related to the concept of cross-selling is „one-stop-shopping". The goal is to satisfy a customer's multiple and complementary demands in one (virtual) place. Adapted to institutions of higher education "one-stop-shopping" means to offer all services for program members through a single user interface such as, for example, a web portal.

Fig. 1 shows on the right hand side ("Perspective of a University") which steps are suitable for cross-selling. Furthermore, the hypothesis is presented that services in acquisition phase I and education phase I influence the probability of successful up-selling in acquisition phase II: The better the university's services during the bachelor studies are, the higher the probability is that the student applies to a following program at the same university.

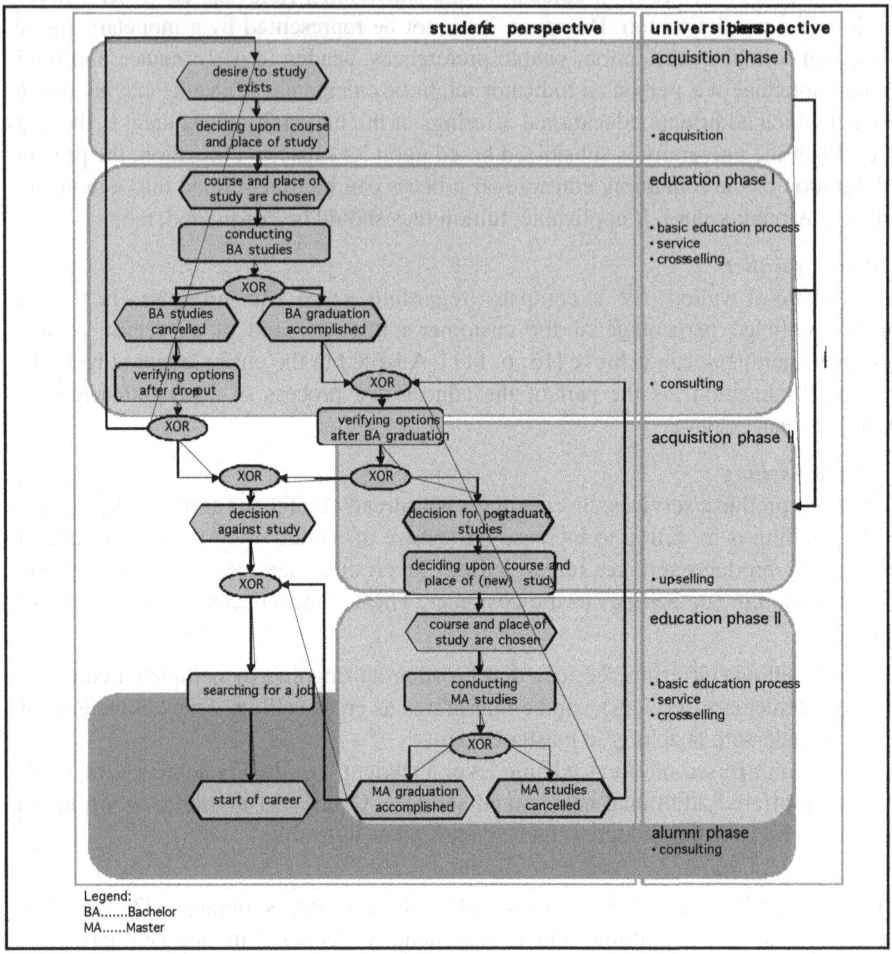

Fig. 1: Educational process throughout bachelor and master programs

Applying the term customer here as well as transferring CRM concepts to universities has limitations. A corresponding comparison between companies and institutions of higher education can be found in Fig. 2. Besides varying objectives and retention strategies, the target groups or, more precisely, the rationale leading to target groups for CRM actions differ. Enterprises are implementing selective CRM strategies [17, p. 3]; actions for customer retention are applied to (potentially) profitable customer relations only. For universities this would mean to offer certain services only to a subset of their students selected basing on their "customer value". Taking into account the goals of the Bologna declaration, such a strategy cannot be applied, at least not at government funded universities.

CRM application area / Criteria	Enterprise	University
objectives	business objectives (e.g. profit, turn over)	• fulfilment of the educational task • capacity utilisation • generation of additional income
means to achieve custome r retention	• emotional attachment • product quality • service quality • switching barriers	• emotional attachment • product quality • service quality
target group	profitable customers/ client relationships	all students

Fig. 2: Comparison of CRM concepts deployed by enterprises and universities

5 Designing an Integration Architecture for the Deployment of CRM at Universities

In this section central requirements are being outlined that have to be met when implementing a CRM strategy at a university. The discussion is restricted to the support of bachelor and master programs, i.e. functions "BA studies accomplished" and "MA studies accomplished" of the event-driven process chain presented in Fig. 1. Covering additional educational phases (e.g. accomplishing two bachelor programs) are possible too. In the following, an architecture is presented that can integrate new systems (especially for CRM functionality) and legacy systems.

5.1 Requirements

A CRM strategy for institutions of higher educational has to solve two core problems. On the one hand, isolated service processes of different organizational units have to be aligned. Integrating the services towards a coherent overall process should be done by the university („One-Stop-Shopping") and not by the students. The entire educational process could be event-driven. The subscription to a specific program could automatically trigger other processes, e.g. the display of related classes offered in the current semester. Depending on the student´s choice other services could follow.

On the other hand, following a successful integration – and this is the specific potential of this approach – additional value added services could be offered in order to intensify the student's relationship with the university. Examples for those services are personalized messages regarding:

- subscription deadlines of classes relevant to the individual student,
- classes that complement classes the student has already attended,

- developments in the educational process (academic performance) endangering successful studies toward the degree,
- guest lectures and other events which are, based on their content and related to the current course of study, especially relevant to the student,
- employment opportunities fitting to the educational status,
- location changes or class cancellations.

It is possible to deliver these messages by SMS or E-Mail. Some universities in Europe already offer such services.[1]

5.2 Architectural outline

To be able to implement the requirements mentioned above, the university's IT systems have to be connected. Especially, data about the students from existing and separated data sources have to be integrated into a consistent customer view. In the following we illustrate in detail the functionality of the architecture depicted in Fig. 3.

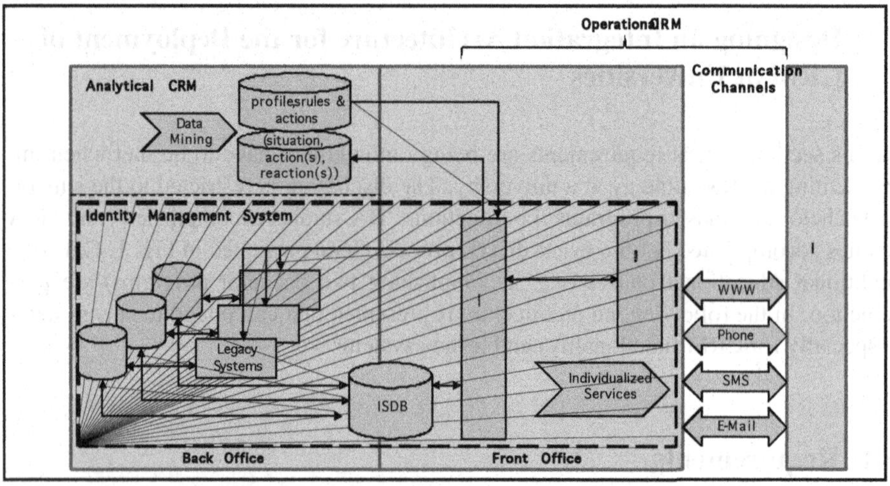

Fig. 3: Architecture for the implementation of CRM concepts at universities

The core of the architecture is an integrated student data base (ISDB). It is the interface between the back office and front office systems and contains all integrated data on the students. The ISDB should be synchronized on time with the legacy systems (examination office system etc.) to assure short refresh periods. If the legacy systems provide sufficient availability (up time) and accessibility the ISDB can be implemented as a federated database system thus avoiding data replication.

In an additional database (depicted in the left hand side of the figure) profiles, rules and actions are stored to compare individual student data with the profiles to de-

1 http://www.ethbib.ethz.ch/service/sms.html; http://www.ub.uni-passau.de/e-mail-benachrichtigung.html; http://www.isu.uzh.ch/cms/marketing/marketingmanagement/e-learning/smsservice.html, https://unisms.unisg.ch/

duct and take, based on the rules, specific actions. The profiles are generalized situations with assigned actions. The actions are designed to provide services (value) to the students that fit to their current situation.

Generating these profiles, rules and actions, which are part of analytical CRM, can be based on hypotheses in a first step. Later on, it is possible to deduct information of the CRM actions and the students' reactions with data mining techniques. These data (tuple "situation, action(s), reaction(s)") are transferred through the CRM system to the analytical CRM system and processed. The outcome of this feedback is a so called "closed loop", that can be used for the individualized services, e.g. in a call center or for generating SMS and e-mails. The use of e-business actions at universities was already suggested by Kidwell et al. in *"Is Your Campus Ready for E-Business?"* [13, p. 27].

Process integration can be achieved by implementing a workflow management component. This component is included in the described architecture and assures that processes initialized by the students are connected seamlessly. At the same time the students can use a web portal (which uses information from the CRM system) providing access to the back office legacy systems. Thus, comfortable self service functions can be used and challenges for first year students as described by *Heiling* are eliminated [7, p. 44]. Additionally, a full service accessible at a single point is offered [7, p. 53] ("one-stop-shopping").

The architecture outlined above does not differ fundamentally from CRM architectures in the commercial area; the use of standard components (CRM software, portal technology) is possible. The main challenges are to compose reasonable service processes, to integrate the data of the different applications, and of course to fulfill the requirements mentioned before in chapter 5.1.

6 Future Work and Conclusion

The architecture presented in this paper is very similar to common CRM architectures. The increasing competition resulting from the Bologna process forces universities to transform themselves into educational service providers for students. This transformation will eventually lead to the adaptation and implementation of CRM concepts. Universities can achieve unique selling propositions and enhance student retention by means of advanced CRM methods such as, for example, data mining. It can be expected that this will render innovative services to students possible in the near future.

Besides a refinement of the architecture and an evaluation how the typical legacy systems at universities can be coupled with state-of-the-art CRM applications, the retention effect has to be further investigated and verified. It is intuitively plausible that student-centered educational processes are causing this effect; also the first empirical results are showing this (compare [18] as well as the results of the Technical University of Dresden [19, p. 33]). Nevertheless, further research has to be done on the students´ perception of integrated and innovative services as added value and on assumed retention effects.

The adaptation of CRM concepts at a university raises privacy protection issues especially when academic record data is involved. Therefore, retention efforts through CRM are dependent on the students´ consent to integrate and analyze their data. It has to be investigated if students are concurring with such a use of their data.

Based on the presented concepts the term "customer" can be extended to cover additional groups of stakeholders [20], e.g. companies using the universities' educational services for personnel development.

Finally, the assumption can be made, that implementing CRM concepts at a university also has positive effects on winning and retaining academic and professional personnel, because a professional working environment can be provided and administrative work can be done more easily. This hypothesis should also be proved by empirical research.

Bibliography

1. Bologna Declaration of 19 June 1999: Joint declaration of the European Ministers of Education. http://www.bologna-berlin2003.de/pdf/bologna_declaration.pdf. Accessed 21 April 2008
2. Rektorenkonferenz der Schweizer Universitäten (CRUS): Regelung für die Zulassung zu den Spezialisierten Masterstudiengängen an den schweizerischen Universitäten. www.crus.ch/dms.php?id=2285. Accessed 21 April 2008 (in German)
3. Ferriss A L (1965) Predicting Graduate Student Migration. In: Social Forces 43 (3):310-319
4. Teichler U, Jahr V (2001) Mobility During the Course of Study and After Graduation. European Journal of Education 36 (4):443-458
5. Briedis K (2005) Der Bachelor als Sprungbrett? Erste Ergebnisse zum Verbleib von Absolventen mit Bachelorabschluss. In: Leszczensky M, Wolter A (ed.) Der Bologna-Prozess im Spiegel der HIS-Hochschulforschung, Kurzinformation HIS, Hannover (in German)
6. Amrhein D (1998) Die Universität als Dienstleistungsunternehmen, Deutscher Universitäts-Verlag, Wiesbaden (in German)
7. Heiling J (2004) Studierendenzentrierte Dienstleistungen. In: Zentrale Studienberatung der Universität Hannover (ed.) Ressourcenorientierte Studienberatung - zwischen methodischem Konzept und ökonomischem Kalkül, Proceedings „Fachtagung der Gesellschaft für Information, Beratung und Therapie an Hochschulen e.V. GIBeT" 3rd to 6th of March 2004, pp. 61-75 (in German)
8. Kudrass T (2005) Integration heterogener Datenbanken am Beispiel eines Hochschul-Informationssystems. In: Jantke K P, Fähnrich K P, Wittig W S (ed.) Marktplatz Internet: Von e-Learning bis e-Payment, Proceedings 13th LIT 2005 (13. Leipziger Informatik-Tage) Bonner Köllen, Bonn, pp. 287-296 (in German)
9. Pausits A (2006) Student Relationship Management in der akademischen Weiterbildung Dissertation, Universität Flensburg (in German)
10. Tapp A, Hicks K, Stone M (2004) Direct and database marketing and customer relationship management in recruiting students for higher education. In: International Journal of Nonprofit and Voluntary Sector Marketing 9 (4):335-345
11. Seidman A (1991) The Evaluation of a Pre/Post Admissions/Counseling Process at a Suburban Community College: Impact on Student Satisfaction with the Faculty and the Institution, Retention, and Academic Performance. In: College and University 66 (4):223-232
12. Tinto V (1998) Colleges as Communities: Taking Research on Student Persistence Seriously. In: The Review of Higher Education 21(2):167-177

13. Kidwell J, Mattie J, Sousa M (2000) Prepare your Campus for E-Business – Tips for crafting a successful strategy. In: Educause Quarterly 2:21-29
14. Rapp R (2000) Customer Relationship Management. Campus, Frankfurt/New York (in German)
15. Gerth N (2001) Zur Bedeutung eines neuen Informationsmanagements für den CRM-Erfolg. In: Link J (ed.) Customer Relationship Management. Springer, Berlin et al. (in German)
16. Scheer A W (2000) ARIS - Business Process Modeling. Springer, Berlin et al.
17. Link J (2001) Grundlagen und Perspektiven des Customer Relationship Management. In: Link J (ed.) Customer Relationship Management. Springer, Berlin et al. (in German)
18. Wyss, A.: Kundenbeziehungsmanagement im universitaeren Bereich: Eine empirische Untersuchung zur Wirksamkeit von Kundenbeziehungsmassnahmen. Lizentiatsarbeit, Institute of Information Systems, University of Bern 2006 (in German).
19. Festge F, Meyer M, Schwaiger M (2005) Die Zufriedenheit mit dem Studium der Betriebswirtschaftslehre an der Technischen Universität Dresden. Schriften zur Empirischen Forschung und Quantitativen Unternehmensplanung. 22.2005, Ludwig-Maximilians-Universität München (in German)
20. Fayerman M (2002) Customer Relationship Management. In: New Directions for Institutional Research 113:57-67

e-Government in the Finnish Early Childhood Education: An Analysis of Current Status and Challenges

Annukka Vahtera

Turku Centre for Computer Science, Turku School of Economics,
Information Systems Science, Rehtorinpellonkatu 3, FI-20500 Turku, Finland
annukka.vahtera@tse.fi

Abstract. With the increasing number of citizens accessing the Internet, governments at all levels around the world have no other choice but to utilize information technology, especially the Internet, to provide improved services to their citizens. This paper studies and analyzes the status and challenges of e-government services within early childhood education context in ten of the largest municipalities in Finland. The study draws upon previous research on e-government stage models and e-government challenges. Our analysis indicates that there is significant development work in progress in the field of early childhood education and e-government in many Finnish municipalities. Many of them have reached relatively mature stage in developing early childhood education e-services. The paper also discusses the challenges municipalities face when they try to implement e-government services. Overall, the paper tries to provide examples and ideas for researchers and practitioners for developing better quality early childhood education e-government services.

1 Introduction

The role of IT is not only limited to the private sector. In the public sector, e-government has become one of the key challenges for both governments and municipalities. E-government refers to the use of information technology in the public decision making and in the delivery of public services [1]. Public sector has faced with many challenges in the recent years. Public sector pursues to improve its

---

Please use the following format when citing this chapter:

Vahtera, A., 2008, in IFIP International Federation for Information Processing, Volume 286; Towards Sustainable Society on Ubiquitous Networks, eds. Oya, M., Uda, R., Yasunobu, C., (Boston: Springer), pp. 233–244.

productivity and effectiveness by rethinking missions, re-engineering processes and implementing information technology solutions [2]. Pressure concerns the whole public sector, but several studies show that social care sector is not yet a great user of information technology. This paper examines e-government services within early childhood education (ECE) in Finland, which are considered to be to a large degree in its infancy. Early childhood education refers to children's educational interaction before the compulsory school age of seven years. We are especially interested in the evolution and current status of e-government in this area.

In order to hasten the development of Finnish information society, the Finnish Government launched a policy program called 'Government Information Society Program' in 2003. The aim of the program is to improve competitiveness and productivity, to promote social and regional equality, and to improve citizens' well-being and quality of life through effective use of information and communications technologies [3]. These aims also concern the Finnish day care and early childhood education development. Early childhood education should be involved in the development of Finnish information society, and in the transformation of operational environment. Information technology enables for example new working practices in day care, more effective communication between different early childhood education actors and better quality education.

Early childhood education should also respond to the altered demand of its customers – i.e. families with children. The wide use of Internet and different kinds of electronic services has also increased the demand for e-services in the public sector. That is why early childhood education should change its operation models to better respond to these recent changes.

Finland is often been ranked as one of the leader countries in exploiting information and communication technology to revise its economy and to reform its public administration [4-6], but for some reason early childhood education has not been at the head of this development. However, after the launch of 'Government Information Society Program' in 2003, the development of Finnish e-government has been spread to early childhood education area as well, and many e-government development projects have taken wind under their wings. This paper examines thus this recent development by studying the early childhood education and its e-government services in ten largest municipalities in Finland.

The paper is organized as follows: in the next section, we present different e-government stage models. In section 3 we introduce different e-government challenges. The research context – early childhood education – is presented in section 4. In section 5 we introduce the methodology and cases. The analysis of the status and challenges are discussed in section 6. Finally we draw some conclusions and propose research limitations.

2 e-Government Stage Models

E-government literature demonstrates that many e-government initiatives have been failures [7, 8]. In order to help public administrators to manage often chaotic e-government initiatives, a few e-government stage models have been proposed to understand the development from traditional administration to e-government. The most referred models are Layne and Lee's four-stage model [8], United Nation's five-stage model [9] and Hiller and Bélanger's five-stage model [10]. These models are discussed in the following subsections.

Layne and Lee's four-stage model [8]

Based on technical, organizational, and managerial feasibilities of several examples, Layne and Lee [8] found e-government to be an evolutionary phenomenon, and therefore e-government initiatives should be accordingly derived and implemented. In this regard, Layne and Lee [8] presented the four stages of a growth model for e-government as: 1) cataloguing, 2) transaction, 3) vertical integration, and 4) horizontal integration. These four stages are discussed below.

Stage I: *Cataloguing*. In this stage, governments create a 'state website' due to the pressure from the media, technology-literate employees, demanding citizens, and other stakeholders. At this stage, governments do not have much Internet expertise, and they minimize the risk by doing a small project. The main reason for 'electronic cataloguing' is the citizens' and businesses' access to Internet: as they access information on services from the private sector from the Internet, they expect the same from the government. Therefore governments put parts of the government's non-transactional information on the site. The typical government department website at this stage contains description of the department, some downloadable forms, and some links to other pages. Therefore it establishes a departmental 'presence'.

Stage II: *Transaction*. This stage extends the capability of cataloguing and empowers citizens to deal with their governments online anytime, saving hours of paperwork, the inconvenience of traveling to a government office and time spent waiting on lines. Communication becomes now two-way communication: instead of simply having the ability to download forms, people can fill out forms online and government responds by providing confirmations, receipts, etc.

Stage III: *Vertical integration*. This stage initiates the transformation of government services rather that automating and digitizing existing processes. There should be permanent changes in the government processes themselves, because in the long run, the full benefit of e-government will be realized only if organizational changes accompany technological changes. After online transaction services become more mature, citizens' expectations will increase. This requires integration of scattered government functions at different levels.

Stage IV: *Horizontal integration*. This stage focuses on integrating different functions from separate systems so as to provide citizens a unified and seamless service. The horizontal integration across different functions of government will be driven by visions of efficiency and effectiveness in using information technology, but pulled by citizens' demands on more service oriented government functions. Such integration will provide citizens "one stop shopping".

United Nations' five-stage model [9]

Arguing that the purpose of e-government is to provide efficient web-based public service, the UN [9] suggested a five stages e-government model, which is ascending in nature and builds upon the previous level of sophistication of citizen services online. The five stages are emerging presence, enhanced presence, interactive presence, transactional presence, and networked presence. These five stages are defined as follows:

Stage I: *Emerging presence*. A single or a few independent government website provide limited and basic information.

Stage II: *Enhanced presence*. Government provides current, specialized and dynamic information. Though more sophisticated, the interaction is still primarily one- way from government to citizen.

Stage III: *Interactive presence*. Online services enter the interactive mode with services to enhance convenience of the citizen such as downloadable forms and applications. The government officials can be contacted by e-mail, telephone and post. The site is updated with greater regularity to keep the information up to date for the public..

Stage IV: *Transactional presence*. This stage allows two-way interaction between the citizen and government. Citizens have the capability to conduct complete and secure actions through a single government website.

Stage V: *Networked presence*. Stage V represents the most sophisticated level in the online e-government initiatives. It can be characterized by an integration of G2G, G2C and C2G (and reverse) interactions. Governments utilize a single and universal website to provide a one-stop portal in which users can immediately and conveniently access all kinds of available services.

Hiller and Bélanger's five-stage model [10] and Moon's five-stage model [11]

Hiller and Bélanger [10] identified a five-stage model, which reflect the degree of technical sophistication and interaction with users – information, two-way communication, transaction, integration and participation. Despite some minor changes, Moon [11] adapted Hiller and Bélanger's five stage model. The model consists of the following stages:

Stage I: *Information*. Stage I is the most basic form of e-government, which uses IT for disseminating information, simply by posting information and data on the websites for citizens to view.

Stage II: *Two-way communication*. In this stage, government sites allow citizens to communicate with the government and make simple requests and changes. Government agencies allowing online requests provide sites with fill-in forms, but the information is not returned online, but sent by regular mail or e-mail.

Stage III: *Transaction*. In stage III, the government allows online services and financial transactions, which used to be performed by public servants.

Stage IV: *Integration*. In stage IV, all the government services are integrated vertically (intergovernmental integration) and horizontally (intragovernmental integration) to enhance efficiency, user friendliness, and effectiveness. This can be accomplished with a single portal that citizens can use to access services they need no matter which agencies or departments offer them. This stage is challenging because it requires a tremendous amount of time and resources to integrate online and back-office systems.

Stage V: *Participation*. Stage V involves the promotion of web-based political participation, which includes online voting, online registration, online public forums, and online opinion surveys. While the previous stages are related to web-based public services in the administrative arena, the fifth stage highlights web-based political activities by citizens.

It should be noted, that these e-government stage models are only conceptual tools to examine the evolution of e-government. The real adoption of e-government may follow a different linear progression. For example, a government may pursue various components of e-government simultaneously [11].

3 e-Government Challenges

E-government also faces several challenges. Chen [12] has categorized these challenges as follows:

- *Organizational and cultural inertia.* Many public entities are not exactly known for their efficiency and willingness to adopt changes. Problems such as the organizational bureaucracy and lack of clear communication and collaboration culture need to be resolved before any successful e-government initiatives can be adopted.
- *Government and legal regulations.* There are often numerous laws and regulations at all government levels which are intended to specify rights or duties or to carry out a supervisory or balancing functions. Despite their well-intended nature, they can inhibit innovations.
- *Security and privacy.* E-government applications must protect the privacy within an open and often not-so-secure Internet environment. This applies to e-business too, but governments have an extra burden of guaranteeing security and privacy for citizens.
- *Disparate and out-dated information infrastructures and systems.* Many government departments experience budget restrictions which lead up to out-of-date information infrastructure and systems.
- *Lack of IT funding and personnel.* IT spending is often not a priority in government units, which can be seen in small investments in ICT and staff training.

Similarly, OECD [13] has identified external obstacles to e-government, namely: 1) legislative and regulatory barriers; 2) budgetary barriers: 3) technical barriers; and 4) the digital divide. Legislative and regulatory barriers, budgetary barriers and technical barriers are all analogous to Chen's categorization, whereas the latter obstacle refers to the access to ICT and the Internet. According to OECD, generally the most disadvantaged citizens have the lowest levels of access, and at the same time they are the ones who have the highest levels of interaction with government. If these individuals can not access e-government services, they will miss out on the benefits of e-government.

4 Research Context

In Finland, every child has a subjective right to receive public day care and the municipalities have the obligation to organize day care according to the demand. The concept early childhood education (ECE) refers to the care of children under compulsory school age (ages 0–6). Public day care is mostly organized in day care centers (approx. 70 % of the children) and family childcare, which offer full day, full year service, including evening, night and weekend childcare for children whose parents are either working or studying. The main goal in day care is to promote child's healthy growth, development and learning skills. Day care should also support parents raising their children [14].

Early childhood education in Finland is a well-developed system and much appreciated by the parents. Early childhood education is assured by public investments, and quality regulations are clear and strictly enforced. Charges for day care are based on a percentage of the family's gross income. The charge for a municipal day care place cannot be more than 200 € a month (in 2008) [15]. Early childhood education emphasizes the importance of co-operation between different administrations in relation to the organization of early childhood education and care services for children and parents as well as the educational partnership of parents and personnel [16].

According to a recent study, there were approximately 186 000 children in day care, which represents over 50 per cent of the children under compulsory school age in Finland. In 2005, municipal day care employed 57 000 employees. In all, Finnish social care employed 101 000 employees in 2005, thus day care workers represent a considerable proportion of municipal workforce [17].

5 Research Design

Data collection

This study examines and analyzes the status of e-government service development in early childhood education in ten largest municipalities in Finland. The rationalization for selecting 10 largest municipalities into this study lies behind the innovation adoption literature, which suggests a positive relationship between size – in this case population – and innovation adoption, i.e. e-government adoption. Therefore, the study selected the following ten Finnish municipalities based on their population in the end of 2006: Helsinki, Espoo, Tampere, Vantaa, Turku, Oulu, Lahti, Kuopio, Jyväskylä, and Pori.

Because there is not much knowledge on e-government services within early childhood education, a qualitative case study was deemed applicable for this study. Yin [18] defines case study as follows: A case study is an empirical inquiry that investigates a contemporary phenomenon within its real-life context, especially when the boundaries between phenomenon and context are not clearly evident. A multisite case study approach was followed in order to understand the processes in different municipalities.

The data was collected using theme interviews and observation. Altogether eight early childhood education experts whose titles varied from Project Managers to Directors of day care center were interviewed. This strategy had the advantage of exploiting different perspectives on the key issues. All the interviews were recorded for more detailed analysis. After the interviews, the audio material were listened and transliterated to enable comparison between cases. The data was completed with observation. We got acquainted with the ECE portals in the above-mentioned cities and analyzed their content. The data collection took place from November 2006 to June 2007.

Case descriptions

Helsinki

Albeit the fact that Helsinki is the largest city in Finland and its capital, the city has not exactly been a forerunner in developing e-government services in ECE. The city has fairly informative ECE-website, but the emphasis is particularly on the distribution of information. The information is regularly updated and the site provides access to many printable forms. However, no electronic forms are available. All the forms are in PDF-format, so there is no possibility to return them electronically. The only more advanced feature is the option for the parents to receive a day care invoice electronically.

Espoo

The second largest city in Finland, Espoo, has clearly put more emphasis on developing e-government services for parents. The ECE website is comprised of several features, such as FAQ of child care services, a comprehensive list of contact information of different district social centers, and a long list of printable forms. The most remarkable function is an electronic daycare application. The application can be filled in and returned on Espoo's webpages. The application also contains a feature which calculates the exact monthly fee of child's day care. In order to use such an e-service, electronic identification is needed. The service generates user name and password, which can be used in all the e-services the city provides (e.g. application for adult learning centers, applying for open job vacancies within the city, etc.).

Tampere

The city of Tampere started a five-year knowledge society program called eTampere in the turn of the millennium. The aim of the program was to transform Tampere into the world's leading city in the research, development and application of knowledge society by strengthening the knowledge base, creating new business activity and introducing new public online services. The program therefore also included the parental services. The purpose of Parental e-services -project was to improve service cost efficiency, quality, fastness and interaction. In other words, the aim was to create valuable electronic services to little children's parents. Among the services generated within the project are electronic application for day care centers and elementary school, electronic notification of open day care places, electronic invoicing, possibility to change one's contact information electronically, electronic application of transfer to another day care center, and electronic cancellation of day care places. The goal is to reduce manual processing in day care management and provide better quality services for parents. Identification is needed to use these e-government services, and the security and privacy is guaranteed by the use of VETUMA, an online identification and payment solution for citizens.

Vantaa, Turku and Pori

The electronic ECE-services are quite similar in the cities of Vantaa, Turku and Pori. As in Helsinki, the emphasis is more on providing information for the citizens, rather than offering them a chance to deal with their ECE-affairs online. There is basic information about different day care centers, and some of them even have their own websites. There is no electronic day care application in Turku and Pori, but the parents in Vantaa have an opportunity to fill in, sign and send the application in electronic format using an online banking network ID or electronic identification card. Similarly to Espoo, also Turku has an electronic application which calculates the amount of family's day care fee.

Oulu

The city of Oulu is known for its technological expertise, and it has attracted many global actors of IT. Therefore Oulu and its surrounding nine municipalities has striven to establish a regional day care operations model which will provide the most advanced day care services in the whole country. The region is famous for its rapid growth in population, and the need for day care services across municipalities is strongly present. The aim is to manage the whole day care application process on the Internet. Families can also receive bills and browse their customer files electronically using their electronic identification cards. In addition, the customers can send and receive information, such as notices of absence, via e-mail or SMS.

Lahti

Lahti's development program, FENIX, focuses on development of software technologies and applications. The main goal is the development of user-friendly application technologies and services for public bodies. As a result, together with the city of Oulu, Lahti is creating a so called citizen's account with which citizens can interact with appropriate authorities online. The citizen's account can be used in a same way as for example an online bank account. One result of this program is an application called 'Mobile-kid'. Mobile-kid is an electronic communication service which connects homes and day care centers. It aims to ease the daily communication between home and day care centers and provide real time information about day care centers' activities. Mobile-kid exploits Internet, e-mail and SMS.

Kuopio

Also the city of Kuopio has started its own development project which deals with electronic day care services. It includes customer-oriented information and communications services, and internal information services for the day care personnel. The idea is to gather up fragmented information services of different actors in day care, and to clarify the electronic communication between them. These actions pursue to more efficient and smooth processes within day care, and to help families to find suitable services for their individual needs. The application form for day care is not available in electronic form yet, but the citizens can give feedback on day care services online.

Jyväskylä

A regional day care development project including Jyväskylä and eight surrounding municipalities was executed in 2005–2007. The idea was to respond to the growing need for day care services in the area. The objective was to produce day care services across municipalities, to clarify different regional day care management models, to develop parent guidance of different day care options, to strengthen service network, to introduce common use of day care information systems, and to detect different costs.

One part of the project was a pilot which tested the consolidation of day care information system, municipal time card system and day care planning system. The idea behind the pilot was that basic personal information about children and personnel and the time they have spent in day care centers would be automatically transferred to day care information system and to the payroll. This data would then act as a basis for different statistics and invoicing the parents. Different planning processes and compilation of statistics are really time-consuming tasks in day care, and along with the system these manual tasks would become much easier and efficient to handle. The director of the pilot day care centre had calculated that the use of the pilot system would save them over 400 working hours per year.

6 Discussion

Although often being criticized for dragging behind the development of other e-government services in Finland, our study shows that early childhood education in many municipalities has recently tried to reach out the gap. All the examined municipalities in our study have at least created some kind of extended presence (UN's stage II) on the Internet, where a citizen can find dynamic, specialized and regularly updated information on ECE services. In fact, our study shows that only one of the studied municipalities – Pori – was still in this early stage of e-government evolution, while the other municipalities appeared to be further on their development.

Several municipalities had taken the step on to the next level, which is interactive presence (UN's stage III; Hiller and Bélanger's stage II). Many of the studied municipalities allow citizens to download different forms online, but the information can not be returned online, but sent by regular mail or visiting the local office. Some of the studied municipalities also try to enhance the convenience of citizens by providing applications which calculated the day care fee, and by offering the possibility to give feedback on day care services online.

Some of the studied municipalities had developed the ECE e-government services even further into transactional stage (Layne and Lee's stage II; UN's stage IV; Hiller and Bélanger's stage III), and developed systems which enable citizens to conduct complete and secure actions through an ECE website. Examples of these services are electronic day care application, electronic invoicing, sending and receiving e-mails and SMS, and receive real time information about day care center's activities. These e-services are available in all the studied municipalities excluding Turku, Pori and Kuopio.

A pleasant example of a genuine attempt to develop mature e-government services was found in Jyväskylä, where they have tried to integrate different functions from separate systems in order to provide citizens and employees a unified and seamless system, which would ease the day care process. The example is a good illustration of horizontal integration (Layne and Lee's stage IV).

The presumption that all the e-government services within ECE are less mature than other e-government services in Finland was therefore to some degree proved wrong. The findings are however affected by the fact that the studied municipalities represented the ten largest municipalities in Finland, and therefore the findings can not be generalized. If the study would have included also smaller municipalities, the findings could have been different and various challenges or obstacles for developing electronic ECE-services would have probably emerged. The findings of our study are summarized in the following table:

Table 1. Summary of the findings

City	e-Government services	e-Government stage
Helsinki	basic information, printable forms, electronic invoice	transactional stage
Espoo	basic information, printable forms, day care fee calculator	interactive presence
Tampere	electronic application, electronic invoice, electronic notification, transfer and cancellation of day care places	transactional stage
Vantaa	basic information, electronic application	transactional stage
Turku	basic information, day care fee calculator	interactive presence
Oulu	electronic application, electronic invoice, e-mails, SMS's	transactional stage
Lahti	basic information, real time information about day care activities, e-mails, SMS's	transactional stage
Kuopio	basic information, electronic feedback	interactive presence
Jyväskylä	basic information, pilot which integrates different day care information systems	horizontal integration
Pori	basic information	extended presence

Although having been quite successful in implementing e-services into ECE, the studied municipalities had faced several challenges of e-government. According to our interviews, the most considerable challenges the municipalities had faced were legal regulations, security and privacy challenges, and the lack of investments in IT. Most of the information in ECE consists of information about the children. There are strict laws about what kind of information about children can be processed electronically, and therefore the question of security and privacy becomes extremely relevant. Many municipalities for example forbid parents to send their children's personal identification numbers via e-mail. Therefore secure transactions and encrypted connections are extremely important; without those the municipalities simply can not provide e-services such as electronic day care application form, which requires child's personal identification number.

Many of the studied municipalities also complained about the small funding in IT. It is virtually impossible to develop modern e-government services in ECE, if the IT infrastructure is out-of-date. The budget in ECE usually goes to other functions than IT, because decision-makers do not often see the potential of ICT in early childhood education. And even though the ECE manages to acquire modern IT, the staff can not often use it efficiently. The Finnish day care personnel's average age is quite high, and their IT skills are quite restricted. In fact, a few recent studies [19, 20] have showed that almost half of the Finnish day care professionals estimate their IT skills to be minor or non-existent. With the lack of funding in staff's IT training, the outcome is not very advantageous.

7 Conclusions

Governments and municipalities have started increasingly to use information and communication technologies in their daily operations. This study examined the use of ICT within the Finnish early childhood education. The study identified areas in which ten largest Finnish municipalities have developed their ECE e-government services. The study therefore provides benchmarks for developing ECE e-government services, and helps municipalities to improve their electronic ECE-services based on the practices in Finland.

As discussed in the previous sections, despite the relatively slow start, the progress towards mature e-government services in ECE in Finland is underway, and it is supported by many regional development projects. Many of the studied municipalities are situated in the higher stages of e-government evolution models: interaction has become two-way between government and citizens, and several municipalities have developed applications which enable online services and financial transactions.

However, the study also has its limitations. The results are limitedly generalized, because the study was conducted just in one country with a minor sample. Nonetheless, the cases described in this paper illustrate the possibilities and challenges many e-government projects especially in the social sector encounter. E-government services should not be seen as obstacles or unavoidable coercion, but as a new way of interacting with citizens and as an opportunity to participate citizens in the governmental processes they are a fundamental part of.

References

1. J.R. Gil-Garcia and I.J. Martinez-Moyano, Understanding the evolution of e-government: The influence of systems of rules on public sector dynamics, *Government Information Quarterly*, Vol.24 (2007), pp. 266-290.
2. M.M. Kamal, IT innovation adoption in the government sector: identifying the critical success factors, *Journal of Enterprise Information Management*, Vol.19 (2006), No.2, pp. 192-222.
3. K. Harjuhahto-Madetoja, V.-V. Ahonen, and S. Hyvärinen, Suomalaista tietoyhteiskuntaa rakentamassa - Hallituksen tietoyhteiskuntaohjelma 2003-2007. 2007, Finnish Government: *Helsinki*.
4. OECD, E-Government in Finland: An Assessment. 2003, Geneve: OECD.
5. Accenture, eGovernment Leadership: High Performance, Maximum Value. The Government Executive Series. 2004: Accenture.
6. Accenture, Leadership in Customer Service: Delivering on the Promise. Government Executive Series. 2007: Accenture.
7. M.P. Gupta and D. Jana, E-government evaluation: A framework and case study, *Government Information Quarterly*, Vol.20 (2003), pp. 365-387.
8. K. Layne and J. Lee, Developing fully functional E-government: A four stage model, *Government Information Quarterly*, Vol.18 (2001), No.2, pp. 122-136.
9. Benchmarking E-Government: A Global Perspective. 2002: United Nations and American Society for Public Administration.
10. J. Hiller and F. Bélanger, eds. *Privacy Strategies for Electronic Government*. E-government 2001, ed. M.A. Abramson and G.E. Means. 2001, Rowman & Littlefield Publishers: Lanham, MD.
11. M.J. Moon, The Evolution of E-Government among Municipalities: Rhetoric or Reality?, *Public Administration Review*, Vol.62 (2002), No.4, pp. 424-433.
12. H. Chen, Digital Government: technologies and practices, *Decision Support Systems*, Vol.34 (2002), No.3, pp. 223-227.
13. OECD, The e-government imperative: main findings. 2003, Geneve: OECD.
14. Day care Act, in 36/1973. Day care Act 36/1973.
15. OECD, Starting Strong II. Early Childhood Education and Care. 2006, OECD Publishing.
16. Ministry of Social Affairs and Health, Decision in Principle of the Council of State Concerning the National Policy Definition on Early Childhood Education and Care. 2002: *Helsinki*.
17. N. Färkkilä, T. Kahiluoto, and M. Kivistö, Report on the situation of children's daycare. September 2005. Reports of the Ministry of Social Affairs and Health. 2006, Helsinki: Ministry of Social Affairs and Health.
18. R.K. Yin, Case Study Research: Design and Methods. Second ed. Applied Social Research Methods Series, ed. D.S. Foster. 1994, Thousand Oaks: Sage Publications, Inc.
19. S. Mäntylä, Lapsiperheet, IT ja tasa-arvo. Esiselvitys. 2003, City of Tampere: *Tampere*.
20. M. Veikkolainen and P. Hämäläinen, Sosiaali- ja terveydenhuollon henkilöstön tieto- ja viestintätekniikan koulutus- ja oppimateriaalitarve ja koulutuksen kehittämisen haasteet. 2006, Stakes: *Helsinki*.

Network-driven Context in User-driven Innovation

Yumiko Kinoshita[1], Osamu Sudoh[2]

[1]Doctoral Student, The University of Tokyo, Graduate School of Interdisciplinary Informatics

[2]Professor, The University of Tokyo, Graduate School of Interdisciplinary Informatics

Abstract. As new networks such as sensor and grid computing are developed, service providers, intermediaries, and users are exposed to an increasing number of contexts, which is a set of information that affects users' behavior and value system in accordance with a network they belongs to. This paper proposes that citizens' contextual data should be collected based on service quality, satisfaction, and technological acceptance model in administrative IT investment and management framework. The main objectives are that the usage rate of online applications increases, and that multi-channel service delivery and One-stop Portal is efficiently and effectively offered in Japanese e-Gov initiative. We present a methodology of visualizing citizens' trust and continual usage intentions in light of an existing service science model as well as providing governance across multiple administrative agencies and organizations.

1. Introduction

The development of Information Technology (IT) has already come to the point at which we require an enhancement of current socio-economic framework, so called 'open economy'. With the introduction of sensor networks, grid computing, pervasive computing, and sophisticated search and semantic algorithms, individuals belong to an increasing number of networks of completely different natures.

In our existing framework of network analysis, this issue is addressed typically as an environmental and complex ecosystem as well as 'structural attributes' associated with the diverse system [1]. Structure reduces risk in a system. However, users not

---

Please use the following format when citing this chapter:

Kinoshita, Y., Sudoh, O., 2008, in IFIP International Federation for Information Processing, Volume 286; Towards Sustainable Society on Ubiquitous Networks, eds. Oya, M., Uda, R., Yasunobu, C., (Boston: Springer), pp. 245–252.

only involve in production or provision process of products and/or services in a value chain to promote innovation, but they also generate innovation by combining, copying, or switching the contexts they belong to. Contexts are created as a reflection of network, and innovation will occur far more at micro level as the number of network increases. This type of innovation depends less on social or economic structure than the conventional concept of user innovation. Therefore, we must be aware of possible effects of such innovation to bring in our society and economy, and provide tools to promote this user-driven innovation based on the contexts in addition to the analysis of path, distance, or contents provided via network. The following section will discuss the relationship of network, context, and innovation by taking e-Government as a case study.

2. Network-driven Context

In recent years, a research field called 'e-Science' is gathering attention. The service sector consists of approximately 75% of most major economies. Various research initiatives are underway to clarify how to improve the productivity of the service sector and enhance innovative capabilities. Freeman and Soete [2] state that we should reconstruct our understanding on major economic indexes including Gross Domestic Product (GDP) due to the rise of the service economy. Under such conditions, e-Science plays a role to consort efforts for finding a mechanism and achieving agility so that both providers and consumers maximize utility especially in IT services.

From the viewpoint of macroeconomics, it is important to create a service portfolio to provide services with diversification, differentiation, and competitive quality. Service sectors can work together with users to gain maximum return for an area where service is being provided. Some services are not tradable. Therefore, geographical elements must be considered in terms of productivity and opportunities for creating new services. The geospatial elements achieve two goals: to increase return on investment per area and to gain competitiveness in a global market by overcoming locality. To support these objectives, IT is used to create access to network among local entities as well as among actors in the global market. In a 'service ecosystem', which is an important concept for 'Service Science', value networks encompass implications to user's satisfaction regarding the quality of services including both tangibles and intangibles i.e. skills and knowledge of users [3].

From micro-level perspective, agent-based modeling is often used to design web applications. In a complex system, multi-agent systems (MAS) specify the protocols for interaction and agent's strategy [4]. MAS achieve outcome, which is not Pareto-dominated by any other outcome, and maximizes social welfare (ibid.). Such systems are implemented when there are multiple sets of preferences and values for a particular agent. For example, automated guided vehicle interacts with environment to achieve competing goals i.e. optimal speed and comfortableness of driving.

Context is a set of information which affects an agent or member's behavior and the value systems that the agent or member hold over geography and time. An agent or member belongs to several networks, each of which creates a context as its reflection. In US, the federal government is investing in building clinical data management capabilities such as electronic medical record (EMR), personal medical record (PMR), and remote healthcare system using mobile communication devices and sensors. Citizens can access one-stop public service portal, access provider's network, or go to *Medline,* a database of life sciences and biomedical information. Citizens, providers, and payers have different contexts in relation to the networks they belong to. As such, multi-level and multi-layered stakes are involved and innovation occurs when each actor actively engages in identifying contexts and restructuring on their own initiatives.

This is a different type of user innovation from 'prosumers' presented by Toffler [5]. 'Prosumers' involve in production and/or provision process for a particular product or service. On the other hand, user-driven innovation is created by switching, copying, reconfiguring, or combining network-driven contexts. With this in mind, it is necessary that socio-economic infrastructure is equipped with a capability to promote this context-oriented user-driven innovation with the presence of various networks.

3. User-driven Innovation and Micro-level Governance

The relationship of value and choice is under constant pressure for change in the open environment. Therefore, technologies should provide an ability to interpret behaviors of different members or agents in a network. This is a dynamic value recognition mechanism embedded in a system. Semantics and simulation technologies are tools for the communication with the system. Interoperability of different applications and standard protocols has been developed so that organizational activities could reduce multiplicity, or heterogeneity of knowledge, through consensus-building mechanism. However, user-driven innovation requires this multiplicity to be encouraged to increase the rate of knowledge production [6], and reflected to social common capital.

Governance is a part of the social capital, which enhances innovative capability of our society and economy. Social capital can be considered from the viewpoint of private and social effects, for example, in the case of healthcare according to Uzawa [7]. The private effect is expressed by the function of the ability of labor and a factor of production. It is optimized according to a utility function, in which an individual person chooses a combination of medical care and its quality subject to a budget constraint. Market equilibrium is achieved based on 'the sum of the levels of medical care provided by all medical institutions', production, labor, wage, demand and price of goods and services (ibid.). As for governance, it is a process of exercising control over the task of information processing in a hierarchy or organizational context [8]. Therefore, governance relates to the hierarchy, in which firms and organizations affect production and other factors.

Governance for network-driven context should be less hierarchical or structural so that user-driven innovation is obtained. Aoki [8] refers to 'relational contingent governance' with regard to the case of venture capital. If a user involves in innovation process as an entrepreneur, governance must be provided as a form of (virtual) symmetry. Symmetry is a method to manipulate structure, system, or domain with no observable change. When symmetrical contexts are presented within a network in addition to the relation of members or agents, users are exposed to the governance mechanism similar to the 'tournament effect' (ibid.). As for public services including healthcare, government agencies have a role to play in providing governance for contexts on behalf of individual member or agent in the network as a social common capital based on mutual trust so that structural void is filled within networks.

The trustworthiness for each service provided by e-government infrastructure is determined by service quality, technical ability, benevolence, and integrity according to Benbasat et al. [9] who surveyed 647 e-government services in Canada. 'Empathy' and 'benevolence' are similar concepts to context. Both of which show the weakest correlation to 'user's trust' and 'continual use intention' among the other attributes (ibid.). It is assumed that the importance of context is not fully recognized by either users or government agencies. This situation poses an important question to ask. Is the existing e-government infrastructure equipped with necessary functions and management scheme to enhance public services and facilitate user innovation in the above-mentioned network-driven context? The following section will review e-Government policy in Japan by focusing on one-stop portal and multi-channel service delivery from the viewpoint of IT investment and capital management.

4. Socio-economic Architecture and Innovation

In Japan, New IT Reform Strategy, developed in 2006, aims at developing the most efficient and usable e-Government in the world [10]. The first target is to increase the usage rate of online applications to 50% by 2010. Secondly, the government will optimize operations and systems through cross-agency cooperation including the coordination of front and back offices. To achieve these goals, the government will particularly emphasize performance-based evaluation and Plan, Do, Check and Action (PDCA) cycle. By 2010, a standard model for service infrastructure will be developed, and One-stop Service Portal will be launched (See *Figure 1*). A part of such efforts is the visualization of administrative service value from user's viewpoint.

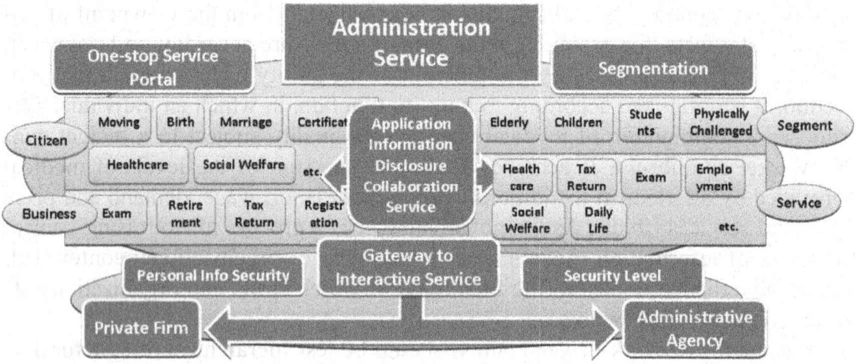

Figure 1 One-stop Service Portal and User Segmentation (Source: Created based on [11])

4.1 Context-based Process Management for Administrative Services

What is the best method for IT investment and capital management for the project of

One-stop Portal and multichannel service delivery so that the benefit is visualized for users? The current evaluation system focuses on qualitative assessment based on user's expected value and perceived value. To manage the One-stop Service Portal in the most efficient and effective manner as well as to achieve user-driven innovation in the network-driven context, the process assessment can be improved as follows.

A proposed method is to extract and manage contextual information from the current system as *Figure 2*. Administrative organizations have improved their process and business toward government-wide optimization. Agency collects information on individual users, technological capability, and user's value systems with regard to a particular service, the agency designs appropriate service at micro level, and visualize values from user's viewpoint in the process evaluation. The overall benefits is captured in the impact evaluation from the viewpoint of economic, social, strategic, political, and innovative benefits [10] at macro level (for both users and the agency).

Through this process, multiple agencies coordinate their contracts to identify common service components to reduce overall investment costs and facilitate service delivery. In this proposed method, government agencies manage the cost and benefit of users based on context more than activity, process, component, or project. Administrative agencies may achieve the next level of transformation after activity-based reform and strategic organizational reform, in which IT investment and management can be implemented thoroughly *from user's viewpoint at an organizational level.*

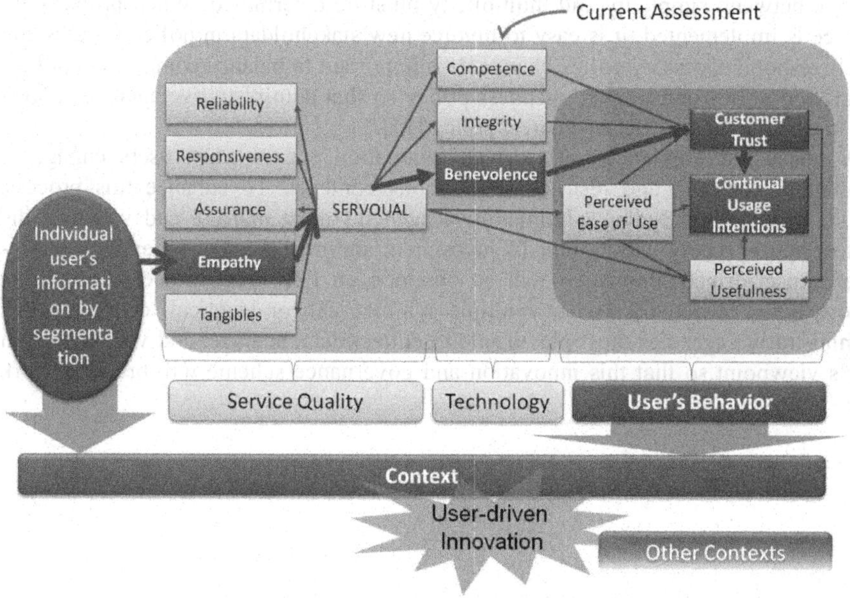

Figure 2 Context-based Management Approach for e-Government (Source: Created based on [9])

4.2 Governance for Context-based Management

Japan's IT management and evaluation scheme is influenced primarily by U.S. Enterprise Architecture model. The above-mentioned context management can be understood within the framework of Federal Enterprise Architecture (FEA) Performance Reference Model (PRM) of Office of Management and Budget. In PRM, IT investment is planned, budgeted, and executed to achieve the lowest life-cycle cost and least risk [11]. The context-based assessment should be particularly useful for mixed life-cycle investment so that IT investment can be managed consistently across multiple systems. In addition, an interagency acquisition is often made based on a multi-agency or government-wide contract to manage one investment project. Such multi-agency collaboration investments require Line of Business (LoB) initiatives as well as Chief Information Officers (CIOs) to consort their efforts to analyze duplicate investments, gaps and opportunities. Because the context-based approach enables us to manage administrative service based on more than an activity or component, it will provide users with a clear picture on what stake they have with the investment.

When regulatory policy has a strong guidance for action across agencies, administrative agencies cope with the issue of multi-layered, multi-level stakes through regulatory power sharing based on certainty, proportionality, and procedures [14]. To overcome the challenge and serve diffuse interests rather than focusing on narrow program interests, IT plays a role to distinguish variables and common areas with regard to the value of administrative services. The variables identified through the context-based management are controlled by power sharing by LoB or CIOs. Thus, the balance between simplicity and multiplicity must be determined. When proper governance is implemented, it is easy to involve new stakeholders in policy debates and timely respond necessary policy change. It is important to balance competition policy, integration policy and market openness policy so that administrative agencies play a role to enforce the conflict-of-interest policy [14].

As discussed previously, user-driven innovation occurs when users engage in combining, copying, and restructuring various contexts. To enhance this process, service providers including administrative agencies must manage and visualize the context appropriately within their IT investment and management schemes. Governance of user-driven innovation will be obtained on P2P (peer-to-peer) bases over various types of networks when multiple symmetrical (or identical) contexts exist. Administrative agencies must play a role to collect data, analyze, and visualize from user's viewpoint so that this innovation and governance scheme will properly work (See *Figure 3*).

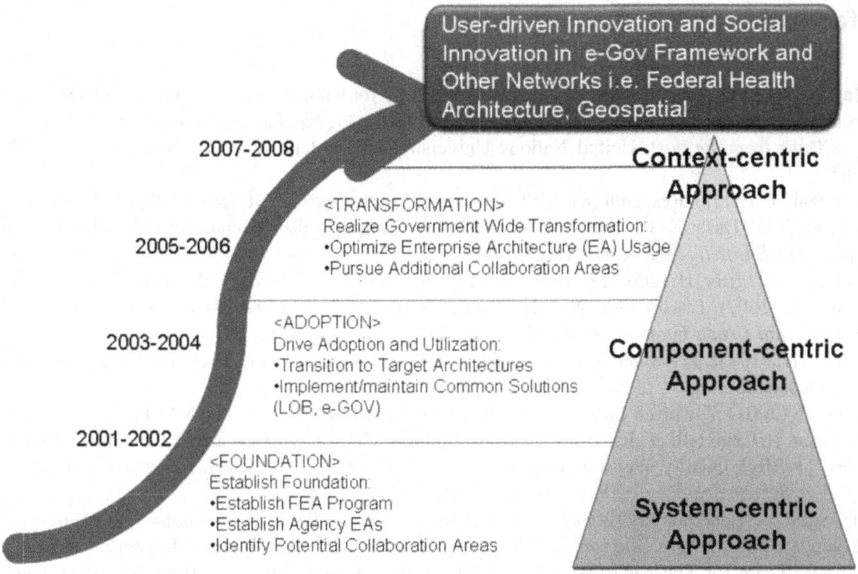

Figure 3 Federal Enterprise Architecture and Context (Source: Created based on [13, 15])

5. Conclusion

This paper argues the method of IT investment and management i.e. e-Government and social issues. This attempt will contribute to the most convenient and effective e-Government from user's viewpoint. The concept of context can be implemented in administrative IT investment and management framework to increase the usage rate of online applications, and to offer multi-channel service delivery and One-stop Portal. As we have seen, network-driven context and user-driven innovation will bring the following benefits. First, the context data is clearly identified and visualized so that public service is provided from user's viewpoint. Secondly, the micro-level governance is implemented.

Lastly, it is also clear that the micro-level governance through providing the symmetrical mechanism must be further studied. Past researches mainly discuss value creation process and the role of services from the viewpoint of industry structure, value chain, and networks. Analysis of pathway, value clustering, and sub-networks have been focused on. The importance of context, which is a product of existing networks, should be carefully considered also. Collaborative, open innovation can be enhanced by integrating network-driven context and user-driven innovation as a form of governance and socio-economic infrastructure. Therefore, this argument is prerequisite for enhancing open innovation based on user's active engagement, and developing socio-economic framework based on service industries including administrative services. From this perspective, the relationship between network and context must be studied further so that research findings can be implemented in our network society as an institutional mechanism.

Reference

1. May, M. R., Levin, A. S., Sugihara, G. (2008). Ecology for bankers. *Nature*, 451(21), 893-895.
2. Freeman, C., Soete, L. (2007). *Developing science, technology and innovation indicators: what we can learn from the past*. United Nations University; UNU-Merit Working Paper Series #2007-001.
3. Sawatani, Y. (2007). Research Service Ecosystems. *Proceedings of PICMET 2007*, 2763-2768.
4. Parkes, C. D., Dash, K. R., Jennings, R. N. (2003). Computational-Mechanism Design: A Call to Arms. *IEEE Intelligent Systems*, 18(6), 40-47.
5. Toffler, A., Toffler, H. (2006). *Evolutionary Wealth*. New York: Currency Doubleday.
6. Fujita, M. (2007). Towards The New Economic Geography In The Brain Power Society, *Regional Science and Urban Economics*, 37(2007), 482-490.
7. Uzawa, H. (2005). *Economic Analysis of Social Common Capital*. New York: Cambridge University Press, 322-358.
8. Aoki, M. (2001). *Toward a Comparative Institutional Analysis*. Boston: The MIT Press.
9. Benbasat, I., Cenfetelli, T. R., Tan, C. (2008). Building Citizen Trust towards e-Government Services: Do High Quality Websites Matter?. *Proceedings of the 41st Hawaii International Conference on System Sciences – 2008*, 1-10.
10. IT Strategic Headquarters (2006). *New IT Reform Strategy: Realizing Ubiquitous and Universal Network Society Where Everyone Can Enjoy the Benefits of IT*. Japan Prime Minister's Office.
11. Project Team for The Next Generation e-Public Service Infrastructure (2008). Resource document. The Government of Japan. http://www.kantei.go.jp/jp/singi/it2/nextg/meeting/dai3/pdf/siryou2.pdf Accessed 13 April 2008.
12. Sudoh, O., Gotoh, R., Akatsu, M., Yoshikawa, H., Nakagawa, T., Kinoshita, Y. (2007). Performance Measurement and Evaluation Framework for e-Government (To Be). In Public Service Analysis Group (eds.), *e-Government Evaluation Committee's Report for the 2nd meeting* (26 July 2007). Division of University Corporate Relations, The University of Tokyo.
13. The Office of Management and Budget Office of E-Government and Information Technology (2007). *FEA Consolidated Reference Model, Document Version 2.3*. Executive Office of the President.
14. OECD (2006). Public Governance. In OECD, *Policy Framework for Investment: A Review of Good Practices*, 233-258.
15. The Office of Management and Budget Office, (2005). *Enabling Citizen-Centered Electronic Government 2005 - 2006 FEA PMO Action Plan*. Executive Office of the President, March 2005.

Does E-government Trust in e-Commerce when Investigating Trust? A Review of Trust Literature in E-Commerce and e-government Domains

Matti Mäntymäki

Turku School of Economics, Information Systems Science
Rehtorinpellonkatu 3, FI-20500 Turku, Finland
matti.mantymaki@tse.fi

Abstract. Trust has been acknowledged to be an important determinant of e-commerce acceptance. Therefore, understanding the nature and importance of trust is momentous in promoting e-government adoption. This paper reviews the trust discussion in business-to-consumer (B2C) e-commerce and government-to-individuals (G2IS) e-government. The aim of the paper is to identify potential differences as well as common denominators in order to introduce aspects that could potentially mutually benefit the research in the e-government and e-commerce domains. The main findings of the study are: 1. both domains trust largely conceptualize as multidimensional construct. 2. In the e-government field, trust is more often also empirically investigated as more than only one variable. 3. In the e-government literature, two main discourses related to trust were identified; trust in government in general, and trust in e-government, referring to the technology aspects.

1 Introduction

Trust has been identified as an important factor in explaining customer's adoption of e-commerce and e-services.[1][2; 3] Pavlou and Fygenson (2006, 133) articulated in their study on B2C e-commerce trust being perhaps the most interesting and empirically influential belief associated with getting information and purchasing products.[4]As stated by numerous authors, trust has been in the interest of several disciplines such as marketing, social psychology, sociology, management and marketing. [5][2]

Please use the following format when citing this chapter:

Mäntymäki, M., 2008, in IFIP International Federation for Information Processing, Volume 286; Towards Sustainable Society on Ubiquitous Networks, eds. Oya, M., Uda, R., Yasunobu, C., (Boston: Springer), pp. 253–264.

The multi-dimensional of trust nature has been widely acknowledged [cf. e.g. 6]. Moreover, the conceptual complexity and thus the difficulties in finding a universal definition of trust have been addressed. [5] Despite these challenges, numerous studies in the e-commerce domain have contributed to increasing understanding on the nature and role of trust as well as its antecedents and consequences.

According to OECD (2003), e-government can be defined as "the use of ICTs, and particularly the Internet, as a tool to achieve better government". According to Lee, Tan, Xin and Trimi (2005) e-government is mainly concerned with providing high quality public services and value-added information to citizens.[9] In this study, e-commerce is defined rather broadly to encompass products and services

E-government has become an emerging field of research in the recent years. [7] E-government can be categorized in several ways, depending on the services offered and the target group of the offering. In this paper, we conceptualize e-government as the services that a governmental organization provides to individuals, referring to the categorization (G2IS) by Bélanger & Hiller (2006).[8]

This paper investigates the trust literature in business-to-consumer (B2C) e-commerce and G2IS e-government fields of research. The aim is to identify potential differences as well as common denominators in order to introduce aspects that could potentially mutually benefit the research in the e-government and e-commerce domains. Thus, the paper contributes the e-government research by presenting an overview of the trust discussion within the domain and reflecting it to the respective literature from e-commerce. In practical terms, this is done by reviewing prior literature and presenting the findings in a structured form.

This study focuses on business-to-consumer (B2C) e-commerce and e-services. Similarly, the e-government domain is restricted to electronic services the government provides to citizens. Thus, services targeted to corporate customers (B2B and G2B) are excluded from this study, as well as C2C e-commerce.

2 Trust in B2C e-Commerce and G2IS e-Government Literature

As stated by Cheung et al (2005, 8), trust and perceived risk have been extensively investigated in relation to online purchase intentions.[10] IT acceptance has evolved as one of the most influential streams of research within the IS discipline [11]Several models have been developed to investigate and explain users' acceptance of new technologies[12; 13] However, in the IS research IS continuance and post-adoption behavior have become an emergent topic in the recent years which is also reflected in the reviewed trust literature. [14; 15][16; 17]

In ProQuest database a search using terms 'e-commerce' and 'trust' returns 1745 results, when limiting the search to academic articles the number of hits drops to 166. Conducting the search with 'e-government' and 'trust' the number total number of hits is 65 of which 18 are peer reviewed.

In the first round of the review, a keyword-based search was done in ProQuest/Abi/Inform, EbscoHost, Emerald and Elsevier ScienceDirect databases. Keywords 'trust' and 'e-government', 'trust' and electronic government', and finally, 'trust', 'government', and 'internet' were used. The first round of the review revealed that the academic discussion around e-government is fragmented across several forums. Therefore, two one dedicated e-government journals, Electronic Government, and International Journal and Electronic Journal of e-Government were included in the second round consisting of systematic review of the key publications as suggested by Webster & Watson (2002)[18]. The review of e-commerce trust literature was done solely using keywords 'trust' and 'e-commerce' and 'trust' and 'electronic commerce'.

The reviewed e-commerce trust literature has been divided into three rather wide categories, studies discussing trust in e-commerce adoption and studies focusing on ongoing customer relationships after the initial adoption or acceptance has taken place, i.e. the post-adoption phase. The third category consists of literature reviews and conceptual papers. Self-evidently, the table does not contain all the literature that has been published, but the purpose is to give an overview of trust literature in the e-commerce domain. The aim of the categorization is used to somewhat compress and systematize the way the results are presented. The reviewed e-commerce trust literature is presented in tables 1, 2 & 3 and the e-government literature in table 4.

Table 1. B2C e-commerce studies focusing on trust in initial acceptance

Studies on adoption and acceptance	**View of trust**	**Findings**	**Theoretical framework**
Pavlou [3] Lim et al. (2006)[19] Pavlou et al. (2006)[4] Gefen et al.(2003)[21] Gefen & Straub (2003)[22] Pavlou et. al. (2007)[23] Hampton-Sosa & Koufaris (2005) [20] Bhattacherjee (2002)[1] McKnight et al. (2002)[6]	Set of trusting beliefs, operationalized as a single variable [3] Trusting belifes + trust propensity as variables [20] Multidimensional, Also operationalized as multidimensional [1] [6]	TAM+trust+risk determinants of purchase intentions and actual purchases [3] Trust increases willingness to buy [19] Trust influences attitudes and controllability over getting information and purchasing [4] Trust integrated to TAM [21] [22] Trust impacts purchase intentions indirectly through perceived uncertainty [23] Initial trust as a mediator between web site appeal and usefulness and intention to use a web site, trust propensity an antecedent of initial trust [20] Develops and test a scale for measuring trust [1] Familiarity Willingness to transact [1] Tests and validates the framework developed by McKnight [6]	TAM [3] TRA [19] TPB [4] TAM [21] [22] Principal-agent theory [23] TAM [20] Trust literature from several disciplines TRA [6]

Table 2. B2C e-commerce studies focusing on trust after the initial acceptance

Studies	**View of trust**	**Findings**	**Theoretical framework**
Li et al. (2006a)[29] Thatcher & George (2004)[30] Gummerus et al. (2004)[31] Cyr et al. (2007)[32] Anderson & Srinivasan (2003)[33] Floh & Treiblmaier (2006)[34] Pennanen et al. 2007 [35] Wang & Head (2006) [36] Gefen (2002)[37] Mukherjee & Nath (2007) [38] Luarn & Lin (2003)[28]	Operationalized as a single variable, however the authors discuss that trust is not un-dimensional [29] Trust in the Internet [30] Operationalized as a single variable Operationalized as a single variable Operationalized as a single variable, yet the multidimensional nature of trust is discussed [32] Operationalized as a single variable [33] Operationalized as a single variable [34] Multidimensional, Evolving [35] Multidimensional, Operationalized as a single variable [36] Operationalized as a single variable Reliability and empathy investigated within servqual [37] Multidimensional, Operationalized as a single variable Set of specific beliefs (integrity, benevolence, competence and predictability) Operationalized as a single variable [28]	Commitment a stronger predictor for stickiness thantrust. The impact of trust also mediated by commitment [29] After a certain level of experience, trust in the Internet not correlated to loyalty. [30] Service quality-trust-satisfaction-loyalty chain. Trust as a mediator between service quality dimensions and customer satisfaction [31] Trust mediates between perceived social presence and e-loyalty [32] Trust mediates between E-satisfaction and e-loyalty [33] Trust mediates the impact of service quality and web site quality on loyalty. [34] Presents a framework for consumer e-trust building process [35] Trust has an impact on relationship intention [36] Trust important also among veteran customers, servqual an antecedent of trust [37] Privacy the most important determinant of trust. Also communication is important.[38] Commitment as a powerful mediator between trust, satisfaction, perceived value and loyalty [28]	Investment model for interpersonal relationships & commitment trust theory [29] TRA [30] SERVQUAL [29] TAM [32] N/A [33] [34] [36] Qualitative study, [35] SERVQUAL [37] Commitment-trust theory [38] Trust-commitment framework [28]

Table 3. B2C e-commerce literature reviews on trust

Studies	View of trust	Findings
Wang & Emurian[24]	Multidimensional, [24] [2] [27] [25]	Framework for trust inducing features [24]
Tan & Sutherland (2004)[25]	Proposed operationalization one-dimensional [26]	In IS literature, trust is often seen as one-dimensional, only focusing on the interpersonal aspect, ignoring the dispositional and institutional dimension. [25]
Holsapple & Sasidharan[26]	Multidimensional, Dynamic [5]	Proposes a research model that includes subjective norm, computer anxiety and computer self-efficacy to the TAM framework. [26]
Grabner-Kräuter & Kaluscha (2003) [5]		Conceptual challenges in empirical studies, different definitions & concepts, comparing empirical studies difficult [5]
McKnight & Chervany (2001)[2]		Comprehensive conceptualization of trust [2]
Kim et al. (2005)[27]		Comparison of academics' and practitioners' perspectives of trust. Content analysis, semantic network analysis. [27]

Table 4. G2IS e-government literature discussing trust

Studies	View of trust	Findings	Theoretical framework
Carter & Bélanger (2005)[39]	Multidimensional, Operationalized as a single variable [39]	Compatibility, ease of use and trustworthiness significant predictors of intention to use. [39]	Integrated DOI + TAM + trustworthiness [39]
Schaupp & Carter (2005)[40]	Multidimensional, Operationalized as a single variable [40]	Compatibility, perceived usefulness and trust the predictors of internet voting among young citizens. [40]	Integrated DOI + TAM + trust [40]
Horst, Kuttscreuter & Gutteling (2007)[41]	Trust in relation to risk [41]	Trust in e-government main determinant of PU. [41]	Applied TBP framework [41]
Bélanger & Carter (2008)[7]	Multidimensional, also operationalized as multidimensional, including disposition to trust [7]	Trust of the Internet and trust of the government influence the intention to use. [7]	TRA [7]
Tolbert & Mossberger (2006)[42]	Trust and confidence in government Multi-dimensional, process-based and institutional-based. [42]	E-government can increase process-based trust by improving interaction with citizens. [42]	N/A [42]
Grimsley & Meehan (2007)[43]	Community perspectives of trust, trust in relation to public value [43]	Trust is related to feeling of being well-informed, greater personal control and sense of influence or contingency [43].	Interpretive approach to IS evaluation. [43]
Welch, Hinnant & Moon (2004)[44]	Trust in government Multi-dimensional Fiduciary, mutual and social trust [44]	Visiting local government web site lead to enhanced trust in local government. [44]	N/A [44]
Li, Hess & Valacich (2008) [45]	Multidimensional, Also empirically investigated as multidimensional [45]	Cognitive base trust (reputation) and calculative base have a significant impact on adoption whereas e.g. personality base and institutional based had a smaller effect.	Trust + TRA [45]
Gilbert, Balestrini & Littleboy (2004)[46]	One-dimensional [46]	(Lack of) Trust were found to be an adoption barrier [46]	DOI+TAM+SERVQUAL [46]
Gonzales, Gasco & Llopis (2007)[47]	One-dimensional [47]	Trust creation as a final phase e-government evolution [47]	Case study [47]

3 Discussion

Implications for research and practice

E-government is still a relatively new area of research. The first e-government articles presented in this paper were published in 2004.Thus, compared to rather large number of studies on trust within the e-commerce field of research, the trust discussion within the e-government domain is relatively meagre.

As stated earlier, the complex nature and challenges in defining of trust have been articulated by several authors. [cf. e.g. 5; 48] As articulated by e.g. McKnight et al. 2001, trust can be viewed to have dispositional, interpersonal and institutional dimensions and neither of these dimensions is by nature monolithic. Despite most of the authors acknowledge the fact that trust is a multi-dimensional construct, in most of the listed e-commerce studies trust is operationalized as a single variable. In the e-government field, relatively more studies empirically investigate trust as a multidimensional construct. This interesting finding may be explained by the fact that the research on trust within the e-government domain has benefited from prior trust research within e-commerce and e-services.

In the reviewed e-government literature, two main areas of trust discussion were identified. Trust in e-government [cf. e.g. 39] refers to individuals' perception of the trustworthiness of the technology used in producing and delivering the governmental service whereas trust in government [cf. e.g. 42; 44; 49] reflects individuals' perception on trustworthiness of the government in a wider perspective, including the political system and administration.

In the e-commerce literature, trust has been extensively discussed in relation to adoption.[10] However, particularly the recent e-commerce research includes examples of studies investigating trust also related to continuous use and customer loyalty. [cf. e.g. 13; 29] In the e-government literature the emphasis has so far been rather on exploring the adoption than continuous use of e-government services. This can be explained by the fact that the e-government per se is a relatively new phenomenon and therefore, investigating citizens' initial adoption is of particular importance. When looking back to the early days of trust research within the e-commerce domain, which is a more mature field of research, one can interpret that e-government research will evolve similarly from adoption towards focusing more on continuous use.

As regards the theoretical frameworks, multiple background theories have been used in the reviewed studies. In the presented e-commerce studies, quantitative analysis and literature reviews are in an important position. Quantitative research methods dominate also the reviewed e-government literature on trust. The e-government studies largely utilize the conceptualizations of trust from the e-commerce literature which may explain the lack of literature reviews focusing on trust in the e-government literature.

From a managerial perspective, trust is an issue of great significance in both a-commerce and e-government areas, influencing not only the initial adoption but also the subsequent phases of the customer relationship. Since the role of trust evolves, it is a dynamic construct. Developing differentiated means for nurturing trust for novice and experienced users could potentially help to built enduring relationships with the users.

E-government has reported to provide several benefits from both the citizens' and government's perspective in form of costs savings and improving the availability of the service. (cf. e.g. Gonzales et al. 2007.)[47] Moreover, as stated by e.g. Welch et al. (2005) [44], use of e-government can increases citizens' overall trust in government. As trust has been identified to have an influence on e-commerce adoption, building trust is an important issue also from a managerial perspective.

Limitations

As with every research, also this study has its limitations. First of all, the risk with literature reviews is that important contributions are for some reason not included in the scrutiny. To reduce this risk, a systematic review of two dedicated e-government journals was conducted. However, since the e-government discussion is fragmented across several journals, the systematic approach did not create much additional value.

As the focus of this study was more on the e-government side, only a fraction of trust literature from e-commerce domain was selectively included in this review. Since both e-commerce and e-government are published on same forums, conducting a systematic review of e.g. ten key e-commerce journals would be a natural step to continue this path of research.

Directions for future research

This paper has investigated trust discussion in e-commerce and e-government fields. A potential avenue for further investigation would be to include e-health in the focus of the study. This could provide a more comprehensive picture of the trust discussion in the e-area.

One potential avenue to enrich the view of trust in the e-government domain would be to investigate trust from political science perspective. Introducing the concept of power from political science would potentially offer insight on how power and authority influence may trust in the e-government context.

Since trust is a dynamic construct, its role probably evolves after the initial adoption has taken place. So far, only very studies have done systematic attempts to investigate the dynamics of trust.

Moreover, attempts to put a price tag on trust would be interesting, i.e. what cost and/or benefit of nurturing trust. This issue has been investigated to some extent related to electronic marketplaces [50] but not extensively related to e-government. Thus, gaining a better understanding on the financial consequences of trust would be an insightful avenue for research also in the e-government domain.

4 Conclusions

The aim of the paper was to review B2C e-commerce and e-services and G2IS e-government trust literature in order to find differences as well as common denominators that could identify potential paths for further research and help to understand the present state of trust discussion within the two domains. The reviewed trust literature was divided into four categories, findings were discussed from a theoretical and managerial perspective and avenues for additional research suggested.

References

1. Bhattacherjee, A. (2002). Individual trust in online firms: Scale development and initial test. *Journal of Management Information Systems, 19*(1), 211-241.
2. Mcknight, D. H. (2001). What trust means in E-commerce customer relationships: An interdisciplinary conceptual typology. *International Journal of Electronic Commerce, 6*(2), 35-59.
3. Pavlou, P. A. (2003). Consumer acceptance of electronic commerce: Integrating trust and risk with the technology acceptance model. *International Journal of Electronic Commerce, 7*(3), 101-134.
4. Pavlou, P. A., & Fygenson, M. (2006). Understanding and predicting electronic commerce adoption: An extension of the theory of planned behavior. *MIS Quarterly, 30*(1), 115-143.
5. Grabner-Kräuter, S., & Kaluscha, E. A. (2003). Empirical research in on-line trust: A review and critical assessment. *International Journal of Human-Computer Studies, 58*(6), 783-812.
6. McKnight, D. H. (2002). Developing and validating trust measures for e-commerce: An integrative typology. *Information Systems Research, 13*(3), 334-359.
7. Bélanger, F., & Carter, L. Trust and risk in e-government adoption. *The Journal of Strategic Information Systems, In Press, Corrected Proof*
8. Belanger, F., & Hiller, J. S. (2006). A framework for e-government: Privacy implications. *Business Process Management Journal, 12*(1), 48.
9. Lee, S. M., Tan, X., & Trimi, S. (2005). Current practices of leading e-government countries. *Association for Computing Machinery.Communications of the ACM, 48*(10), 99.
10. Cheung, C. M. K. (2005). A critical review of online consumer behavior: Empirical research. *Journal of Electronic Commerce in Organizations, 3*(4), 1-19.
11. Jasperson, J. (., Carter, P. E., & Zmud, R. W. (2005). A comprehensive conceptualization of post-adoptive behaviors associated with information technology enabled work systems. *MIS Quarterly, 29*(3), 525-557.
12. Venkatesh, V. (2003). User acceptance of information technology: Toward a unified view. *MIS Quarterly, 27*(3), 425-478.
13. Premkumar, G., & Bhattacherjee, A. (2008). Explaining information technology usage: A test of competing models. *Omega, 36*(1), 64-75.
14. Bhattacherjee, A. (2001). An empirical analysis of the antecedents of electronic commerce service continuance. *Decision Support Systems, 32*(2), 201-214.
15. Bhattacherjee, A. (2001). Understanding information systems continuance: An expectation-confirmation model. *MIS Quarterly; Minneapolis, 25*(3), 351-370.
16. Parthasarathy, M. (1998). Understanding post-adoption behavior in the context of online services. *Information Systems Research, 9*(4), 362-379.
17. Spiller, J., Vlasic, A., & Yetton, P. (2007). Post-adoption behavior of users of internet service providers. *Information & Management, 44*(6), 513-523.

18. Webster, J., & Watson, R. T. (2002). Analyzing the past to prepare for the future: Writing a literature review. *MIS Quarterly, 26*(2), 13-23.
19. Lim, K. H., Sia, C. L., Lee, M. K. O., & Benbasat, I. (2006). Do I trust you online, and if so, will I buy? an empirical study of two trust-building strategies. *Journal of Management Information Systems, 23*(2), 233-266.
20. Hampton-Sosa, W., & Koufaris, M. (2005). The effect of web site perceptions on initial trust in the owner company. *International Journal of Electronic Commerce, 10*(1), 55-81.
21. Gefen, D., Karahanna, E., & Straub, D. W. (2003). Trust and TAM in online shopping: An integrated model. *MIS Quarterly; Minneapolis, 27*(1), 51-90.
22. Gefen, D., & Straub, D. W. (2003). Managing user trust in B2C e-services. *E - Service Journal; Bloomington, 2*(2), 7.
23. Pavlou, P. A., Huigang Liang, & Yajiong Xue. (2007). Understanding and mitigating uncertainty in online exchange relationships: A principal--agent perspective. *MIS Quarterly, 31*(1), 105-136.
24. Wang, Y. D., & Emurian, H. H. (2005). An overview of online trust: Concepts, elements, and implications. *Computers in Human Behavior, 21*(1), 105-125.
25. Tan, F. B., & Sutherland, P. (2004). Online consumer trust: A multi-dimensional model. *Journal of Electronic Commerce in Organizations, 2*(3), 40.
26. Holsapple, C. W., & Sasidharan, S. (2005). The dynamics of trust in B2C e-commerce: A research model and agenda. *Information Systems and eBusiness Management, 3*(4), 377.
27. Kim, D. J., Song, Y. I., Baynov, S. B., & Rao, H. R. (2005). A multidimensional trust formation model in B-to-C e-commerce: A conceptual framework and content analyses of academia/practitioner perspectives. *Decision Support Systems, 40*(2), 143.
28. Luarn, P., & Lin, H. (2003). A customer loyalty model for E-service context. *Journal of Electronic Commerce Research, 4*(4), 156-167.
29. Li, D., Browne, G. J., & Chau, P. Y. K. (2006). An empirical investigation of web site use using a commitment-based model. *Decision Sciences, 37*(3), 427-444.
30. Thatcher, J. B., & George, J. F. (2004). Commitment, trust, and social involvement: An exploratory study of antecedents to web shopper loyalty. *Journal of Organizational Computing and Electronic Commerce, 14*(4), 243.
31. Gummerus, J., Liljander, V., Pura, M., & van Riel, A. (2004). Customer loyalty to content-based web sites: The case of an online health-care service. *The Journal of Services Marketing, 18*(2/3), 175.
32. Cyr, D. The role of social presence in establishing loyalty in e-service environments. *Interacting with Computers, 19*(1), 43-56.
33. Anderson, R. E., & Srinivasan, S. S. (2003). E-satisfaction and E-loyalty: A contingency framework. *Psychology & Marketing, 20*(2), 123-138.
34. Floh, A., & Treiblmaier, H. (2006). What keeps the E-banking customer loyal? a multigroup analysis of the moderating role of consumer characteristics on E-loyalty in the financial service industry. *Journal of Electronic Commerce Research, 7*(2), 97.
35. Pennanen, K., Tiainen, T., & Luomala, H. T. (2007). A qualitative exploration of a consumer's value-based e-trust building process. *Qualitative Market Research, 10*(1), 28.
36. Wang, F., & Head, M. (2007). How can the web help build customer relationships?: An empirical study on e-tailing. *Information & Management, 44*(2), 115.
37. Gefen, D. (2002). Customer loyalty in E-commerce. *Journal of the Association for Information Systems, 3*, 27-51.
38. Mukherjee, A., & Nath, P. (2007). Role of electronic trust in online retailing. *European Journal of Marketing, 41*(9), 1173-1202.
39 Carter, L., & Bélanger, F. (2005). The utilization of e-government services: Citizen trust, innovation and acceptance factors. *Information Systems Journal, 15*(1), 5-25.
40 Schaupp, L. C., & Carter, L. (2005). E-voting: From apathy to adoption. *Journal of Enterprise Information Management, 18*(5/6), 586.

41 Horst, M., Kuttschreuter, M., & Gutteling, J. M. (2007). Perceived usefulness, personal experiences, risk perception and trust as determinants of adoption of e-government services in the netherlands. *Computers in Human Behavior, 23*(4), 1838-1852.
42 Tolbert, C. J., & Mossberger, K. (2006). The effects of E-government on trust and confidence in government. *Public Administration Review, 66*(3), 354.
43 Grimsley, M., & Meehan, A. (2007). e-government information systems: Evaluation-led design for public value and client trust. *European Journal of Information Systems, 16*(2), 134.
44 Welch, E. W. (2005). Linking citizen satisfaction with E-government and trust in government. *Journal of Public Administration Research and Theory, 15*(3), 371.
45 Li, X., Hess, T. J., & Valacich, J. S. Why do we trust new technology? A study of initial trust formation with organizational information systems. *The Journal of Strategic Information Systems, In Press, Corrected Proof*
46 Gilbert, D., Balestrini, P., & Littleboy, D. (2004). Barriers and benefits in the adoption of e-government. *The International Journal of Public Sector Management, 17*(4/5), 286.
47 Gonzalez, R., Gasco, J., & Llopis, J. (2007). E-government success: Some principles from a spanish case study. *Industrial Management + Data Systems, 107*(6), 845.
48 Cowles, D. L. (1997). The role of trust in customer relationships: Asking the right questions. *Management Decision, 35*(4), 273-282.
49 West, D. M. (2004). E-government and the transformation of service delivery and citizen attitudes. *Public Administration Review, 64*(1), 15.
50 Pavlou, P. A., & Dimoka, A. (2006). The nature and role of feedback text comments in online marketplaces: Implications for trust building, price premiums, and seller differentiation. *Information Systems Research, 17*(4), 392-414.

Effects of Information Communication Technology on Urban and Rural Service Sectors: An Empirical Analysis of Japanese Economic Geography

Hideyuki Tanaka, Takeshi Okamoto

The University of Tokyo, Graduate School of Interdisciplinary of Information Studies,

7-3-1, Hongo, Bunkyo-ku, Tokyo, Japan

Abstract. The present paper investigates the impacts of information communication technology (ICT) on economic geography by focusing on the Japanese service sectors. The authors empirically assess the effects of ICT on the urban and rural service sectors using Japanese economic data. There are two main findings. The first indicates that the service sectors in urban areas agglomerated from 2000 to 2006. The second is that the ICT environment might affect the location of the service sectors; an especially dense ICT service could accelerate agglomeration in urban areas. However, the effects of the ICT-related environment on the location of the service sectors are different in urban and rural areas. A dense ICT service environment might disperse service sectors in a rural area.

1. Introduction

The present paper investigates the impacts of information communication technology (ICT) on economic geography by focusing on the Japanese service sectors.[1] Service sectors have become the main engine of the world economy, accounting for approximately 70% of aggregate production and employment in OECD countries (OECD 2005). In Japan, the service sector share of total employment has risen from

[1] Section 4 will show the types of service industries included in present analysis.

Please use the following format when citing this chapter:

Tanaka, H., Okamoto, T., 2008, in IFIP International Federation for Information Processing, Volume 286; Towards Sustainable Society on Ubiquitous Networks, eds. Oya, M., Uda, R., Yasunobu, C., (Boston: Springer), pp. 265–277.

47% in 1970 to 67% in 2005[2]. The service sectors play a major role in the Japanese economy and affect the country's urban structure.

From a geographical viewpoint, service sectors were previously concentrated in urban areas because of the sectors' focus on the spatial distribution of the demand for their services (Tabuchi and Thisse 2006). One of the characteristics of service is direct or face-to-face interaction between provider and consumer, which is difficult to provide beyond a certain distance. The share of the service sector market in the thirteen largest Japanese cities[3] was more than ten points larger than the remaining cities combined in 2006[4].

ICT affects several aspects of the service sectors. The development of ICT has reduced communication and coordination costs across distances. Services can be provided from a distance using ICT, including e-commerce, digital music, and on-line support. A significant cost reduction could induce or accelerate sector agglomeration in urban areas based on the core-periphery argument (Krugman 1991). The productivity of the sectors has also been advanced by ICT. Historically, improvement of service sector productivity has been difficult. The labor intensiveness of the services provided has made productivity advancements more difficult than in the manufacturing sector, for which productivity improvements could be made through mechanization. This phenomenon, known as Baumol's cost disease, has been altered through ICT, which provides opportunities for the service sector innovation (Baumol 1961). Innovative sectors have been shown to prosper in large, diverse metropolitan areas (Henderson et al. 1995). Consequently, sector expansion and agglomeration in urban areas may be facilitated by ICT.

The research question explored in the present study is whether ICT accelerates or deters service sector agglomeration. The impact of ICT on the urban structure has been disputed for more than a decade, as is described in Section 2. However, previous quantitative empirical studies have not assessed the impacts on service sector agglomeration. In addition, few empirical studies of ICT and urban agglomeration have been based on quantitative data collected in Japan. The authors intend to contribute to economic geography by using recent Japanese empirical data to evaluate the role of ICT in the service sectors. The remainder of the paper is organized as follows. Section two surveys related literature, section three describes the methodology used in the empirical analyses. Section four summarizes the Japanese statistical data and the empirical analyses. Section five assesses the agglomeration of the service sectors and section six investigates impacts of ICT on service sector agglomeration. The authors discuss the results in section seven and conclude the research in section eight.

---

[2] The figures are based on the 2005 National Census of Japan.

[3] The thirteen cities are consistent with the data used in the empirical analyses. The cities are the ordinance-designated cities as of 2000: Sapporo, Sendai, Chiba, Tokyo-special wards, Yokohama, Kawasaki, Nagoya, Kyoto, Osaka, Hiroshima, Kitakyushu, and Fukuoka.

[4] The service sectors account for 84% of the employment in the 13 largest cities and 72% in the remaining urbanized areas, based on the 2006 Establishment and Enterprise Census.

2. Related Literature

The role of ICT in determining the location of economic activity has been evaluated previously. One of the main arguments addresses whether ICT is a substitute for or a complement to face-to-face interaction. If the former effect is indicated, economic activity is liberated from geographic limitations. If ICT complements personal interaction, services should remain concentrated in urban areas (Gaspar and Glaeser 1998).

Empirical research has identified two effects of ICT on the need for face-to-face communication. The first type (Type I) investigates the effects of ICT adoption on urban agglomeration. Using data for U.S. ICT workers, Kolko (2002) contends that ICT raises the speed of spatial dispersion and lowers the level of industry concentration by controlling the distribution of educated workers. Ioannides et al. (2008) present international data supporting the assertion that increases in the number of telephone lines per capita encourage spatial dispersion of population. Contrary to these results, which suggest a substitution effect, Biteux-Orain and Guillain (2004) reveal that a complement effect exists in addition to the substitute effect in face-to-face interaction based on French data.

The second effect (Type II) deals with the influence of the urban environment on ICT adoption. Zook (2002) argued that the regional distribution of venture capital investment played a central role in determining the location of new Internet startups. Pons-Novell and Viladecans-Marsal (2006) conducted a survey in the province of Barcelona and showed that off-line commercial distribution in cities affected the Internet availability. Forman et al. (2003, 2005a, b) introduced a new outlook on the face-to-face argument based on the General Purpose Technology (GPT) theory (Bresnahan and Trajtenberg 1995). They identified two purposes for adopting the Internet in business; one is participation and the other is enhancement. Examples of the former are e-mail and web-browsing, i.e. the basic purposes, and those of the latter are e-commerce and security, i.e. the complex purposes. Their empirical studies show that the urban environment affects ICT adoption when the latter purpose is sought. ICT users require support by skilled labor or technical support such as system engineers, software consultancy, and IT system integrators. Urban settings make it possible to supply the dense technical supports for firms by means of face-to-face interactions. Furthermore, firms in urban areas could effectively adopt ICT as GPT and change their business model or organization.

Recent empirical works shed light on ICT-related service sectors (hereafter, ICT service sector) demonstrating that technical or professional support by the ICT service sectors plays a key role in the effective implementation of IT systems for business use. The ICT service sectors are concentrated in urban areas. Isaksen (2004) explains the reasons for the clustering of the Norwegian software sector in the Oslo area based on the need for face-to-face support. Aslesen and Isaksen (2007) reveal that urban firms use consultancy services more frequently than those located outside of urban areas. Arora and Forman (2007) show that the magnitude of local ICT services significantly influences the decision to out-source software programming and design.

Prior studies deal with the relationship between ICT adoption and urban structure or between the ICT-related urban environments and ICT adoption (Table 2.1). The present authors aim to verify the relationship between the ICT-related urban environments and urban structure (Type III) and focus on local ICT service sectors as an ICT-related urban environment. Furthermore, the goal of the present study is to determine whether the urban ICT environment affects urban structure through latent technology adoption.

Table 2.1
Prior studies and the authors study

ICT-related urban environments (a)	ICT adoption (b)	Urban structure (c)
	Type I (b<=>c) Kolko(2002), Ioannides et al.(2008), Biteux-Orain and Guillain (2004)	
Type II (a<=>b) Zook (2002), Pons-Novell and Viladecans-Marsal (2006), Forman et al. (2003,2005a,b), Arora and Forman (2007), Aslesen and Isaksen(2007)		
Type III (a<=>c) Research by the authors		

3. Methodology

The basic economic model of the present research is based on the summaries of three theories regarding dynamic externalities in urban environments provided in Glaeser et al. (1992). The first theory is the Marshall-Arrow-Romer (MAR) externality. The first externality concerns knowledge spillovers between firms in an industry (localization). The concentration of an industry in a city helps firms to share knowledge spillovers and enhances the growth of that industry and city. The theory predicts that a local monopoly is better for growth than local competition because the flow of ideas to other firms is restricted by local monopoly. The second theory is the Porter (1990) externality. The theory states that knowledge spillovers in specialized, geographically concentrated industries stimulate growth. In contrast, local competition fosters the pursuit and rapid adoption of innovation (competition). The third theory is Jacobs' (1969) study of diverse urban economies, in which the most important knowledge transfers come from outside the core industry. The externality is derived from a buildup of knowledge or ideas associated with historical diversity. Similar to Porter (1990), Jacobs (1969) favors local competition. Glaeser et al.(1992) extended three theories into the following model.

$A_t f(l_t)$ is the production function of a firm in a certain industry, where A_t represents the overall level of technology at time t measured nominally, and l_t is the labor input at time t. Each firm in this industry takes technology, prices, and wages, w_t, as given and maximizes equation (3-1).

$A_t f(l_t) - w_t\, l_t$ (3-1)

Labor input is set so as to equate the marginal product of labor to its wage, as in equation (3-2).

$A_t f'(l_t) = w_t$ (3-2)

(3-2) can be rewritten in terms of growth as equation (3-3).

$\log(A_{t+1} / A_t) = \log(w_{t+1} / w_t) - \log(f'(l_{t+1}) / f'(l_t))$ (3-3)

A_t contains national and local technology (3-4).

$A_t = A_{local}\, A_{national}$ (3-4)

$\log(A_{t+1} / A_t) = \log(A_{local,t+1} / A_{local,t}) + \log(A_{national,t+1} / A_{nationall,t})$ (3-5)

The local technology is assumed to grow at a rate exogenous to the firm but is dependent on various technological externalities present in this industry in the city, as in equation (3-6)

$\log(A_{local,t+1} / A_{local,t}) = g(\text{specialization, competition, diversity, initial conditions}) + e_{t+1}$ (3-6)

If we set $f(l) = l^{1-\alpha}$, $0 < a < 1$, we can obtain equation (3-7)

$\alpha \log(l_{t+1} / l_t) = -\log(w_{t+1} / w_t) + \log(A_{national,t+1} / A_{nationall,t}) + g(\text{specialization, competition, diversity, initial conditions}) + e_{t+1}$ (3-7)

Equation (3-7) allows us to associate the growth of employment in a particular industry in a city with measures of technological externalities given by the above theories. In the following section, we will empirically assess the effect of the ICT-related environment as one of the initial conditions based on equation (3-7).

4. Data

The data set is composed of four Japanese government statistics: the Establishment and Enterprise Census conducted by the Ministry of Internal Affairs and Communications (MIC); the Population Census conducted by MIC; the Survey of Selected Service Industries conducted by the Ministry of Economy, Trade and Industry (METI); and the Basic Survey on Wage Structure conducted by the Ministry of Health, Labor and Welfare (MHLW).

The data set contains information on employment, payroll, number of establishments, and education by two-digit sector. The authors obtained wages by dividing payroll by employment. The limitations of the data structure require that we use data for the 13 ordinance-designated cities and 47 prefectures. Data from prefectures that contain a major city/cities exclude the data for the city/cities. There are 60 statistical divisions in the data. The service sectors are classified according to the Japan Standard Industrial Classification, and include sectors H (Information and Communications) to Q (Services, N.E.C), excluding I (Transport). The one-digit sector I is omitted because payrolls data could not be obtained. Furthermore, the following two-digit sectors are excluded because of changes in the classifications in 2004: 37, 40, 41, 68, 69, 78, 94. Although, there could be a maximum 2,640 area-sectors, we finalized 2,578 area-sectors as basic observations because certain area-sectors have no employment. In the following sections, we exclude outliers beyond mean plus standard deviation (SD) x 4 or below mean minus SDx4 for some variables.

Following Glaeser et al. (1992) and Kolko (2002), the authors use a natural logarithm of the sector-area employment growth rate from year 2000 to year 2006 as a proxy for agglomeration (or dispersion). The dependent variable is lnEmpG.

$\ln EmpG_{ix}$: $\ln Emp_{ix}^{2006}$-$\ln Emp_{ix}^{2000}$: employment growth from 2000 to 2006

Independent variables are defined as follows. The first three variables correspond, respectively, to specialization, competition, and diversity in equation (3-7).

Spc_{ix}=$Emp_{ix}^{2000}/Emp_{i}^{2000}$: specialization
Cmp_{ix}=$(Firm_{ix}^{2000}/Emp_{ix}^{2000})/(Firm_{i}^{2000}/Emp_{i}^{2000})$: competition
Div_{ix}=$-\Sigma_{j\neq i}(Emp_{jx}^{2000}/Emp_{x}^{2000}-Emp_{j}^{2000}/Emp^{2000})^2$: diversity
$\ln Wage_{ix}$: natural logarithm of $wage_{ix}^{2000}$
Grw_{ix}: natural logarithm of $\Sigma_{y,y\neq x}\ emp_{iy}^{2006}/\ \Sigma_{y,y\neq x}\ emp_{iy}^{2000}$: industrial growth
$\ln Emp_{ix}^{2000}$: natural logarithm of Emp_{ix}^{2000}
Edu_{ix}: fraction of emp_{ix}^{2000} with a bachelor degree
$\ln(ICTS_{x}^{2000}/\ln Emp_{x}^{2000})$: natural logarithm of fraction of $ICTS_{x}^{2000}$ in Emp_{x}^{2000}
where
Emp: employment
Emp_x: employment excluding agriculture and government in area x
Firm: number of establishments
ICTS: employment of ICT service sector
i: sector indexes
x: area indexes
f: firm indexes

5. Analysis 1: Service Sector Agglomeration

In the current section, the authors assess service sector agglomeration. The evaluation utilizes sample data that consist of all service sectors, including the ICT service sector. Summaries of the statistics and the correlation of variables are shown in Table 5.1 and Table 5.2, respectively.

Table 5.1
Variable means and standard deviations

Variable	Mean	SD	Max	Min
$\ln EmpG_{ix}$	.035	.307	1.370	-1.247
$Specialization_{ix}$	.014	.013	.130	.000
$Competition_{ix}$	1.209	.427	3.600	.280
$Diversity_{ix}$	-.003	.001	-.001	-.007
$\ln Wage_{ix}$	15.274	.145	15.741	14.951
$Industry\ growth_{ix}$	.040	.227	.764	-.283
$\ln Emp_{ix}^{2000}$	8.483	1.544	12.439	3.425
$\ln Edu_{ix}$	-1.623	.807	-.278	-7.637

Observations: 2525

Table 5.2
Correlation of variables

	$\ln EmpG_{ix}$	Spc_{ix}	Cmp_{ix}	Div_{ix}	$\ln Wage_{ix}$	Grw_{ix}	$\ln Emp_{ix}^{2000}$	$\ln Edu_{ix}$
$\ln EmpG_{ix}$	1							
Spc_{ix}	-.001	1						
Cmp_{ix}	.037	-.383	1					
Div_{ix}	.006	-.160	-.027	1				
$\ln Wage_{ix}$	-.123	.331	-.087	.081	1			
Grw_{ix}	.791	.047	-.053	-.002	-.085	1		
$\ln Emp_{ix}^{2000}$	-.038	.453	-.529	.022	-.092	-.030	1	
$\ln Edu_{ix}$	.085	.032	.140	.061	.383	.093	-.327	1

$\ln Emp^{2000}$ is used as an explanatory variable. If the coefficient of the variable is significantly positive, this indicates that the higher the employment in service sector i in area x, the more employment grows. This relationship leads to agglomeration.

The results are shown in Table 5.3. The coefficients for $\ln Emp_{ix}^{2000}$ are significantly positive in column (1) and (2). However, the coefficient in column (3) is not significant. These results support the notion that the service sectors are agglomerating in Japan, but only in urban areas and not throughout the country.

In the next section, we investigate the effect of the ICT environment on service sector agglomeration.

Table 5.3
City-Industry employment growth between 2000 and 2006

Variable	Dependent variable: $\ln EmpG_{ix}$ (1)	(2)	(3)
$Specialization_{ix}$	-.073	-1.042	.564
	(.358)	(.586)	(.711)
$Competition_{ix}$	.065	.064	.066
	(.010)	(.027)	(.014)
$Diversity_{ix}$	3.200	-5.359	8.063
	(3.065)	(7.935)	(5.174)
$\ln Wage_{ix}$	-.119	.052	-.161
	(.031)	(.084)	(.039)
$Industry\ growth_{ix}$	1.067	.958	1.096
	(.017)	(.036)	(.021)
$\ln Emp_{ix}^{2000}$	.008	.025	.001
	(.003)	(.007)	(.004)
$\ln Edu_{ix}$	.013	-.003	.016
	(.005)	(.013)	(.006)
Constant	1.700	-1.102	2.408
	(.479)	(1.304)	(.616)
Adjusted R^2	.635	.563	.668
Observations	2525	543	1555

Column (1): Over all of Japan; Column (2): 13 cities; Column (3): 36 prefectures that do not have any major cities.

6. Analysis 2: Impacts of the ICT Service Sector

To determine the effects of ICT on service sector agglomeration in urban areas, this section investigates the relationship between the ICT-related environment and the urban structural changes, focusing on service sectors.

The variable $\ln(ICTS_x^{2000}/\ln Emp_x^{2000})$ is added in this analysis. This variable is a proxy for the ICT-related environment. Firms in areas with high ICTS proportion could easily access ICT support services. The firms might use ICT effectively with co-invention, or innovation, creating a business model or organization that is more suitable for ICT. Consequently, those firms may grow more than those in the area with a low-ICTS proportion.

Tables 6.1 and 6.2 show summaries of statistics and the correlation of variables by date in major cities, respectively.

Table 6.1
Summary of statistics (13 cities)

Variable	Mean	SD	Max	Min
$\ln EmpG_{ix}$	.005	.283	1.036	-.875
$Specialization_{ix}$	.029	.050	.491	.001
$Competition_{ix}$	.904	.325	3.257	.280
$Diversity_{ix}$	-.003	.001	-.000	-.007
$\ln Wage_{ix}$	15.364	.122	15.741	15.192
$Industry\ growth_{ix}$	.035	.227	.759	.333
$\ln Emp_{ix}^{2000}$	8.842	1.563	12.913	3.802
$\ln Edu_{ix}$	-1.363	.689	-.311	-3.978
$\ln(ICTS_x^{2000}/Emp_x^{2000})$	-4.288	.626	-2.81	-5.227

Observations: 551

Table 6.2
Correlation of variables(13 cities)

	$\ln EmpG_{ix}$	Spc_{ix}	Cmp_{ix}	Div_{ix}	$\ln Wage_{ix}$	Grw_{ix}	$\ln Emp_{ix}^{00}$	$\ln Edu_{ix}$	$\ln(ICTS_x^{00}/Emp_x^{00})$
$\ln EmpG_{ix}$	1								
Spc_{ix}	-.013	1							
Cmp_{ix}	-.038	-.238	1						
Div_{ix}	-.019	-.594	.116	1					
$\ln Wage_{ix}$	-.063	.478	-.139	-.401	1				
Grw_{ix}	.737	-.055	-.094	.010	-.828	1			
$\ln Emp_{ix}^{2000}$	.031	.400	-.318	-.329	.067	-.084	1		
$\ln Edu_{ix}$	-.009	.135	.122	-.016	.272	.022	-.270	1	
$\ln(ICTS_x^{2000}/Emp_x^{2000})$	.052	.347	-.143	-.623	.362	-.018	.171	.093	1

Observations: 551

The results are provided in Table 6.3. The data in columns (1) and (2) consist of all service sectors, excluding the ICT service sector in major cities. The estimate of the variable, $\ln Emp_{ix}^{2000}$, in column (1) shows that service sectors have also agglomerated although the ICT service sector is excluded from the sample. The ICT service impact can be seen in the estimation of the variable, $\ln(ICTS_x^{2000}/Emp_x^{2000})$, which is significantly positive. This result supports the contention that the ICT-related environment affects service sector agglomeration in urban areas. The more ICT service industries located in an area, the more accelerated is the agglomeration of the other service sectors.

In addition, the authors assessed the impact of ICT services on service sectors in rural areas. Column (3) shows those results. The coefficient of $\ln(ICTS_x^{2000}/Emp_x$

^{2000}) is negative. Although the significance level is between 5% and 10%, the ICT environment might negatively affect the location of the service sectors in rural areas. The more ICT service sectors located in an area, the more probable the other service sectors might disperse rather than agglomerate.

Table 6.3
City-Industry employment growth between 2000 and 2006

	Dependent variable: $\ln EmpG_{ix}$		
Variable	(1)	(2)	(3)
$Specialization_{ix}$	-.005	.063	.029
	(.226)	(.227)	(.770)
$Competition_{ix}$	.061	.069	.082
	(.0270)	(.027)	(.014)
$Diversity_{ix}$	1.118	13.380	9.649
	(7.215)	(8.537)	(5.159)
$\ln Wage_{ix}$	.0120	-.019	-.170
	(.080)	(.081)	(.039)
$Industry\ growth_{ix}$	.941	.943	1.106
	(.036)	(.036)	(.020)
$\ln Emp_{ix}^{2000}$	.021	.021	.005
	(.006)	(.006)	(.004)
$\ln Edu_{ix}$	-.001	-.004	.022
	(.013)	(.013)	(.006)
$\ln(ICTS_x^{2000}/Emp_x^{2000})$	-	.045	-.018
	-	(.017)	(.010)
Constant	-.455	.233	2.400
	(1.241)	(1.262)	(.618)
Adjusted R^2	.551	.556	.679
Observations	551	551	1515

Column (1) and (2): 13 cities; Column (3): 36 prefectures that do not have any major cities.

7. Discussion

The results of analysis 1 suggest that the service sectors in urban areas might agglomerate. However, the authors could not verify the spatial distribution direction of the rural service sectors.

The results of analysis 2 suggest two different effects of the ICT environment on service sector location. In urban areas, a dense ICT service environment might accelerate the agglomeration of other service sectors. In contrast, a dense service environment in a rural area might accelerate dispersion of other service sectors, although the significant level is not particularly high.

The combination of the two analyses resulted in the authors' contention that the ICT environment or ICT itself accelerates a structural change in the location of the service sectors; from rural to urban. Furthermore, we should identify the ICT effect on economic geography. Figure 7.1 summarizes the above assertion.

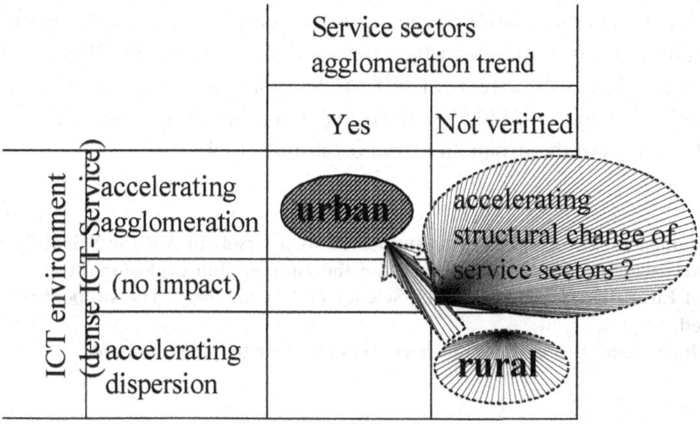

Fig. 7.1
Effects of ICT on urban and rural service sectors

8. Conclusions

The current research empirically assesses the effects of ICT on urban and rural service sectors using Japanese economic data. There are two main findings. The first conclusion is that service sectors in urban areas agglomerated from 2000 to 2006. The second is that the ICT environment might affect the location of the service sectors. In particular, an especially dense ICT service could accelerate agglomeration in urban areas. Furthermore, the effects of the ICT-related environment on the location of the service sectors might be different in urban and rural areas. A denser ICT service environment might disperse service sectors in a rural area.

The following three viewpoints were identified as the geographic impacts in the ICT research area. The first is the empirical assessment of the relationship between the ICT environment and urban structure. As shown in Table 2.1, prior literature evaluated the relationship between ICT adoption and the urban structure or between the ICT environment and ICT adoption. The present paper introduces a new perspective to this research area. The second contribution is the empirical assessment of the ICT effects on the agglomeration of service sectors. Prior ICT geographical analyses did not directly investigate the sectors' agglomeration. The third contribution is the analysis of the Japanese ICT environment and economic geography. Previously, few empirical studies dealt with the relationship between ICT and the Japanese economic geography.

The present paper has three limitations. Firstly, the authors' analyses are based on two points in the time series, 2000-2006, due to lack of statistics. A future study based on longer time series would be needed to assess the present conclusion. Secondly, the present paper could verify the effects of ICT in rural areas by statistically but weakly significant results. The direction of rural services location will be discussed in future studies. Thirdly, the present paper focuses on the Japanese service sectors. One of the characteristics of the Japanese economic geography is the dispersion of the manufacturing sector in urban areas (Mano and Otsuka 2000) and future research should address the effects of ICT on the urban and rural manufacturing sectors. An evaluation of the combined service and manufacturing research will depict the structural changes in the urban and rural economies of Japan.

Acknowledgments **The research was supported by a Grant-in-Aid for Scientific Research on Priority Areas, "New IT Infrastructure for the Information-explosion Era", funded by the Ministry of Education, Culture, Sports, Science and Technology. The support is gratefully acknowledged.**

The authors thank two anonymous reviewers for their helpful comments.

References

Arora, A. & Forman, C. (2007). Proximity and information technology outsourcing: How local are IT services markets? *Journal of Management Information Systems*, 24(2), 73-102.

Aslesen, H. W. & Isaksen A. (2007). Knowledge intensive business services and urban industrial development. *Service Industrial Journal*, 27(3), 321-338.

Baumol, W. J. (1961:1977), *Economic theory and operations analysis*, Englewood Cliffs, N.J. : Prentice-Hal.

Biteux-Orain, C. & Guillain R. (2004). Changes in the intrametropolitan location of producer services in Ile-de-France (1978-1997): Do information technologies promote a more dispersed spatial pattern? *Urban Geography*, 25(6), 550-578.

Bresnahan, T. F. & Trajtenberg, M. (1995). General purpose technologies 'Engines of Growth'? *Journal of Econometrics*, 65, 83-108.

Forman, C., Goldfarb, A., Greenstein, S. (2003). The geographic dispersion of commercial Internet use. In Cranor, S. F. & Wildman, S.S.(Eds.), *Rethinking rights and regulations: Institutional responses to new communications technologies* (pp.113-145). Cambridge, Mass: MIT Press.

Forman, C., Goldfarb, A. Greenstein, S. (2005a). How did location affect adoption of the commercial Internet? Global village vs. urban leadership. *Journal of Urban Economics*,58, 389-420.

Forman, C., Goldfarb, A. and Greenstein, S.(2005b). Geographic location and the diffusion of Internet technology. *Electronic Commerce Research and Applications*, 4, 1-13.

Gaspar, J. & Glaeser, E.L (1998). Information technology and the future of cities. *Journal of urban economics*, 43, 136-156.

Glaeser, E. L. , Kallal, H.D., Scheinkman, J.A., Shleifer, A. (1992). Growth in Cities. *The Journal of Political Economy*, 100(6), Centennial Issue. 1126-1152.

Henderson, V., Kuncoro, A., Turner, M. (1995). Industrial development in cities. *Journal of Political Economy*, 103(5), 1067-1090.

Ioannides, Y. M., Overman, H.G., Rossi-Hansberg, E., Schmidheiny, K. (2008). The effect of information and communication technologies on urban structure. *Economic Policy*, April, 201-242.

Isaksen, A. (2004). Knowledge-based clusters and urban location: The clustering of software consultancy in Oslo. *Urban Studies*, 41(5), 1157-1174.

Jacobs, J. (1969), *The economy of cities*, New York: Vintage.

Krugman, P. (1991). Increasing returns and economic geography. *Journal of Political Economy*, 99(3), 483-499.

Kolko, J. (2002). Silicon mountains, silicon molehills: Geographic concentration and convergence of Internet industries in the US. *Information Economics and Policy*, 14, 211-232.

Mano, Y. & Otsuka, K. (2000). Agglomeration economies and geographical concentration of industries: A case study of manufacturing sectors. *Journal of the Japanese and International Economies*, 14, 189-203.

OECD (2005), *Enhancing the performance of the service sector*, Paris: OECD.

Pons-Novell, J. & Viladecans-Marsal, E. (2006). Cities and the Internet: The end of distance? *Journal of Urban Technology*, 13(1), 109-132.

Porter, M. E. (1990), *The competitive advantage of the nations*, New York: Free Press.

Tabuchi, T. & Thisse, J. (2006). Regional specialization, urban hierarchy, and commuting costs. *International Economic Review*, 47(4), 1295-1317.

Zook, M. A. (2002). Grounded capital: Venture financing and the geography of the Internet industry, 1994-2000. *Journal of Economic Geography*, 2(2), 151-177.

The Age-Divide in E-Government – Data, Interpretations, Theory Fragments

Björn Niehaves, Jörg Becker

European Research Center for Information Systems, University of Muenster,
Leonardo-Campus 3, 48149 Muenster, Germany,

{Becker, Bjoern.Niehaves}@ercis.uni-muenster.de

Abstract. 14 of the world's 15 'oldest' countries (largest percentage of people age 65 plus) are to be found in Europe. While E-Government is currently establishing as the most important public sector reform strategy in the EU (Lisbon Agenda), age is a factor which strongly affects E-Government usage. Under the label of 'E-Inclusion' EU policies seeks to solve also age-related digital divide issues. This paper seeks to explore the age-divide in E-Government and discusses 2006 Eurostat data on online service usage. The case of Germany will be given as example.

1 Introduction

Population aging is one of the greatest challenges to societies in Europe! Some claim it is a sign of the success of Western societies: as medicine, sanitation, and agricultural production have improved, life expectancy has risen. This, combined with plunging birth rates, is causing what is called the 'demographic transition'. One of the biggest impacts of this transition is population aging. Europe has seen both mortality and fertility fall since the 19th century. Since the 1960s, however, fertility has declined even more dramatically. Europe now has so many elderly people and so few newborns that, as a consequence, population aging has established itself as a long-term trend that will continue for generations to come. Today, 14 –besides Japan– of the world's 15 'oldest' countries – those with the largest percentage of elderly people (age 65 or older) – are in Europe. In Italy, Europe's oldest country by these standards, around 19.5 % of the population is elderly. In other European countries, including Germany, Greece, Sweden, Bulgaria, Belgium, and Portugal, the percentage of elderly is over 17 %. In Spain, Estonia, Latvia, Croatia, France, UK, and Finland their

Please use the following format when citing this chapter:

Niehaves, B., Becker, J., 2008, in IFIP International Federation for Information Processing, Volume 286; Towards Sustainable Society on Ubiquitous Networks, eds. Oya, M., Uda, R., Yasunobu, C., (Boston: Springer), pp. 279–287.

share is larger than 16 % (Population Reference Bureau, 2006). Population aging is not only a challenge in Europe, but it is indeed a European Challenge.

While E-Government is establishing as the most important public sector reform strategy, age is a factor which strongly affects E-Government usage! A key element of public sector reforms in the EU (European Union) is E-Government (Electronic Government) which can be defined as the use of information technology in governments. In the move of the Lisbon-Agenda, all EU member states have committed to implementing an E-Government-oriented strategy of public administration modernisation. Web-based information and communication technologies are intended to become the primary channel for public service delivery. According to the European Commission, in 2004 an average of 84% of all public services was available online in the EU member states. Despite such positive efforts to provide E-Government services, analyses of usage numbers and user structures indicate that digital exclusion today is primarily a demand side rather than a supply side issue. Here, especially senior citizens are still potentially very much excluded from participation in electronic services.

Against this background, the aim of this paper is to investigate into the digital divide in E-Government taking into account the specific perspective of senior citizens. Here, we seek to develop complexity of age-aware E-Government rather than to reduce complexity in terms of, for instance, an age-aware Technology Acceptance Model for E-Government. Thus, the research method chosen is that of a descriptive-statistical analysis followed by a comprehensive interpretation. Such interpretive discussion is aimed at contributing to a foundation of a preliminary theory of age-aware E-Government. Therefore, we will contrast different types of online service usage data, including general internet usage, E-Commerce usage as well as E-Government usage. Taking the exemplary case of Germany, we seek to address the research question of *"What is the current state of inclusive E-Government, especially from the perspective of senior citizens, and which factors could explain a possible inclusion gap to which extent?"*

In order to address this research question, the following section will relate our analysis to prior studies and the existing literature. Section 3 presents the research methodology, focusing on a quantitative analysis of comprehensive Eurostat data from digital divide group perspectives. Following a comparative presentation and discussion of relevant data, a comprehensive data interpretation seeks to offer explanations for inclusion gaps in (German) E-Government and identify potential operational strategies to overcome a digital divide in E-Government (Section 4). The paper will conclude with a summary of results and an outlook to potentially fruitful avenues for future research (Section 5).

2 Related Work

2.1 Demographic Transition

According to Hauser & Duncan (1959), demography can be defined as „the study of the size, territorial distribution, and composition of population, changes therein, and the components of such changes, which may be identified as natality, mortality, territorial movement (migration), and social mobility (change of status)“ (p.2). Here, literature identifies three specifically major factors underlying to the development of demography: a) fertility, b) mortality, and c) migrations (Kaufmann 2005). Accordingly, demographic transition can be understood as the progressive alteration of these determinants. Especially fertility and mortality have undergone significant changes in most industrialized countries. On the one hand, fertility has been declining due to, for instance, changed life models or family planning and the possibilities of birth control and abortion (Hill and Kopp 2000). Morgan & Hagewen (2005) state that fertility transitions "[...] are complete in many developed countries and are in progress in much of the rest of the world. The transition model has three stages: relatively high and stable fertility, followed by a period of fertility decline, and then followed by relatively low and stable fertility (p. 231). While life expectancy is rising and populating experiences normal aging, less young people are succeeding which results in an overall aging of the society in these countries. The old-age dependency ratio that sets the number of people aged over 60 years in relation to the number of people aged between 20 and 60 years dramatically increased by two to three times its size in some industrialized countries (Birg 2005). Therefore, societal aging can be identified as a major element of demographic transition in industrialized countries (Niehaves et al. 2008).

2.2 E-Inclusion

These trends pose several challenges to the development of E-Government strategies. One of these challenges is the digital divide, in this context understood as an emerging polarization phenomenon in society, creating a gap between those who do have access to and use the potentialities of information and communication technologies, and those who do not (European Commission 2004a). The demographic gap refers, amongst others, to the fact that senior people often do not use ICT on a regular basis (E-Aging, Becker et al. 2008). The reasons for this gap results from a multitude of several challenges which senior people often face. These include for instance isolation, physical disabilities, or low retirement pension (Kraner 2004). Disabilities can debar people from actively using information technology. For the usage of online services the most important disabilities to consider are visual handicaps, cognitive defects and limitations of motor skills. Geographical differences refer to gaps in ICT usage between different regions. Socio-economic gaps include differences in occupation, income and education whereas ethnical and cultural gaps identify barriers in the ICT usage of migrants and ethnical minorities.

Here, E-Inclusion focuses on the elimination of these barriers for the use of ICT. The declaration of Riga gives the following definition of E-Inclusion: "'eInclusion' means both inclusive ICT and the use of ICT to achieve wider inclusion objectives. It focuses on participation of all individuals and communities in all aspects of the information society. eInclusion policy, therefore, aims at reducing gaps in ICT usage and promoting the use of ICT to overcome exclusion, and improve economic performance, employment opportunities, quality of life, social participation and cohesion." (European Union 2006, p. 1) The main focus of E-Inclusion is on creating accessible services over ICT. This effort can be divided into accessibility and usability aspects (Kraner 2004). Accessibility means the possibility for handicapped people to access the relevant service. This includes for instance creating opportunities for Braille support on web-sites and general thoughts about compatibility with older technologies. Usability focuses on the user-friendliness of a web-service. According to EU's "Top of the web" report, the main criteria for this effort includes easy discovery and fast navigation within a website, easy use of the service, satisfying speed and a clear language that is easy to understand (European Commission 2004b).

2.3 Effects of Aging

Aging is certainly one of the most important aspects to consider when creating or adapting E-Government strategies. According to Davis' Technology Acceptance Model (TAM), the two main dimensions of technology acceptance are perceived usefulness and perceived ease of use (Davis et al. 1989). The perceived usefulness on the one hand has the biggest influence on the actual usage. Older people are lacking the awareness of advantages related to ICT usage because they are easily satisfied with their current possibilities and cannot imagine how ICT could improve their lives (Morris and Venkatesh 2000). They have a critical attitude towards the usage of new technologies because they did not get used to them throughout their working lives. They appreciate the face-to-face contact and fear that new media will contribute to their isolation. The perceived ease of use, on the other hand, is usually declining with an increasing age. An impairment of vision implies difficulties in recognizing details especially if they are presented on a computer screen (Shirley 2004). Furthermore, it is harder for the elderly to adapt necessary skills because they have problems to understand complex new processes. A recent study showed that especially older people feel "more often than the others that the work pace, things to be remembered, rules to be taken into consideration, difficulty of tasks, and monitoring of their work had increased" (European Commission, p. 98).

Against this discussion, it is to investigate into the question of if age is a factor which in a certain way specifically affects E-Government usage or if age generally affects all types of online service usage in a similar way. In order to analyse the potential specific effects of age on E-Government usage, we will contrast internet and E-Commerce usage with E-Government usage both from the perspective of the total population and the group of senior citizens.

3 Research Methodology

In order to answer the research question and populate the model, a descriptive-statistical quantitative analysis of Eurostat data from 2006 (Eurostat 2007) on individual internet-based service usage was conducted. A methodological description of the survey is given by the European Commission (European Commission 2006). While such data is secondary data and publicly available, a specific investigation into the in- and exclusiveness in European, and specifically German E-Government has not yet been undertaken. Consequently, the analysis of such comprehensive and high quality and comprehensive data (sample size: n=21.160) offers great potential to shed new light on the question of the status-quo of inclusive E-Government and on the question of which factors could explain possible inclusion gaps. Table 1 shows questions used to collect the data for the different variables.

Table 1. (Individual) Usage of Internet, E-Commerce, E-Banking, and E-Government and Corresponding Questions.

Analysis Dimension	Question
Internet	I have used the Internet in the last 3 months
E-Commerce	I bought or ordered goods or services, over the Internet, for non-work use, in the last 3 months
E-Government	I have used Internet, in the last 3 months, for obtaining information from public authorities web sites

Moreover, in order to allow for a deeper analysis of non-usage of E-Government services, reasons for non-usage (on an individual basis) are taken into account and range from non-availability of services over concerns about data security, privacy or costs to complexity of (electronic) public services (see Table 2). These two analysis dimensions (usage data and reasons for non-usage) are contrastively discussed taking into account the population average and the group of senior citizens (within the Eurostat data defined of age 55-74).

Table 2. (Individual) Reasons for Non-Usage of E-Government and Corresponding Questions.

Reason	Question
Service not available / to difficult to find	I'm not using Internet for dealing with public services or administrations, because: The services I need are not available on-line or difficult to find
Personal contact missed	I'm not using Internet for dealing with public services or administrations, because: I miss personal contact
Immediate response missed	I'm not using Internet for dealing with public services or administrations, because: I miss immediate response
Concerned about data security	I'm not using Internet for dealing with public services or administrations, because: I'm concerned about protection and security of my data
Concerned about additional costs	I'm not using Internet for dealing with public services or administrations, because: I'm concerned about additional costs
Too complex	I'm not using Internet for dealing with public services or administrations, because: it's too complex
Other reasons	I'm not using Internet for dealing with public services or administrations, because of other reasons

4 The Age-Divide in E-Government

Analysing in- and exclusiveness of electronic public service delivery in Germany, data on internet, E-Commerce, and E-Government usage was contrasted (see Table 3). While 69% the total population used the internet during the last three months, only 37% of senior citizens did so. In the total population, a gap of 10% can be identified between E-Commerce (38%) and E-Government (28%) usage. This gap is significantly smaller regarding the group of senior citizens which used E-Commerce in 15% and E-Government in 12% of the cases.

Table 3. Usage Data of Online Services in Germany

	Total population	Senior Citizens (Age 55-74)
Internet	69%	37%
E-Commerce	38%	15%
E-Government	28%	12%

In addition, the E-Commerce and E-Government usage was seen in relation to only the onliners in the total population and in the group of senior citizens. In the total population, 55.1% of onliners used E-Commerce and 41% of onliners used E-Government. In the group of senior citizens, 40.5% of onliners used E-Commerce and 32.4% used E-Government. Relating these two service-specific figure between the total population and senior citizens shows that even if a senior citizen is already online, the probability that she or he uses E-Commerce or E-Government Services is still lower than in the total population (0.74 resp. 0.79; see table 4).

Table 4. eService Usage Ratio of Senior Onliners & Total Population Onliners (Germany).

	Total population	Senior Citizens (Age 55-74)
E-Commerce	1.00 (55,1%)	0.74[a] (40,5%)
E-Government	1.00 (41%)	0.79 (32,4%)

Source: Data based on Eurostat (2006).

a - eService Usage Ratio describes the relation of specific eService usage within a certain digital divide group to eService usage among the average population, e.g., (SeniorCit.-CommerceUsers/ SeniorCit.Onliners) / (Aver.Pop.E-CommerceUsers/Aver.Pop.Onliners); (15%/37%)/(38%/69%)=0.74

Analysing the specific reasons for non-usage in such digital divide group perspectives led to the following key findings. As for the population average, missing personal contact, concerns about data security, and the complexity of services are considered as major reasons for E-Government non-usage among digital divide groups in Germany. Concerns about data security were mentioned as reasons for non-usage of E-Government 1.27 times more often by senior citizens than by population average. The complexity of E-Government services was mentioned as a reason for non-usage 1.24 times more often by senior citizens than by population average. This leaves the four major reasons for senior citizens to not use E-Government services to be: missing personal contact, concerns about data security, service complexity, and concerns about additional costs (see Table 5).

Table 5. Reason for Not Using E-Government Services (Germany).

	Total Population	Senior citizens (Age 55-74)
Service not available / too difficult to find	1 (21%)	0.78[a] (16%)
Personal contact missed	1 (48%)	1.08 (52%)
Concerned about data security	1 (40%)	0.93 (37%)
Concerned about additional costs	1 (13%)	1.27 (17%)
Too complex	1 (24%)	1.24 (30%)
Other reasons	1 (16%)	0.89 (14%)

Source: Data based on Eurostat (2006).

a - Relation to population average used to highlight group specific reasons
E.g., 0,78 (Senior citizens, Reason: Service not available) represents 16% (0,78*21%=16%) of the senior citizens giving that very reason.

Especially concerns about additional costs, complexity, and missing personal contact have been mentioned by senior citizens more often than by population average. Here, it might me argued that these three reasons for non-usage would in a similar way affect both E-Commerce and E-Government usage. For instance, E-Commerce might not be a desirable alternative to shopping in a physical store as personal contact is missing here as well. E-Commerce also includes services of certain complexity, e.g. auctioning for and buying an item online. Additional costs can be interpreted as costs of additional infrastructure necessary to be able to use the internet (69% population average, 37% senior citizens) and then to use specific services such as E-Government.

As a consequence, the data presented might be interpreted in a way that there is a smaller gap between E-Commerce and E-Government usage in the group of senior citizens than in the total population. It might, comparing these two eServices, not only be specific problems of E-Government which E-Government managers have to tackle when looking for creating age-aware inclusive E-Government solution. Major E-Government problems, as the data suggests, include those which affect general internet usage (e.g., infrastructure (cost) problems) as well as usage of complex online services in general, such as E-Commerce and E-Government (e.g., complexity and the missing possibility to ask someone certain questions which may arise during service usage).

Nonetheless, we argue that at current there is still major potential left in E-Government for including senior citizens. This could contain, for instance, senior citizen-specific design of life events or designing more one-stop-government-oriented solutions (Wimmer 2002) which are easier to access and to understand, as extensive knowledge of public administration structures and lengthy search processes for E-Government services are not necessary. Here, potentially the EU service directive, which has to implemented in EU member states by end of 2009, could pave the road not only for a one-stop-government for businesses, but also for (senior) citizens. Here, good-practices of age-aware inclusive E-Government, for instance, 'Seniorenlotse' (www.seniorenlotse.bremen.de), 'CitizenAdvice' (www.citizensadvice.org.uk), or senior citizen portals (such as www.seniors. gov.au) could provide potentially fruitful starting points.

5 Summary and Future Research

From the perspective of E-Government managers, there is an uncertainty of which measures to undertake in order to increase inclusiveness of electronic public service delivery. One can identify several problem streams, issues and barriers overlapping and adding upon one another creating the current picture of prevailing E-Government exclusiveness. Regarding the perspective of senior citizens, major reasons for them for not using E-Government services are not necessarily E-Government-specific but affect general internet usage (e.g., infrastructure costs) as well as usage of (other) complex online services such as E-Commerce (e.g., complexity or missing personal contact). This reflects the fact that, in Germany, the gap between E-Commerce and E-Government usage for senior citizens is 3% while it is 10% for the total population. Future research is necessary as the above given findings can only be regarded as a basic starting point, for instance, in terms of comprehensive qualitative and comparative studies on local age-aware E-Government.

References

Becker et. al.: "E-Inclusion – Digitale Integration durch E-Government", Münster, 2008.

Birg, H.: "Die demographische Zeitenwende. Der Bevölkerungsrückgang in Deutschland und Europa", München, 2005.

Davis, F.D., Bagozzi, R.P. and Warshaw, P.R.: "User Acceptance of Computer Technology – A comparision of two theoretical models", Management Science Vol. 35 No. 8, August 1989, pp. 989-1003.

European Commission: "eInclusion@EU: Strengthening eInclusion & eAccessibility across Europe. Analytic framework - eInclusion and eAccessibility priority issues", 2004a.

European Commission: "Top of the web. User Satisfaction and Usage Survey of E-Government services", Kopenhagen, 2004b.

European Commission: "Methodological manual for statistics on the Informations Society". Office for Official Publications of the European Communities, Luxembourg, 2006.

European Union: "Ministerial Declaration - Approved Unanimously on 11 June 2006", Riga, 2006.

Eurostat: "Statistics on households/individuals and the information society". Eurostat Office. 2007.

Hauser, P., and D. Duncan, D.: "The Study of Population. An Inventory and Appraisal", Chicago, 1959.

Kaufmann, F.: "Schrumpfende Gesellschaft. Vom Bevölkerungsrückgang und seinen Folgen", Frankfurt, 2005.

Kraner, S.: "Bridging the Digital Divide in E-Government." Zürich 2004.

Morgan, S. and Hagewen, K.: "Fertility", Handbook of Population, D. Poston, and M. Micklin, New York, 2005, pp. 229-249.

Morris, M.G. and Venkatesh, V.: "Age Differences in Technology Adoption Decisions: Implications for a Changing Work Force", Personnel Psychology Vol. 53 No. 2, 2000, pp. 375-403.

Niehaves, B., Ortbach, K., Becker, J.: "The Demographic Challenge: Aging and Depopulation and their Consequences for E-Government – A Case Study". Unpublished Manuscript. Muenster (2008)

Population Reference Bureau: "World Population Data Sheet", Washington DC, USA, 2006.

Shirley, A.B.: "E-Government Visual Accessibility for Older Adult Users", Social Science Computer Review Vol. 22 No 1, 2004, pp. 11-23.

Wimmer, M. A.: Integrated Service Modelling for Online One-Stop Government. Electronic Markets 12 (2002) 149-156

Software Piracy in Chilean e-Society

Ranjan B. Kini

MIS, Indiana University Northwest, USA,

Abstract. The Business Software Alliance and their counterparts in the global market are determined to make significant progress in curbing the Software Piracy globally. Their aggressive pursuit in their endeavor has produced results in bringing down the piracy rate. However, despite the highly net-ready Chile being part of the Latin American region still leads in the software piracy rate. In this study, a micro-level research is performed on the convenient sample of Chilean graduate students to measure their moral intensity towards piracy. The results show that Chileans are at the lower level of moral intensity toward Software Piracy. This suggests that more work needs to be done in educating Chileans in curbing the software piracy and its impact on the economy and business environment.

1. Introduction

As the stage for transforming the current society into an e-Society is gradually built, a challenge that will continue to exacerbate e-Citizens as well as companies will be the continued piracy of digital goods. Digital Piracy is a challenge that both the software industry and the digital content industry continue to face until there is global understanding and value recognition of intellectual property. In educating the e-citizens, the industries involved in producing such products have

---

Please use the following format when citing this chapter:

Kini, B. R., 2008, in IFIP International Federation for Information Processing, Volume 286; Towards Sustainable Society on Ubiquitous Networks, eds. Oya, M., Uda, R., Yasunobu, C., (Boston: Springer), pp. 289–301.

been aggressive in the recent years to introduce some traditional and innovative techniques. For example, Business Software Alliance (a software industry alliance formed to curb the piracy), has been going around the globe establishing local presence to influence national laws and policies in curbing any form of piracy. Using the carrot and stick approach BSA has been trying to be effective for the last decade. The reports published by various global institutions have documented that digital piracy is rather declining at a very small rate in different countries. However, there is also a sense that dollar value of the piracy cost has remained high. Thus, curbing the digital piracy is still clearly an important objective to organizations such as BSA along with other organizations belonging to Alliance for Digital Progress. [2]

Among the organizations forming the coalition to stop the digital piracy, BSA has been the most aggressive organization. BSA, a coalition of software companies is the leading organization in targeting companies and individuals pirating software. Pirating software has been a common phenomenon for the last two decades. However, as the growth in the technology adoption and the diffusion of such technology around globe progresses there have been increases in the software piracy. According to BSA's Global Piracy Study in 2006, although efforts by BSA contributed in the reduction of piracy rate in the annual numbers, because of the growth in PC adoption in the developing countries, the overall average piracy rate remained the same at 35 percent. The report also indicates that the dollar value of piracy, in fact, increased in 2006 by 15 percent or 5 billion US Dollars. The piracy rate ranged from 21 percent in the US to 95 percent in Armenia. [6] The study estimates that in 2006 for every 2USD worth of software purchased legally there was 1USD worth of software bought illegally. Furthermore, the study estimates that for about the half the countries (of total 102) they studied for every 1USD spent on software legally, about 2USD was spent to acquire illegally. The study reports that situation with countries with high piracy rate is ever worse. [6] The study makes a projection that in the next four years global software piracy may reach 180 billion USD.

The BSA study reports based on their four annual studies that variation in piracy rate in different regions is influenced by factor such as "… *the strength of intellectual property protection, the availability of pirated software, and cultural differences*". The study also reports the piracy rates within the countries are affected by characteristics such as industry, demographics, type of software (system or application), and size

(SMB) of businesses. The BSA study recommends that countries can use the following five steps to curb the piracy; shifting public attitude towards software piracy by education and awareness, adopting and enforcing World Intellectual Property Organization laws, creating strong and workable enforcement mechanisms, supporting the enforcement mechanisms through dedicated resources, and the country governments leading antipiracy efforts within their own governments. [6]

In the digital age, the opportunities for the piracy to worsen are high. Software piracy, a small sub set of digital piracy alone is expected to be nearly 50 billion USD per year by 2010. [6] The concern for to curb such phenomenon has motivated many academic research studies both at the macro level and micro level. At the macro level, studies have been conducted to identify the influence of cultural factors, legal environment, corporate environment, and ICT maturity level of the country. [4][5][9][14][17][18][19]. While, the micro level studies have focused more on influence of demographic factors, ethical models, moral intensity and individual behavior, etc. Both macro level and micro-level studies have contributed to the academic as well as practitioner world in identifying and understanding factors to focus when deploying resources to curb software piracy locally as well as nationally. In this study, author's motivation is to study the perception of software piracy and to measure the moral intensity among the citizens of the leading ICT ready country in Latin America, Chile. [7][11][12][14][16]

2. Literature

Chile is acknowledged as the most *wired* or the most e-Ready country in Latin America, according to the 2006 Economist Intelligence Unit Rankings. It is ranked higher than many European Countries in its Network Readiness in 2006 according to World Economic Forum Report. [8] Chile is also commended by many global economic watch groups for their action in advancing the country towards ICT readiness. Chileans through public and private partnership are determined in becoming a leader in ICT use in Latin America. In establishing its robust digital agenda, Chile has established many initiatives focusing on Access, Digital literacy, e-Government, e-transactions (e-Business), and Legal framework. Digital literacy or human resource development is what the government coordinator for ICT considers as the biggest challenge. Chile has recognized ICT as an important instrument to gain economic growth and maturity. In establishing these goals, Chile has recognized that it needs to get itself ready in the transformation process from being a resource-based economy to a knowledge-based economy. [3][10]

Currently, there is limited research available on digital piracy or software piracy in Chile. From the above discussion, it is clear that intensity and pervasiveness of software piracy is highly correlated with ICT maturity, economic development, and cultural understanding of intellectual property and related issues. Chile, considered one of the most developed countries in Latin America, according to BSA is having 68 percent piracy rate while it indicates Latin American region has second highest average in software piracy rate of 66 percent. Chile is indicated to have higher piracy than Columbia, Brazil, and Equador. [6] This is in contrast to many of the local Chilean Spanish newspapers indicating that Chile was having 68 percent in 1994 but because of the government efforts, it fell to 56 in 1997, 59 in 1999, 53 in 2000, and 51 in 2005. According to various articles in newspapers, Chileans pirate software from all socio-economic groups and all sizes of businesses. Some articles mentioned large companies had 35 percent piracy rate while small and medium sized companies had piracy rate of 80 percent. Chilean *Asociacion Chilena De Distribuidores De Software A. G. (ADS),* the Chilean Software Distribution Association has been actively working with Chilean government to educate citizens about piracy, assess the impact of piracy on tax revenues, impact on labor market, ability to attract foreign investments, etc. Despite the fact that most software can be bought from *Mercado Persa* (illegal market) at a very low price relative to legal price, ADS believes that it is primarily cultural factors that drive Chileans and businesses to pirate. In 2000, Chilean government estimated over 50 million USD of tax revenues were lost annually because of piracy, and in 2007 it estimates losing 163 million USD of tax revenues. Both the Chilean government and ADS have proposed voluntary certification and audits for companies. ADS hopes to have 5000 companies audited and self-regulate themselves. It had only 400 companies certified in 2005. [1]

In this study, as mentioned above, the author's intent is to measure the moral intensity towards software piracy among Chileans. According to ADS, cultural factors drive most Chileans to pirate the software. Thus, the study attempts to contribute in understanding the perception of

Chileans regarding pervasiveness of software piracy and contributes in assessing the moral intensity of subjects towards software piracy. [1]

For this research the term Software Piracy, uses the commonly used definition *making unauthorized copies of software by individuals or businesses for resale or to use in workplace, school, or home; and,* Softlifting uses the definition *as illegal copying of software by individuals for personal use but not for resale as in software piracy.* Based on the prior research and studies [12] the questionnaire useful in measuring moral intensity towards software piracy in other studies is used in this study. [12]

3. Research

In attempting to measure the moral intensity and community effects, authors developed a survey questionnaire that included 11 demographic related questions and 40 Softlifting related questions, as shown in *Appendix A.* In this exploratory study, authors used a convenient sample of MBA students from a leading private university in Santiago, Chile. This survey was first translated in to Spanish and reverse translated for accuracy. The questionnaire was then administered to a small group of students to pretest the questionnaire and correct interpretation. All of these students are fulltime working students. The data was collected between January and May 2005. This is a captive crowd; hence, a little bias is expected. Although this is not a good representative sample of Chilean population, this however is a sample of educated population with a tendency to have highest number in levels of income and highest level of ICT adoption rate. All students were informed that participation was voluntary and that individual student responses will remain completely anonymous. The students were asked to rate the question items on Likert scale to 1 to 5, 1 being *Strongly disagree* and 5 being *Strongly agree.* It should be pointed out the items I43, I44 and I49 are reverse coded and interpreted appropriately. The authors collected 185 valid responses from the university students. The analysis and findings based on responses to 20 items of the total 49 items specifically related to the students or subjects are discussed in the following sections.

4. Findings

The focus of this study is to capture the perception of students who may be at different levels of Kohlberg's moral stages of development. *(Appendix B)* Although there were 41 questions, in this study the analysis is performed on responses to the relevant 20 questions. The findings discussed below are based on 183 responses.

The intensity of moral development depends on the way individual rationalizes the decision. In the earlier research, it has been identified that often the moral stage of development of an individual can be transient and situation dependent. Accordingly, there has been some research that indicates that Software Piracy is one such situation. That is, in case of Software Piracy an individual can drop in the level of stage of moral development. [10][11][12]

From Table 1, one can depict a typical respondent in this study as 31-40 years old, male, graduate student, has extensive experience with computer, holds a managerial position, and uses software mostly on the job. (Table 1) The Table 2 shows average scores for each of the items. The response to the item V55 with a mean estimate of 8711 copies (for 100 legal copies of software) seems irrational even for students, especially when reports indicate that there are 68 copies for every 100 copies. This perception can distort the true understanding of the situation by the respondent. The distortion may be reflected in their responses to I13 and I12 with high means. With respondents scoring means below 3 for I48, I47 and I36 they have shown that they are above the Level 1 of moral development although slipped below by scoring higher for I12 and I13. With low mean scores for I43, I49 and I44 (reverse scored items) respondents show that they are aware of the consequences but their level of moral development relating to software piracy drives them to be adventurous and drop to Stage 2 as evidenced by I12 and I13 scores.

The correlation Table 3 without any surprises indicates that respondents are consistent in their moral development. The highly significant and high correlations among items representing different levels and stages clearly indicate these respondents do possess a low level of moral intensity towards software piracy. These findings are preliminary. The data will need to be further analyzed with more robust statistical techniques to gain more insights.

1 Comments

The perception of Chileans is that Software Piracy is not a major issue. Everyone is doing it and in general, it is all right to do it is common theme. The responses analyzed in this study are from an educated and higher socio-economic class population. The preliminary evidence from this study suggests that more needs to be performed in terms of educating the public in informing about the Intellectual property and benefits thereof to the economic development, government, labor market and foreign investment.

The level of moral development of individuals is influenced by various factors. Thus, although one should commend Chile for being the technology leader in Latin America, it needs to use appropriate nationwide approach in raising the moral intensity towards Software Piracy (and Digital Piracy), so there will be more rapid reduction of the piracy rate while it continues to be technology leader.

Acknowledgement: Authors would like to thank Rotary International and District 6540 for their support through University Professor Grant in completing this study while at University Adolfo Ibanez, Santiago, Chile.

References

1. ADS (2008) http://www.ads.cl/
2. Alliance, (2008) http://www.alliancefordigitalprogress.org/content/?p=CoalitionMembers
3. Álvarez, C. (2005) "ICT as a part of Chile's Strategy for Development: Present Issues and Challenges", *DIGITAL AGENDA*, Deputy Minister of Economy, Government Coordinator for ICT, CHILE.
4. Banerjee, D. (2003) Software Piracy: a Strategic Analysis and Policy Instruments, *International Journal of Industrial Organization* 21 (1) 97-127.
5. Banerjee, D., Khalid, A.M. and Sturm, J. (2005) Social-economic Development and Software Piracy: an Empirical Assessment, *Applied Economics* 37, 2091-2097.
6. Business Software Alliance (2007) *2006 Piracy Study*. http://w3.bsa.org/globalstudy//upload/2007-Global-Piracy-Study-EN.pdf
7. Cronan, T.P., Foltz, C.B., and Jones, T.W. (2006) Piracy, Computer Crime, and IS Misuse at the University *Communications of the ACM* 49 (6) 84-90.
8. Dutta, S., Lanvin B., and Paula F. (2005) Global Information Technology Report 2004-2005, *World Economic Forum*.
9. Husted, B.W. (2000) The Impact of National Culture on Software Piracy *Journal of Business Ethics* 26(3) 197-211.
10. Kini, R. B. (2007) Vendor Availability: A Key Factor for Outsourcing in Chilean ICT Sector, *Information Management & Computer Security*.
11. Kini, R. B., Ramakrishna, H. V., and Vijayraman, B. S. (2004) Shaping of Moral Intensity Regarding Software Piracy: A Comparison Between Thailand and U.S. Students, *Journal of Business Ethics*.
12. Kini, R. B., Rominger A. R., and Vijayraman, B. S. (2000) An Empirical Study of Software Piracy and Moral Intensity Among University Students, *Journal of Computer Information Systems* XXXX(3) 62-72.
13. Kohlberg, L. "Stage and sequence: The Cognitive Developmental Approach to Socialization", in *Handbook of Socialization Theory & Research*, D. Growling (ed.), Rand McNally, 1969.
14. Leonard, L.N.K., Cronan, T.P. and Kreie, J. (2004) What Influences IT Ethical Behaviour Intentions--Planned Behaviour, Reasoned Action, Perceived Importance, or Individual Characteristics? *Information & Management* 42 (1) 143-158.
15. Marron, D.B. and Steel, D.G. (2000) Which Countries Protect Intellectual Property? The Case of Software Piracy, *Economic Inquiry* 38(2) 159-174.
16. Peace, A.G., Galletta, D.F. and Thong, J.Y.L. (2003) Software Piracy in the Workplace: A Model and Empirical Test *Journal of Management Information Systems* 20 (1) 153-177.
17. Ronkainen, I.A. and Guerrero-Cusumano, J.-L. (2001) Correlates of Intellectual Property Violation *Multinational Business Review* 9(1) 59-65.
18. Shore, B., Venkatachalam, A.R., Solorzano, E., Burn, J.M., Hassan, S.Z. and Janczewski, L.J. (2001) Softlifting and Piracy: Behaviour across Cultures *Technology in Society* 23 (4) 563-581.
19. Yang, D. and Sonmez, M. (2007) Economic and Cultural Impact on Intellectual Property Violations: A Study of Software Piracy *Journal of World Trade* 41 (4) 731-750.

Table – 1: Demographic Data

Variable	Categories	Number
Age Group	Under 19	0
	19-21	1
	22-25	7
	26-30	42
	31-40	96
	Over 40	25
Gender	Male	119
	Female	52
Program	Graduate	144
	Undergraduate	26
Computer	Has at Home	162
Computing Experience	None	2
	Basic	28
	Extensive	113
	Advanced	28
Current Employment	Clerical	0
	Supervisory	25
	Managerial	81
	Professional	55
Using Software for	On the job	140
	Classroom use	6
	Personal use	23
	Advanced	0

Table 2: Descriptive Statistics

	N	Min.	Max.	Mean	Std. Dev	
V55	169	0	1000000	8711	77586	I think for every 100 legal copies of software in the market there are at least _____ illegal copies made of the same software in Chile.
I13	183	1	5	**4.251**	0.840	**I believe most *students* copy commercial software instead of buying it.**
I28	183	1	5	3.934	0.929	I think it is alright for *a student* to use a university owned software at home to complete university assignments.
I12	183	1	5	**3.820**	1.019	**I believe most *people* copy commercial software instead of buying it.**
I34	184	1	5	3.625	1.048	I think it is alright for *a student* to use university computer and software for their benefits as long as it has no adverse effect on others.
I22	184	1	5	3.462	1.086	I think it is alright for *a student* to use university computers and software for their social organizations.
I46	183	1	5	3.328	1.049	I think it is alright for *me* to "try out" software so long as I intend to buy it in the future.
I25	183	1	5	3.306	1.215	I think it is all right for *a student* to copy commercial software to evaluate it for possible purchase.
I19	184	1	5	3.228	1.211	I think is alright for *a student* to use university computers and software for non-university activities.
I45	184	1	5	**3.114**	1.175	**I think it alright for *me* to use copied software if I would not buy it in any case.**
I31	184	1	5	3.098	1.141	I think it is alright for *a student* to use a university owned software at home for personal use.
I35	181	1	5	3.077	1.142	I think it is alright for *a student* to use university computer and software for their benefits as long as it has only minor adverse effect on others.
I16	184	1	5	**3.011**	1.145	**I think it is alright for *a student* to copy commercial software instead of buying it.**
I48	184	1	5	2.516	1.106	I think it is alright for *me* to copy commercial software because it is unlikely that I will be caught
I47	183	1	5	2.503	1.084	I think it is alright for *me* to copy commercial software if most people do it.
I36	184	1	5	2.495	1.197	I think it is alright for *a student* to use university computer and software for their benefits regardless of its effect on others.
I43R	184	0	4	1.620	1.249	I think it is illegal for a *student* to copy commercial software instead of buying it.
I49R	184	0	5	1.348	1.232	I do not think it is right to copy commercial software.
I44R	184	0	4	1.310	1.209	I think it is illegal for *anybody* to copy commercial software instead of buying it.

Strongly Disagree 1 R – is reverse scored

Disagree 2

No Opinion 3

Agree 4

Strongly Agree 5

Table 3: Pearson Correlation Coefficients

	I 12	I 13	I 16	I 19	I 22	I 25	I 28	I 31	I 34	I 35	I 36	I43 R	I44 R	I 45	I 47	I 48
I 12	1															
I 13	.50 **	1														
I 16	.20 **	.25 **	1													
I 22	.24 **	.17 *		.59 **	1											
I 25			.36 **	.18 *	.19 **	1										
I 28	.16 *		.28 **		.23 **	.27 **	1									
I 31	.14 *	.20 **	.23 **	.36 **	.38 **	.32 **	.42 **	1								
I 34	.25 **	.16 *	.14 *	.42 **	.52 **	.19 *	.36 **	.48 **	1							
I 35	.15 *			.27 **	.22 **		.16 *	.32 **	.48 **	1						
I 36				.18 *				.24 **	.27 **	.73 **	1					
I44 R												.56 **	1			
I 45	.19 **	.23 **	.45 **			.23 **	.27 **	.26 **	.14 *			.19 **	.14 *	1		
I 46							.16 *								.19 **	
I 47		.22 **	.32 **					.17 *		.21 **	.16 *	.21 **	.27 **	.51 **	1	
I 48		.19 **	.25 **			.15 *				.18 *			.27 **	.43 **	.77 **	1
I 49			.19 **			.20 **		.15 *			.14 *	.18 *	.39 **	.38 **	.29 **	.16 *
V 55													.16 (*)			

**. Correlation is significant at the 0.01 level (2-tailed).

*. Correlation is significant at the 0.05 level (2-tailed).

Appendix A
SOFTWARE COPYING Questionnaire [12]

For the following items, the authors asked the respondents to circle, based on their beliefs and feelings, the appropriate choice of one of the Likert scale choices as given below:

Strongly Disagree Disagree No opinion Agree Strongly Agree
1 2 3 4 5

I12. I believe most *people* copy commercial software instead of buying it.
I13. I believe most *students* copy commercial software instead of buying it.
I16. I think it is alright for *a student* to copy commercial software instead of buying it.
I19. I think is alright for *a student* to use university computers and software for non-university activities.
I22. I think it is alright for *a student* to use university computers and software for their social organizations.
I25. I think it is all right for *a student* to copy commercial software to evaluate it for possible purchase.
I28. I think it is alright for *a student* to use a university owned software at home to complete university assignments.
I31. I think it is alright for *a student* to use a university owned software at home for personal use.
I34. I think it is alright for *a student* to use university computer and software for their benefits as long as it has no adverse effect on others.
I35. I think it is alright for *a student* to use university computer and software for their benefits as long as it has only minor adverse effect on others.
I36. I think it is alright for *a student* to use university computer and software for their benefits regardless of its effect on others.
I43. I think it is illegal for a *student* to copy commercial software instead of buying it.
I44. I think it is illegal for *anybody* to copy commercial software instead of buying it.
I45. I think it alright for *me* to use copied software if I would not buy it in any case.
I46. I think it is alright for *me* to "try out" software so long as I intend to buy it in the future.
I47. I think it is alright for *me* to copy commercial software if most people do it.
I48. I think it is alright for *me* to copy commercial software because it is unlikely that I will be caught.
I49. I do not think it is right to copy commercial software.
V55. I think for every 100 legal copies of software in the market there are at least ____ illegal copies made of the same software in the U.S.

Appendix B

Kohlberg's levels of Moral Development [12][13]

Level 1- Preconventional Level: Individuals begin their moral development with an internal focus, first to avoid punishment then to achieve some level of self-gratification.
Stage 1 - Action is motivated by avoidance of punishment and "conscience" is irrational fear of punishment.
Stage 2 - Action is motivated by desire for reward or benefit. Possible guilt reactions are ignored and punishment viewed in a pragmatic manner. (Differentiates own fear, pleasure, or pain from punishment-consequences.)

Level 2 - Conventional Level: At this point in the development process individuals focus more on a group. This is the level at which peer pressure begins to exert its influence. An individual who develops beyond the stage of peer pressure will begin to look at rules as defining behavior.
Stage 3 - Action motivated by anticipation of disapproval of others, actual or imagined - hypothetical. (e.g., guilt).
Stage 4 - Action motivated by anticipation of dishonor, i.e., institutional blame for failure of duty, and by guilt over concrete harm done to others.

Level 3 - Postconventional level: This is the point at which individuals are more concerned with ramifications toward society in general.
Stage 5 - Concern about maintaining respect of equals and of the community.
Stage 6 - Concern about self-condemnation for violating one's own principles.

Items relevant to Kohlberg's Stages

Stage 2: I12, I13, I36, I48
Stage 3: I16, I19, I22, I45, I47
Stage 4: I25, I28, I31, I35, I43, I44, I46
Stage 5: I34
Stage 6: I49

A Computing System to Assist Business Leaders in Making Ethical Decisions

Reggie Davidrajuh

University of Stavanger Department of
Electrical Engineering and Computer Science
PO Box 8002, Norway

Email: reggie.davidrajuh@uis.no

Abstract. This paper explores whether it is possible to build a computing system that can make ethical decisions autonomously, and if it is possible, then what it takes to build such a system. Firstly, this paper introduces ethical business decision-making, and also explains the reason for building an autonomous computing system that can assist business leaders. Secondly, a literature study is presented on the existing models for ethical decision-making; from the literature study, and with the help the stakeholder analysis (ethical theories that are relevant to the business environment), a new model is proposed. Thirdly, based on the new model, this paper proposes building an autonomous computing system; the proposed system has a layered architecture. This paper concludes that if such a system is built then inherently it has to be an adaptive system in order to cope with ever changing environment.

1. Introduction

The collapses of Enron, WorldCom, Arthur Andersen, Martha Stewart's stock sales, etc. have made us aware of the seriousness of ethical implications of business decisions. These days, business decision makers must incorporate ethics in their business decisions. However, confronting ethical dilemmas and making ethical decisions are not easy as:

- There are no magic formulas available to help the decision makers solving ethical dilemmas they confront

Please use the following format when citing this chapter:

Davidrajuh, R., 2008, in IFIP International Federation for Information Processing, Volume 286; Towards Sustainable Society on Ubiquitous Networks, eds. Oya, M., Uda, R., Yasunobu, C., (Boston: Springer), pp. 303–314.

- When confronting ethical issues, huge number of variables (from sociology, psychology, economics, business, laws & regulations, etc.) that have to be considered. Hence, without any computing aid, it is not easy for decision makers to make an 'optimal' solution

Thus, this paper proposes an autonomous system to help decision makers incorporate ethics in their business decisions. In order to develop such a system:

Firstly, it is necessary to get a systems perspective of ethical business decision-making in the networked economy: what are the elements and environments involved in the decision-making process, how the elements are connected or related to each other, how the elements, environments, and the interconnections can influence each other, etc.

Secondly, it is necessary to devise a model for the autonomous computing system for decision-making.

Thirdly, a validation of the model has to be done; whether suitable enabling technology is available to realize such a system? Will it be possible to program the system? Etc.

2. Why a Computing System?

Despite the growing interest in ethical decision-making, there is considerable disagreement about the appropriate way to define business ethics, and business ethical leadership, and the ways to asses the ethical decisions (Yukl, 2006; Heifetz, 1994).

Generally, ethical business decision making is such a difficult process, so much that business leaders use their moral standards to evaluate their ethical decisions as good or bad depending on what extend to which the outcomes of their decisions violate basic laws of society, denies others their rights, endangers the health and lives of other people, or involves attempts to deceive and exploit others for personal benefits. This paper proposes implementing business ethical decision-making processes as computer software so that it can help solving the following problems associated with ethical decision-making:

Ambiguous process: Ethical decision-making is an ambiguous process that appears to include a huge number of highly interconnected Webs of sub-processes. This is due to the existence of several criteria that are relevant for judging ethical decisions, including the person's values, the person's stage of moral development, conscious intentions, freedom of choice, use of ethical and unethical behavior, and the probable outcomes of the ethical decisions (Yukl, 2006).

Dependency on moral development: Kohlberg (1984) proposed a model to describe how people progress through six sequential stages of cognitive moral development as they grow from child to an adult. With each successive stage, the person develops a broader understanding of the principles of justice, social responsibility, and human rights. Unlike physical maturation, moral development is not inevitable, and some people become fixated at a particular stage. A leader who is at a higher level of development is usually regarded as more ethical than one at a lower level of development; the level of moral development of leaders has an impact on ethical decision-making in business organizations (Trevino, 1986; Trevino and Youngblood, 1990).

Uncertainty in problem identification: An important leadership function is to help frame problems by clarifying key issues, encouraging dissenting views, distinguishing cases from symptoms, and identifying complex interdependencies (Yukl, 2006). In ethical decision-making, identifying and acknowledging key problems and issues is no easy task; a computer program may facilitate leaders systematically identify problems, acknowledge, delegate to followers, and solve problems.

Environmental influences: Ethical behavior occurs in a social context and it can be strongly influenced by aspects of the situation (Trevino, 1986; Trevino et al, 1998). Business leaders' personality and cognitive moral development interact with aspects of the situation in the ethical decision-making. That is, ethical decisions can be explained better by consideration of both the individual and the situation than either variable alone (Yukl, 2006).

Formal Assurance: Burns (1978) and Heifetz (1994) describe leadership as both a dyadic and collective process. Leaders influence individuals, and they also mobilize collective efforts to accomplish adaptive work. The type of influence used by leaders includes not only use of rationality and appeal to values, but also formal authority. Leaders can use their authority to direct attentions to problems, frame issues, structure decision processes, mediate conflicts, allocate resources to support problem solving, and delegate specific responsibilities to individuals or groups. Though formal authority is not necessary as emergent leaders acquire informal authority by taking responsibility for exercising leadership institutions where it is needed, Heifetz (1994) emphasizes that meaningful change requires shared leadership, and it can not be accomplished by a single, heroic individual. A significant and formal assurance from a computer program could function as a solid backing to leaders to put into practice their decisions.

Empirical research on ethical issue in leadership is relatively new topic, and much still needs to be learned about it (Yukl, 2006). Kahn (1990) proposed an agenda of research questions that would help to bridge the apparent gap between normative concepts (defining ethical behavior) and contextual concepts (the conditions influencing ethical behavior). The objective is to produce knowledge that strengthens both the theory and practice of ethical conduct in Organizations. Examples of relevant research questions include language used to frame and communicate ethical issues, the conditions under which conversations about ethics are likely to occur, the process by which ethical dilemmas and disagreements are resolved, the process by which ethical principles are adapted to changing conditions, and the ways that leaders influence ethical awareness, dialogue, and consensus.

This paper proposes a natural extension to the line of thought of Kahn (1990); the proposal is to implement the process of ethical business decision-making as a computing system, so that a systematic analysis of the process can be done.

3. Modeling Ethical Decision-Making

First, a literature study is given on the existing models for ethical decision-making in the networked economy. From the literature study, a new model for ethical decision-making is developed.

3.1 Existing Models for Ethical Decision-Making

3.1.1 A Model Based on Four Constraints

In business environments, there are many constraints that can guide and shape business transactions. Lessig (1999) presents a model describing four constraints that regulate the ethical behavior of cyberspace activities.

The first constraint is the law. Laws are rules or commands imposed by the government that are enforced through ex post sanctions; ex post sanction means that law retroactively makes criminal conduct not criminal when performed, but increases the punishment for crimes already committed. The second constraint is the market. The market regulates through the price it sets for goods and services.

The third constraint is the code (*aka* architectural constraint). The architectural constraints are physical constraints, natural or man-made, restricts the freedom of business transactions. The fourth constraint is the social norms. Social norms are informal expressions of a community that defines a well-defined sense of normalcy and expects the members of the community to follow. An example for social norm under business context is the dress code.

3.1.2 Modified Model by Spinello

The model by Lessig (1999) incorporated ethics under the broad category of "social norms"; social norms have only cultural or community value. Spinello (2003) argues that the fundamental principles of ethics are metanorms and they have universal validity, and hence should not be classified as social norms. In the modified model by Spinello, ethics is given a directive role, that is, ethics should guide and direct the ways in which the constraints such as laws, the market, code, and social norms, exercise their regulatory power.

3.1.3 A Model Based on Six Environments

Walstrom (2006) conducted an empirical study to investigate factors that impact on ethical decision-making processes regarding information ethics. Walstrom (2006) found that the two factors that had predominant impact were:

- The social environment: religious values, cultural values, and social values
- The government/legal environment: legislation, administrative agencies, judicial systems, etc.

However, there exist four other factors too that exercise influence on ethical decision-making (Boomer et al, 1987):

- Personal environment: individual attributes including personal goals, motivation, position, demography,

- Private environment: peer group, family, and their influences,
- Professional environment: code of conduct, professional meetings, licensing,
- Work environment: corporate goals, stated policy, corporate culture.

3.1.4 A Model Emphasizing Personal Environment

On contrary to the model by Walstrom (2006) that is based on six environments emphasizing social and legal environments, Haines and Leonard (2007) suggests that the impact of the personal and private environments have a greater influence in certain ethical problems.

3.2 Theoretical Basis for Developing a New Model

It is easy to see that the existing models presented in the previous subsection are only for qualitative reasoning; and that these models can not be used towards realization of computer systems that can make autonomous decisions, as the models do not facilitate inclusion of mathematical modules for computation. Thus, in this subsection, a new model for ethical decision-making is developed; the main reason for developing the new model is to build a computing system that can autonomously make ethical decisions.

Although there are no magic formulas to start with, it is helpful to have a framework with which the ethical decision-making process can be organized (Silbiger, 2007); stakeholder analysis is a framework that helps us identify various elements involved in the decisions.

3.2.1 Stakeholder Analysis

Under stakeholder analysis, three theories of ethics are applied in business environments. These are stockholder theory, stakeholder theory, and social contract theory. These theories and their interpretations and implications are given below:

Stockholder Theory: According to the stockholder theory, the stockholders contribute capital to the businesses; corporate leaders act as agents in advancing the stockholders interests (Pearlson and Saunders, 2006). According to the originator of this theory, the only social responsibility of business and hence the agents, is to use the resources to engage in business activities designed to increase profits for the stockholders; profit making must be done by open and free competition, without deception or fraud (Friedman, 1962; Pearlson and Saunders, 2006).

Stakeholder Theory: According to the Stakeholder theory, in addition to the obligation to the stockholder, agents are also responsible for taking care of the interests of *all the stakeholders* of the business; the term stakeholder refers to any group that vitally affects the survival and success of the corporation (e.g. employees, suppliers, distributors, customers) or whose interest the corporation vitally affects (e.g. the local community, customers) (Smith and Hasnas, 1999). This means, unlike stockholder theory that primarily look into the interests of stockholders, stakeholder theory balances the rights of all stakeholders (Pearlson and Saunders, 2006).

Social Contract Theory: Both stockholder theory and stakeholder theory do not talk about the society; according to the social contract theory, agents are responsible for taking care of the needs of a society without thinking about corporate or other complex business arrangements. Social contract theory forces the agents to interact in a way that business transactions bring benefits to the members of a society. Hence, society can grant legal recognition ('social contract') to a corporation to allow it to employ social resources toward given ends (Smith and Hasnas, 1999). The social contract allows a corporation to exist and demands that agents create more value to the society than they consume for the business transactions.

Summary of Stakeholder Analysis: By skimming through the three theories of business ethics, one can see that these three theories related. The social contract theory is the most restrictive one, demanding that the whole society should be taken care of by the agents when they conduct business exchanges. The stakeholder theory is lesser restrictive than the social contract theory, as instead it demands that all the stakeholders of the business (not the whole society) should be taken care of. Finally, the stockholder theory is the least restrictive one, as it demands that only the stockholders are to be taken care of by the agents. In summary, stakeholder analysis presented above suggests that first we draw a list of all the elements (stockholders, customers, etc.) potentially effected by an ethical decision; then, we evaluate net economic benefits that the ethical decision will cause on each elements on the list.

3.3 The New Model

Based on the stakeholder analysis presented in section 2 and on the literature study on the existing models for ethical decision-making, presented in section 3, we formulate a new model consisting of the following processes:

Initialization: Identifying the main elements (stakeholders) and the environments involved in the ethical issue.

Establishing the connected system: Determining the rights and responsibilities of each element and the relative weights of each element, thus establishing the connection between the elements.

The process of measurement: Setting up the governing equations that that combines the elements and the environments, and measuring the harms and benefits to each element, and finally, making decisions based on the net harms and benefits to the elements involved in the issue.

3.3.1 Identifying the Primitive Elements of the Model

There are a number of elements already identified in the literature: Lessig (1999) identifies four elements such as laws, the market, code, and social norms, as the primitive elements of a system for ethical business decision-making. Walstrom (2006) identifies six elements such as social environment, legal (or government) environ-

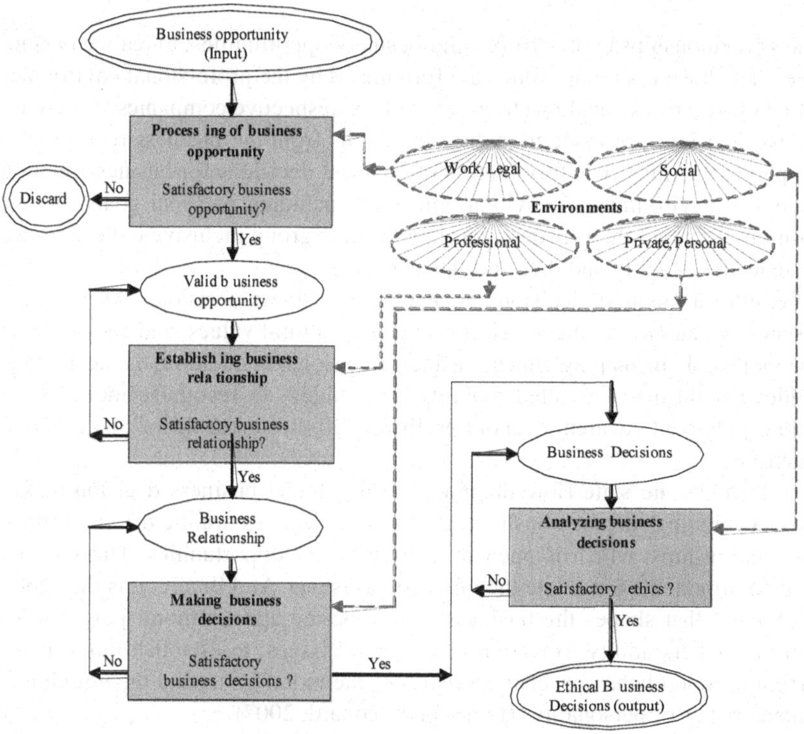

Figure 1 : State flow diagram for ethical business decisi on-making

ment, personal environment, private environment, professional environment, and work environment, as the primitive elements. In addition to all these elements, the literature also sites the following primitive elements: interacting agents, leaders, shareholders, etc.

3.3.2 Establishing the Connections in the Model

Before we start thinking about the internal connections of the system, let us identify the sources (or the external disturbances that agitate the system to produce an output) and the output of the system. Business opportunities are the sources of the system. Obviously, without business opportunities there won't be any ethical business decisions; ethical business decisions are the output of the system.

Given below is a step-by-step formulation of the connections between the primitive elements of the system:

When the input (a business opportunity) is fed into the systems, the legal environment and the work environment (business goals and objectives, etc.) must recognize the business opportunity as a valid one. For example, when a company in US receives a business opportunity from a company in Cuba, the legal environment will reject the opportunity. In some other cases, an opportunity may be rejected because the opportunity does not satisfy business goals and objectives (work environment) of a company.

Business relationships evolve from valid business opportunities, to realize business exchanges. The business relationships are formulated by the professional environment (code of conduct, professional meetings, etc.) of the respective companies involved.

Business decisions are made to strengthen profits from the business relationships. A major player that influence formulation of business decisions for business relations is the personal environment (individual attributes including personal goals, motivation, position, etc.) and the private environment (peer group inclusive colleagues and immediate leaders, family and their influences).

Finally, ethical business decisions evolve from business decisions. As Walstrom (2006) states, social environment (religious values, cultural values, and social values) plays the major role in shaping ethical business decisions. In addition, the agent's personal ethics (might also be called morality - the ability to recognize moral issues, make moral judgment, awareness about profit for "all the stakeholders", etc.) play en important role.

Figure 1 shows the state flow diagram for the ethical business decision-making processes. As figure 1 depicts, business goals and objectives are the driving force of business relationships, which is opened up by business opportunities. The six socio economic environments formulate the business decisions. And finally, it is the agent's moral judgment that shapes the business decisions; the agent's moral judgment depends on his or hers ability to recognize the moral issues, to establish moral intent, engagement in moral behavior, characteristics of the moral issue, and the individual's own characteristics or personality (Haines and Leonard, 2007).

4. Developing the Proposed Computing System

The architecture of the computing system is a hybrid architecture based on previous works on autonomous and adaptive business systems; se Muller et al (1995), Fasli (2007), and Woolridge (1999) for some of the architectures. The architecture consists of three distinguishable layers, such as Planning layer, Inference layer, and Data layer.

4.1 Planning Layer

The planning layer uses the models to predict potential outcome of a scenario. First it checks the overall validity of the business opportunity (see figure-1); it then generates goals which are associated with ethical business strategies. Subsequently, business goals are propagated down to the inference layer, which uses the data layer to make decisions. The inference layer hosts a number of inference engines. The data layer mainly consists of a knowledge base.

4.2 Inference Layer

In figure 1, oval shaped components are passive components (such as input buffers for incoming business opportunities, intermediate buffers for storing intermediate decisions made, and output buffers for storing final decisions, etc). Rectangular components are active components, such as inference engines for decision-making. In figure-1, four inference engines are visible: 1) Processing of business opportunity, 2) Establishing business relationships, 3) Making business decisions, and 4) Analyzing business decisions. These inference engines are the main components of the inference layer.

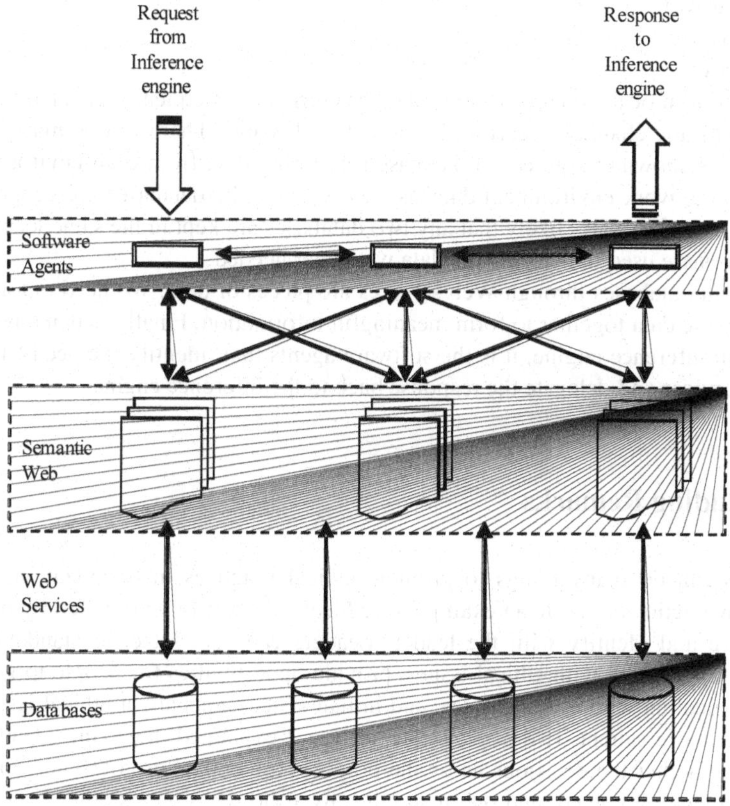

Figure-2: The data layer that consists of many brokers working together

The inference engines are equipped with mathematical models for decision-making. We believe that it is possible establish mathematical models to measure net economic benefits even for the complex problems like ethical issues, as the necessary enabling technologies are already available. We can utilize fuzzy logic (Ross, 2004; Tsoukalas and Uhrig, 1997) to code the mathematical models; the reason for proposing the use fuzzy logic is that fuzzy logic filters away inaccuracies in the input parameters; in addition, compared to pure mathematical approaches (such as mixed integer programming, linear programming, etc), with fuzzy logic it is easy to model a system.

4.3 Data Layer

Figure-2 shows details of the data layer, which consists of several brokers:
The software agents
Semantic Web
Web Services
Databases

At the bottom of the data layer rests data bases that are frequently updated to synchronize with the changes occurring in the external world. There can be many databases (e.g. as shown in figure-1, a database for storing data from each environment, legal database, work environment database, etc.). Since the databases are geographically distributed (it is less likely that any two databases are kept in the same location), Web services are used to delegate the data whenever needed.

Data from databases through Web services are pieces of data. We need ontologies to integrate the data together to form meaningful information. Finally, when a request comes from inference engine, it is the software agents that identify the needs, locate the Web services and delegate the response back to the inference engine.

5. Concluding Remarks

Leaders can do many things to promote ethical practices in organizations. The leader's own actions provide an example of ethical behavior to be imitated by people who admire and identify with the leader. Leaders can also set clear standard and guidelines for dealing with ethical issues, provide opportunities for people to get advice about dealing with ethical issues, and initiate discussions about ethical issues to make them more salient. However, as the section 2 explained, how can a leader be sure about whether the decisions he or she proposes are ethical or not? There are too many parameters involved, and one man ethically valid decisions is other man's unethical decision. This paper proposes an autonomous computing system to assist leaders making ethical decision.

The system proposed in figure-2 should not be assumed as a static system as it may looks like. The databases shown in the figure are static databases, but frequently updated by a set of software agents that can learn about the environment, and the changes in the environment. Use of software agents gives the autonomous property to the proposed computing system.

References

Boomer, M., Clarence, G., and Tuttle, M. (1987) A behavioral Model of Ethical and Unethical decision Making. Journal of Business Ethics, 6(4), (May 1987), pp. 265-280

Burns, J. (1978) Leadership. New York: Harper & Row

Cassandras, G. and LaFortune, S. (1999). Introduction to Discrete Event Systems. Hague, Kluwer Academic Publications

Dickson, M., Smith, D. Grojean, M., and Ehrhart, M. (2001) An organizational climate regarding ethics: The outcome of leader values and the practices that reflect them. Leadership Quarterly, 12, 197-217

Fasli, M. (2007) Agent Technology for e-commerce. Wiley

Friedman, M. (1962) Capitalism and Freedom. Chicago: University of Chicago Press

Haines, R. and Leonard, L. (2007). Individual characteristics and ethical decision-making in an IT context. Industrial Management & Data Systems, 107 (1), pp. 5-21

Heifetz, R. (1994) Leadership without easy answers. Cambridge, MA: Belnap Press of Harvard University Press

Kahn, W (1990) Toward an agenda for business ethics research. Academy of Management Review, 15, 311-328

Kohlberg, L. (1984) The psychology of moral development. New York: Harper & Row

Lessig, L. (1999) Code and Other Laws of Cyberspace. New York: Basic Books

Muller, J., Pischel, M., and Thiel, M. (1995) Modelling reactive behaviour in vertically layered agent architecture. In Wooldridge, M. and Jennings, N., editors, Intelligent Agents: Agent Theories, Architectures, and Languages (ATAL), LNAI Volume 890, pages 261-276, Springer, Berlin

Pearlson, K. and Saunders, C. (2006) Managing & Using Information Systems: A strategic Approach. 3ed., Wiley

Peterson, J. (1981) Petri Net Theory and the Modeling of Systems. Prentice-Hall, N.J.

Ross, T. (2004). Fuzzy logic with Engineering Applications. 2. ed. John Wiley & Sons

Silbiger, S. (2007). The 10-Day MBA. Piatkus, London.

Smith, H. And Hasnas, J. (1999) Ethics and Information Systems: The Corporate Domain. MIS Quarterly, 23 (1), (Mar. 1999), pp. 109-127

Spinello, R. (2003) CyberEthics: Morality and Law in Cyberspace. 2nd ed. Jones and Bartlett Publishers

Trevino, L. (1986) Ethical decision making in organizations: A person-situation interactionist model. Academy of Management Review, 11, 601-617

Trevino, L. Butterfield, K. and McCabe, D. (1998) The ethical context in organizations: Influences on employee attitudes and behaviors. Business Ethics Quarterly, 8(3), 447-476

Trevino, L. and Youngblood, S. (1990) Bad apples in bad barrels: a casual approach. Journal of Applied Psychology, 75, 378-385

Tsoukalas L. and Uhrig, R. (1997). Fuzzy and Neural Approaches in Engineering. John Wiley and Sons

Walstrom, K (2006) Social and legal impacts on information ethics decision making. Journal of Computer Information Systems, XLVII (2), (Winter 2006-2007), pp. 1-8

Wooldridge, M. (1999) Intelligent Agents. In Weiss, G., editor, Multiagent Systems: A modern approach to Distributed Artificial Intelligence, pages 27-77. The MIT Press, Cambridge, MA

Yukl, G. (2006) Leadership in organizations. 6th Ed. Pearson / Prentice-Hall.

Local Government ICT Platform
Standardization Activities of ICT Systems and Services for Offering High Value-added Service by Interacting Local Governments, Regional Institutions and Private Sector

Akihira Yoshimoto, Shu-ichi Muto, Genichi Kaneda, Kazuaki Ohara, Masahiko Nakayama, Atsushi Hirao, Hidekazu Masaki, and Daisuke Miyamoto

The Association for Promotion of Public Local Information and Communication,

2-9-14, Torano-mon, Minato-ward, Tokyo 105-0001, Japan

Abstract. As Japanese local governments are facing severe financial situation, reduction of administration cost with use of ICT is in burning necessity. However, electronic local government has not been promoted smoothly in Japan, since ICT systems have been introduced without sufficient business process reengineering. On the other hand, the citizens' needs for enhancing public services have increased. In order to respond the citizens' needs with the fiscal constraint, enriching public online service by the service interaction between local governments and regional institutions and private sector is indispensable. The Association for Promotion of Public Local Information and Communication (APPLIC), its members are local governments and private companies, has promoted the standardization activities of Local Government ICT Platform, which enables smooth interaction of data and services and brings solutions to the problems. By applying the standard specifications, business operation in local governments will be streamlined, and local governments and regional entities will be able to provide high value-added services such as one-stop service to citizens. This paper describes problems Japanese local governments have regarding the public service utilizing the ICT, activity of APPLIC to establish and promote Local Government ICT Platform for alleviating the problems, and the effect and architecture of Local Government ICT Platform.

Please use the following format when citing this chapter:

Yoshimoto, A., Muto, S., Kaneda, G., Ohara, K., Nakayama M., Hirao, A., Masaki, H., Miyamoto D., 2008; in IFIP International Federation for Information Processing, Volume 286, Towards Sustainable Society on Ubiquitous Networks, eds. Oya, M., Uda, R., Yasunobu, C., (Boston: Springer), pp. 315–326.

1. Introduction

In Japan, as aging society with fewer children proceeds, realization of the rich and collaborative society is aspired, which citizens and companies in region can share their knowledge and know-how, and esteem individual value and lifestyle.

By the progress of building of IT infrastructure based on e-Japan Strategy, ubiquitous network society has come that anyone can use ICT for anything always at anywhere. ICT also plays important role for the management of private companies and governmental agencies. In recent years the Japanese central government has carried out measures to realize "one-stop electronic administration for citizens" and "regional revitalization". Major measures are described in Table 1.1 [1,2,3,4,5,6,7,8].

Table 1.1. Japanese government measures for e-government and e-local government

Published Date	Document Title	Published Agency
January 2006	New ICT Reform Strategy	IT Strategic Headquarters
March 2007	New e-Municipality Promotion Guideline	Ministry of Internal Affairs and Communications
April 2007	ICT Policy Package of New IT Reform Strategy	IT Strategic Headquarters
July 2007	Priority Policy Program 2007	IT Strategic Headquarters
November 2007	Regional Reproduction Strategy	Headquarters for the Regional Revitalization
February 2008	Urgent Program for Regional Revitalization by ICT	IT Strategic Headquarters
April 2008	ICT Policy Roadmap	IT Strategic Headquarters

However, electronic local government has not been promoted smoothly in Japan, since local governments have introduced the ICT systems without sufficient implementation of business process reengineering. On the contrary, the ICT systems based on procedures of conventional administrative office work that paper documents are centered, or the ICT systems that don't adequately meet the convenience and usability of citizens have established. In addition, due to the stagnation of the Japanese economy that has continued for years and hollowing out of domestic manufacturing in region, the tax revenue of local government has curbed. The subsidy from Japanese central government has also been cut along with the promotion of decentralization. Providing administrative service convenient for citizens by utilizing the ICT systems, under the circumstance of severe financial situation, is in burning necessity for the majority of local governments.

This paper presents the activity towards solving the problems Japanese local governments have regarding enhancing regional public services, with efficient use and expenditure of ICT systems. It is the activity to establish and promote Local Government ICT Platform, which is the standard specification documents for interacting and combining various services on network and building new services, based on the concept of Service Oriented Architecture (SOA). The goal of the activity is to streamline business operation in the local governments with minimum administrative costs and enhance convenience of citizens, by offering interactive public services such as one-stop service. One-stop service is defined as the service conducted and terminated by single application of service.

The content of the paper includes the problems the Japanese local governments face, the introduction of the association tackling the problems, and the effect, system and architecture of Local Government ICT Platform. The remainder of this paper is organized as follows: Section 2 shows the present situation and the difficulties of Japanese local governments. Section 3 shows the brief explanation of the association that forms and promotes Local Government ICT Platform. Section 4 shows the outline and the effect of the standard specification, and section 5 shows its architecture and functions.

2. Current Problems of Local Government

Local governments hold difficulties regarding offering proper administrative service and managing regions. The main problems are introduced in this section: improvement of public services, reduction of ICT costs, increase in efficiency of administrative affairs, and the promotion of ICT industry in region.

2.1 Improvement of Public Services

The explosive spread of the Internet enables citizens to receive various services through the Internet. However, regarding administrative services, offering of services with the viewpoint of convenience for citizens has not sufficiently achieved, and the realization of high value-added public service is long awaited.

The typical example of high value-added public service is one-stop service, which the citizen can automatically receive the information regarding the administrative services related to the citizen, and can simultaneously apply applications not only to central and regional governments but also to regional institutions and companies from regional portal site. The one-stop service boosts the convenience of citizens especially at the time the major events in lifetime, such as moving, marriage, birth of child, death of relevant and retirement.

2.2 Reduction of ICT Costs

Many local governments apply general-purpose computers to ICT systems conventionally. General-purpose computer adopts centralized system and the process and management of data is done at central computer. As the years have passed, system modification in accordance to law amendment and addition of system functions has repeated, and inside of the general-purpose computer has become black box that system engineers cannot easily understand and modify the ICT system.

Since the number of the engineers who are able to maintain the general-purpose computer has decreased, concern regarding the stability of the maintenance work comes up and the operation and maintenance cost has increased.

Furthermore, it is almost impossible for the other system vendors to reconstruct the system, since there is no designing standard for general-purpose computer. As the system vendor who is able to modify the ICT system is restricted to the original constructor, competition does not exist and the reduction of ICT system cost is difficult to occur.

Even though reconstruction of general-purpose computer and interaction between other systems are realized, they further increase the dependence to the original constructor, as specification of the system depends on the vendor. The effort of continuous use of system inhibits construction of ICT system that multiple system vendors participate in, and impedes proper procurement.

2.3 Increase in Efficiency of Administrative Affairs

Local governments used to develop systems optimal only for specific business, and there are many cases that the adopted technologies differ depend on system vendors or the timing of procurement. It makes the interaction between ICT systems difficult, and causes double input and double management of data. For instance, when a family moves in to the region and turns in application forms to a number of divisions of the local government, every division needs to input the same data such as name and address, since the interoperability of data is not achieved. Similarly, the employee of the local government has to ensure data consistency between the ICT systems of different divisions in certain intervals.

The interaction of data has not achieved until today, and the double input and double management of data causes inefficiency of the administrative office work.

2.4 Promotion of ICT Industry in Region

Many of system vendors in region have had few opportunities to acquire the information regarding measure of informatization that central and local governments promote. In many cases they tend to get subcontracted work of system construction, and are not in the situation of actively taking part in informatization in region, including construction of electronic local government. It is desired that local governments enable to conduct procurement more openly and with smaller unit, so that the opportunity of regional system vendors increases and it leads to employment expansion and economic growth of the region.

3. Formulation of Local Government ICT Platform by APPLIC

Table 3.1. Vision, mission and major activities of APPLIC

Vision	-Collaborative promotion of regional community information policy by public and private - Building regional society which citizens get high value-added service by the use of various ICT equipments
Mission	-Open and collaborative work by local governments and companies -Interaction with policy of Japanese government
Major activities	-Drastic reform of information system of local governments -Building the ICT Platform which openly interacts information systems of regional institutions and companies -Maintenance and promoting public applications such as disaster prevention, medical treatment, education, etc. -Holding personnel training and seminars for the promotion of regional community information -Further maintenance of the public ICT networks and promotion of interconnection of the networks - Construction of a public ICT network that connects all prefectures in Japan

Table 3.2. Major roles of APPLIC committees

The technical committee	- Establishment and management of Local Government ICT Platform standard specification document from the viewpoint of business, technology, interconnection and GIS
The application committee	- Formulation of recommended specifications that local governments could commonly adopt such as disaster prevention, health and welfare, education - Formulation of data interaction specification
The diffusion promotion committee	-Planning, preparation, and presentation of seminars to promote the Local Government ICT Platform -Diffusion of knowledge and know-how and the training of talented people
The information and telecommunications infrastructure committee	-Share of the information on maintenance situation regarding information and telecommunications infrastructure - Examination of the promotion method regarding infrastructure maintenance toward building regional public network and broadband network all over Japan

In order to solve the problems described in section 2 by promoting the examination regarding the realization of electronic local government and the regional informatization, the Association for Promotion of Public Local Information and Communication (APPLIC) was established in 2006. The members of APPLIC are local governments, private enterprises and academic experts who voluntarily participate in the examination process. The vision, mission and major activities of APPLIC are described in Table 3.1.

APPLIC specifically consists of four committees: the technical committee, the application committee, the diffusion and promotion committee, and the information and telecommunications infrastructure committee. The major roles are described in Table 3.2.

In the technical committee, in order to realize the smooth interaction of data and service within and between the local governments, and to realize one-stop service in region, the examination and establishment of Local Government ICT Platform is taken place, and APPLIC has released its standard specification documents on its website. The outline and effect of Local Government ICT Platform is explained in the following section.

4. The Outline and Effect of Local Government ICT Platform

4.1 The Outline of Local Government ICT Platform

For bringing solutions to the problems explained in section 2, APPLIC has set up Local Government ICT Platform. Local Government ICT Platform establishes standard specification for interacting data and various services on the network and building new services, based on the concept of SOA. Local Government ICT Platform does not include the creation of the standard platform system itself [9].

Local Government ICT Platform is established based on the viewpoint of operation and technology of administrative services. It establishes the standard of the data exchanged and the standard of the technology of exchanging the data (Figure 4.1). By conforming to Local Government ICT Platform, regional institutions and private enterprises will be able to provide various services through portal sites, such as information offering service on certain topics and application processing service on the time of moving or other important events. The service provider interacts with local government, utility enterprises such as electricity and post office and public enterprises via online to process the applications received from citizens.

Procurement authority such as local governments and regional institutions utilize local Government ICT Platform, for examination of system configuration. System vendors utilize local Government ICT Platform too, for development of system products and solutions.

The activity of building and rebuilding systems or releasing products conforming to Local Government ICT Platform is beginning to spread. As of June 2008, the development of system conforming to Local Government ICT Platform is on the way in several advanced local governments, and several other local governments are making plans to apply the standard. They request information and proposal regarding development and modification of system based on the standard.

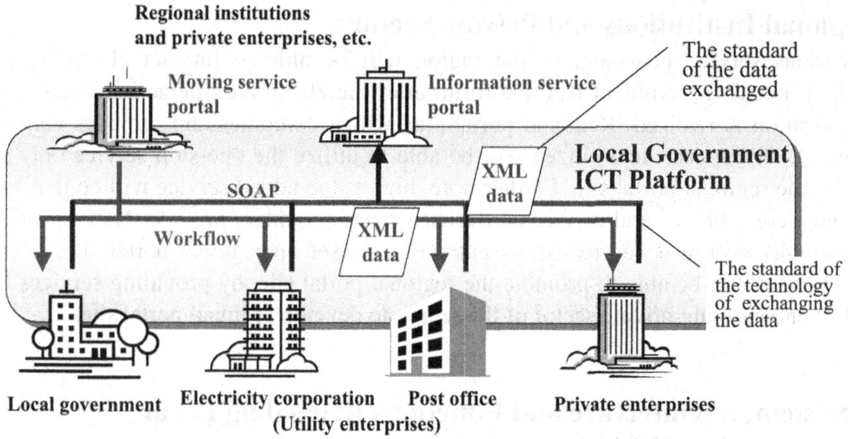

Fig. 4.1. Interaction between local governments, regional institutions and private sector by utilizing Local Government ICT Platform

There are more than twenty local governments that prepare budget for FY2009 to concern Local Government ICT Platform, and more than sixty local governments schedule to include budgeting in their medium-term plan. Also, there are 20 system vendors who have announced that they will release the products conforming to Local Government ICT Platform, and 12 consulting companies have announced that they can deal with consulting relates to the standard.

4.2 The Effect of Local Government ICT Platform

By adopting Local Government ICT Platform several effects will be brought to local governments and regions. In this section we describe two effects: electronic interaction within local government and one-stop online services between local governments and regional institutions and public sector.

4.2.1 Electronic Interaction within Local Government

The electronic interaction of business functions, such as receipt, process and approval, etc. of electronic application within the local government will be achieved by introducing Local Government ICT Platform. Conventionally, when citizen turns in several application forms to multiple divisions in local government, employee of each division punches in the information to its own ICT systems. The double input of information is one of the causes of inefficiency in administrative affairs. By realizing electronic interaction through Local Government ICT Platform, the workload of employee will be cut enormously.

4.2.2 One-stop Online Services between Local Governments, Regional Institutions and Private Sector

Various service providers of the region will be able to interact electronically through Local Government ICT Platform, after the electronic interaction within the organization is realized. Regional portal site, which combines and provides various services, will appear, and citizen will be able to utilize the one-stop service only to access the regional portal site. Furthermore, high value-added service will be realized by interacting the several services different service providers provide. New business opportunity will also be created, as entrepreneurs set up regional portal site. Local government will be able to promote the regional portal site, by providing services itself or encouraging private sector of the region to develop regional portal sites.

5. System, Architecture and Functions Regarding Local Government ICT Platform

System of documents, architecture and its outline of functions regarding Local Government ICT Platform are described in this section.

5. 1 System of Documents Regarding Local Government ICT Platform

Local Government ICT Platform standard specification consists of five specifications, one guideline and two other statements. System of documents regarding Local Government ICT Platform is shown in Figure 5.1.

As business model standard, Standard Specification regarding Local Government Business Application Unit regulates interface specification of major business application units required for the interaction of data and service. As service interaction technology standard, Standard Specification regarding Architecture and Standard Specification regarding Platform Communication regulates specification of requirements and protocol, etc. of platform applications that support service interaction. The version one of these standard specifications that aims for realizing the interaction within local government is released in 2007, and the version two that aims for realizing interaction between public and private sector is released in 2008.

Specification regarding GIS Common Service regulates specification for building business units and applications utilizing GIS. Specification regarding Confirmation of Conformity and Interconnection regulates specification used to confirm conformity of various products and interconnection of the conformed products. These specifications are newly released in 2008 [10].

Guideline of Local Government ICT Platform compiles the matters, which should be concerned by procurement authorities who introduce service platform and business application conformed to Local Government ICT Platform.

Fundamental Statement regarding Local Government ICT Platform describes the basic concept and the aim of Local Government ICT Platform, and Operational Regulations regarding Local Government ICT Platform describes establishment, modification and release methods of the standard.

These documents are released at APPLIC website, and will be revised continuously.

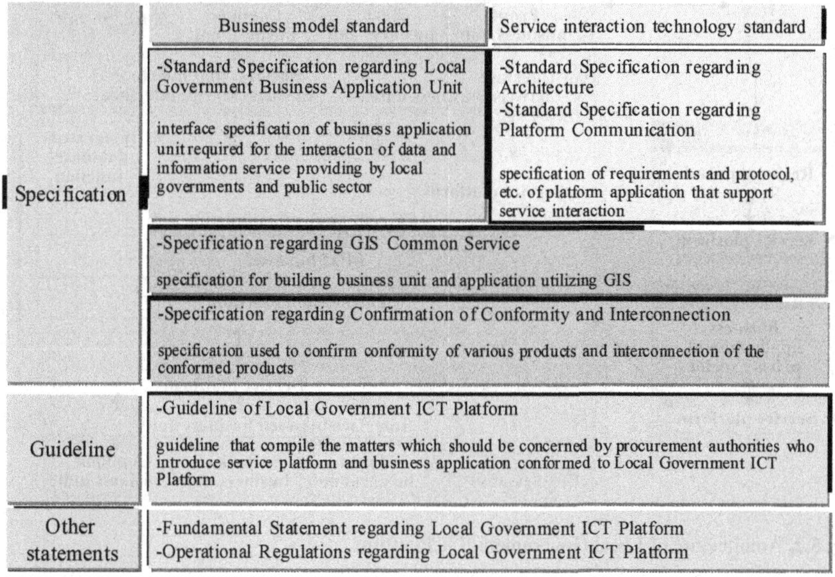
Specification
Business model standard
Service interaction technology standard
-Standard Specification regarding Local Government Business Application Unit
interface specification of business application unit required for the interaction of data and information service providing by local governments and public sector
-Standard Specification regarding Architecture
-Standard Specification regarding Platform Communication
specification of requirements and protocol, etc. of platform application that support service interaction
-Specification regarding GIS Common Service
specification for building business unit and application utilizing GIS
-Specification regarding Confirmation of Conformity and Interconnection
specification used to confirm conformity of various products and interconnection of the conformed products
Guideline
-Guideline of Local Government ICT Platform
guideline that compile the matters which should be concerned by procurement authorities who introduce service platform and business application conformed to Local Government ICT Platform
Other statements
-Fundamental Statement regarding Local Government ICT Platform
-Operational Regulations regarding Local Government ICT Platform

Fig. 5.1. System of documents regarding Local Government ICT Platform

5.2 Architecture and Functions of Local Government ICT Platform

Architecture of Local Government ICT Platform is shown in Figure 5.2. Local Government ICT Platform consists of business units and service platform. Business unit consists of business unit interface necessary for interaction between business units, and business service interface necessary for realizing one-stop service. Service platform consists of platform communication function, integrated database function, business process management function and platform common function. The outline of these functions is described afterward.

The technologies applied in Local Government ICT Platform are separated into essential technologies and optional technologies. In order to realize one-stop service, different sites or differently implemented business units have to interact smoothly, so the essential technologies are the technologies indispensable to connect each site or business unit in communication level. They are specified based on the technologies formed by international standardization organizations such as W3C (World Wide Web Consortium) and OASIS (Organization for the Advancement of Structured Information Standards), and the conditions on which companies adopt the technologies to their products. Also, necessity for local governments is examined to specify the technological subset. Optional technologies are the technologies required depend on the service implementation requirements. They include technologies for reinforcing communication level depending on service requirements, and for realizing platform common functions necessary for connection between different sites.

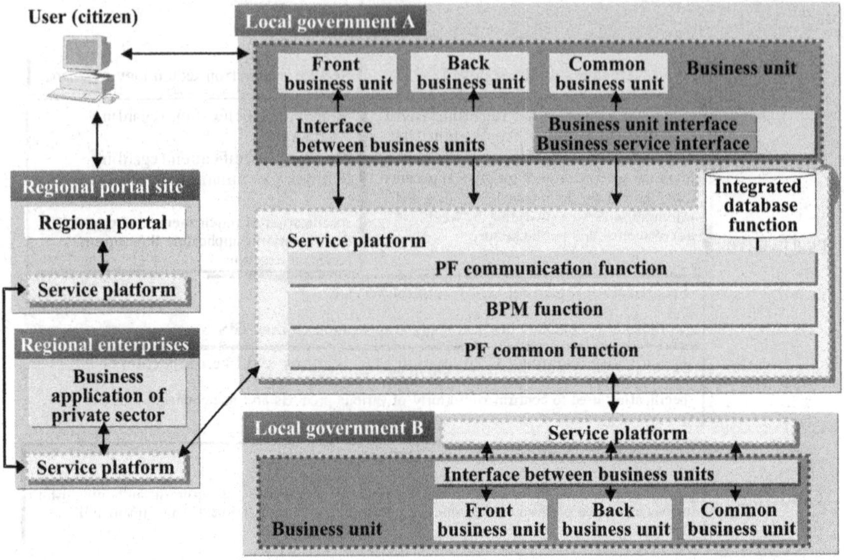

Fig. 5.2. Architecture of Local Government ICT Platform

5.2.1 Platform Communication Function

Platform communication function is service communication function based on international standard SOAP (Simple Object Access Protocol). Security and high reliability communication function, etc. can be applied as an option. Platform communication function serves as premise software of other system configuration units such as business units, business process management (BPM) function and integrated database function and does not compose system configuration unit independently.

The essential technologies of platform communication function are as follows: IPv4 for Internet protocol, SOAP1.1 for basic messaging, XML Schema1.0 for business documents definition, etc. The optional technologies of platform communication function are as follows: embedded text and SwA (SOAP messages with Attachments) for messaging with attachment files, SSL3.0, TLS1.0 for security of data transmission channel, etc.

5.2.2 Integrated Database Function

The integrated database is the mechanism that use and refer data unitary between business units. The platform communication function is the premise software, since information is offered from service call of SOAP to the integrated database. In order to interact with business units, it mounts the interface the standardized business unit mounts, which are necessary for interaction. There are two mounting methods: database system disclosure method and common interface method. Integrated database function is an option.

5.2.3 Business Process Management Function

BPM function manages execution of business process. It executes business process by calling service interface the business units offer, based on the business process definition determined on the basis of the international standard WS-BPEL (Web Services Business Process Execution Language Version 2.0). It has business service interface called by business units, the client of the business process execution. The platform communication function is the premise software, since the service communication is carried out. The BPM function is an option utilized in the case of executing sequential services one after the other, and is indispensable for offering one-stop service.

5.2.4 Platform Common Function

Platform common function is an option. The major technologies adopted here are monitoring function and service authentication and approval function, which have newly developed for the standard. Monitoring function is used to carry out process between multiple sites and to confirm the status of requested processing of the other site. The technology used here is the technology of collecting effective information in the case of avoiding processing troubles in advance, and formulating improvement of systems and services. Service authentication and approval function is used when the single sign-on is required between the sites that have different ID system. The technologies used here is the technology of preventing identification of multiple accounts under the same.

5.2.5 Business Unit

Business unit processes specific business independently. The platform communication function is the premise software, since the service communication is carried out. It has business unit interface, which is called from other business units or BPM function. It has business service interface, which is called from BPM function, in the case of realizing one-stop service interacting with BPM function. Some business units accept application and service from user or external organizations. They call for common business units, background business units or BPM function, and offer the result of processing.

6. Conclusion

In this paper we describe the necessity and efforts of establishing Local Government ICT Platform, in consideration of the policy of the Japanese central government and the problems Japanese local governments face regarding the promotion of electronic government. The outline of the specific standard is also introduced. We will continue promotion activities of Local Government ICT Platform and encourage local governments, regional institutions and system vendors to correctly understand its effect and adopt them. Operation, maintenance and enhancement of Local Government ICT Platform will also be conducted continually, based on the feedback we get from local governments and system vendors who adopt the standard.

References

1. IT strategic Headquarters, e-Japan Strategy, 2001.
2. IT strategic Headquarters, New ICT Reform Strategy, 2006.
3. IT strategic Headquarters, ICT Policy Package of New IT Reform Strategy, 2007.
4. IT strategic Headquarters, Priority Policy Program 2007, 2007.
5. IT strategic Headquarters, Urgent Program for Regional Revitalization by ICT, 2008.
6. IT strategic Headquarters, ICT Policy Roadmap, 2008.
7. Headquarters for the Regional Revitalization, Regional Reproduction Strategy, 2007.
8. Ministry of Internal Affairs and Communications, New e-Municipality Promotion Guideline, 2007.
9. The Association for Promotion of Public Local Information and Communication, Local Government ICT Platform fundamental description document V3.0, 2008.
10. The Association for Promotion of Public Local Information and Communication, Local Government ICT Platform standard specification document V2.0, 2008.

Service Interaction Platform Technologies Providing High Value-added ICT Services

Takashi Kai, Atsushi Hirao, Daisuke Miyamoto, Yuko Ueda

Hitachi Co., Ltd., Public Systems Division,

1-6-27 Shin-suna, Koutou-ward, Tokyo 136-8632, Japan

Abstract. In ubiquitous network society, various kinds of entities offer online services. For the user's convenience, providing high value-added service such as one-stop online service is in urgent need. One-stop services transform citizens' daily lives more convenient by, for example, improving online application procedures to local governments and companies. Service interaction platform technology, which securely and flexibly combines various kinds of services operated under different sites or established under different system architectures, is essential to realize high value-added services. In this paper we propose the core components of service interaction platform technology, and its effectiveness measured through demonstration experiments. The scenario of moving is applied in the experiments.

1. Introduction

The number of Internet user in Japan is increasing rapidly as the explosive spread of broadband and mobile network terminals. Today the Internet is becoming a fundamental social infrastructure, and the state of service offered by the Internet has changed. People use the Internet not only for collecting and exchanging information, but also for applications and transactions. Citizens hope a number of services can be provided through the Internet, including application procedures to central and local governments.

From e-Japan Strategy II [1], Japanese government has shifted the policies to increase users' convenience, and the Ministry of Internal Affairs and Communications

Please use the following format when citing this chapter:

Kai, T., Hirao, A., Miyamoto, D., Ueda, Y., 2008, in IFIP International Federation for Information Processing, Volume 286; Towards Sustainable Society on Ubiquitous Networks, eds. Oya, M., Uda, R., Yasunobu, C., (Boston: Springer), pp. 327–340.

promotes u-Japan Policy [2] along with the strategy. The target of U-Japan Policy is the realization of the ubiquitous network society by 2010, which anyone can always connect to network for anything and at anywhere. Toward the target, various measures have carried out for the realization of "one-stop electronic administration for citizens".

Regarding application procedures to governments, it is expected that the broad range of administrative procedure will be offered online together with service of private sector. It will enormously increase citizens' convenience and efficiency of local governments, if citizen can file applications for all kinds of public and private services online, without going out to windows or writing down same information several times in different application forms.

We define such one-stop online service as high value-added service, as citizens can apply for governments and companies at one time from anywhere, which had been impossible for a long time. One-stop service means that certain service is conducted and completed by single application of service. Here, service includes collecting information and processing applications.

In this paper, we propose service interaction platform technology, which is necessary to realize high value-added services. The remainder of this paper is organized as follows: Section 2 shows the example of the benefit of high value-added service. Section 3 shows the existent problems and the outline of core component of service interaction platform technology. Section 4 shows the effectiveness of the technology measured by demonstration experiments. Section 5 shows conclusion and future activity to disperse the technology.

2. Aims of the Research: Providing High Value-Added Services

Service interaction platform technology is necessary for offering high value-added services to user. In this chapter we exemplify the benefit of high value-added services with one-stop online moving case, and explain the specific scenario applied in the demonstration experiments.

2.1 The Benefit of High Value-Added Services: the Case of One-Stop Online Moving Service

High value-added service such as one-stop online service increases convenience of citizens and efficiency of office work of local governments. Citizen can conduct application procedures to governments and companies by single application via online. At the same time, the employee of local governments can refer and confirm information of other regional governments through the online inquiry. As an example of the benefits brought by one-stop online service, we explain the present image and the future image of application procedures at the time of moving.

In the case of moving, there are plenty of applications to be done. For instance, citizen has to turn in application form of change-of-address registration to civic affairs division and welfare division, and application form of allowance for children to child support division in the local government the citizen moves in (Fig. 2.1).

Change-of-residence registration is also required to banks and other companies. In addition, cancellation and new application of electricity, gas, water service, etc., must be done to utility companies. In present, citizen has to go to window of local government and companies, and submit separate application form at each window, writing down same information many times. Employee of local government that citizen moves in (local government A) has to inquire of local government the citizen moves out (local government B) by phone, if the application submitted by the citizen requires reference or confirmation of the information local government B has.

In such a case, one-stop online service increases citizens' convenience by great deal. For instance, citizen can access to regional portal site and apply applications to local government A, utility companies and banks electronically from home. It reduces the time to visit each window and write down same information repeatedly. Citizen can also confirm the progress of process from portal site.

One-stop online service also increases the efficiency of office work of local governments and companies. Local governments, utility companies and banks can receive the applications and return the results electronically. Moreover, Local government A can refer and confirm the information of local government B through the network. Conventionally citizen has to get a proof of earnings of previous year from government B and turn it in to government A to get allowance for child, and the employee of local government A has to manually input the data to child allowance system. As there are plenty of necessary attached documents, this is one of the reasons that processing application takes time. However, in one-stop online service, local government A can refer and confirm information of earnings on screen of child allowance system by service interaction of both local governments.

2.2 Scenario Applied in the Demonstration Experiments

In demonstration experiments, the scenario of one-stop online moving service is applied. We assume that a family moves from local government B to local government A. The family applies changing address to civic affairs division and welfare division of local government A, bank and electric power company, and applies allowance for children to child support division of local government A.

The specific flow of process and information is described in Fig. 2.1. The family accesses to regional portal site, fills necessary information in application forms and turns them in electronically. Regional portal site receives the submitted applications and the business process management (BPM) function controls the process of one-stop service between local government A and B, bank and electric power company. Through the Internet the BPM function distributes the applications to local government A, bank, electric power company respectively. To bank the application is distributed after local government A finishes the procedures, since bank needs the address information local government A confirms.

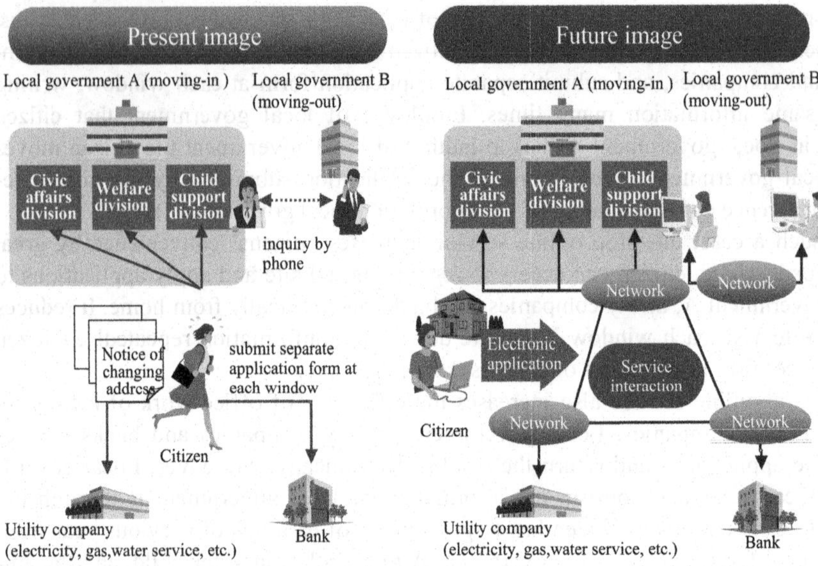

Fig. 1.1. Present and future image of moving service

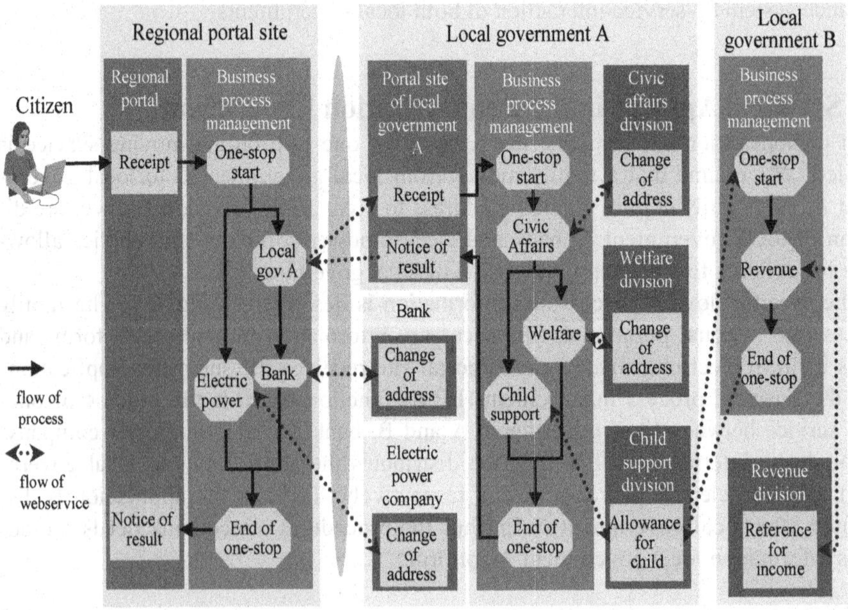

Fig. 2.1. Flow of process and web service in one-stop online moving service

In local government A, bank and electric power company, procedures are processed internally. In local government A, portal site receives the application data, and BPM function controls the process of one-stop service between civic affairs, welfare and child support division. After civic affairs division registers the address of the family, welfare division registers the address and child support division processes the application of allowance for child. In order to judge whether the allowance is applicable, child support division of local government A asks revenue division of local government B to refer the previous year's income of the family. With the information acquired from local government B, child support division processes proper procedures. When one-stop service within local government A is finished, it returns the notice of result to BPM function of regional portal site.

Application of changing address to bank and electric power company is also processed the same way. When one-stop service between local government A and B, bank and electric power company has finished, regional portal site returns the result to the family, and the family can confirm the result from the screen of regional portal site. Regional portal site shows the progress information of applications, when the family asks for the result in the middle of one-stop service.

3. Outline of Service Interaction Platform Technology

There are technical problems peculiar to online one-stop service between multiple sites. We have divided the problems from the aspects of service development, service supply and service administration, and have developed core component technologies that provide solution to each of those problems. They are design pattern technology, authentication interaction platform technology and integrated monitoring technology [3]. In this section we describe the existent problems concerning online one-stop service, and the outline of core components of service interaction platform technology.

3.1 Design Pattern Technology

In order to design web service between multiple sites, the developer needs to grasp the specifications of each site and consider the best way of these combinations. It takes man-hour, and it is also difficult to make use of know-how of past projects. Design pattern technology is developed to increase the efficiency of designing interactive web service.

Design pattern is a model form of designing system, which includes business process of one-stop service and interaction of systems. Design pattern technology is the technology that streamlines design, defines and verifies operation of the interactive service over multiple sites, and is applicable to the phase of designing interactive service, generating definition and verifying operation.

In design phase of interactive web service, functional requirements and non-functional requirements such as performance, reliability and security, should be defined. Conventionally system engineer manually understands the requirements, creates a suitable model and defines the web service. There are tools that streamline these processes, however, only functional requirements are described with these existent tools. Engineer has to define non-functional requirements by their own, usually based on know-how from past projects. In order to describe non-functional requirements, design pattern technology regulates design pattern language, the describing method of non-functional requirements. By utilizing design pattern language, non-functional requirements are described as expanded description of XML, and design pattern can have non-functional information together with functional information.

In definition creation phase, the technology provides designing tool, with which engineer can automatically generate BPEL (Business Process Execution Language) that defines business process of interactive service, and WSDL (Web Service Description Language) that defines interface of services, by selecting appropriate design patterns from pattern pool and specifying certain conditions. Process of definition creation becomes efficient, by storing the design patterns that have been developed in past projects and reuse them to new projects. The technology also provides the tool, which converts BPEL and WSDL from and to UML (Unified Modeling Language), the general description of designing document. As the definition written by UML is convertible to BPEL and WSDL, previously generated definitions in other projects are applicable to the web service, and the contrary is also realized.

In operation verification phase, the technology automatically generates service simulator, which is necessary for verifying the operation of the generated web service.

With this technology, engineer with scarce experience can understand and design interactive web service between multiple sites easily, and the developed design patterns and definitions are reusable to future projects. Design of web service becomes efficient, and thus the efficiency of design enormously improves (Fig. 3.1).

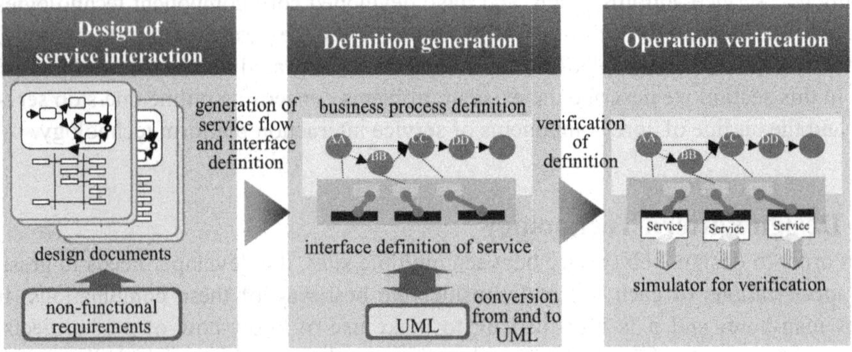

Fig. 3.1. Outline of design pattern technology

3.2 Authentication Interaction Technology

For the users' convenience, it is aspired that user can get one-stop online service by single sign-on, which enables to gain access to the multiple services by getting authentication only one time. However, the risk of drain of privacy information becomes higher in one-stop service, because if user's identification data (ID) of single site is leaked, identification of multiple sites becomes possible, and the information registered at various sites can be gathered and abused. Authentication interaction technology is developed in order to prevent the drain of personal information in one-stop interactive service.

Authentication interaction is achieved by setting up authentication center, which manages every user's log-in ID and temporary IDs and sends temporary ID by request of each site. Log-in ID is the unique identification user uses to access the account of regional portal site and get interactive web services. Temporary ID is the unique identification of user used in the communication between authentication center, regional portal site and service providers. Temporary ID is transformed to real ID within each site. Real ID is the unique identification of user used in each site.

Specific mechanism of authentication interaction is shown in Fig. 3.2. When user A wants to get services provided by site A and B, the user accesses to regional portal site and put in log-in ID (123) and password for the regional portal site (#1). At authentication center, authentication interaction function connects the log-in ID (123) to user A's temporary ID of regional portal site (zzz) (#2). The temporary ID (zzz) is sent to regional portal site, authentication interaction function of regional portal site receives the ID, and the temporary ID (zzz) is connected to real ID of user A (ZZZ) inside the regional portal site (#3). Regional portal site calls service of site A with user A's temporary ID of regional portal (zzz). At site A authentication interaction function receives the ID (zzz) and asks authentication center for the temporary ID of site A whose temporary ID of regional portal is zzz (#4). The temporary ID of site A (aaa) is sent to site A, and authentication interaction function of site A connects the temporary ID (aaa) to real ID of user A (AAA) inside site A (#5). The same mechanism of temporary ID (bbb) and real ID (BBB) works for site B (#6 and #7). When the services of site A and B are terminated, regional portal site returns the result of one-stop service to User A.

The characteristic of the technology is that real IDs of certain user differ at each site and are managed only within the site, and authentication center does not know any of real IDs. Therefore, even though the communication between authentication center and sites is tapped, it doesn't connect to the leak of identifiable information of user. By applying the technology, disclosure of personal information is minimized, and user can utilize safe interactive one-stop service by logging in to regional portal site only once.

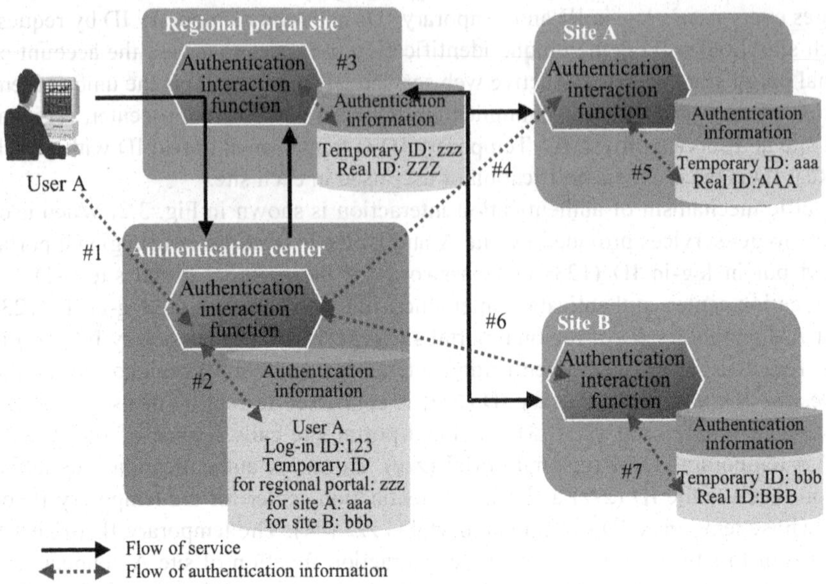

Fig. 3.2. Image of authentication interaction technology

3.3 Integrated Monitoring Technology

In one-stop online service between multiple sites, the data exchanged between sites increases. The increase of data affects performance of whole interactive services, and the management cost of interactive service becomes higher. Easy understanding of system operation situation and early detection of system resource failure are necessary for providing stable online one-stop service. Integrated monitoring technology is the technology that collects system resource data from different sites, integrates and analyzes them and provides appropriate system configuration plan. System resource is the resource of CPU or network ports, used at the time of execution of business process and services.

The technology regulates interface, provides tools and monitors. Firstly, the technology regulates the integrated monitored data and managed information interface, which are based on web service specification. As conventional technologies adopt various forms of system resource data, the unified form of data and its interface is necessary. Secondly, the technology develops the tool that generates and set in the module, which converts system resource data in various formats to integrated monitored data. The technology also provides monitor that visualize the resource utilization efficiency of multiple systems in different sites. Moreover, the technology develops integrated managed information analysis tool, which analyzes the collected integrated monitored data and generates system configuration plan, for more efficient use of system resource. The tool features considering cycle of operation load together with peak of operation load, which the existent similar technologies have not achieved. As it considers the peak information of certain interval of time, more reliable system configuration plan is calculated.

Concretely, monitoring information service function collects resource data from server in site A, B and C respectively. The data are converted to integrated monitored data, sent to surveillance center via the Internet. The data are integrated, visualized and analyzed, so that service administrator at surveillance center can easily understand the utilization rate of system resource in multiple sites, and draw better system configuration plan (Fig. 3.3). Therefore the efficient and stable offering of interactive service is realized.

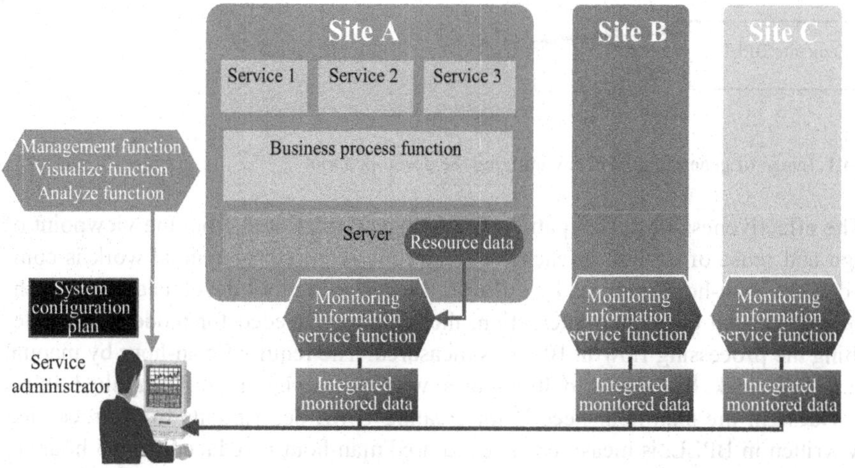

Fig. 3.3. Image of integrated monitoring technology

4.Effectiveness of Service Interaction Platform Technology

In this section we describe effectiveness of the core component technologies of service interaction platform technology. The effectiveness is measured through the demonstration experiments. One-stop online moving service scenario explained in the section 2 is applied to the experiments.

4.1 Effectiveness of Design Pattern Technology

Designing process includes modeling processing flow, generating BPEL definition and verifying BPEL operation. In modeling processing flow, engineer usually depicts flow based on BPMN (Business Process Modeling Notation), standardized description of business process. The image of BPMN depicted by the designing tool, which the design pattern technology develops, is shown in Fig. 4.1. Engineer firstly chooses appropriate design pattern from design pattern pool, and depicts processing flow. When engineer confirms the flow and orders to generate BPEL, BPEL with information of non-functional requirements is generated automatically.

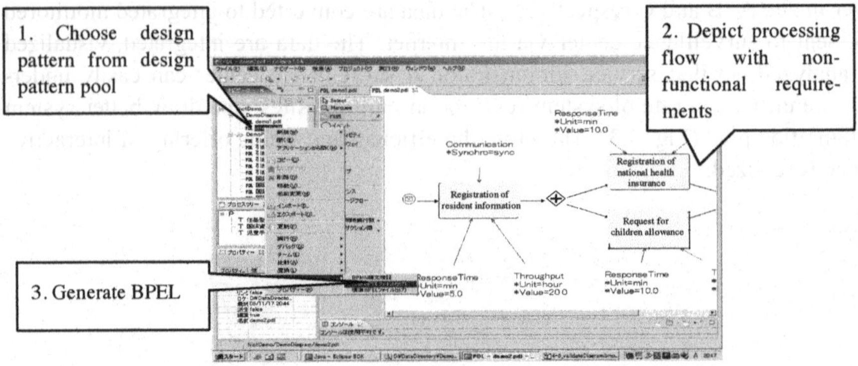

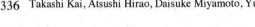

Fig. 4.1. Image of generating BPEL by utilizing the developed tool

The effectiveness of design pattern technology is measured from the viewpoint of design and reuse of design. In each case, the time required by manual work is compared to the man-hour required by utilizing the designing tool developed by the technology. In design of service interaction, the man-hour needed for modeling and describing the processing flow in BPEL is measured. The required man-hour by manual work is one week. It shortens to 30 minutes, when the designing tool is applied. In reuse of design, the man-hour needed for creating UML descriptions from processing flow written in BPEL, is measured. The required man-hour is reduced from 3 hours to 2 minutes, when the designing tool is applied (Table 4.1).

Designing web service is indispensable procedure for offering one-stop moving service. The total time and cost of designing interactive services, such as collaborative one-stop service between local governments and companies, will be extremely smaller by applying the developed technology. Engineer can use the reduced time to deeper understanding of generated designs and planning better services, etc. In addition, as engineer can automatically convert UML descriptions to BPEL definitions and vice versa, the design know-how accumulated in other projects can be easily utilized for own project. It contributes to better productivity of designing work.

In the demonstration experiment, man-hour for detailed design work is not taken into consideration. In actual development, the additional man-hour is expected to be required, as detailed design work becomes necessary. For instance, at the time of calling service, the definition creation work for data conversion becomes necessary. Man-hour based on actual development should be examined by each project.

Table 4.1. Man-hour requirement comparisons of conventional method and design pattern technology

No.	Process	Result of experiment			
		Conventional method		Design pattern technology	
		Method	Man-hour	Method	Man-hour
1	Design of service interaction	Describe processing flow by manual work	1 week	Choose appropriate design pattern from design pattern pool	30 minutes
2	Creation of UML	Create UML descriptions by manual work	3 hours	Generate UML descriptions automatically	2 minutes

4.2 Effectiveness of Authentication Interaction Technology

The possibility of authentication interaction is measured based on the user ID information shown in Table 4.2. Regional portal site, local government and electric power company have real ID and temporary ID, respectively. Authentication center manages log-in ID and three temporary IDs. There is also bank, but other way of authentication is conducted at bank. Application pattern is five patterns, which are several combinations of operations executed in local government, electric power company and bank, based on online one-stop moving service scenario. Rejection of application is included in some application patterns. It is proved that in each application pattern authentication is executed correctly and operation is concluded properly. Therefore, user can utilize one-stop service by single sign-on to regional portal site, at the same time preventing leak of personal information.

Table 4.2. ID information applied in demonstration experiment

Site name	Log-in ID/ Real user ID	Temporary user ID
Authentication center	idp_user1	chiiki_user1_sp (for regional portal site)
		portal_user1_sp (for local government)
		denryoku_user1_sp (for electric power company)
Regional portal site	chiiki_user1	chiiki_user1_sp
Local government	portal_user1	portal_user1_sp
Electric power company	denryoku_user1	denryoku_user1sp

4.3 Effectiveness of Integrated Monitoring Technology

The effect of integrated monitoring technology is measured from the viewpoint of calculation of appropriate system configuration plan. Integrated management information analysis tool analyzes the collected integrated monitored data and calculates the appropriate system configuration plan for local government A.

The environment of demonstration experiment is shown in Fig. 4.2. There is monitoring information service function, which collects system resource data from operational servers in local government A, converts them to integrated monitored data and send to surveillance client terminal via the virtual private network. Surveillance client terminal supervises and analyzes integrated monitored data of local government A.

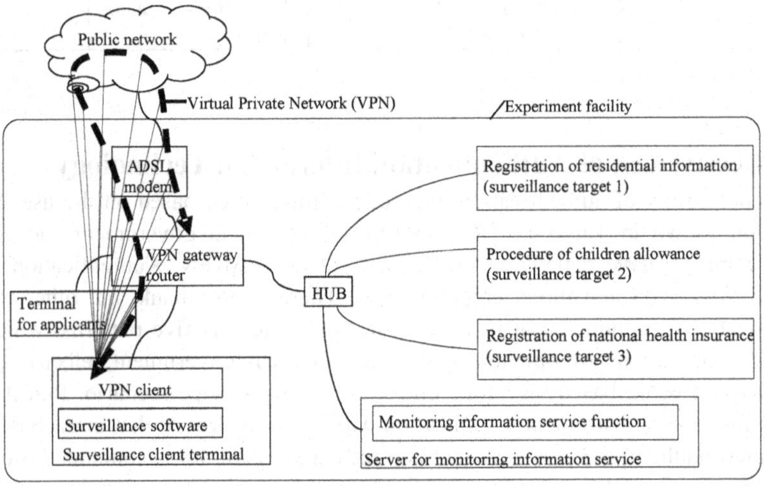

Fig. 4.2. Demonstration experiment environment regarding integrated monitoring technology

Condition in the experiment is as follows. The operations executed in local government A are registration of residential information, procedure of children allowance and registration of national health insurance. One physical server is used for each operation. Application pattern is eight patterns, which is the combination of three operations. Applications are filed in certain interval, and the number of applications filed on Wednesday is six times more compared to other days of the week. The number of applications examined changes in every 30minutes. Ten applications are examined in first 30 minutes, fifteen applications in second 30 minutes, twenty applications in third 30 minutes, and twenty-five applications in last 30 minutes.

Utilization efficiency is calculated by the following formula.

Utilization efficiency =(total sum of average amount of resource used / total sum of resource) *100

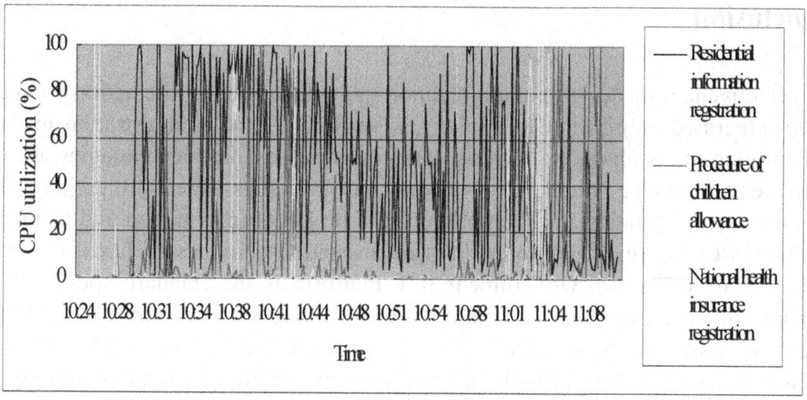

Fig. 4.3. CPU Utilization on Wednesday

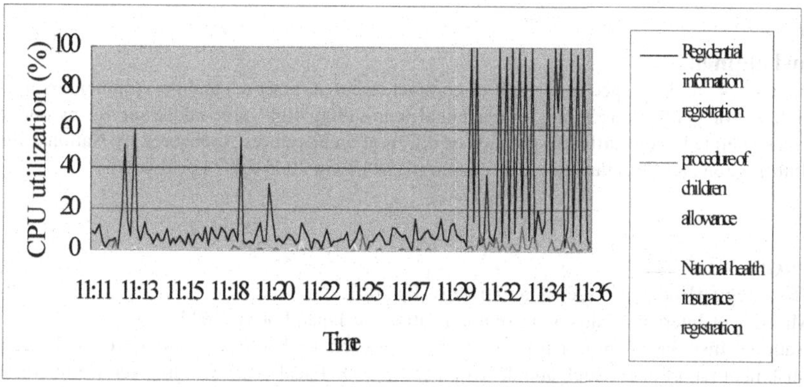

Fig. 4.4. CPU utilization on the other days of the week

Fig. 4.3 and Fig. 4.4 show CPU Utilization of three physical servers in certain time interval on Wednesday and on the other days of the week. The cumulative CPU utilization of three servers on Wednesday is more than 200%. Therefore, three sets of server are necessary. On the other hand, on the other days of the week, the cumulative CPU utilization is less than 100% and single server can conduct the three operations. After the system concentration, average utilization efficiency of CPU increases from 8.0% to 8.8%. In other words, utilization efficiency ratio improves approximately 10%.

By utilizing the technology, service administrator at surveillance center can grasp the utilization efficiency of system resource in single site and plan more efficient system configuration. The technology is also applicable in the situation that the systems are dispersed in multiple sites. Thus service administrator can easily understand the condition of system resource and provide stable one-stop service.

5. Conclusion

The effectiveness of design pattern technology, authentication interaction technology and integrated monitoring technology is verified by the demonstration experiments applying one-stop online moving service scenario. These technologies are indispensable for service interaction between multiple sites. We will propose the technologies to Association for Promotion of Public Local Information and Communication (APPLIC), which promotes the standardization activities of Local Government ICT Platform. Local Government ICT Platform is the standard specification documents for interacting and combining various services on network and building new services, based on the concept of Service Oriented Architecture (SOA). We will contribute to the realization of high value-added service through proposal activity of the technologies and commitment to APPLIC.

Acknowledgments

The technologies are developed as a result of contract research 'research and development regarding service interaction platform technologies that enables providing high value-added service by interacting services operated under different policies or different architectures' sponsored by National Institute of Information and Communication Technology (NICT) in 2005-2007 fiscal year.

References

1. IT strategic Headquarters, e-Japan Strategy II, 2003.
2. Ministry of Internal Affairs and Communications, u-Japan Policy, 2004.
3. National Institute of Information and Communication Technology, Contract research accomplishment report of research and development in 2007 fiscal year regarding service interaction platform technologies that enables providing high value-added service by interacting services operated under different policies or different architectures, 2008.

Realizing Interoperable Infrastructure for Electronic Business Systems and Local Government Systems

Kazunori Iwasa[1]**, Masahiko Narita**[2]**, Makiko Shimamura**[1]

[1]Strategy and Planning Division, Software Unit, Fujitsu Limited
3-9-18 Shinyokohama, Kohoku-ku, Yokohama, 222-0033, Japan
E-mail: {kiwasa, maki.shimamura}@jp.fujitsu.com

[2]Department of Information Systems Architecture
Advanced Instirute of Industrial Technology
1-10-40 Higashi Ohi, Shinagawa-ku, Tokyo, 140-0011, Japan
E-mail: narita-masahiko@aiit.ac.jp

Abstract. Web Services and related open standard technologies are key technologies for system infrastructure in industry systems and local government systems. There are many projects that have adopted these technologies in the local government systems and also in B2B systems in various industries. We found that one of the key requirements to promote these standards in industries is pull messaging for client/server systems, since many small and medium enterprises can't afford server systems. To achieve this, we have standardized Pull messaging specification as a part of ebXML (Electronic Business using eXtensible Markup Language) Messaging Services Specification Version3.0, with inputs of industries requirements. We also have developed Conformance test tool and additional test assertions for ebMS3.0 to promote interoperable implementation for ebMS3.0, and executed interoperability test. In this experience, we have found interoperability issues in open source. We will investigate this issue further, and continue giving feedbacks to implementations and prototype. We believe this experience regarding Pull messaging technology will be valuable for local government systems in the future, when it is going to expand its infrastructure to connect with medium and small entities.

Please use the following format when citing this chapter:

Iwasa, K., Narita, M., Shimamura, M., 2008, in IFIP International Federation for Information Processing, Volume 286; Towards Sustainable Society on Ubiquitous Networks, eds. Oya, M., Uda, R., Yasunobu, C., (Boston: Springer), pp. 341–352.

1 Introduction

Web Service and relating open standard technologies are going to be one of the most important key technology for system infrastructures recently, because of 1) the openness of the key technologies, e.g., XML, Internet, SOAP and other Web Services related Specifications, 2) increasing a number of products and services that support Web Services and relating technologies, and 3) user demands to openness, flexibility of business data format, system architecture, and trading partners. Many industries are going to adopt Web Services technologies and its relating technologies in their system infrastructure when they standardize the industry standard of electronic business trading among enterprises in the industry. It is also adopted in the public service system infrastructure of local government in Japan. For this reason, interoperability of these infrastructures is critical to develop a system, since such systems should be able to communicate with a lot of other different systems, developed by various vendors. This paper describes concrete example of Web Services adoption in industries and local government in Japan, issues and lessons learned from standardization and interoperability verification for a standard messaging protocol, and the future activities to promote these technologies in industries and local government further.

2 Web Services in the Local Government Systems

There is a Japanese government project to adopt Web Services in the local government systems. Ministry of Internal Affairs and Communications, and the Association for Promotion of Public Local Information and Communication jointly sponsor this project. This project was initiated in 2005 to develop a Public Local Information Platform that will be the base of the nationwide local government information systems.

2.1 Overview of the Public Local Information Platform

The Public Local Information Platform is a set of specification to define common platform to provide integrated/communicated local information services from local government and/or private companies. Traditionally, Japanese local government has different systems for each department: electronic application, personnel and payment, pension, public welfare, tax, and others. It has been common to exchange data manually or by paper between different departments. To enable data exchange and operational interaction between systems in a different department, they are going to connect each application on a common system communication platform that adopt Web Services and relating open standard technologies. This system enables to share services and operations. For instance, when you move, it is required to submit various documents to the local government. It includes: Notification of change of address, address change application for the National Health Insurance and the National Pension Plan, application for changing location of light automobile, application for childcare allowance, taxation certificate, and others. It is possible to provide one-stop service solution if each system that supports the above application: the basic resident register system, light automotive tax system, child-care allowance system, nursing care and public welfare system, electronic application system and others are communicated on the local information platform.

2.2 Goal of the Local Information Platform and its Requirements

The goal of the Local Information Platform includes: 1) increasing convenience of government services by providing communicated services within a local government, inter-local government, and between local government and private sector, and creating a new business opportunity with this change, 2) decreasing a system cost by adopting an open standard technologies like Web Services, which enables more choices of software/service provider, and 3) reusing the existing local government systems. Therefore the standardization of the services, a platform that is adopting open standard technologies, and interoperability is the requirements for this platform.

2.3 Web Services as a Platform of Local Government Systems

The Local Information Platform specification is going to define common vocabulary, standard business documents and business process to cover wide range of local government services including: Basic Resident Register, National Health Insurance, Child-care Allowance, Seal Registration, Property Tax, Resident Tax, Corporate Tax, National Pension Plan, Elder Care, Care Insurance, School Attendance, Census Registration, Personnel and Compensation, Document Management, and others. [4]

Local Information Platform also defines to use standardized Web Services technologies, since the system should be able to communicate with different systems from different vendors. For instances, it defines to use a standard communication protocols including reliable messaging and security, since those functions - guaranteed delivery, duplicate elimination message ordering and message security are critical to develop real business systems. It also defines specification for business process execution and management, authentication for service interaction, and system monitoring.

The Local Information Platform is currently for server systems for large entities. And it may be a future requirement to support smaller entities that can't afford server systems. In that case, client/server systems with pull messaging, that client asked a message to receive in the server, will be required in the future.

3 Web Services in the Industry

In contrast with the previous section, this section describes how the Web Services and B2B messaging standards are used in the vertical industry. It also describes how we have developed a standard specification to meet industry requirements.

3.1 Industry Adoption for B2B Standard Messaging Protocol

- Retail Industry: Japanese retail industry has defined their standard protocol - "Japan Chain-stores Association (JCA) Protocol". And it is widely used in the industry from 1980s. It is pull messaging that client asks for a message to receive. Adoption rate between retail stores and wholesale/manufacture is more than 90%. DSRI (the Distribution Systems Research Institute) has defined Pull Messaging extension for "SOAP-RPC" to migrate it to Web Services technologies. They have executed POC in 2004. Japanese retail industry also decided to adopt ebMS2.0 for standard messaging protocol in the industry recently. [1]

- Manufacturing Industry: Japan Electronics and Information Technology Industries Association (JEITA) ECALGA project has standardized an industry standard specification for parts procurement system from 2003. It is adopting ebMS2.0 and many systems are in-services. JEITA also defined messaging model for client / server model to develop JEITA client recently as described in the Fig. 3.1.

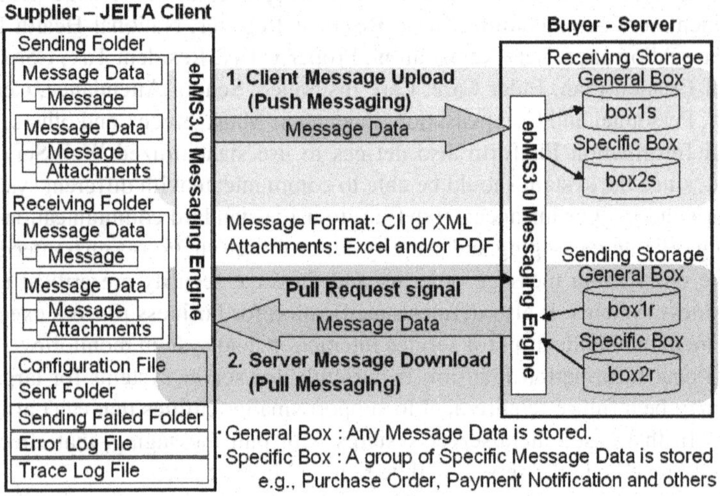

Fig. 3.1. JEITA Client and its messaging model *

* The fig. 3.1 is translated to English and merged from two figures that were originally created by JEITA member in Japanese [6].

- Common XML/EDI Practice Promotion Council (COXEC) is promoting EDI services with ASP model. They have defined "Common XML/EDI Framework" in December 2005.

3.2 Challenge to Increase B2B Adoption Rate in SMEs

The above three industries are promoting the industry standard specification. However one of the big obstacles for them to increase adoption rate of B2B messaging standard is the low adoption rate of the B2B standard in the Small and Medium Enterprises (SMEs). There was ISO standard for B2B messaging protocol i.e., ebXML Message Services 2.0. However it was standardized mainly for server-to-server messaging. It requires the receiving PC stand by to receive an incoming message. There was a big demand of B2B messaging standard for client/server model to promote B2B standard in SMEs.

3.3 Requirements to Promote B2B in SMEs

There are some requirements to promote B2B messaging standard in SMEs:

- The system should be easy to adopt. Most SMEs are not adopting real time processing. Currently, they are not required to process data in real time. They are not required to connect the Internet 24X7. They need light-weight system to allow them exchange data on the Internet easily.
- A single system should be able to use for all trading partner. Although legacy Web-EDI is affordable, it requires to use different Web EDI systems for each trading partner. Sometimes it requires to pay multiple system fee or connection fee for multiple Web-EDI systems. It requires to input data manually. It is expensive in terms of human resources.
- The system should be easy to use. SMEs have no enough resources for system maintenances or operation. It should be easy to exchange messages like FAX.
- Messaging data in client system should be reused in other systems. Legacy Web EDI systems don't allow to reuse data, since all data is stored in server. [3]

3.4 Resolution: Standardizing Pull Messaging Protocol for Client/Server System

To meet these requirements, we have standardized Pull messaging specification for Client-Server messaging model. The figure 3.2 shows how the Pull messaging works.

In this figure, the Responding MSH on the left side is going to send a message to the Initiating MSH on the right side. However Responding MSH doesn't initiate a message connection, but put the message in the local storage. The Initiating MSH will send a Pull Signal Message regularly to get a message. If there is a message for the Initiating MSH on the Responding MSH, then the message is delivered to the Initiating MSH on the response of the underlying protocol e.g., HTTP Response, if the underlying protocol is HTTP. This model is applicable for client / server model. The Initiating MSH is the client in this case. This is useful when the client has no global IP address, or client can't accept an incoming connection for the restriction of the firewall.

It realizes affordable adoption of B2B messaging infrastructure and easy maintenance. The Pull messaging specification was submitted to OASIS ebXML Messaging Services TC, and it was standardized as a part of ebXML Messaging Services specification Version 3.0 (ebMS3.0). This feature is one of the major enhancements of ebMS3.0 from ebMS2.0, since ebMS2.0 supports server-to-server messaging only. Pull messaging is legacy EDI friendly and it doesn't require changing the system architecture, although it is not real time messaging. The client system doesn't have to wake up 24X7. It doesn't require global IP address costing you a lot. Therefore Pull messaging meets requirements from SMEs and it

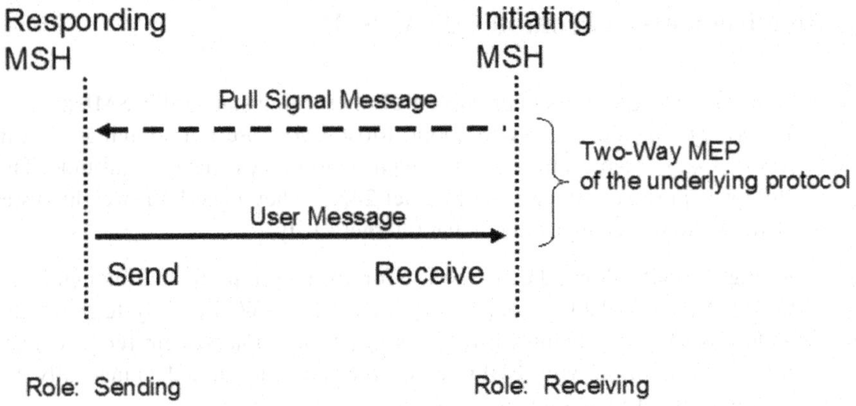

Fig. 3.2. Pull Messaging Model [7]

realizes affordable adoption cost and easy maintenance for B2B system. To standardize the Pull messaging specification, we also have gotten requirements from JEITA, COXEC, and other industries. The requirements includes:

- A simple authentication for client. The ebMS2.0 requires certificate for authentication. But the bar is too high for some SMEs. Therefore ebMS3.0 added simpler authentication - ID and Password authentication for SMEs.
- Prioritized / Categorized messaging. This feature let client choose a category of messages to receive.
- Reliable messaging. It requires resending a lost message and recovering after system down. It should not be depend on the application.

There requirements are submitted to OASIS ebXML Messaging Services TC, and standardized as a part of ebMS3.0 specification. With this achievement, JEITA and COXEC have adopted the ebMS3.0 with Pull Messaging for their client / server messaging model, as described in the Figure 3.1.

4 Verification and Promotion of the Specification

In the previous two sections, it was described some examples of Web Services in the local government systems and some vertical industries. The common requirements to the technologies they have chosen are: 1) it should be a standard technology, and 2) assurance of interoperability of implementation, since a system needs to communicate with other systems developed by other vendors.

Currently, local government system is not targeted for small and medium organizations that can't maintain server. On the other hand, vertical industries are trying to promote electronic trading to SMEs, since many SMEs have not yet adopted electronic trading. In the previous section, it was described that Pull messaging standard specification was standardized as a part of OASIS ebMS3.0 specification to meet industry requirement that wish to promote B2B in SMEs. However standardizing a specification is not the end of resolution, since it is more important to make various implementations interoperable when they have implemented the standard specification. This section describes how we are ensuring conformance and interoperability of the standard specification we have standardized.

4.1 Conformance Test Tool for Web Services is Developed

There is a conformance test tool for Web Services technologies that we have developed to promote interoperable Web Services implementation. We have tested reliable messaging specification and implementation with this test tool and executed interoperability test for local government system application before.

4.2 Supporting ebMS3.0 with the Conformance Test tool

To help implementers of ebMS3.0 test their implementations, and promote interoperable implementation, we have developed ebMS3.0 test assertions for the confor

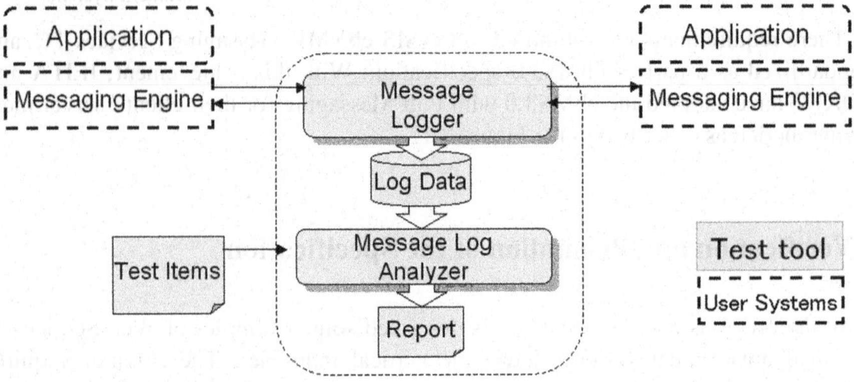

Fig. 4.1. Architecture of Conformance Test Tool

mance test tool. It supports all elements and attributes of the ebMS3.0 specification with 111 test assertions. The architecture of this conformance test tool is follows:

4.3 Interoperability Verification for ebMS3.0

We have executed interoperability test among three implementations on March 2008. Two of them are clients and one of them is a server. Each implementation have been developed as follows:

Table 4.1. Implementation overview

	Client A	Client B	Server C
Java	JDK1.5.0_14	JDK1.5.0_11	JDK1.6.0.14
HTTP	HTTP1.0	HTTP1.0	HTTP1.1
SOAP engine*	Apache Axis1.3	Apache Axis1.3	Apache Axis2

* The SOAP engine that each implementation adopted for generating, sending and receiving SOAP messages.

Please note each of these three implementations has adopted open source implementation -apache Axis, but the version is not same between server implementation and clients.

For this interoperability test, we have defined the following two major test scenarios. These test scenarios are very simple but include typical client server messaging scenarios that will be used widely in various industries.

Table 4.2. Test Scenarios

Test cases	Test description
SC1: Client sends a message to Server - Push messaging	
SC1-1	One-way Reliable Messaging with one payload
SC1-2	One-way Reliable Messaging with three payloads
SC2: Client receive a message from Server - Pull messaging	
SC2-1	One-way Pull Reliable Messaging with no message
SC2-2	One-way Pull Reliable Messaging with one payload
SC2-3	One-way Pull Reliable Messaging with three payloads

4.4 The Current Status of the Test Results

Test Results for Client A and Server C is follows:

The UserMessage in the table includes all elements and attributes under the ebMS3.0 UserMessage element that includes business message.
The SignalMessage is the table includes all elements and attributes under the

Table 4.3. Test Results for Client A and Server C

Test category	Test Items	SC1-X				SC2-X			
		P*	F*	W*	N*	P*	F*	W*	N*
Messaging	6	6	0	0	0	6	0	0	0
UserMessage	69	56	0	0	13	0	0	0	69
SignalMessage	36	0	0	0	36	14	0	0	22

* P:Passed, F:Failed, W:Warning, N:Not tested

ebMS3.0 SignalMessage element that include signal message like PullRequest - indication to pulling a message.

Messaging in the table is indicate the Messaging element in ebMS3.0 that is the most outer element of the ebMS3.0 message.

Test Results for Client B and Server C is follows:

Table 4.4. Test Results for Client B and Server C

Test category	Test Items	SC1-X				SC2-X			
		P*	F*	W*	N*	P*	F*	W*	N*
Messaging	6	6	0	0	0	6	0	0	0
UserMessage	69	48	0	0	21	0	0	0	69
SignalMessage	36	0	0	0	36	14	0	0	22

* P:Passed, F:Failed, W:Warning, N:Not tested

Please note that the above test results showed a portion of tests we have successfully tested. There are some interoperable issues for this test. For instance, it was failed to complete sending SC1-x messages, since there was error occurred to save a received message in the server. The reason may be the incompatibility between Axis1.3 and Axis2, but need further investigation. However the message sent was captured by the testing tool and analyzed. The above test results showed the result of the analyzed message, although it was not saved in the server correctly.

4.5 Observation of the Test Results

From the test result above, we found that format of all message tested were correct. In detail, there is no test item that was failed or warned in Table 4.3 and Table 4.4. There are six test items for "Messaging" test category in Table 4.3. And it showed us that the tested message have passed all six test items. For "UserMessage" Test categories, 56 out of 69 test items were successfully passed the test. There are 13 test items that were not tested, since the tested message is not including such elements or attributes. Thus, about 65% of the test items were tested in this test, and all of them were successfully passed. We can conclude the test messages generated in this test were compliant with ebMS3.0 specification.

There are also interoperability issues in this test. The error was occurred during the process of Axis2 in the server. Axis2 tried to save attachments in the temporally file, but for some reason, it couldn't save the second MIME part and the after. One of the possible reasons is incompatibility of MIME implementation between Axis1.3 and Axis2. This issue should be further investigated. Currently it is the middle of migration from Axis1.x to Axis2, so both implementations exist in the market. We need to be careful about interoperability issues caused from such situation.

In summary, we have developed test assertions for the conformance test tool to test pull messaging in ebMS3.0. We tried to test existing implementations and prototype for ebMS3.0 with this testing tool. At this point, we have gained experience for incompatibility of the open source. We will continue the investigation of the issues and we will give feedbacks to implementation and prototype.

5. Conclusion and Future Activities

As described in section2, Local government is adopting Web Services technologies as a key infrastructure in the Local Information Platform. In industries, there are attempt to promote B2B standard technologies to Small and Medium Enterprises. One of the key requirements to promote B2B systems to SMEs is Pull messaging for Client/Server systems. It is one possibility that the Local Information Platform is also require Pull messaging to promote the platform more widely. For instance, it may expand the platform to connect with small systems, i.e., it may want to allow: 1) certified public tax accountant office to connect to the platform with a client system, 2)small health clinic to connect some systems on the platform in the future, and others. In such cases, it may be possible to reuse the technologies the industry have developed, or get some hints from such experiences. We also have developed conformance test tool for Web Services and additional test assertions for ebMS3.0. We have tried interoperability test with existing ebMS3.0 implementations and prototype. We have gained knowledge about incompatibility of open source. The test tool also is applicable to other projects in the future, since it is publicly available.

It is important the industries validate and promote interoperable standard technology for pull messaging. We would like to contribute for this direction by promoting interoperability testing in Japan, Asia or in the world.

We believe this experience regarding Pull messaging technology will be valuable for local government systems in the future, when it is going to expand its infrastructure to connect with medium and small entities. In this case, the experiences and knowledge we get with this activity in industries can be applied in local government systems in the future.

Acknowledgements

These activities are part of the "Digital Information Appliance Interoperability Technology Project (Development of Remote Management Platform for Information Appliances)" sponsored by NEDO (New Energy and Industrial Technology Development Organization) in Japan.

References

1. Masahiko Narita, et al., Developing a Messaging Specification for EDI on Internet for SME and Its Standardization, IEICE, Vol.J89-D, No.10, pp.2237-2245, 2006
2. Masahiko Narita, et al., Verifying the Reliability of Web Services Interactions for the Robot Communication Platform, Tokyo Metropolitan University, Journal of Advanced Computaiational Intelligence and Intelligent Informatics (JACIII), Vol.12, No.1 pp77-84, January 2008
3. Kazunori Iwasa, et al., Promoting e-Business and Web Services Standards to SMEs in Japan, and Asia, OASIS, 2007
4. Masahiko Narita, et al., Verification for the Interoperability of Web Services for Municipality Systems, Advanced Institute of Industrial Technology, Bulletin of Advanced Institute of Industrial Technology, October 2007
5. Small and Medium Enterprise Agency, Ministry of Economy, Trade and Industry, White Paper on Small and Medium Enterprises in Japan, Japan Small Business Research Institute, 2007 http://www.chusho.meti.go.jp/pamflet/hakusyo/h19/download/2007hakusho_eng.pdf
6. Kazunori Iwasa, et al., ebXML Messaging Services Ver3.0 Interoperability test specification, ECOM, 2008

7. Pete Winzel, et al., OASIS ebXML Messaging Services Version3.0: Part 1, Core Features, OASIS Standard, OASIS, 2007
8. Information Sciences Institute, University of Southern California, Internet Protocol, DARPA Internet Program Protocol Specification, IETF, RFC791, 1981
9. Information Sciences Institute, University of Southern California, Transmission Control Protocol, IETF, RFC793, 1981
10. R. Fielding, et al., Hypertext Transfer Protocol -- HTTP/1.1, IETF, RFC2616, 1999
11. Tim Bray, et al., Extensible Markup Language (XML) 1.0 (Fourth Edition) W3C Recommendation, W3C, 2006
12. Tim Bray, et al., Namespaces in XML 1.0 (Second Edition) W3C Recommendation, W3C, 2006
13. Henry S. Thompson, et al., XML Schema Part 1: Structures Second Edition W3C Recommendation, W3C, 2004
14. Don Box, et al., Simple Object Access Protocol (SOAP) 1.1 W3C Note, W3C, 2000
15. Nilo Mitra, et al., SOAP Version 1.2 Part 0: Primer (Second Edition) W3C Recommendation, W3C, 2007
16. Martin Gudgin, et al., SOAP Version 1.2 Part 1: Messaging Framework (Second Edition) W3C Recommendation, W3C, 2007
17. Martin Gudgin, et al., SOAP Version 1.2 Part 2: Adjuncts (Second Edition) W3C Recommendation, W3C, 2007
18. Kazunori Iwasa, et al., WS-Reliability1.1 OASIS Standard, OASIS, 2004
19. Doug Davis, et al., WS-Reliable Messaging Version1.1 OASIS Standard incorporating Approved Errata, OASIS, 2008

Group Support in Collaborative Networks Organizations for Ambient Assisted Living

Paulo Novais[1], Ricardo Costa[2], Davide Carneiro[1], José Machado[1], Luís Lima[2], José Neves[1]

[1] DI-CCTC, Universidade do Minho, Braga, Portugal

[2] College of Management and Technology - Polytechnic of Porto, Felgueiras, Portugal

Abstract. Collaborative Work plays an important role in today's organizations and normally in areas where decisions must be made. However, any decision that involves a collective or group of decision makers is, by itself, complex. In this work we present the VirtualECare project, built in terms of an intelligent multi-agent system able to monitor, interact and serve its customers, which are, normally, in need of care services, and assisted with tools based on open standards, like OSGi an R-OSGi.

1. Introduction

In the last years there has been a substantially increase in the number of people needed of intensive care, especially among the elderly, a happening that is related to population ageing [1]. However, this is not exclusive of the elderly, as diseases as obesity, diabetes, and blood pressure have been increasing among young adults [2]. While a new realism, it has to be dealt with by the health sector, and particularly by the public one. Thus, the implication of finding or not new and cost effective ways for health care delivery are of particular importance, especially when one want them not to be removed from their "habitat" [3]. Following this line of thinking, the VirtualECare project [4] is presented in section 2, like similar ones that preceded it [5]. In this paper we are going to center our efforts on the Group Decision modules of the VirtualECare project.

Please use the following format when citing this chapter:

Novais, P., Costa, R., Carneiro, D., Machado, J., Lima, L., Neves, J., 2008, in IFIP International Federation for Information Processing, Volume 286; Towards Sustainable Society on Ubiquitous Networks, eds. Oya, M., Uda, R., Yasunobu, C., (Boston: Springer), pp. 353–362.

In the last years we have assisted to a growing interest in combining the advances in information society - computing, telecommunications and presentation – in order to create Group Decision Support Systems (GDSS). Indeed, the new economy, along with increased competition in today's complex business environments, takes the companies to seek complementarities in order to increase competitiveness and reduce risks. Under these scenarios, planning takes a major role in a company life. However, effective planning depends on the generation and analysis of ideas (innovative or not) and, as a result, the idea or brainwave making and management processes are crucial.

Our objective is to apply the GDSS approach to problem solving to a new area. We believe that the use of GDSS in the healthcare arena will allow professionals to achieve better results in the analysis of one's Electronically Clinical Profile records (ECPs). This achievement is vital, regarding the explosion of knowledge and skills, together with the need to use limited resources and get better results.

2. VirtualECare

The VirtualECare project main objective is to present an intelligent multi-agent system able to monitor, interact and provide its customers with health care services of the utmost excellence. This system will be interconnected, not only to other healthcare institutions, but also with leisure centers, training facilities, shops and patient relatives, just to name a few.

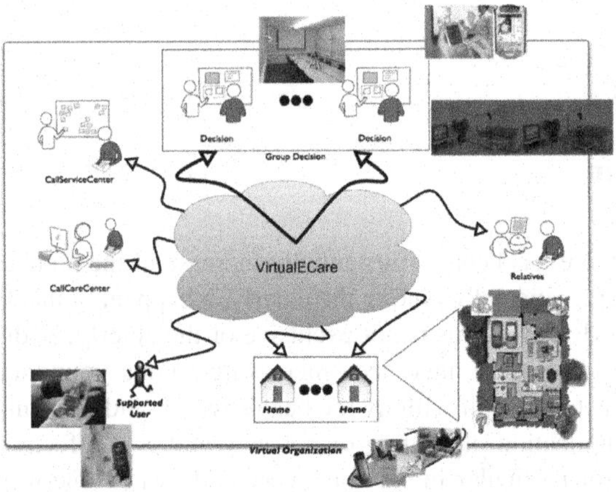

Fig. 1. The VirtualECare Architecture

The VirtualECare Architecture is a distributed one with their different modules interconnected through a network (e.g. LAN, MAN, WAN), each one with a different role (Figure 1). A top-level description of the architecture machinery is given below:

- SupportedUser – elderly people with special health care needs, whose clinical data is sent to the CallCareCenter and redirected to the Group Decision Support System;

- Home – the elderly natural environment, provided with sensors, with the clinical data being sent to the Group Decision Support System through the CallCareCenter, with the remaining one being redirected to the CallServiceCenter;
- Group Decision – it is in charge of all the decisions taken at the VirtualECare platform (our work will be centered on this key module);
- CallServiceCenter – Entity with all the necessary computational and qualified personal assets, capable of receiving and analyze the different data and take the necessary actions according to it;
- CallCareCenter – Entity in charge of computational and qualified personal resources (i.e. healthcare professionals and auxiliary staff), capable of receiving and analyze the clinical data, and take the necessary actions, accordingly;
- Relatives – individuals that may have an effective role on the organized assignment of the tasks of their love ones, being able to give valued information about them and to intervene, in a complementary way, in recognized emergency (e.g., loneliness).

In order to the Group Decision Support System to make its work, it has to collect the judgment of specialized staff (e.g., nurses, paediatrics, cardiologists). There is also the need to have a digital profile of the SupportedUser, allowing for a better understanding of his/her special needs. In this profile one may have quite a few types of relevant information, ranging from the patient Electronic Clinic Process to their own personal preferences (e.g. musical, gastronomic) passing by their own personal experiences, which can be used to better understand and satisfy their needs and expectatives.

This solution will help healthcare providers to integrate, analyze, and manage complex and disparate clinical, research and administrative knowledge. It will provide tools and methodologies for creating an information-on-demand environment that can improve quality-of-living, safety, and quality of patient care.

3. Group Support in Collaborative Networks Organizations

By definition, any Collaborative Network Organization (CNO) may support collaborative work, which presupposes the existence of a group of people that has as mission the completion of a specific task [6]. The number of elements involved in the group may be variable, as well as its perseverance. The group members may be at different places, meet in an asynchronous way and may belong to different organizations. Collaborative work has not only inherent advantages (e.g., greater pool of knowledge, different world perspectives, increased acceptance), but there are also some drawbacks (e.g., social pressure, domination, goal displacement, group thinking) [7].

Group Decision Support Systems (GDSS) intend, as we shall see, to support collaborative work. In this work we will call "meeting" to all the processes necessary to the completion of a specific collaborative task. A meeting is a consequence or an objective of the interaction between two or more persons [8]. Physically, a meeting can be realized in one of the four scenarios: same time / same place, same time / different places, different times / same place and different times / different places. Each one of these scenarios will require from the GDSS a different kind of support.

Until now we discusses collaborative work and present group members as the only persons involved in the process, however, it is very common to see a third element taking part in the course of action, the facilitator. The meeting facilitator is a person welcomed by all the members of the group, neutral and without authority to make decisions, which intervenes in the process in order to support the group in the identification of a problem and in the finding of a solution, in order to increase group efficiency [8].

According to Dubs and Hayne [9], a meeting has three distinct phases, as it is depicted in Figure 2.

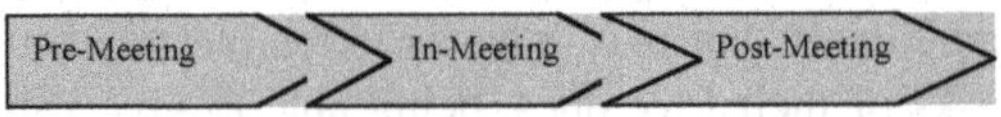

Fig. 2. Meeting Phases

In the Pre-Meeting phase the facilitator prepares the meeting, i.e., establishes the meeting goals, proceeds with the group formation (being in no doubt that all the participants have the necessary background), selects the best supporting tools, informs the meeting members about the goals and distributes the meeting materials.

In the In-Meeting phase the participants will be working in order to accomplish the meeting goals, and the facilitator has the task of monitor the elapsing of the meeting (e.g., to observe the relationship between the group members) and to intervene if necessary.

In the Post-Meeting phase, it is important to evaluate the results achieved by the group, as well as by how much each group member is acquit with the achieved results (satisfied/unsatisfied). Still, in this phase, it is very important to identify and store information that can be useful in future meetings (e.g., how to actualize the participant's profile for future selection).

Quite a few modules compose the VirtualECare Group Decision Architecture as it is depicted in Figure 3:

- Setup module – will be operated by a facilitator during the pre-meeting phase that will do several configuration and parameterization activities;
- Multi-criteria module – will be operated by a facilitator during the pre-meeting phase, being in charge of the definition of the evaluation criteria and scales and, eventually, in deleting dominated alternatives;
- Argumentation module - This module is based on the IBIS (Issue Based Information System) argumentation model developed by Rittel and his colleagues in the early 70's. According to this model, an argument is a statement or an opinion, which may support or pointed out one or more thoughts (Figure 4).
- Voting module - This module is responsible for allowing each intervenient of the decision group component to "vote" for his/her preferred option, normally the one most similar to his/her "belief" (Figure 4).

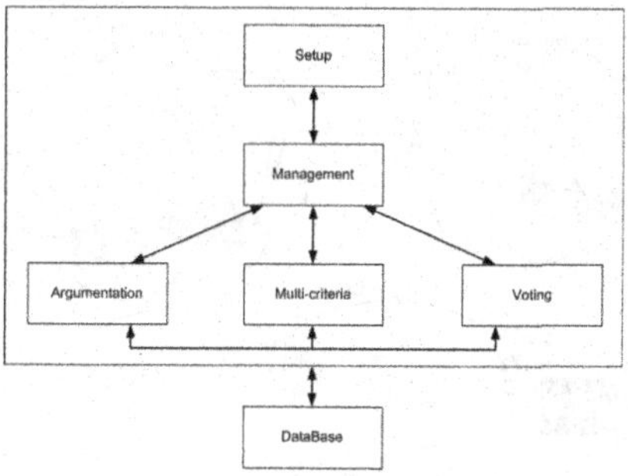

Fig. 3. VirtualECare Group Decision Architecture

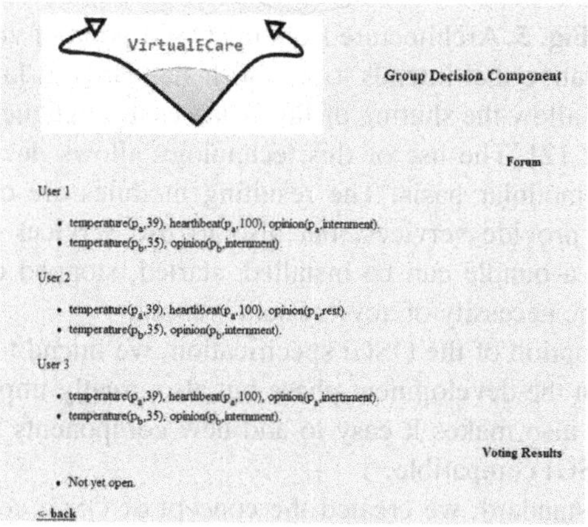

Fig. 4. Forum

4. Implement Issues

The Group Decision is made of different machinery, which must be interconnected, despite their differences. As the decision can be based on information obtained from physical sensors, software agents, external entities and other sources, finding a way of unifying these heterogeneous sources of information is a very important task. To address this challenge, we adopted a service-based architecture relying on OSGi [10] (Figure 5).

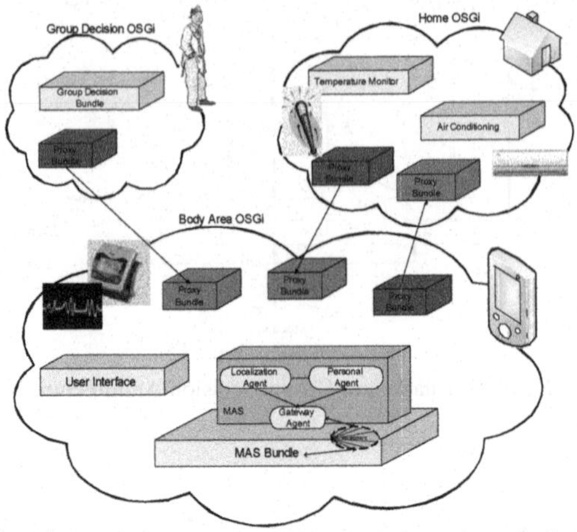

Fig. 5. Architecture from the OSGI point of view

OSGi is an initiative that intends to establish standards in Java Programming [11, 12], more specific, allow the sharing of Java Classes through the adoption of the services paradigm [11, 12]. The use of this technology allows developers to build Java Applications in a modular basis. The resulting modules are called bundles, which may, not only to provide services, but also to use services provided from other bundles. In OSGi, a bundle can be installed, started, stopped or uninstalled in run-time and without the necessity of any "system" reboot.

Through the adoption of the OSGi specification, we intend to adopt standards that will not only fasten the development phase but also greatly improve the dynamics of the architecture. It also makes it easy to add new components to our architecture as long as they are OSGi compatible.

Following this standard, we created the concept of OSGi cell. An OSGi cell is a collection of bundles, which provide and use services needed for accomplishing their tasks. In this specific case, the conclusion of the group decision is taken through the interaction of the bundles inside the group decision cell. Moreover, we hide the different components needed for the group decision (Multi-Agent Systems, physical sensors, among others) behind bundles, so they can interact among themselves.

4.1 - Unifying the sources of information

As assumed before, the sources of information may, and probably will, be very heterogeneous. Therefore, the exchange of information among the several parties is a difficult task. By "hiding" each one of these components behind bundles, we ensure that they will all speak the same language. That brings us, however, the additional work of making each different component bundle compatible. Our objective is to make each bundle able to offer services and functionalities of the component "behind" it, and provide those services to any other component that may need them, to ensure its normal operation.

4.2 - Sensors

A physical sensor for instance does not need, under this setting and approach, to use any service from other workings, since it simply provides the information it reads from the environment. Therefore, bundles, which implement sensors, are just required to present the service on which the sensor is specialized. This is the simplest bundle which, each time the service is requested, reads the value that the sensor makes available on that particular moment (real time), converts it to a standard format (e.g. float, integer, etc.) and returns that value as the result of the service invocation. Indeed, we are able to build a meteorological station bundle in which there are several outside sensors, such as wind, rain, luminosity and humidity sensors. The meteorological station bundle can receive the information relative to all of the sensors and the register services, each one corresponding to one of the sensors. In this way, any other bundle of the OSGi cell can use the information from the weather forecast, simply by requesting the respective service from the meteorological bundle.

4.3 - Human Experts

Another elements that make part of the GDSS are the human experts. These are specialized assets that may apply their knowledge and experience in specific areas on the decision making process. We can think of a physician, as an example. The physician is faced with a set symptoms presented by his/her patient, the respective clinical history, sets the list of problems and provides the respective plan of action (treatment). In this case, the bundle behind the physician is quite complex. Whenever the physician is asked to present a diagnose, he/she must have access to his/her Clinical Electronic Process) [13]. Therefore, the physician bundle must contact the relevant services (such as services provided by the patient's personal agent or by the hospital's clinical registry) and provide the relevant information to the physician. This bundle, besides registering the physician service, also needs to draw on services from other bundles, bundles that may, eventually, be outside the OSGi cell (e.g. the personal agent of the patient is probably running on its hand held device) (the interface between the physician and the bundle may be as simple as a GUI that shows the data acquired from other bundles and where the physician may write its conclusions).

4.4 - Multi-Agent Systems

Multi-Agent Systems are a key component in a GDSS platform and we must have a way of integrating such technology with the rest of the bundles. The objective is to allow an agent to run in a way that its functionalities (e.g. methods) can be provided as services to other bundles. It would not be advisable to convert each agent into an OSGi bundle since that would increase development time and throw away the advantages of MAS. Our choice was to create a bundle behind each agent, the MAS bundle. This bundle can deal with one or more agents and implement the methods declared in the interface of those agents as services of their own. Moreover, this bundle must be able of start and stop agents, which will correspond to the start and stop of the services being provided by those agents. The bundle is responsible for, after receiving an invocation for an offered service from any other bundle, to forward the invocation to the correspondent agent and delivering the result of the invocation. Note that an agent, when trying to satisfy a method invocation, can possibly need to use services from other bundles that are currently available, so agents can also access services through this MAS bundle.

We are now ready to make a more detailed description of the MAS bundle. It has two methods for controlling the bundle that will be used by the client or administrator to start or stop the bundle. This corresponds to starting a container and the necessary agents and killing them, respectively. As this MAS bundle registers the services of the agents it creates, it declares the public methods of the agents on its interface so that they are visible to the other bundles as regular services. As for the interface between the MAS bundle and the Jade System, a JadeGateway agent is being used. This agent is created when the bundle is started, along with the other agents. Its task is to act as a bridge between Jade and non-Jade code. Whenever a request from a service arrives to the MAS bundle, it knows to which agent that request should be forwarded. A shared object (which we call blackboard and contains some fields such as the name of the recipient agent or the method to be invoked) is created and sent to the gateway agent. The gateway agent then contacts the recipient agent, invoking the requested method and waiting for the answer. After having received the answer, it is written to the blackboard and the command is released. At this point, the MAS bundle resumes the execution and the result of the invocation can be read from the blackboard and returned as the result of the invocation of the service from another bundle. Likewise, if an agent needs to use a service from another bundle, it contacts the MAS bundle, which is responsible for contacting the correct bundle; invoking the service and forwarding the result back to the agent. Finally, the MAS bundle implements a method for shutting down the agent container, which corresponds to uninstall all the services being provided by the agents.

The more specific issue of the interaction between agents inside each platform is also addressed. Agent communication is indeed a very important subject since it implies directly with the performance and behavior of the whole system. FIPA establishes several agent-related standards, being one of them the Agent Communication Language (FIPA-ACL). This standard defines how to syntactically and semantically construct a message. It specifies the parameters a message should have (e.g. sender, content, performative) and how to use them. The communication between the agents of our architecture complies with FIPA-ACL standard. By doing so, we solve some challenges and enlarge the compatibility of our architecture with outside agents that follow the same standard. At this point, any agent that complies with FIPA-ACL can run inside a container that is controlled by a MAS bundle and at the moment it starts, the methods declared on its interface are added as one more service provided by the bundle.

5. Interconnecting

We have already seen how to adapt some of the most important components in our GDSS platform in order to be OSGi compatible and how to enable them to communicate. There must be, however, a way for users of this platform to access the service or services that are, eventually, remotely provided. This is where R-OSGi comes into play.

The main idea behind R-OSGi is for remote services to be accessed by bundles, like they would be if they were local ones, in a completely transparent way. What we do is to add an additional bundle to each cell that provides at least a remote service. This bundle is responsible for checking the service registry of the OSGi cell it is in, and searches for services which should be provided remotely, and announce them in an external port. Remote bundles, which want to subscribe its services, will make a connection to that port and subscribe it. Moreover, each cell should also start a bundle for each service (or bundle of services) it wants to remotely access. This bundle subscribes the remote service as soon as it is needed and registers it in the local OSGi cell, as if it was the bundle providing it. After that, any local bundle can use the service without the need to know if it is accessing a remote or a local service. When adopting R-OSGi, we not only have a way of providing the group decision service. We also expand the group decision capacity, since the main bundle or the other bundles will be able of using external resources (bundles in other OSGi cells), if needed.

It is now clear that the service of the GDSS should be made remotely available, so that the users can have access to it through R-OSGi. There is, therefore, a main bundle on which the decision is made. This bundle registers the main service of the GDSS and the proxy bundle starts providing it remotely. Behind this main bundle of course, there can be a MAS, an expert or any other mechanism for making the decision. When the service is invoked, this decision mechanism, through the main bundle it is in, contacts the relevant bundles (local or remotes), collects the data it needs to make a decision and returns the result of the judgment.

6. Conclusion

In the healthcare arena one aims at a distinguished deliverance of healthcare services to the population in general, and the elderly in particular, without delocalizing or messing up with their routines. Indeed, in this paper it is described a VirtualECare project, with special incidence on its GDSS features, that support asynchronous and distributed meetings, aiming at multi-criteria decision problems, in order to answer to questions being referred to above.

We have also show how we use OSGi to implement a GDSS mechanism, on which we may integrate several different components, enabling them to work together. Moreover, by using R-OSGi, we are able to remotely provide this service and extend the group decision abilities by enabling it to use external services, greatly expanding its potential.

References

1 'Healthcare 2015: Win-win or lose-lose?', in Healthcare 2015: Win-win or lose-lose?' (IBM Global Business Services, 2006.

2 Riva, G.: 'Ambient Intelligence in Health Care', CYBERPSYCHOLOGY & BEHAVIOR, 6, (3), 2003

3 Marreiros G., Novais P., Machado J., Ramos C. e Neves J., An Agent Based Approach to Group Decision Simulation using Argumentation, in Proceedings of the Agent Based Computing: Workshop III - ABC 2006, Wisla, Poland.

4 Costa R., Novais P., Machado J., Alberto C., Neves J., Inter-organization Cooperation for Care of the Elderly, in Integration and Innovation Orient to E-Society, Wang W., Li Y, Duan Z., Yan L., Li H., Yang X., (Eds), Springer-Verlag,Series: IFIP International Federation for Information Processing, ISBN: 978-0-387-75493-2, 2007.

5 Camarinha-Matos, L.M., Castolo, O., and Rosas, J.: 'A multi-agent based platform for virtual communities in elderly care', 2003.

6 Camarinha-Matos, L.: 'New collaborative organizations and their research needs', 2003.

7 Marreiros G., Santos R., Ramos C., Neves J., Novais P., Machado J. and Bulas-Cruz J., Ambient Intelligence in Emotion Based Ubiquitous Decision Making, International Joint Conference on Artificial Intelligence (IJCAI 2007) - 2nd Workshop on Artificial Intelligence Techniques for Ambient Intelligence (AITAmI'07), Hyderabad, India, 2007.

8 Schwarz, R.M.: 'The Skilled Facilitator: Practical Wisdom for Developing Effective Groups' (Jossey Bass, 1994. 1994)

9 Dubs, S., and Hayne, S.C.: 'Distributed facilitation: a concept whose time has come?', 1992.

10 Carneiro, D., Costa, R., and Novais, P.: '(R-)OSGi: The VirtualECare Open Framework', 2008.

11 Initiative, O.S.G.: 'Osgi Service Platform, Release 3' (IOS Press, 2003. 2003)

12 Chen, K., and Gong, L.: 'Programming Open Service Gateways with Java Embedded Server(TM) Technology' (Prentice Hall PTR, 2001. 2001)

13 Machado J., Abelha A., Neves J. e Santos M., Ambient Intelligence in Medicine, in proceedings of the IEEE-Biocas 2006, Biomedical Circuits and Systems Conference, Healthcare Technology, Imperial College, London, UK.

Index of Authors

Index of Authors